The Rise and Fall of the Religious Left

COLUMBIA SERIES ON RELIGION AND POLITICS

COLUMBIA SERIES ON RELIGION AND POLITICS

The Columbia Series on Religion and Politics, edited by Gastón Espinosa (Claremont McKenna College) and Chester Gillis (Georgetown University), addresses the growing demand for scholarship on the intersection of religion and politics in a world in which religion attempts to influence politics and politics regularly must consider the effects of religion. The series examines the influence religion exercises in public life on areas including politics, environmental policy, social policy, law, church-state relations, foreign policy, race, class, gender, and culture. Written by experts in a variety of fields, the series explores the historical and contemporary intersection of religion and politics in the United States and globally.

Mark Hulsether, *Religion, Culture, and Politics in the Twentieth-Century United States*

Gastón Espinosa, ed., *Religion and the American Presidency: George Washington to George W. Bush with Commentary and Primary Sources*

Richard B. Miller, *Terror, Religion, and Liberal Social Criticism*

Gary Dorrien, *Economy, Difference, Empire: Social Ethics for Social Justice*

John M. Owen IV and J. Judd Owen, eds., *Religion, the Enlightenment, and the New Global Order*

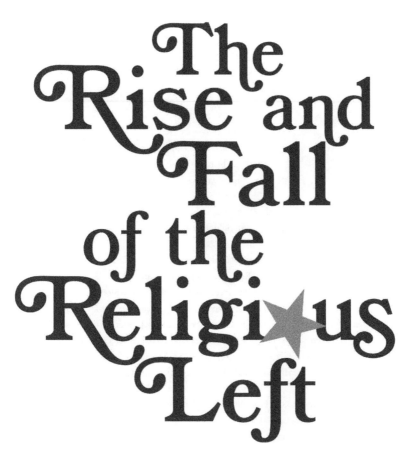

The Rise and Fall of the Religious Left

Politics, Television, and Popular Culture in the 1970s and Beyond

L. Benjamin Rolsky

Columbia University Press/New York

Columbia University Press

Publishers Since 1893

New York   Chichester, West Sussex

cup.columbia.edu

Library of Congress Cataloging-in-Publication Data

Names: Rolsky, L. Benjamin, author.

Title: The rise and fall of the religious left : politics, television, and

popular culture in the 1970s and beyond / L. Benjamin Rolsky.

Description: New York : Columbia University Press, 2019. | Series: Columbia series

on religion and politics | Includes bibliographical references and index.

Identifiers: LCCN 2019025148 (print) | LCCN 2019025149 (ebook) |

ISBN 9780231193627 (cloth) | ISBN 9780231193634 (paperback) |

ISBN 9780231550420 (ebook)

Subjects: LCSH: Liberalism—Religious aspects—Christianity. |

Liberalism (Religion)—United States. | Popular culture—United States—

History—20th century. | Popular culture—Religious aspects—Christianity. |

Lear, Norman—Influence. | Religious right.

Classification: LCC BR1615 .R65 2019 (print) | LCC BR1615 (ebook) |

DDC 306.6/773082—dc23

LC record available at https://lccn.loc.gov/2019025148

LC ebook record available at https://lccn.loc.gov/2019025149

Cover design: Noah Arlow

TO MY WIFE, LINDSEY, AND MY DAUGHTER, AUDREY JACQUELINE, who continue to make me the academic, and the man, that I am today

Our founders clearly intended that there be a level of separation between church and state. I was just trying to build a wall of understanding, of common sense—to go along with the notion that it's a poor idea to mix politics and religion—and a good idea—to back that caution with laws that make that clear.

—Norman Lear, "I Am a Jew and Proud of It"

Contents

Acknowledgments

Despite growing up in the 1990s, I was raised on 1970s television. Programs such as *The Mary Tyler Moore Show*, *MASH*, *Taxi*, and *All in the Family* served as our weekly entertainment day after day, month after month, and year after year. Because I was born well after these shows originally aired, much of this upbringing unfolded against the popularity of *Seinfeld*, *Friends*, and other national ratings giants on network TV. More importantly, these viewing practices took place deep in the woods of Montana, at the base of Big Mountain, where our closest neighbors were bear, moose, mountain lion, and deer. My family and I also watched innumerable televised sporting events including the World Series, the Super Bowl, and the NBA Finals. Without fail, someone would inevitably thank God or Jesus Christ for the strength to hit the game-winning home run, make the game-winning basket, or conduct the final drive to the end zone before time expired. Soon after, my parents would begin lambasting the television—confused and angered by the "out-of-place" theology articulated upon the highest stages of competition. Why were they so upset? Why were there "appropriate" places for such utterances? Were they otherwise "inappropriate," these voices of Christian witness in the public square? It has taken most of my academic life to figure out a series of answers to such conundrums. In many ways, this book represents the best answers I have been able to come up with thus far.

Chronologically speaking, the first person to ever place my name in the same sentence as "an ivy" was my high school American history teacher, L. Mark Sweeney. His classes were brutal, but they gave me a sense of what rigor was like at that level and what it could be like moving forward. I then met the likes of Mark Montesano, Tisa Wenger, Ken Morrison, and Karen Bruhn while attending

Arizona State University as an undergrad. Reading *I and Thou* for an entire semester left an indelible mark on my intellectual development and my ability to parse out challenging lines of prose and text. The following years led me to Claremont School of Theology and Yale Divinity School. My mentor to this day, Gaston Espinosa, introduced me to the fine arts of argumentation, documentation, and elaboration all within the confines of the "single-spaced page." Later, Tisa Wenger would again provide me with indispensable advice about the academy and how best to think about my various writing projects. In fact, it was Tisa whom I first told about my thinking on Norman Lear, American liberalism, and the study of religion. She could not have been more supportive. Combined with the theoretical freedom of courses with Kathryn Lofton, such an education laid the proverbial groundwork for what was to come during my coursework at Drew University. My time as a student at Drew gave me the space to pursue my analytical passions to the highest degree and the funds to do research at the Bancroft Library at the University of California at Berkeley in the archives of People for the American Way. Kathy Brown stood by me through thick and thin—even when it came to my all-important stipend as her longtime student assistant and colleague in the classroom.

I have been fortunate enough to be able to share my work with countless centers, universities, and colloquia. In many ways, my time in front of students and faculty at Princeton University, Yale University, and Columbia University went a long way toward sharpening and honing my prose and overall argument both within and across the manuscript. In particular, my time in Columbia's Religion in America seminar as part of the University Seminars gave me the confidence and funding needed to pursue the project I truly wanted. For this I will be forever grateful. In addition, Jason Sexton and Ed Blum awarded me with the Best Student Paper Award as part of the Symposium on Religion in California at UC Berkeley. In 2007, I attended my first AAR (American Academy of Religion) conference in sunny San Diego. Not only did such a world forever wed me and my interests to the scholarly pursuit of religion, I was also able to taste what being part of a such a community would mean for the foreseeable future. Like many, I could never do justice to the countless hallway conversations and late-night debates I have had with close friends and colleagues since. While the following list is not meant to be exhaustive, it nevertheless speaks to how grateful I am for the time and energies of such a group of scholars. Without the consistent feedback by the following individuals, this book would have turned out completely different: John Modern, Finbarr Curtis, Chip Callahan, Tisa Wenger, K. Healan Gaston, Paul Harvey, Randall Balmer, Wallace Best, Judith Weisenfeld, Mark Edwards, Edwin Aponte, Laura Jakubowski Aponte, David Watt, David Walker,

Laura Levitt, Gary Laderman, Christopher Allison, Bobby Smiley, Adam James, and Billy Blackmon II.

My time with Columbia University Press has been a true blessing. From the very beginning, Wendy Lochner heard "a voice" in the writing, one that she had not heard before, and one that she wanted to hear more of. Her timely suggestions made the following book into the coherent, passionate piece of writing that readers hold before them. Once again, Gaston Espinosa guided my writing and composition through the proposal phase and into the writing stage as I continued to rewrite and rewrite and rewrite. Finally, my two external reviewers were very kind with their comments, encouraging me to pursue what I wanted without the need for technical revisions. In this regard, I would like to thank the broader network of support that has made much of my education possible: Laura and Bob Rolsky as well as Steve and Bobbi Duckers, Nan, and Pop. I would not be the scholar I am today without the conversations we have had over the years about Archie, Norman, and American liberalism broadly considered. I would also like to thank the Norman Lear Center and Norman Lear himself for his time and energy for the two bicoastal interview sessions we conducted in his home and in his Manhattan apartment. And, lastly, my immediate family has given me everything—time, love, and support. My wife, Lindsey, and my daughter, Audrey, have been beacons of light in otherwise stormy times. Their love continues to drive me to do better.

The Rise and Fall of the Religious Left

Introduction

Religious Liberalism, American Politics, and Public Life

In the fall of 1984, *Harper's* magazine hosted a spirited exchange of letters between renowned television producer and writer Norman Lear and then President Ronald Reagan. The magazine first published Lear's letter to President Reagan followed by Reagan's handwritten response to Lear. "Dear Mr. President," Lear began, "I am deeply troubled by what seems to be an endorsement of the so-called Christian Nation movement in many of your recent speeches. While I fully respect (and would fight to protect) your right to whatever spiritual and religious beliefs you prefer, I am concerned that you not use the office of the presidency as Evangelist in Chief or to further the notion that any particular group of Americans is to be accorded special standing because it practices any religion." Lear willingly accepted the fact that Americans, including the president himself, had the constitutional right to express themselves freely, yet he nevertheless thought that politically conservative religions were attempting to curtail those very same individual liberties in an act of religious tyranny. "Mr. President," Lear elaborated, "without freedom *from* religion we could have no freedom *of* religion."[1]

The president's prompt response assured Lear that he had no intention of representing what Lear called "the Christian Nation movement" in any of his social policy decisions. "I certainly do not support the notion that any group of citizens is to be accorded special standing 'because it practices any religion,'" Reagan declared. "The goal of our nation must always be to achieve the ultimate in individual freedom consistent with an orderly society." Despite Reagan's philosophical differences with Lear, his description would prove quite prescient since his notion of an "orderly society" and the values and ethics through which it could be realized would contribute to defining two very important developments in late twentieth-century America: the emergence of the culture wars as both idea and social phenomenon and the terms of a new conservative consensus.[2] More important, the discussion between Lear and Reagan spoke to the impact of Southern California and the larger Sunbelt on postwar American religious life as understood from the soundstages and writing rooms of "the Dream Factory," known otherwise as Hollywood.[3] Due in large part to the clarity of their respective positions, the argument between Lear and Reagan was nothing less than dramatic as a former television writer went head-to-head with a former actor over the means and ends of the orderly society in a pivotal moment in late twentieth-century America.

In many ways, Lear's disagreement with Reagan was the product of nearly a decade of organizing and activism in defense of what was popularly referred to as "the American Way."[4] Lear had been on the collective radar of conservative activists, journalists, and organizers since the premiere of his 1971 hit situation comedy *All in the Family*. Despite, or because of, the inclusion of the word "family" in the show's title, the program faced virulent criticism for its naive or "indecent" material by some of conservatism's most well-respected names, including writer William F. Buckley Jr. and evangelist Jerry Falwell.[5] In fact, Falwell would later declare Lear to be the "number one enemy of the family in America" during the show's run on CBS. This seemingly innocuous difference in opinion between Lear and Falwell over the nature of television programming, however, effectively illuminates the contested character of the American family at the time and the ways in which liberals and conservatives understood it during what scholars refer to as the "culture wars."[6] It also speaks to the liberal religious reliance on culture in order to make political claims about public life and how best to regulate it in contested times.

Lear's religio-political work became especially significant in these contests when he and other Hollywood writers sued the FCC (Federal Communications Commission), along with television networks NBC, CBS, and ABC, over a perceived curtailment of their freedom of expression as a result of adopting "the Family Viewing Hour" in prime time. Despite the largely conservative notion of family that would help mobilize a generation of voters, it was Lear who inaugurated the decade with his vision of family and family values as part of the federally protected public interest on network television. In this way, Lear's activism was indicative of a broader style of organizing and argumentation commonly referred to as the "Religious Left" or "Spiritual Left" in American public life, a style that viewed the public square as its own creation and one deserving federal protection and regulation in the name of the public interest.[7]

Lear's involvement in the entertainment industry drew his and others' attention to the activities of conservative Protestants and their protests *much earlier* than many of the journalists, academics, and political commentators who would later encounter them in the public square as part of a story or formal study of "the Christian Right."[8] As such, Lear's decision to found the nonprofit organization People for the American Way (PFAW) in 1981 came out of his observations and careful analyses of right-wing organizations, speakers, and preachers—namely those who constituted the ascending "electronic church" and the Moral Majority. In this sense, Lear can be understood as one of the more significant interpreters of the "New Right," "the Religious Right," and "the New Christian Right" in the recent American past as understood from the vantage of the burgeoning Religious Left.[9] These phrases functioned not only as terms of historically contingent description for Lear and his supporters but also as powerful rhetorical stereotypes of conservative religiosity run rampant in the public square.[10]

Due to the publicity and character of Lear's arguments, his religio-political writings and activism were defended vociferously throughout the 1970s and 1980s by interfaith organizations such as the National Council of Christians and Jews (NCCJ) and mainline Protestant organizations including the National Council of Churches (NCC) and the *Christian Century*.[11] In light of this support, Lear first decided to compose a satirical movie based on the lives of two preachers in order to articulate his criticisms of the Christian Right and its methods of exclusionary politics and tax evasion.[12] Despite the assistance of fellow comedy writers Robin Williams and Richard Pryor, Lear decided to go in a different direction due to the urgency he felt from the growing collective weight of televangelist influence over American media. "One day, while working to realize the film we envisioned, my concern reached its peak. I had tuned in to Jimmy Swaggart and caught the reverend, Bible in hand, railing about a constitutional issue that was due to come before the Supreme Court and asking his 'godly' viewers to pray for the removal of a certain justice," Lear recalled. "That was the last straw for me—I had to do something."[13]

Lear was not the only one to be disgusted by what he saw on the television screen during this period, yet it is *his* story, and the story of those who supported him, that remain to be told in the recent history of American religion and the wars of culture that have characterized subsequent American political debate since the 1960s. On the one hand, this is a story about cultural victory, one signifying a given community's ability to shape and even dictate culture to those eager to consume it.[14] On the other, it is a story about what may be gained by this power over the long term and what is lost in the short term in the realm of politics itself as understood as the deliberation and negotiation of power by means rarely agreed upon by the combatants. In this sense, those who defended public reason's ability to govern public discourse by deploying it against their political enemies were making an argument about how the public square should be constituted and on whose terms. As illustrated by the following analysis of Norman Lear's career in media and nonprofit activism, this vision, broad as it might have been, ultimately lacked the capacity to include those whom it seemed to care about most: most notably Archie Bunker himself.

In other words, whether it was publisher William Rusher, political operative Kevin Phillips, or Archie Bunker, Lear and his various supporters within the Religious Left had difficulty seeing past the caricatures that Lear was partly responsible for creating of conservatism in the public square. In this sense, many of the struggles and challenges that American religious liberals have experienced in the years since can be understood as largely self-inflicted in nature as they gradually lost the ability to speak to the masses due to the successes of Lear's form of popular yet relevant entertainment on a mass scale. In many ways, this study demonstrates why such irony remains largely unrealized to this day and, as such, unexamined in both popular and academic imaginations.

ARGUMENT AND OBJECTIVES

This book illuminates how our contemporary political moment has become so polarized since the tumultuous events of the 1960s through the use of culture and its adjudication in public based on the spiritual directives of largely oppositional political religions.[15] For the purposes of this analysis, the word "culture" describes the various artistic productions, Lear's and others', that were disseminated over the airwaves by American television networks in prime time. In particular, my work examines the *spiritual politics* surrounding this type of cultural production in late twentieth-century America authored by the likes of Lear but also by his fellow supporters in what could be understood as the Religious Left, including journalist Bill Moyers, television writer Larry Gelbart, and church historian Martin Marty. While the following analysis focuses primarily on Lear, his connections to Gelbart, Marty, and Catholic theologian Theodore Hesburgh spoke volumes about how the Religious Left organized itself based on a diversity of viewpoints and religious traditions including Protestant Christianity, Judaism, and liberal democracy itself. Lear's dominance of American television throughout the 1970s spoke to the mainstream ascent of his civil religious vision of the nation, one that saw religious pluralism as a foundation of liberal democracy. At the same time, such dominance also spoke to a fundamental flaw within liberal religious argumentation and organizing: its inability to seriously engage either the sources or content of arguments authored by conservative political elites and populist heroes alike.

Many of my historical subjects relied on the language of "the spirit" and "the spiritual" to both voice their religious concerns in public *and* add rhetorical weight to their public declarations regardless of political orientation. I contend that this particular usage of "spirit" reflected a longer tradition of ethical or mystical liberalism typically associated with the history of American spirituality dating back to the eighteenth century.[16] For Lear's interfaith nonprofit People for the American Way in particular, the most important aspect of religious liberalism was its attempt to monitor potentially abrasive language in the public square while facilitating civil deliberation on behalf of the nation's religious minorities.[17]

In light of this brief historical background, my larger critical inquiry examines Norman Lear's religio-political vision in order to identify the broader contours of what I'm calling the "spiritual politics of the Religious Left." Lear's career in Hollywood serves as the paradigmatic example of liberal religious mobilization in the recent past in its opposition to the proliferation of conservative, and at times militant, Protestantism in the public sphere.[18] I argue that Lear's television career, including the groundbreaking *All in the Family*, communicated a consensus-values-driven project of preserving a more civil and religiously tolerant America, first through his programming and later through his nonprofit organization PFAW.[19] This type of liberal activism, one that has been profoundly overshadowed by scholarly attention to "the Christian Right," functioned as an articulation of civil religious ideals over and against the perceived divisiveness and abrasive cultural and religious politics of American conservatism in general, and conservative Protestantism in particular.[20]

Seemingly designed for the purposes of entertainment itself, this story of religio-cultural contestation unfolded on the screens of color televisions across the country through various comedic forms of entertainment. In fact, television itself achieved much of its social power during this time within the very families that both the Left and the Right appealed to through prime-time programming, situation comedies, and the variety show special in the name of federally protected entertainment.[21] As such, I argue that a new televisual arena of contest and debate emerged during this period in the fierce battle between Lear (and PFAW) and various conservative Protestant televangelists over who would define the public script of American religious life. For many journalists, politicians, and entertainers at the time, this was nothing less than a "holy war" over the medium and the communicative power of television itself.

Lear's religio-political activism, however, was not simply the product of American religious liberalism itself. His cultural work certainly represented a broader current of mobilized spiritual activism during this period, but he was also a "theatrical liberal."[22] This latter dimension of Lear's writing and television projects effectively highlights their Jewish characteristics as self-fashioning endeavors carried out within largely Protestant spaces where the theater is always and already sacred. "The power of this popular culture resides not in its secular neutrality," argues scholar of religion Andrea Most, "but in its specific spiritual vision, one that makes use of secular cultural modes to express a morally coherent worldview."[23] As such, Lear is best understood as a religious liberal who deployed a spiritual politics in American public life because he was deeply concerned with civic activism, correcting unjust societal structures and authoring controversial programming in the name of the public interest.[24] For Lear, "the spirit" implied behavior that was "in the spirit of," implying action or activity carried out "in the spirit" of fairness, equality, or social justice. Like other religious liberals, Lear also tended to see "spirit" as that which undergirded religion itself in all its diverse, global forms.[25]

Much of Lear's activism, including PFAW, depended on his connections to similarly thinking Hollywood actors and his willingness to use television as a means of arguing for spiritual and religious tolerance as an alternative to the abrasive style of Christian Right televangelists. As such, Lear and others' spiritual labors in the various spaces of American politics during the 1970s and 1980s depended on a clear understanding of liberal sentiment undergirding the vitality of the public square.[26] In this regard, Lear shared a great deal with his supporters within the Religious Left, including Father Theodore Hesburgh from Notre Dame and Donald and Peggy L. Shriver from Union Theological Seminary, who also worried about the religio-political implications of conservative Christianity in American public life.[27]

For these members of what neoconservative writers would call America's "knowledge industry," developing an appreciation for "the spirit" was inseparable from defining the "broader values" of American democracy itself. In fact, this industry's shared commitment to addressing injustice in American society reflected the very same liberal mindset found in progressive evangelical circles.[28] Lear's fundamentally liberal vision of American public life possessed the same social investment in the common good, suggesting that there was much more to the civic vitality of the period's Spiritual Left than scholars have previously acknowledged.[29] In this sense, we can understand Lear's project as part of a custodial impulse to protect the public square from potentially harmful inhabitants, however he defined them.[30] For Lear and his fellow religious liberals, "The return of a more progressive political order goes hand in hand with the vitality and integrity of religious liberalism."[31]

In this sense, we can understand Lear as a particular type of postwar liberal—one who combined the rigors and expectations of public reason and civil religion with a profound sense of empathy for religious and political difference in the public square.[32] A child of the New Deal era, Lear understood the role of government in American society as a largely necessary and positive one in addressing various societal ills, including rampant capitalism and religious discrimination. As a result, the time he spent in his childhood listening to the diatribes of one Father Charles Coughlin on the crystal radio left an enduring mark on Lear and shaped his later crusades against representatives of the Christian Right in the name of "pluralism." "Liberals viewed tolerance and inclusion as a means of acculturation," argues historian Cheryl Greenberg. "Since those freed from oppression would naturally embrace society's values, pluralists did not see this as coercive or incompatible with the goals of personal liberation."[33]

In this sense, instead of investigating a singular or monolithic form of liberalism in the recent past, scholars of American liberalism have instead spoken of multiple *liberalisms* that have shaped the political life of the nation across the twentieth century. In Lear's case, it would be most accurate to say that his writings combined a New Deal emphasis on pluralism and tolerance with a postwar attention to cosmopolitanism, which tended to foreground relativism and rationalism over the local or the provincial in the public square. Following the tumultuous events of the 1960s, American liberalism changed drastically as it began to transition from a socioeconomic emphasis on class to a largely symbolic attention to culture. As a result, liberals began to become more conversant with certain economic classes of individuals over others in terms of both legislation and daily interactions with one's fellow citizens as the proverbial movement got off the ground and into the streets of the nation writ large. On the verge of the 1970s, liberalism's rise seemed to be undeterred, at least for the time being.

Such a transition, however, came at a political and social cost—one that Lear's spiritual politics represent to the proverbial *T* to this day. "When they turned to culture," argues historian Jennifer Burns, "liberals lost the ability to understand how conservatives connected with a larger audience, for they stopped taking conservative arguments seriously."[34] On the one hand, liberals like Lear possessed a great deal of optimism relative to the people as a whole—imagined or otherwise. Given the right information, most Americans were utterly and completely capable of making the right and thus informed decision when it came to voting. On the other hand, due to the power of public figures such as Father Coughlin, liberals like Lear feared the irrational potential of "the people" to become "the masses" under the direction of a charismatic leader such as Coughlin, or later Adolf Hitler.

As a result, when conservative Protestants began mobilizing on behalf of "born-again" political candidates in the name of a "Moral Majority" or a "Christian Right" in the 1970s, religious liberals like Lear illustrated the oftentimes harsh and exclusionary tendencies within liberal democratic forms of governance by labeling them religious extremists or calling their beliefs "bad religion." While this description did not physically keep conservative individuals out of the public square, it nevertheless labeled them as unfit subjects due to a lack of political maturity. Indeed, Lear may have tolerated individuals like Jerry Falwell and Pat Robertson, but tolerance and toleration of difference worked in two directions—anyone could enter the public square, but only those who played by its rules were left alone by the state and its powers of public reason. Those who possessed overly provincial or inaccessible grounds of argumentation, such as religious "fundamentalists," were required to translate their claims into ones equally accessible to by all. "Local politics became increasingly marked by arguments over 'reverse racism' and by laments about 'limousine liberals' or 'bleeding hearts,' elite liberal leaders who they claimed abandoned their concern for the working or middle class for law and order, for merit, rules, or morality."[35]

While this sentiment aptly described the feelings and actions of those living in "middle America" as part of Nixon's "silent majority," there was no better representative of this larger phenomenon than one of Lear's most iconic television characters—Archie Bunker. Lear foregrounded Archie and his Coughlin-like diatribes not because he *agreed with them* but rather because he wanted to make his audiences think about their own potential prejudices and assumptions that might have led to offensive or discriminatory behavior toward racial or religious minorities. This optimism, however, could only be realized if the very same audiences saw Archie as a subject of satire and self-examination—two of the most important tools utilized by religious liberals like Lear in addressing societal ills through media.

As such, Lear's portrayal of Archie on *All in the Family* was a quintessentially *liberal* one in the sense that Archie's voice was included within the deliberative space known as the sitcom but functioned as a prop within a given episode's plot to further a broader didactic purpose—to educate through satirical appropriation of white working-class views, stereotypes, and politics. The content of such argumentation reflected a type of post-1960s liberalism that privileged "the other" and its marginalized knowledge in addition to emphasizing "cultural politics that were more [often] suitable to academe than to public debate or electoral politics."[36] It also spoke to what could be understood as Lear's fundamentally "liberal faith" by emphasizing two of its core beliefs—that ideas possess a context and that those ideas must be continually reexamined in light of contemporaneous circumstances.[37] In this way, Lear's rise to fame and power within the entertainment industry mirrored his growing influence within the Religious Left. Yet this ascent was only made possible by a wider constellation of assumptions about the masses and their largely unpredictable and conservative tendencies when confronted by totalitarian power. It is in this sense that I speak of a rise and gradual fall of liberal engagement with the popular—Lear addressed it weekly through his programming, but he did so from within his own religio-political framework.

This type of civic spirituality, or spiritual reflection, did not limit itself to exclusively Jewish or Protestant modes of communication and instruction. In fact, Jewish entertainers readily borrowed concepts and ideas from other traditions, "drawing on aspects of liberal Protestantism and blues spirituality" that were "easily misunderstood by orthodox Christians as expressions of a religiously vacant (and hence debased) liberal secularism."[38] As a result, to conservative evangelists such as Pat Robertson and Jerry Falwell, Lear's spiritual politics was virtually *unintelligible* as a form of religious practice in the public square beyond the familiar accusation of "secular humanism." For sociologist Wade Clark Roof, this epistemic incommensurability is the product of differing knowledge systems: one that foregrounds the content of religion when speaking of the public good and another that prioritizes the civic principles that govern religion as part of the public interest.[39] While supportive of the former theoretically, Lear and his fellow liberals ultimately preferred and defended the latter because they saw themselves as protecting the public square and its First Amendment freedoms from what they understood as theocratic malcontents.

What made Lear's spiritual politics different from other liberal entertainers and writers was that he wanted to entertain and make people laugh *about something* by using the genre of the situation comedy to express satirical analyses of America and its turbulent society.[40] I argue that Lear's understanding of "relevance" and his deployment of satire as well as his consequent programming materialized as a direct product of his own religious biography or spiritual vision as an influential religious liberal with his own "moral order of American public life."[41] Like his liberal Protestant supporters within the Religious Left, he believed "'religion' named the excessive, fallible, and temporal residue that has gummed up the search for genuine spirituality and prophetic justice making."[42] Lear's desire to educate and entertain about something, a form of prime-time televisual didacticism, both reflected and laid the groundwork for the liberal values he sought to maintain in American public life, including civility, religious tolerance, and the separation of church and state, as part of his spiritual politics. This process became especially visible once Lear moved out from behind the camera and entered the fray of early-1980s American politics, a religio-political landscape more reflective of the nation's neoliberal future than its fading New Deal past.

My objective in this book is to apply the same critical attention that scholars have typically given "the Christian Right" and conservative Protestantism to what I and others have identified as the Spiritual or Religious Left through a case study of Norman Lear's religio-political vision and career in media and nonprofit activism.[43] One of the goals of this study is to illuminate a politics of religious liberalism using a diverse array of Lear's writings, his television work, and the literature of his nonprofit organization People for the American Way.[44] Both the political Right and the Left relied on the resources and personalities of Southern California at the time in order to further their religio-political ends in public, yet it has been the political and Christian Right that has to this point dominated studies of media, politics, and religion in the field of American religious history.

As a result, Lear's style of Hollywood-based religious liberalism has been concealed from our collective, historiographic view.[45] Lear is a significant figure in American religious history, along with his various interfaith supporters, because he both documented the rise of the Christian Right and produced knowledge about its organization(s), membership, and leadership in the form of sitcom episodes, public service announcements, prime-time television specials, and nonprofit organizations. His work was also indicative of a growing community of religious liberals who sought to protect the public interest by way of entertainment and the prime-time sitcom as part of a broader Religious Left in the recent past. As such, Lear's writings and cultural productions can be understood as contributing to the contemporary history of American religious liberalism as well as to the entity that scholars and journalists have identified as "the Christian Right" since the late 1970s. In fact, I argue that it is virtually impossible to understand the creation of the latter without knowing the spiritual politics of the former as a product of one of the most contentious periods in American political history.

SCHOLASTIC INTERVENTIONS

This book is at once a history of the Religious Left as understood through Norman Lear's spiritual politics *and* a religious history of the Christian Right. This is largely the case because representatives of the Christian Right influenced Lear's ability to disseminate his spiritual vision of civic life over the airwaves through network television and its prime-time listings. The execution of this narrative, one that takes the form of thematically oriented yet historically grounded case studies of Lear's career in media, is a reflection of Lear's own encounters with various representatives of the New Right and the New Christian Right. As a result, some chapters will feature material on conservative Protestant leaders such as Jerry Falwell, Jimmy Swaggart, or Donald Wildmon, but others will not, or not to the same degree. Both the New Right and the New Christian Right shadowed much of Lear's programming due to its controversial content, which Lear understood as censorship and thus a violation of the First Amendment. As such, my narrative is a braided one in that it primarily documents the movements of Lear and his supporters, but to properly accomplish this, I must also include their conservative *counter*movements when and if they arose to complete the picture of Lear's significance in American public life in the recent religious past.

I argue that what scholars have traditionally called "the Christian Right" would be better understood less as a monolithic religio-political entity and more as a disparate collection of individual, organizational, and grassroots interests working on behalf of a broadly conservative political and cultural agenda set by nationally oriented New Right strategists and policy specialists.[46] In this sense, yet-to-be composed studies of conservative strategists such as Howard Phillips and Richard A. Viguerie should accompany those of their organizational foot soldiers, namely individuals such as Jerry Falwell and Pat Robertson, in order to better understand the social power of the Christian Right in the public square.[47] As historian Neil J. Young argues, "The New Right combined its radically free market impulses with a strident cultural conservatism, most visible through rabid opposition to abortion, gay rights, and the ERA, to create a potent political force with roots reaching back to the campaigns for Barry Goldwater, Richard Nixon, and George Wallace."[48]

In this sense, New Right strategists themselves maintained many of the rhetorical connections between the New Right of the 1960s and 1970s and the Old Right of the 1930s as part of a larger political agenda for the 1980s.[49] Despite the fact that "the Christian Right," as a term, is arguably as much a liberal/modernist construction as it is a conservative one, it can also be understood as another fundamentalist and business-oriented attempt to create a "theological vessel that individuals could fill with their own doctrinal particulars."[50] Once viewed from this vantage, we are better able to understand "the Christian Right" less as a description of empirical reality and more as a product of both liberal and conservative commentary and discourse in the name of electoral gain.[51] As such, Lear's and others' analyses from within the Religious Left serve as the quintessential example of this process by reflecting both the empirically grounded observation and the hyperbolic exaggeration as part of the first of two "evangelical scares" in the recent American past.[52]

In addition to studies of the Christian Right, the interpretive evidence for this project draws primarily on two subfields within the study of America's religious history: culture wars studies and American religious liberalism. Both of these subfields are well developed in their own rights, yet their contributions become most evident when they are brought together so as to elucidate Lear's spiritual vision of civic life in its historical context, namely from within the culture wars themselves and its terms of religio-political engagement. Like the larger field of American religion and politics, culture wars studies remain fixated upon conservative Christianity and its social and cultural power in public. This literature not only leaves underexplored the spiritual counteropposition to such conservative power, namely Lear's spiritual vision, it also leaves unexamined the place of liberalism as a form of religious establishment in the United States since the social programming of Franklin Delano Roosevelt in the 1930s. This book contributes to these ongoing conversations by examining the fundamental role that Lear's vision played in the attempted liberal maintenance and later eventual conservative redefinition of midcentury consensus by representatives of the Christian Right and its political architects during the 1970s.

Unfortunately for Lear and his progressive supporters, the nature of conflict following the 1960s had shifted into a cultural register of the personal over and against one designed for explicitly public expression and consumption.[53] As a result, the culture wars were nothing if not negotiations over which forms of culture would be allowed to exist within increasingly calcifying politics of resentment and metonymy. Lear's satirical programming was oftentimes at the center of these debates regarding television, including violence and television's varied impact on American society. His writing functioned seamlessly within the "public interest" for some, yet for others it contributed to an already substantive list of pornographic television programs that American television networks continued to broadcast each and every week. In essence, each side of the religio-political debate, regardless of membership, found traction for its claims and arguments because of culture and its power to function politically in public.

This is arguably why such contests were understood as largely *cultural* during this time, namely because American politics itself began to manifest in and proliferate through newly utilized cultural registers including prime-time television and the situation comedy. "The key to understanding the political fallout of this pivotal era," argues historian Matthew Lassiter, "is that cultural explanations triumphed over economic ones in setting the terms of public debate and determining the direction of public policies."[54]

Despite arguments to the contrary, I contend that political and spiritual liberals like Lear have shaped the terms of these culture wars, along with their conservative activist detractors since the 1960s, due to their familiarity with various forms of popular culture and their ability to politicize a given social subject or issue for public consumption. How you received Archie Bunker as a viewer said everything about the manner in which taste emerged as a contested category during the culture wars, which for some called for immediate legislative action on Capitol Hill. This was especially the case for those who composed "relevance programming" during the early 1970s, including television producers such as Grant Tinker (*Mary Tyler Moore*), Norman Lear (*All in the Family*), and Larry Gelbart (*MASH*). In this sense, liberals may in fact continue to win the culture wars, but at what cost to their own electoral futures?[55]

These writers often voiced their disdain for the Christian Right, its reliance on mass media, and its articulation of political claims in public in terms resembling manners, etiquette, or taste.[56] This discomfort was intimately connected to the fact that "religion" itself was already a protected category for liberals during this period and for liberal democracy more broadly, one that appeared in public only under specific linguistic conditions such that its partisan potential could not manifest too strongly in the process of public reasoning.[57] The Christian Right in general, and the electronic church in particular, violated virtually all of these unspoken measures assumed to be at the heart of American public life and its proper functioning.

No one was more attuned to these developments than Norman Lear and his immediate contemporaries within the Religious Left because they were both victims of and commentators on conservative Protestant evangelists and their attempts to boycott the network's primary advertisers. The disintegration of America's aspirational midcentury consensus, a process intensified by the writings of conservatives, neoconservatives, and Protestant conservatives throughout the 1960s, revealed the fact that the various means of cultural production utilized by Lear were fast becoming the most important sources of social capital during the culture wars. As such, they served as sources of immense power and influence over how the nation transitioned from the turbulence of the 1960s to the divisive war years both at home and abroad during the early 1970s.

In both his situation comedies (*All in the Family*) and his political organizing (PFAW), Lear constructed a makeshift civics classroom out of performance space: the Bunker's living room and the variety show stage. He displayed and gave voice to his liberal understanding of the fundamental social and cultural challenges of the day in each setting through character dialogue and plot. This insight becomes clearest when the descriptions of relevance programming merge with the narratives of American religious liberalism and the Religious Left in the twentieth century. In particular, Lear's pluralist vision found its motivation in the potential of humanity to work through its divisions for the good of the larger whole. In this sense, first *All in the Family* and later PFAW served as powerful media-based outlets for Lear's crusade against religious and racial intolerance in the United States. In his less public moments, however, Lear would gather with close friends at his home in Vermont, the former home of poet Robert Frost, in order to deliberate over the day's current events and social challenges through civil debate. An intellectual luminary, Frost, as well as his writings and his home, served as the most appropriate source of spiritual inspiration for Lear and his fellow "spiritual gropers" to meet and seek together as "one step removed from religion generally."[58]

Despite the clarity of Lear's spiritual practices, including mystical exploration, relevance programming, and liberal religious pilgrimage, my depiction of the spiritual politics of American religious liberalism and the Religious Left remains incomplete without an examination of liberalism's exclusionary tendencies, especially when it concerned conservative persons of faith in the public square.[59] When confronted by evangelists who "graded" television programs based on various decency measures, Hollywood necessarily and lawfully defended its own freedom of expression. This defense, however, often meant protecting the Hollywood writer's ability to satirize through a prophetic voice of social criticism and liberal critique. In times of civic and spiritual unrest, conservative religiosity became a favorite subject of ridicule for writers in both the entertainment and knowledge industries. As a result, when Lear wrote or spoke about the Christian Right and its activities, he unknowingly contributed to a longer tradition of "framing" conservative religiosity dating back to the Scopes trial of 1925 and the radio diatribes of Father Charles Coughlin in the 1930s.[60]

When Lear and others began hearing from conservative activists during the 1970s, they inaugurated their own chapter of social theory and analysis of conservative religiosity within a longer story, one that centered on a constituency of Protestant Americans who had finally "matured" enough to become involved in American politics.[61] This interpretation was not anomalous to mainline, interfaith, or Hollywood circles of religious liberals; it was rather *the* interpretation that guided much of their commentary on and responses to conservative mobilization in the American public square. It also defined the intellectual assumptions of the Religious Left when it came to the Christian Right and its seemingly threatening presence in the public square. As such, these arguments might have undergirded the Religious Left's rise to prominence in the form of Lear and his cultural productions during this period, but they also contributed to the very same Left's decline and eventual fall in the wake of Carter's defeat by Reagan and the New Right's successful reappropriation of single-issue advocacy on behalf of the rights of the unborn.

LEAR, LIBERALISM, AND AMERICAN PUBLIC LIFE: A HYPOTHESIS

Lear's story is a significant one for scholars of post–World War II American religion because it assists us in understanding the demographic shift that took place within American Christianity as an instance of "religious restructuring."[62] Lear's commitment to social justice, as witnessed weekly in his programming, arguably mirrored the commitments by countless priests, pastors, and rabbis who traveled to the American South to march on behalf of civil rights as part of the Religious Left. For one commentator at the time, these decisions laid the groundwork for one of the "deepest schisms in the churches since the Protestant Reformation."[63] Lear's style of relevance programming, a by-product of both the relevance activism of the 1960s and his own preference for dramatic writing, mediated much of this conflict for hundreds of millions of people through his didactic comedies that explored racial bigotry and religious discrimination in the name of the public interest.

The significance of Lear's criticisms of the Christian Right and its politics can be additionally understood as one of many within a "whistle-blower" tradition of American public life. Whistle-blowers sound the alarm when they sense that a conservative Protestant is about to upend the First Amendment in the name of theocratic rule. For these individuals, including Lear, "'religion' is not benevolent but dangerous, a divisive and disruptive presence in public life which deflects attention from material concerns or accepted forms of recognition onto scrims and screens that lure people from real world engagement with promise of messianic glory." Within these conditions, "religion" does not corrupt its surroundings. Instead, it is "what corrupts and corrodes the secular, rational character of American ideals and procedures."[64] One of these ideals, one that Lear would later enshrine in his nonprofit organization, was the notion of pluralism in both its civic and religious manifestations. Preachers like Falwell tended to disagree with this assumed value within liberal notions of consensus, which is why his programming oftentimes received greater scrutiny from the FCC and why Lear's did not.

These disagreements revolved around the understudied yet nevertheless significant notion of "the public interest," a principle developed in the 1930s by the
FCC to guide the programming content of those who possessed a license to such
a scarce resource as the airwaves. Because an understanding of pluralism was
already built into the public interest as evidence of its content serving "public
importance," I argue that Lear's programming more often than not slipped past
federal regulations because his writing engaged subjects of public concern through
his interest in pluralism of both voice and program, thereby fulfilling the federally mandated public interest requirement. In other words, to broadcast Lear's
programs as a network, which meant hosting weekly discussions about controversial subject matter in prime time, was to program in and on behalf of the public interest because the content of the programming (the controversy/pluralism)
matched its purpose (diversity of opinions/raising awareness). As a result, Lear
used "the public interest" as leverage to defend his own programming and its subject matter in the name of the public interest, which included didactic story
lines on bigotry, religion, and the women's movement.

Set against this particular religio-political backdrop, the emergence of the
Christian Right as historical subject and media narrative is a significant historiographic artifact of the 1970s as a product of the nation's introduction to evangelicals and their newly defined politics, both liberal and conservative. Much of
this encounter took place through various media including television, feature
films, satire, and the situation comedy—a nexus of creativity and cultural influence Lear was all too familiar with. These representations did not simply reflect
the ephemeral world of the popular; instead, these debates contested many of the
fundamental assumptions guiding the relationship between religion and politics
in American public life and the appropriate grounds for voicing "private" morality *as* "public" deliberation.

Relative to Lear and his interfaith activism, the Christian Right would be better understood both as a collection of organizations, groups, and individuals
who organized on a grassroots level *and* as rhetorical shorthand for a group of
people led not only by televangelists but also by savvy political advisers who over-
saw all administrative and organizational logistics.[65] In this sense, the Christian
Right has been, and continues to be, a unique work of both human and God—
human-made yet, for many, divinely inspired.[66]

Put another way, this book shifts our scholarly attention away from what has
dominated the field of American religion and politics (the Christian Right) to
reveal something novel about the contentious relationship between the center
(religious liberalism) and the periphery (conservative Protestantism) in American public life. My hypothesis is that the culture wars can be best understood as

a fierce contest between competing notions of consensus and the terms deployed to define them—one set dependent on the once powerful welfare state and the other thriving due to an ascendant neoliberal economic regime epitomized in the economic politics of the Reagan administration.[67] Lear's consensus-based establishment position at the heart of America's entertainment industry served as the oppositional foundation for his political activism against the dangers he saw developing in televangelist rhetoric and in their political activism. The subsequent cultural fault lines that emerged from this confrontation, ones identified by sociologist James Davison Hunter in the early 1990s as the culture wars, helped to shape our current forms of religio-political debate, revealing much about the tumultuous nature of American public life over the past half century.[68]

These were not wars over economic or American foreign policy but rather wars over culture and the federal policies that were supposed to arbitrate the proper and the improper, to differentiate the tasteful from the tasteless, and most important, to protect the civil from those who did not know how to be so. This was nothing short of a battle over cultural *power*—the power to disseminate, the power to broadcast, and the power to mobilize in the name of American Ways and Moral Majorities.[69] The Religious Left utilized the then recently formulated notion of "civil religion" in order to explain its rationale for valuing religious pluralism and the calls of one's neighbor over and against those made in the name of the unborn fetus.[70] What was properly "biblical" and what was not were at the center of these debates—and Lear was front and center.

Each chapter possesses its own content and method of execution. I combine historical narrative and ideological analysis in order to better understand Lear's religio-political vision of American civic life as a historical-critical enterprise.[71] Toward this end, each chapter functions as a layer of analysis when it comes to elucidating Lear's cultural productions as products of the spiritual politics of the Religious Left. Chapter 1 introduces the reader to Lear's understanding of the appropriate relationship between religion, American politics, and spirituality as a religious liberal. In the process, I establish a connection between Lear's individual story and those told by scholars of American religious liberalism in order to identify *how* Lear's religious liberalism manifested in public as a form of spiritual politics through his television writing and nonprofit organizing.

My preference for "spiritual" over "religious" when describing Lear's liberalism is a reflection of his own emphases, which tended to orient themselves toward "the spirit" instead of a particular institution or concept like "religion."[72] Lear's politics, however, remains incompletely described without the appropriate acknowledgement of its exclusionary tendencies when it came to conservative religiosity. As such, we can identify Lear as both a political and a social theorist of the Religious Left in his attempts to understand the Christian Right according to largely liberal notions of progress and maturity. Lear's ability to "voice a larger vision for the nation" began and ended with the content of his arguments and spiritual descriptions of American civic life, which included public citations of William James and a double-vision perspective for evaluating and pursuing relevance in the public square.[73]

Chapter 2 examines these descriptions and illustrations of American public life as they were understood by American audiences through the genre of the situation comedy. Lear's most well-known sitcom, *All in the Family*, premiered on CBS in 1971, thereby inaugurating a tradition of prime-time television best described as "relevance programming." Reacting to the largely apolitical programming of the 1960s, Lear established both relevance and topicality as viable narrative structures as he became one of television's earliest auteurs, or showrunners, for situation comedies in the most highly sought-after time slot—prime time.[74] He did so because both narrative concepts were direct products of Lear's religious liberalism as well as his *theatrical* liberalism. As an auteur, Lear influenced the writing, producing, directing, and casting of his various programs including *All in the Family*, *Maude*, and *Sanford and Son* throughout the 1970s.

I contend that Lear extended the theatrical Jewish tradition of cultural and artistic production to the medium of television as millions of Americans each and every week tuned into his shows. For some, this number reached upwards of a quarter of the country at one time. Lear's style of satirical social commentary, as witnessed through the diatribes and arguments of the Bunker family, represented a form of "spiritual storytelling" in prime time, a narrative that was as didactic as it was entertaining. This chapter locates Lear's pluralist project in prime time through ideological analysis of plot and character development as seen in *All in the Family*.[75] This was not simply television; this was television with a purpose, but was it universally understood as such? In many ways, the successes of *All in the Family* as both commercial product and didactic entertainment came at the expense of white working-class life and its own socioeconomic complexities. Those at home certainly laughed *at* Archie, but were they willing to admit that they had laughed *with* him as well? Despite the cynicism that surrounded the production of "Archie for President" bumper stickers and T-shirts soon after the show's inaugural season, they nevertheless spoke to a cosmopolitan mindset that saw Bunker's views as anything but destined for the dustbin of history. Such support, and its resonances with today's cultural divisions, deserve our continued analytical and descriptive attention.

Chapter 3 examines how prime-time television itself became a contested, political space during the culture wars. Building on the previous chapter's analyses of

Lear's television programming, this chapter investigates the relationship between the television networks, Hollywood, and the federal government when it came to the airwaves and their respective regulation. The chapter takes Lear's story back to the days of the crystal radio, Father Charles Coughlin, and FDR in order to describe the historic federal preference for mainline or interfaith partners when it came to programming "in the public interest." I argue that the way in which the FCC defined the public interest ideally suited Lear's programming rationale as programs about "issues of public concern." Unfortunately for Lear and his supporters in the Religious Left, the public interest was far from a consensus ideal during the 1970s. With the rise of televangelism and the electronic church came liberal and conservative reactions of support and derision. In this new world of boycotts and advocacy groups, prime-time television was target number one for evangelists like Falwell, Robertson, and Swaggart in their attempts to rescue the nation from its own cultural depravity. In this culture war, Lear was enemy number one.

The fourth chapter foregrounds Lear's nonprofit organization People for the American Way as a form of interfaith activism during the ascendance of a conservative age. I examine how Lear's nonprofit was an application of his religious liberalism to American politics as an expression of the Religious Left's *spiritual* politics. I also explore how this work was part of a larger "advocacy moment" in the recent history of the American past as organizations such as the Moral Majority and PFAW began reorganizing the religious landscape according to opposing camps and their respective "family values." As a result, PFAW functioned as the civic and spiritual culmination of Lear's religious liberalism, first witnessed on *All in the Family* and later articulated in variety show specials on network television in prime time. I conclude that PFAW was one of the foremost interfaith nonprofits of the Religious Left during the 1980s as the product of one man's quest to protect the public square from the rhetorical iniquities uttered by the likes of Coughlin, Falwell, and Robertson.

The last chapter brings the story of Lear's spiritual politics to a close by examining the Lear authored ABC variety show *I Love Liberty* as an example of what I call "liberal theatrics." This concept is tied closely to the work of scholar of religion Andrea Most and her notion of "theatrical liberalism" as a uniquely Jewish articulation of American ideals. Lear deployed the variety-show setting, along with the power of Hollywood itself, to make an argument about America's best self in opposition to the America portrayed by Falwell and others. Lear's description, however, ultimately belied his own intentions by reinforcing consensus ideals of religious pluralism and civic deliberation over and against the exclusionary tactics of Falwell and his supporters. As a result, when Falwell requested to be a part of Lear's program, he was systematically turned away from the festivities. The show exemplified the rationale behind Lear's television and nonprofit programming because it was designed to raise awareness in the name of relevance and the spirit of fair play, largely at the expense of conservative argumentation. Former senator Barry Goldwater took part in the show as part of its celebrity-laden lineup, but he did so largely as a punchline—not unlike Bunker himself.

In short, this book tells a story about the conflict between differing understandings of American public life in the recent religious past, ones that continue to impact the nature of civic deliberation today and our ability to exchange ideas with one another as members of the public square. The term "spiritual politics" reflects this analytical and categorical work because it captures the nature of religio-political conflict at the time by demonstrating the reliance on and preference for "the spirit" by actors across the political spectrum. Despite the fact that Lear and Falwell may have used the same terms in their various writings, they most certainly meant different things by them. As such, my use of the term not only speaks to conservative articulations during this period but, more important, reflects how the Religious Left understood politics as an extension of the life of the spirit and the search for the common good.

Instead of assigning blame to one religio-political side or the other, the subsequent analysis illustrates how both parties have been culpable for today's polarized populace for reasons both political and religious. It also illustrates how Lear's successes in the realms of popular culture and nonprofit activism ironically came at the expense of his ability to speak to the very masses he programmed for throughout the 1970s. In other words, the Religious Left's rise through culture and its deployment in the public square foretold its decline and eventual fall; Lear's arguments were heard in prime time, but they and others would not stay there for long. In time, late-night talk shows hosted by sardonic comedians came to be seen as some of the more viable spaces for liberal politics due to the satire and social commentary they contained. Despite the cultural influence that accompanied such productions, it paled in comparison to the power attained by those who sought to dismantle the New Deal order by addressing the very audiences that consumed Lear's shows. And for many, Archie had a point.

I

Norman Lear, the Christian Right, and the Spiritual Politics of the Religious Left

On January 21, 1987, the *Christian Century* published a short piece by former senior editor and church historian Martin E. Marty titled "A Profile of Norman Lear: Another Pilgrim's Progress." Looking back on a storied career in television production and writing, Marty relied on the image of the pilgrim, and his proverbial journey, to describe Lear's eclectic spiritual practices and writings and their positive relationship to American civic life. This was valuable information in light of the ongoing criticisms of Lear and his "atheist" programming authored by conservative televangelists such as Jerry Falwell and Pat Robertson. Beginning in the early 1970s, both Lear and his programs were targeted specifically, including *Maude* and *All in the Family*, as evidence of Lear's depraved sense of taste and decency as a notorious member of the Hollywood community.

Marty's article described Lear as a "seriously religious person" who relied on texts from the "mysticism-spirituality-metaphysics" genre for glimpses of the "transcendent" and "the eternal." Most important, Marty described him as a "prominent, unconventionally religious personality" who had assembled an impressive collection of texts including *Pilgrim at Tinker Creek*, *A Road Less Traveled*, and coffee-table books on Jewish and Buddhist civilizations. For Marty, these spiritual practices demonstrated Lear's " 'fitness' to be in on the debates about civic values and public virtues" that were most relevant to his readers in a decade beset by political and religious strife. In fact, no one was better suited to address the nation's most divisive subjects, such as racism, sexism, and religious discrimination, than television producer and writer Norman Lear.[1]

"In talk of values," Marty observed, "[Lear] regularly moves far beyond the television-producing or support of organizations like People for the American

Way; he voices a *larger vision* for the nation."[2] Marty's words pointed to the fact that the "cultural victory" achieved by religious liberalism in the twentieth century, an argument set forth by sociologist Jay Demerath III and echoed by scholars of American religion, was more than simply a Christian victory.[3] It was also a direct product of Protestant, Jewish, and interfaith organizing in the name of ecumenical cooperation.[4] For Lear and his fellow supporters, these activities reinforced their already firm commitment to both preserving *and* defending America's civic fundamentals as they understood them: separation of church and state, religious tolerance, and diversity of opinion.[5]

For this reason, Lear is a significant figure in the story of American religion because both his entertainment and political careers defended the most dearly held values of American religious liberalism, including the separation of church and state, religious diversity, and the free exchange of ideas, as part of what I identify as the spiritual politics of the Religious Left. I first offer a short biography of Lear in order to provide readers with historical context and a sense of change over time dating back to the 1930s. While the use of narrative is a useful tool in this regard, the design and overall execution of the chapter is less concerned with notions of historical progression and more attentive to thematic continuity when it comes to Lear's writings and analyses of conservative Protestantism in the public square. In this sense, my analysis is less a history of Lear's religious liberalism and more an analytical rendering of it and its most significant characteristics as a reflection of the Religious Left. For example, I draw on the work of liberal theorists of democracy to argue that as a liberal, Lear possessed a spiritual "double vision" or "doubled perspective" that he relied on to evaluate which story lines could function as effective plot points for his situation comedies as vehicles for his religio-political vision.[6] This type of vision reflected not only liberal religious thought but also liberal thought more broadly understood within the United States.[7]

Next, I connect Lear and the Religious Left to the rise of "the electronic church" in order to elucidate the most common biases and stereotypes of the thinking, educated, or "chattering" classes. While religious liberals possessed a deep sympathy for other religions, they were also at times quite stringent about their collective abhorrence for orthodox or conservative religion due to their own discursive "framing." In fact, conservative mobilization and activism during this period resulted in its own form of liberal backlash in the form of Lear's analyses of the Christian Right and later People for the American Way.[8] To conclude the chapter, I illustrate the thematic emphases of Lear's spiritual politics across his published and unpublished writings in order to highlight the commonalities between a longer tradition of American religious liberalism and Lear's cultural productions as seen in prime time.

My usage of the term "spiritual politics" implies both a politics having to do with the "spirit" and a politics that grows out of spiritual practice and values as understood according to "the spirit" of a given rule or guideline, such as fairness or justice. The term also points to the thoroughly contested nature of "the spirit" in American public life at the time. This type of politics, along with its moral grounding and social activism, corresponded to other liberal values that Lear practiced and defended, including empathy for the other, sympathy for religious diversity, and progressive electoral politics. Ironically, Lear's ascendance to political and social prominence following his television career would not have been the same were it not for the oppositional force Lear himself arguably helped to identify—the Christian Right. In this sense, the two formed a symbiotic relationship that continues to fuel progressive and spiritual outreach to this day as part of a Religious Left in American public life.[9]

A SHORT BIOGRAPHY OF NORMAN LEAR

Norman Milton Lear was born July 27, 1922, in New Haven, Connecticut. He spent much of his early life, however, in nearby Hartford as part of an extended Jewish family that included grandparents and uncles. His parents, Herman and Jeanette, both worked in sales, yet it was his father who would have the most lasting impact on Lear as a person and on his career as a situation comedy writer. The Lear home was typically filled to the brim with voices—those of his family and those on the radio. Yiddish and Hebrew turns of phrase as well as the odd obscenity sprinkled Lear's earliest experiences of language, set at a high volume. In particular, his father (often referred to as "King" Lear) loved to listen to speeches, fights, and political diatribes from across the political spectrum, from President Franklin Roosevelt to Catholic priest Charles Coughlin. As Lear is fond of saying, his family lived "at the ends of their nerves and the tops of their lungs."[10]

This particular cultural environment shaped Lear's earliest experiences of America and its citizens regarding their potential for both profound good and evil—for it was this period of his life when Lear first felt like an outsider within the American melting pot. Father Charles Coughlin's unrelenting attacks against American Jews during FDR's presidency gave Lear his first experience of religious discrimination broadcast through the latest means of communications. At the same time, Lear also received an education in how best to govern a diverse people when times were tough. The New Deal and its Social Gospel philosophy demonstrated to Lear the need for federally funded social programming in order to address national and local economic inequalities. He would carry both sets of realizations with him into his career as a television writer and political activist on behalf of the American Way and the nation's First Amendment rights of religious expression.

When Lear was only nine years old, his father went to prison for selling counterfeit bonds. This experience left an indelible mark on the young Lear, one that he has difficulty talking about to this day. It also cultivated space for a deeper relationship to form with his uncle Jack and grandfather Solomon (Shya). In particular, Lear's relationship with his grandfather exposed him to a civic tradition that he would later implement himself in both deed and message through his political activism. Shya had a habit of writing letters to the president of the United States in order to express his deep support of or disagreement with particular policies or viewpoints originating in the Oval Office. This practice shaped Lear's sense of how best to express his own viewpoints on the major political issues of the day in a public setting. Lear particularly enjoyed spending time with his grandparents: "The best time of the year was when my grandparents, Bubbe and Zayde, came to stay with us for the high holidays. Their arrival was preceded days before by two or three barrels of dishes, carefully wrapped in the Yiddish newspapers Zayde had read to the last word."[11] Lear would come to embody both his father's desire to make a quick buck and his grandfather's commitment to civic engagement and expression in his own life through his creative writing on television and his political organizing through the nonprofit organization People for the American Way.

Due to financial constraints, Lear did not think he would be able to attend college as a young aspiring writer. He overcame this obstacle by winning a scholarship in an essay contest titled "The Constitution and Me." Lear's subject was a sensitive one in light of his own experiences with the anti-Semitism of Father Coughlin. As a result, Lear "chose to speak to the specialness of being a member of a minority for whom the constitutional guarantees of equal rights and liberties just might have a more precious meaning."[12] Following his victory, Lear was able to attend Emerson College in Boston, Massachusetts, a university founded as a school of oratory. Lear's college career was cut short, however, when he dropped out and enrolled in the military in 1942.[13] Lear flew more than fifty combat missions as a radio operator and a gunner in the Mediterranean and received the Air Medal for his service behind the rudder. Upon his return, Lear began looking for work in New York as a writer. In the early 1950s, he started writing with comedy writer Ed Simmons in an attempt to move beyond the limitations of writing behind the scenes for others. In time, the writing duo caught the attention of comedy team Martin and Lewis, and they eventually worked on the *Colgate Comedy Hour* throughout the 1950s. In 1958, Lear decided to team up with fellow writer and creator Bud Yorkin in order to establish their own television production company, Tandem Productions.

As Lear established himself as a writer and producer in American television, he began to notice a disturbing trend in 1960s network programming. Unlike many of his counterparts who were simply unhappy with the selection of westerns and hillbillies in prime time, Lear noticed an inherent politics in the programming itself that suggested a great deal about the tumultuous times. Instead of identifying this simply as an example of vapid or "wasteland" programming, Lear argued that the networks themselves were sending a very specific if not explicit message to the American people about the nature of conflict, or lack thereof, in the country's citizenry. For Lear, 1960s programming, as mediated through the predominant network logic of "least objectionable programming possible," displayed an America that was not experiencing any sort of unrest or disturbance along racial, religious, economic, cultural, or psychological lines.

Not content to simply stand by as network television continued to invest in shows that were utterly removed from what was happening around them, Lear took it upon himself to add his own voice to the conversation in the form of situation comedy (letter) writing. Only this time, Lear's writing would not remain confined to letters to the president or to his local congresswoman. Instead, Lear addressed the American people directly out of a deep sense of respect for their collective capacity to think bigger and desire a harder-hitting type of television comedy. Ironically, Lear's most significant impact on American television would not be homegrown but rather based on a British import titled *Till Death Do Us Part*—an appropriately titled sitcom that explored the working class in all its admirable and less admirable qualities. It was from this setting, in addition to Lear's own biography, that the character Archie Bunker emerged as one of the most impactful characters in the history of American television as part of Lear's seminal sitcom *All in the Family*.

Lear's discomfort with the sitcoms of the 1960s was only part of the reason that his show made it onto network television. His arrival onto the prime-time stage came at a time when both writers and executives were looking to do something different regarding content and programming. At a time referred to by historians as "the age of relevance," shows such as *MASH* and *The Mary Tyler Moore Show* joined *All in the Family* as sitcoms that relied on the latest newspaper clippings for their content and plotlines. Compared to what had come before, this new material sought to grab its audiences in a manner unheard of in network sitcom history. Executives exchanged the policy of "least objectionable programming" for "relevance programming" in order to make room for the new, edgier material by the likes of Norman Lear, James L. Brooks (*Mary Tyler Moore*), and Larry Gelbart (*MASH*) while also appealing to a youthful demographic who found value in being "in the know."

As a result, Lear's material relied on contemporaneous events in order to speak to larger pressing issues at the time through his characters and story lines. Even though Lear might not have understood such work as "social" or as communicating "a message," his explorations of racism, women's liberation, American politics, and class nevertheless revealed the intentions of a concerned citizen acting on behalf of the public interest and the common good—as he understood them. Luckily for Lear, his causes would never lack vocal support from those in Hollywood or in the Protestant mainline.[14]

THE ELECTRONIC CHURCH: A PRELIMINARY SKETCH

Marty continued to stand steadfastly by Lear and his spiritual idiosyncrasies well into the 1980s because he knew that Lear had much to offer to those concerned about the nation and the state of its public life.[15] Along with other liberal, theologically minded academics such as Harvard professor Harvey Cox, Marty was skeptical of what he understood as "the electronic church" and its efficacy relative to the more traditional pulpits of larger denominational church settings.[16] In essence, the term "electronic church" referred to the television-based ministries of countless evangelists and preachers in the 1970s and 1980s that were largely conservative in their electoral politics. Lear certainly had this in mind when he used the term, but he also used it in a slightly different manner, namely as evidence for the liberal abhorrence of televised ministries based on their profit motives, assumed tax evasion, and inadequate sense of community.[17] Terms such as "electric church" were also used to condescendingly describe televangelists and their seemingly media-driven work.[18] Like the phrases "the Religious Right" or "the Christian Right," "the electronic church" oftentimes functioned rhetorically as a metonym for conservative Protestantism in the public square.[19]

Televangelist action and speech appeared most ominously to Lear during these years because their very existence characterized a significant reversal of private and public interests. Claims that had once been primarily private (morality/religion) had suddenly become the content of much of the public discourse of the time.[20] In fact, one could argue that the electronic church was the most visible and obvious evidence of the Christian Right and its potential impact on American public life during the late 1970s. In light of this challenge, Lear's task was to defend what he understood as a free-speech-oriented system of public deliberation from the autocratic actions and politics of the emerging Christian Right and its support of political conservatism at both the local and national levels. If unsuccessful, parochial claims by extremist televangelists would continue to divide the American electorate along social and religious lines to the detriment of the most cherished of American political traditions for Lear and his ecumenical supporters—the American Way.[21]

When asked, Lear consistently denied any and all intention of trying to educate his audiences or promote a particular political point of view in any of his shows or published writings. In fact, such inquiries were received by Lear with a smile and a nod: "I'm simply an entertainer." Despite this deflection, Lear's television writing introduced the country to the "relevance programming" form of situation comedy.[22] This type of writing was didactic, dramatic, and most important, relevant—at least to those doing the actual writing. As a result, Lear's programming functioned as a televisual space in prime time that facilitated national discussions about pressing social issues on behalf of America and its constitutional freedoms of speech and the exercise of religion.[23] This attention to cultural relevance was not the by-product of Lear's spiritual labors but, in fact, exemplified his commitment to protecting the diversity of opinion in American public life as a spiritual concern as part of the burgeoning Religious Left.[24] In this sense, Lear's work reflected a "mutual commitment to social action as a fundamental aspect of religious experience."[25]

Lear first demonstrated his multifaceted understanding of religion, politics, and American conservatism in an edited collection for Columbia University's School of Journalism with an essay titled "Liberty and Its Responsibilities."[26] As the title indicates, his writing explores liberty and its responsibilities, an apt subject for someone who monitored and defined public space through his entertaining and sitcom writing. Lear's arguments establish both the general thrust of his vitriol against "moral monopolists" and his overarching theory of the pluralism and tolerance necessary for a healthy liberal democracy. His first sentence elegantly connects his television career to his then burgeoning organizing career as a public figure with a spiritual politics who sought relevance as both a television network value and a religious value. In other words, both network executives and Lear himself saw relevance as beneficial to the bottom line, and to the show's popularity in the public eye. "It is the business of television," Lear contends, "to deal with, to reflect, and to report on the times."[27] Echoing the sentiments of many of his liberal religious contemporaries, Lear argues that television programming cannot simply stand by and reflect the culture that it finds itself in. Like many others who produced sitcoms in the early 1970s, including James L. Brooks and Larry Gelbart, Lear made a point to foster discussion by reporting on what he and his writers had read that very day in the pages of newspapers such as the *New York Times* and *Los Angeles Times*.

In light of this brief history, Lear's cultural work as a religious liberal can be understood as a stern reaction against public conservatism through his defense of airwaves and broadcasting time once assumed to be the exclusive territory of the Protestant mainline. More important, Lear's actions symbolized the activities of a mobilizing rearguard in support of a fragile religious consensus that had remained largely intact over the airwaves since the first Radio Act of the 1930s. This act was particularly important because it was designed to keep all "religious extremists," including Father Charles Coughlin, out of the public interest by keeping them off the air due to their divisive politics and religious intolerance.[28] As a result, the proliferation of televangelists and their ministries throughout the 1970s was an all too familiar story to Lear despite the nearly half century that had passed between his childhood encounter with Coughlin and his career as a producer and nonprofit organizer.[29] "In our time of hardship," Lear reluctantly observes, "we find the New Right and Religious New Right—a new breed of robber barons who have organized to corner the market on morals."[30]

Drawing on the words of Abraham Lincoln and his call to seek God's side during times of political strife, Lear defines a term in "Liberty and Its Responsibilities" that appears consistently in many of his writings on American public life and the Christian Right—the "spirit of liberty." In fact, Lear articulates his own interpretation of how best to balance competing interests in public based largely on the writings of Justice Learned Hand, who defended First Amendments rights in midcentury America.[31] For Hand, "The spirit of liberty is the spirit which seeks to understand the minds of other men and women; the spirit of liberty is a spirit which weighs their interests alongside its own without bias; the spirit of liberty remembers that not even one sparrow falls to earth unheeded; the spirit of liberty is the spirit of Him who, near two thousand years ago, taught mankind a lesson it has never learned, but has never quite forgotten."

Lear champions Hand's values of understanding, unbiased evaluation, and assistance within a larger Jesus Christ–centered message. Like other religious liberals, Lear had no difficulty appropriating the insights of various religious traditions within his own writings on spirituality and American religion; in this case, Lear uses the life Jesus led as an exemplar to others in difficult times. Based on these premises, Lear defines a principle of tolerance that contributes to cooperative living as "a people dedicated to achieving consensus through the expression of diverse and conflicting ideas."[32] This task, however, would prove to be more difficult than Lear could ever have anticipated because of the fundamental disagreement between liberal and conservative actors over the place of religion in American public life.

From Lear's social location in Hollywood, the principle of tolerance "is threatened by that extremist coalition of the New Right and some evangelical fundamentalists who would refuse a hearing to any conflicting opinion because they assume that their certainty is the same as absolute certainty." Lear continues, "To disagree with the conclusions of the New and Religious New Right on numerous matters of morality and politics is to be labeled a poor Christian—or unpatriotic—or anti-family."[33] To Lear, the Christian Right represents an autocratic movement designed to suppress intellectual and religious freedoms protected by the constitution. As he later argues, the most pressing concern is the Right's method of division and judgment rather than the content of its public claims.[34] A politics of certainty rather than of civility threatened Lear's and others' attempts to establish agreed-upon rules for religiously informed public expressions—ones defined and maintained largely by various liberals themselves through social protests during the civil rights and anti–Vietnam War movements in the 1960s and 1970s.[35] In fact, Lear often claimed that his own reform efforts were directly descended from those first applied to public life by the protesters of the movement for civil and human rights.

For scholars of American religious liberalism and the Religious Left, there is an enduring and intimate connection between a liberal spirit of critique and acts of public social engagement, including protests, nonprofit organizing, and boycotts. One of Lear's most pressing concerns when it came to these types of negotiations was airspace; in particular, he was worried about the Christian Right's increasing claims to and control of it on a national scale. His political and ethical concerns, ones that were explored comedically through a variety of Hollywood movies in the early 1980s, found their focus in how the political Right seemed to be on the verge of a media takeover as station after station began broadcasting what Lear heard as hate and at times ethnocentrism.[36] Drawing on an extensive tradition of liberal stereotyping of conservative Protestants in the United States, Lear argued that this generation's evangelists were not cut from the same social cloth as their predecessors. To the contrary—they presented an all new set of challenges for those toiling in the vineyard on behalf of the country's most cherished freedoms of speech and religious practice.

FRAMING THE NEW RIGHT: LEAR AS "DOUBLE-VISION" THEORIST OF CONSERVATIVE RELIGION

Lear's criticisms and analyses of the Christian Right were neither novel nor particularly unexpected. In fact, in many instances they were quite derivative of past rhetoric and tropes developed and employed by progressive academics, writers, and intellectuals as examples of "framing" Christian orthodoxy.[37] Scholars such as Martin Seymour Lipset, Richard Hofstadter, and David Riesman published many antagonistic and ambivalent pieces about "Christian orthodoxy" that not only took advantage of the hostile, antifundamentalist narratives generated in response to the Scopes trial but also took part in composing their own stories of progress and cultural ascendancy over and against a conservative religious threat.

For scholar of government Jon Shields, this "elite class of Progressive-era intellectuals and journalists" focused their analytical attention not simply on particular Christian denominations but instead on an abstracted Christian orthodoxy that threatened the nation's most cherished civic freedoms of constitutionally protected intellectual exploration and articulation. Academics of the 1920s who wrote on the relationship between science and religion following Scopes, including president of Cornell University Andrew Dickson White, laid much of the groundwork for the postwar scholarship of Hofstadter and others by focusing on a "traditionary and provincial faith" that rejected logic and scientific discovery at its own peril. Lear continued this tradition of liberal subject formation in his own writings on "moral monopolists" and "robber barons" within America's marketplace of ideas.

Such bifurcated classifications established many of the intellectual categories that postwar intellectuals and religious liberals would rely on to understand periodic resurgences of conservative Protestantism in the United States. They also laid the groundwork for the Religious Left's fall due to its inability to separate prophetic criticism from conservative condemnation and analysis. As a result, the descriptive affinities between the writings of the 1920s and the postwar period provided a substantial foundation for the analytical descriptions of Lipset, Hofstadter, and later Lear regarding "the dangers of the orthodox mind."[38] For Hofstadter, both Catholic and Protestant fundamentalists shared a "common Puritanism, a mindless militancy, and an ecumenicism of hatred."[39] These phrases, along with normative claims concerning manipulative evangelistic practices (electronic church versus institutional pulpit), would become part of the common parlance for liberal academics, intellectuals, and journalists who studied the various cultural manifestations of conservative Christianity in both popular and professional publications. These proved to be especially significant to liberal writers and producers like Norman Lear because they functioned as the key methods and tropes of "framing" conservative Protestants when they began mobilizing against his programming in the mid-1970s.

Such framing, arguably an expression of liberal religious apprehension over the entrance of Christian orthodoxy into American public life, tells us as much about

Lear's own spiritual politics as his defense of the separation of church and state does. By the time conservative Protestantism began mobilizing in the last quarter of the twentieth century, Lear and others were ready with the subsequent frames: "When the Christian Right finally emerged, intellectuals and elite journalists inherited a well-worn critique of orthodox Christians handed down uncritically from their Progressive heirs and further developed by mid-century scholars."[40] In this sense, Lear is a significant figure for scholars of American religion not only for his liberal religious productions but also for his contributions to the study of the Christian Right itself as a concerned member of the Hollywood community.

Lear often cautioned his listeners not to confuse his religious opponents with those of the past. In "Liberty and Its Responsibilities," Lear argues, "It's important that we do not be misled into thinking that these are simply old-fashioned throwbacks—like Bible-thumping, openly racist, blatantly anti-Semitic rough-hewn whackos of another era," Lear warns. "These are smooth, buttoned-down, middle-class Americans, business-oriented evangelicals, . . . revivalistic salesmen—entrepreneurs—who have a genius for responding to the market's desire for stable values."[41] Not only was Lear aware of a longer tradition of such "Bible thumpers," he also added his own interpretive thrust to an already well-established progressive framing tradition of encapsulating conservative Protestants within various forms of media. As anthropologist Susan Harding has argued, since the 1920s fundamentalists had been victims of "modern discursive practices" and an "apparatus of thought that presents itself in the form of popular 'stereotypes,' media 'images,' and academic 'knowledge.'"[42]

These forms of knowledge were assisted by a "modernist code" that assumed primacy in the manner in which conservative Protestants in general, and fundamentalists in particular, appeared in the public imagination as part of a larger "storyline of liberal progress." It was in this moment that Lear took on the role of educator of his fellow (religious) liberals and political progressives in naming exactly what they were up against in the marketplace of ideas. Perhaps more important, Lear arguably contributed to the creation of the very force he meant to counter by perpetuating its presence in the American public through the very media outlets he himself relied on. By doing so, Lear inadvertently placed restraints on the space that he fought so passionately to protect, namely the larger public discourse he so aptly shaped through his own programming. Lear did his best to counter the division he saw (and, more important, heard) emanating from what he understood as conservative "entrepreneurs of the spirit." Oftentimes, however, Lear's own demands for understanding and unbiased evaluation went unheeded.[43]

As a result, Lear's spiritual liberalism sometimes turned in on itself as an expression of intolerance for the intolerant. This did not mean that he was simply a defender of Americans' free speech. His writings and speeches tell us much about his own reading habits, the ways in which Lear translated spiritual values into political processes, and how religious liberalism found its footing within public spaces of ideas and contestation in the form of spiritual politics. Writing for *USA Today*, Lear argued, "It is not the substance of what is imposed but the imposition itself that is objectionable to free people."[44] Regardless of the assumption Lear made concerning the distinction between form and content, he focused his attention on the means and, more important, the manner in which the Christian Right articulated its claims over the airwaves. To Lear, their divisive and oppositional tactics were to the detriment of the majority of their listeners on both civic and religious grounds. Because of the Christian Right's gains in media and print in the form of televangelism, conservative advocacy groups, and think tanks, nothing less than the means of cultural production were at stake in Lear's bid to remind the country of the American way of doing politics.[45]

Lear's more acerbic moments in public, however, were equally counterbalanced, if not more so, by his reflections on liberal religion itself, which foregrounded empathy, sympathy, and a willingness to search for the deepest recesses of transcendence in everyday life.[46] Echoing the concerns of his progressive midcentury forerunners, Lear "took pride in the modern welfare state as an evolving set of solutions to social problems, testable and adaptable, the antithesis of rigid ideology." For historian George Marsden, liberals were generally pragmatic and also "passionately committed to principles such as individual freedom, free speech, human decency, justice, civil rights, community responsibilities, equality before the law, due process, balance of powers, economic opportunity, and so forth."[47] However, liberal principles or ideas only tell part of the story. Liberal sentiments such as empathy are equally as important to consider—especially in light of Lear's empathetic programming of satire, relevance, and tragic comedy. Echoing the likes of Leigh Schmidt and historian David Hollinger, literary critic Amanda Anderson argues that liberalism's most distinctive feature is its "double-vision" structure of thought and analysis.[48]

For Anderson, liberalism is best understood as a "liberal aesthetic." As such, "Liberalism is best understood . . . as a philosophical and political aspiration conceived in an acute awareness of the challenges and often bleak prospects confronting it."[49] This somewhat paradoxical arrangement leads Anderson to describe liberalism according to a "double-vision structure," which utilizes both moral (self-development) and sociological (mass behavior) insights for much of its explanatory power. In this sense, liberalism encourages the optimism and sympathy associated with its religious counterpart, yet it also fosters feelings of pessimism and irony if the ideal is not realized successfully. "Liberals do not have a monopoly on this split view," argues Anderson, "but it tends to cause them more angst, since there is an ideal of reflective enlightenment in liberalism that cannot rest easily with a gap between a sociological condition seen to characterize what the masses do and believe, and its own progressive ideals."[50]

In other words, due to this gap between economic realities and liberal ideals, political and religious liberals direct much of their energy toward rectifying the difference between what is envisioned and what can actually be realized. Lear and his supporters shared this understanding of religion as inherently relevant to its times. This notion reflected a broader liberal understanding of religion, which for some American Protestants meant an emphasis on works for the sake of others. "Eternity and salvation were less important than moral action, proper behavior, and social and political progress," argues American religious historian Cara Burnidge. "This blurred the lines between sacred and secular behavior as liberals initiated public reforms through voluntarism, legislation, and professional careers."[51]

At times, however, the gap between the real and the idealized cultivated a sense of judgment of those who either resisted such reflective enlightenment or privileged a different set of values concerning their own self-improvement. In cases such as these, the distance between the ideal and the actual determined to a large extent the level of criticism directed at those who remained in the gap or fell short of the ideal according to what Harding refers to as a "storyline of liberal progress." For someone like Norman Lear, this gap between the idealized and the realized fostered simple solutions to complex problems within the American populace—ones suitable to seemingly effortless delivery over the airwaves through a religio-political apparatus such as the electronic church.

Anderson also identifies a number of practices and strategies that support the examined and self-interrogated life of Protestant and spiritual liberalisms including "rigorous scrutiny of principles, assumptions, and belief systems; the questioning of authority and tradition; the dedication to argument, debate, and deliberative processes of legitimation and justification; and the commitment to openness and transparency."[52] Once articulated, these "principles and practices" are turned into "a way of life" as they "are infused into political institutions" as part of a larger liberal project of education.[53] Not only do these characteristics resonate with other descriptions of liberal philosophy and religiosity, they also capture the efforts and values of Lear and others to build a more just and understanding country by way of discussion, argumentation, and most important, civility in public. The influence of Lear's mediating position in prime time as writer and producer from within the Religious Left depended greatly on his ability to execute scrutiny and argument effectively through his television characters as well as through his nonprofit organizing for People for the American Way. In this way, Lear is a productive and substantial example of how religious liberalism mobilizes itself by way of a spiritual politics of rigorous self-examination and visions of the societal ideal.

Anderson's framework seems especially appropriate for someone like Lear, who established much of his early success by composing art on television in prime time through sentiment and empathy—a theatrical imagining of another's pain and discomfort by way of the stage. For religious liberals like Lear, the mutually reinforcing relationship between sentiments such as empathy and idealism within a larger double vision helps explain why liberal religion continues to manifest in public spaces through various forms of spiritual politics both within and outside of the institutional church. Despite the limits of these sentiments, along with the gap between civic ideal and material reality, they nevertheless grounded much of Lear's activism and sitcom writing throughout 1970s along with the nonprofit and interfaith organizing to come later in the name of People for the American Way in the early 1980s. This was one of the many thematic continuities that linked Lear's television writings to his advocacy groups as products of his particular religio-political vision of the public square.

LEAR, LIBERAL RELIGION, AND THE VARIETIES OF RELIGIOUS EXPERIENCE

Despite the bombastic nature of his claims against what he understood as the constitutional improprieties of the Christian Right, Lear's religious liberalism was arguably as public as his televised and printed denunciations of conservatism writ large. In fact, he discussed his passion for seeking "the transcendent," however it appeared to him, in a variety of heavily mediated settings including universities, press clubs, and trade publications like *Time* magazine.[54] In a public address to the National Press Club in Washington, DC, titled "The Search for E Pluribus Unum," Lear addressed the subject of his religious background explicitly. "I am a Jew and I love my people and our culture. . . . But that is not what makes me religious. What makes me religious is the way I experience all of creation; what makes me religious is the way I experience the Almighty, and, perhaps, the way I experience life and the way I try to live it."[55] Not only did Lear's words illuminate a particular understanding of being Jewish, they also demonstrated a "post-"

or "extra-" denominational sensibility within a longer history of American spirituality and liberal religion.

Lear certainly acknowledged the importance of Judaism to his spiritual makeup, but it did not have the last say in influencing how he embodied his liberal religious sensibilities in public. This was a most useful approach to both self-conception and the world's manifold religions—namely to have one foot within a tradition so as to free the other for more exploratory projects of discovery. For historian David Hollinger, not only did liberal self-interrogation create space for exploration and seeking, it also facilitated the impact of secular or nonreligious actors on largely Protestant and religious individuals. By identifying and documenting such self-reflexive behaviors and ways of thinking among less traditionally religious subjects, Hollinger concludes that American religious history becomes less about religion and more about religious engagement(s) between oppositional and sympathetic communities.[56]

Despite the freedom that this "post/extra" language offered Lear, he nevertheless recognized the difficulties in naming himself a "religious" person. "I am reconciled to the fact that not everyone who reads these words will agree that I qualify as a religious person, because I have not expressed myself in a manner they could accept," Lear observed.

> My words lack scripture, theology, ecclesiastical authority. Still . . . I have felt and said that if there was no other reason to believe in God, it would have to be the Havana leaf. I have said the same thing while biting into a ripe peach, a just-ready piece of Crenshaw melon, or a great ear of sweet summer corn. I have experienced God's presence in the faces of my wife, my children, my grandson—and every time throughout my working life when I have gone to bed with a second-act problem and awakened in the morning with the solution.

Lear's willingness to locate experiences of the divine beyond the confines of institutional expressions demonstrates his participation in a longer liberal religious tradition dating back to the writings of Thomas Paine, Walt Whitman, and William James as well as transcendentalists such as Henry David Thoreau.[57] In fact, Lear regularly cited such writers in his public addresses and publications in order to better express his civility-centered vision for the country. In particular, it was James's work that first gave Lear an appreciation for living "between the lines, between the experiences."[58]

James's writings played a very similar role for other reading-minded religious liberals of middlebrow culture because they provided their readers with a way of thinking about the world rather than a particular understanding of that world's human and nonhuman subjects. In this sense, James's work is significant beyond the fact that much of it can be connected to the spiritual philosophy of religious liberalism. He not only contributed heavily to the content of religious liberalism itself, he also has served as a reference for spiritual liberals, including Lear himself, throughout the twentieth century. This suggests that other religious liberals viewed James as a source of authority and enlightenment for their own spiritual development and articulation.[59] Politically speaking, scholars have identified this particular spiritual politics as "ethical mysticism" through which a "spirituality of social vision and transformation" can be realized and enacted in public.[60] Despite the fact that progressive politics did not seamlessly map onto a progressive spirituality, "political progressivism, socioeconomic justice, and mystical interiority" came together in such a way as grounds for the development of a "Spiritual Left" in American religious life.[61]

In addition to James, Lear was also a great admirer of writers such as George Bernard Shaw, Ralph Waldo Emerson, Thomas Berry, Robert Bellah, and Joseph Campbell.[62] In describing his own "spiritual journey" and its essentials, Lear explained, "I take with me every great piece of religious writing I have the strength to carry."[63] In one moment, this might be the words and deeds of Jesus; in another, Lear uses the Yiddish *mama-loshen* to convey his sense of harmony in the universe since "the spiritual life of the human species occupies a much larger, more heterogeneous realm than any one organized religion can lay claim to."[64] For Lear, James's work "positioned religious experience, rather than church, creeds, or systematic theology, at the center of religious life."[65] In many ways, this perspective gave Lear the means through which he was able to articulate a religious sensibility in public despite the dominance of largely Protestant vocabularies for such contested epistemological work.[66] In the end, Lear's advice for deeper spiritual experiences for those still groping for it was simple: "I'd like to propose that you set up your own William James School of Investigative Journalism. This will not be easy, I realize."[67] More about form than content, Lear's usage of James reveals much about how he appropriated James's insights for his own spiritual development—namely as a framework or way of thinking about experience, religion, politics, and spirituality.

When speaking of religious and cultural diversity, Lear's public addresses and writings utilized an important analogy that illustrated how liberal religious traditions understood difference in public life in a key of consensus. Lear limited neither himself nor others to a particular box of religious or spiritual identity. In fact, he encouraged as much exploration as possible since such explorative practices opened the individual up to how diverse the world's spiritual resources were to the traveling pilgrim. "Let's not let religious categories get in the way," Lear suggested. "If one were to look at a very long river, one might see flora and fauna, trees and shrubs of varying nature along the many miles of its banks. If we think of our many and varied religions as uniquely different trees along a thousand mile river—and appreciate that they are all nurtured by the same waters—any member of the press should be able to report on the river, the common nurturer of all of our spiritual traditions and common values."[68] More reliant on essences than on particularities, Lear contended that despite the distinctions differentiating one tradition (or tree) from another, there nevertheless exists a common, fluid denominator that binds varying religions together in accordance with a larger source of spiritual congruence. This sign of appreciation functioned well alongside Lear's own sense of sympathy for the other in cultivating a keen sense of wonder at how diverse human spiritual expression could be.

For thinkers like Lear, no single religion could claim a monopoly on truth, spiritual or otherwise. These ideals "supported spiritual seeking across religious expanses hitherto little explored and helped create a liberal religious culture that opened outward into an eclectic spirituality."[69] Lear's rendering of difference, however, belied the conflict necessary to find the one out of the many. For those who limited the spiritual expanses that beckoned attentive and sympathetic observers by reducing religious traditions down to their voting records, Lear had swift and very unsympathetic remarks that ranged from cautious to downright condemning. The unadulterated imposition of explicitly Christian options within the marketplace of ideas by the Christian Right threatened what Lear saw as essential to American public life—namely the possibility for tolerance, diversity, and understanding within moments of difference.

In this sense, Lear sought a spiritual or discursive form, which included rules governing discussion in the public sphere, for example, rather than content in his confrontations with the Christian Right. Lear's descriptions of the Right as "absolutist" and as "monopolists" gave voice to the sentiment that in order to participate in national conversations, individuals must possess an appreciation for the truths of other voices and opinions. Despite the fact that Lear himself could not extend his own appreciation for the exchange of ideas to those Christian fundamentalists who differed from him, he still regarded such values as essential to seeing the river that united all in its ever-wandering path.

Lear's spiritual vision of American civic life perhaps found its clearest articulation in front of an audience of fellow academic seekers and gropers.[70] In 1989, Martin Marty invited Lear to speak at the largest annual gathering of scholars of religion in the world, the American Academy of Religion (AAR) national conference.[71] Politically speaking, the 1980s had been a very productive decade for Lear. He had launched his nonprofit organization People for the American Way with the help Marty and others, organized the star-studded *I Love Liberty* television special in hopes of fostering nonpartisan discussion of social issues, and established the Business Enterprise Trust for those who had social vision and "moral imagination" in the world of business.[72] Lear's ability to utilize media in the form of the sitcom, the thirty-second spot, and the two-hour special was matched only by Marty's well-honed counsel on how best to reach the American people when discussing contentious issues such as religious freedom and free speech.

Lear titled his AAR plenary talk "Nurturing Spirituality and Religion in an Age of Science and Technology." As expected, he discussed his work with PFAW, the Christian Right, and the means for overall spiritual health. To Lear, the Right threatened the nation's most cherished traditions: pluralism and tolerance. In order to work more cooperatively, Lear suggested focusing on the sacred: "If we can't find what is sacred in that tree, in that butterfly, in each other, then the sacred symbols of our several religions will never satisfy that yearning for connection of which I speak."[73] In short, sacrality transcends religious particularity within nature and the environment as part of a broader, eclectic Lear-authored spirituality.

Due to the perceived intolerance and intransigence of conservative Protestants, Lear emphasized the very same interfaith values that People for the American Way would represent in its own educational activities—church-state separation, pluralism, and ongoing public discourse. Such discussions were also to carry over into the public schools so students could understand just how important religion was to the nation's history and its spiritual formation. For Lear, teachers "must inspire students to nurture that inner world, where humans from the very beginning of the species have shared the same sense of awe and wonder as they groped for meaning." This task had to be accomplished, however, "without preaching a sectarian creed or degenerating into a moral nihilism."[74]

Despite the passion behind these words, it was arguably tempered by a caution all too familiar to one who had experience with conflicts over religion in public. Not only had Lear's organization been accused of partisan politics by his conservative opponents, televangelists had also argued that his television specials and ad spots served as propaganda for a political organization rather than serving an educational one purpose. Lear's qualifying conclusion suggested that there were not only clear answers but right ones to the problems he and others addressed in American public life that stood outside parochial interests and moral skepticism. Unfortunately for Lear, such arguments could not escape their religious particularities.

Lear's blindness to his own notions of consensus and his perspectival singularity, one cultivated by a sense of being more representative of the mainstream than was actually the case, was again apparent in his discussion of schools. "A chorus of diverse voices has grown into a consensus that, yes, we do need to do a better job of teaching about religion in the schools," he argued. "This sentiment is now shared by the National Council of Churches (NCC), the US Catholic Conference, and the American Jewish Congress." Lear's dependence on largely ecumenical Protestant and liberal Jewish institutions signified a religious authority that possessed its own politics and values in the public square. As a result, Lear's religious allegiances to the Protestant mainline, as evidenced by his relationship with church historian Martin Marty, as well as his institutional backing by the NCC aligned him at times more with the cultural and religious investments of an interfaith consensus center than with the political or radical Left.

This tendency would come to define much of Lear's nonprofit work despite his claim to an inclusive and pluralistic American Way. "We must begin to make commitments to higher values, live a moral code that connects us with each other and with eternity," Lear explained in a 1992 interview for the Catholic periodi-cal *Commonweal*. "Ninety percent of Americans believe in a higher meaning—God. It seems so foolish for all the people who care to use religion properly—I mean privately, personally—to cede so much to the fringes to the fundamental-ists and the new-age people." For Lear, religion had rules. Particular expressions and their corresponding formats were allowed while others remained on the side-lines of a discussion larger than any one individual. This was necessary because of the various abuses perpetrated by Christianity's most ardent defenders during Lear's childhood and adult life. If individuals could simply appreciate religion without using it to divide, then a "spirit-led philosophy" could be enacted in politics—one that held toleration, civility, and diversity in very high regard as the basis for American civic life.[75]

CONCLUSION: POLITICS AS POPULAR CULTURE

Unlike many of his spiritual forebears, Norman Lear did not author formal trea-tises or memoirs on the intricacies of sympathy and religion. He never held a position within a university or a church setting in a traditional sense. He also did not attend religious services consistently, Jewish or otherwise. When I asked about his Jewish background, Lear stated that he was grateful for it but that it did not define his religious or spiritual capacities.[76] Such linguistic sidestepping, however, illuminates an alternative approach to the study of religious liberalism—one that asks its first questions outside of institutionally religious spaces. This is a produc-tive method for studying liberal religion and the Religious Left because in order to understand the proliferation of liberal sensibilities through American culture in the twentieth century, one must look to the various "mechanisms of popular religion" for evidence of widespread dissemination as expressions of late twentieth-century American religious middlebrow culture.[77] Such mechanisms, including book clubs, ad spots, television specials, and nonprofit organizations, possessed a power equal to that of more identifiably "religious" or Christian means of information broadcasting.

Cultural productions like Lear's provided their respective audiences with a model for understanding American politics and the debates contained within. In particular, "these cultural portraits not only reflect the religio-political agenda of their creators, they also serve as templates for inhabiting a political world."[78] The specific content of this model originated in the interfaith cooperation that was inherent in the American Way dating back to the interwar period. This suggests that the very notion of consensus itself, something Lear consistently appealed to, was a product of liberally minded religious and spiritual actors writing on behalf of their own self-interests. Unlike other claims to public space, this one in particular seemed to map seamlessly onto broader concerns for the well-being of the nation and its cultural and political institutions. The effort and means necessary for such demographic mapping were considerable, but with mainline resources, in addition to Lear's, a tenable consensus could be established over and against its antithesis, the Christian Right, in the name of the American Way.

Regardless of the venue, prime time or otherwise, Lear's writing was palpable. It made his viewers sit up straight, laugh out loud, and shed the odd tear. It was dramatic, comedic, and theatrical—one-act plays strung together in the form of a situation comedy. As many interpreters have commented, Lear wore his emotions on his sleeve. Empathy for the other, sympathy for religious diversity, and appreciation for religious experience formed the core of Lear's spiritual and religious practice. "I have found that my involvement with People for the American Way has only quickened my spiritual interests. By listening more closely to the deeper message animating so much of the Religious Right's rhetoric, . . . I came to appreciate the depth of spiritual yearning among so many Americans." Lear went on, "The charlatans of TV ministries were, and are, connecting with a vast population of parched souls. Our culture has become a stranger to its own inner needs."[79]

Lear's prescription for the country's ailments was simple: find balance between the bottom line and the inner spirit, cultivate a broadly civil religion in order to establish an arena for public discourse, define the nature of said public discourse as consistently civil regarding religious differences, and support the total separation between church and state in order to avoid a politically sanctioned religious hegemony. Religious and political liberals like Lear can be proud of the fact that many of these realities are, in fact, liberal ones as part of a "cultural victory" in exchange for organizational defeat.[80] The story of Norman Lear's spiritual liberalism is notable, however, not simply for its participation in the cultural victory but also for its resistance to the organizational defeat of liberal and ecumenical Protestantism after the Second World War.

Lear's impact on American religion and politics first became noticeable during the early 1970s when shows such as *All in the Family* and *Maude* began to grace the television screens of Americans in prime time. These shows functioned as mechanisms of popular religion by facilitating televisual space for a discussion of the social issues of the day such as bigotry, feminism, and race in the name of relevance. Lear embarked on yet another spiritual journey when he decided to leave television for the nonprofit realm of education. Once there, with the help of politicians and mainline Protestant religious leaders, Lear built the most significant post–World War II interfaith organization in People for the American Way in order to address the rhetorical iniquities in the public sphere committed by the electronic church.

Like many of his future PFAW programs and campaigns, Lear's television work "provided a springboard for discussion, a conduit for understanding, and a means of obtaining 'nourishment for the soul.' "[81] Prompting discussion was Lear's bread and butter as both a producer and a nonprofit organizer, yet in his own estimation, he was only doing what he thought was best. "Look, I'm a fucking entertainer. We're storytellers. But we *think*. And the things we think of are much harder to deliver on. It's a bitch to get it right."[82] I have argued for understanding Lear and his careers in entertainment and nonprofit organizing as part of a broader spiritual politics, one that is able to move in tandem with fellow religious and theatrical liberals due to their shared notions of stewardship of the public square, seeking as groping, and the separation of church and state. However, Lear's liberalism also tended to turn in on itself when it facilitated the framing of conservative religiosity as spiritually retrograde at best. For many of his supporters, Lear's television programming ultimately got it right more often than not—even if it meant politicizing the very genre he had made possible with topical and relevant programming. *All in the Family* was just this type of show.

2

All in the Family and the Spiritual Politicization of the American Sitcom

Before Lear established his command of the prime-time airwaves, relatively few writers and producers had explored controversial topics over a medium viewed by the entire family. In fact, a noticeable disconnect existed during the 1960s between televised story lines and national events.[1] From the networks' perspective, this was anything but problematic since providing the least objectionable programming to the widest possible audience ruled the day. It took some time for Lear to admit that, relative to the networks, his own programming reflected the interests and social vision of a religious liberal accustomed to the rhythms of Judaism and the extended family, but he eventually acknowledged his own complicity in the backlash against his situation comedies. "When I was asked whether I had a *right* to say the things that were said in the shows, in the early days I would avoid admitting that we did more than entertain," Lear explained. "Then I began to realize that I was 50 years old, a grown man, with responsibilities and attitudes, and why wouldn't I have thoughts and why wouldn't my work express them?"[2]

For Lear and other Hollywood liberals of the period, situation comedy writing functioned as a valuable platform from which to articulate their own sense of right and wrong when it came to American politics and society. In fact, Lear's programming defined the initial contours of this tradition of topicality in prime time as a form of didactic, spiritual storytelling that relied as much on the language of morality and religion as his conservative religious counterparts did. These television narratives in what historians identify as the "age of relevance" utilized contemporaneous events and debates as frameworks for exploring subjects such as race, religion, and gender according to the appropriate ethical and civic parameters of public deliberation.[3] For *Christian Century* editor James Wall, "Lear gives us a comedy with a purpose. He is a village elder . . . successfully telling tribal members gathered about the campfire/tube that individuals are different but valuable. . . . Sly jokes about sex, rather than being intended as dirt, give the inarticulate a way to express affection."[4] Lear's programming possessed a "style of social criticism" all its own, one that oftentimes emanated from his own form of an electronic church, his own "personal bully pulpit."[5] Exemplified by Lear, this brand of televisual criticism was a hallmark of *relevance programming*, a type of prime-time situation comedy writing that used entertainment in an instructional manner to educate the populace on current events and their political ramifications in the public square.

Those who supported Lear and his writing, including Wall and others in the Religious Left, insisted that he not pay too much attention to the calls for less "sex 'n' violence" on television and instead focus on what he did best—offer an enlightened, instructional word on the social controversy of the day.[6] For Wall, Lear's task was simple, the "preaching about moral and social issues in an entertainment setting, purveying his message in a way that captures and retains the attention of more people than does any other preaching we know." These words typified Lear's method of communication as manifested in prime time. Shows like *All in the Family* relied on a form of satirical comedy that created a space for Lear's unique brand of social and cultural criticism. In addition, he utilized satire and irony to "throw a humorous light on our frailties, prejudices, and concerns." More important, "By making them a source of laughter, we hope to show—in a mature fashion—just how absurd they are."[7] These words not only reflected Lear's own rationale for the numerous situation comedies he wrote and produced, they also served as a network-authored disclaimer before the airing of the pilot episode on CBS in 1971.

This chapter examines Lear's prime-time programming—with particular attention paid to *All in the Family* and its critical reception as well as its strategic use of satire—in order to say something about the relationship between spiritual politics, television entertainment, and comedy within a liberal democracy. I argue that as a sitcom showrunner, or auteur, Lear at once introduced new content to prime-time audiences and reflected the broader spiritual clarion call of the decade to be "socially relevant" as part of a "New Morality" in the 1970s.[8] As such, Lear's programming can be understood as part of the same "relevance" moment that applied first to the American churches, both Protestant and Catholic, but nevertheless was designed with the same purpose and aspiration in mind—to remain relevant (that is, topical, in TV speak) in a constantly changing world.[9] In essence, Lear understood the purpose of his chosen medium as an instructional, almost pedagogic instrument to be utilized in the name of awareness and to make a cultural impact on his audience.[10] In order to better understand Lear's ascendancy within ecumenical Protestantism during the 1970s that culminated in the formation of the interfaith nonprofit People for the American Way, we must first address the programming's context as well as its uniquely liberal characteristics and satirical disposition. But, first, a few words about definitions.

Unlike his conservative disparagers, Lear's comedy writing did not identify a particularly *Christian* or *Jewish* perspective on a given topic. Instead, he chose to foreground the form of debate itself, admittedly in its consensus model, as the preferred way of making informed decisions concerning the nation's perennial racial, cultural, and religious challenges. In this way, Lear contributed to two ongoing religious traditions in the United States dating back to the nineteenth century: religious and theatrical liberalism(s).[11] As previously argued, my usage of these terms reflects a larger desire to locate and describe the Jewish characteristics of Lear's spiritual politics within a larger Spiritual Left in late twentieth-century America. As such, Lear's theatrical liberalism shared many of the characteristics that define religious liberalism more broadly, including a cosmopolitan sensibility about religious diversity and an ethical commitment to engaging one's surroundings in the name of moral improvement. In this sense, theatrical liberalism can be understood as a Jewish contribution to the longer history of American religious liberalism dating back to the colonial period.

Another common denominator between the two liberalisms is that they both share a liberal disposition toward religion and religious truths, which includes a willingness to adapt one's religious thought to socioeconomic conditions. As Cara Burnidge argues, "In religion, liberalism refers not to a political paradigm but to philosophical and religious positions with social, economic, and political implications."[12] As a result, the term "liberal religion" may be helpful in describing an understanding of religion outside of any particular Protestant register regarding Lear and his published writings. Moreover, Lear's ability to demonstrate his social awareness through the genre of the situation comedy, which included story lines on abortion, rape, hate crimes, and sexuality, gained further narrative appeal through his appreciation for and execution of public debate as measured sitcom deliberation—even at high volume.

In these moments, the soundstage morphed into a prime-time classroom where the subjects of study were religious toleration, civility, and diversity in front of audiences numbering in the hundreds of millions. Like his Students for a Democratic Society contemporaries, Lear put culture to work in both satirical and ironic modes as a vehicle for his various representations of the American family and the challenges they faced as part of the working class in the midst of significant economic restructuring.[13] As such, I argue that the relationship between

Lear and the Religious Left assumed different dynamics at different times due to his spiritual politics, ranging from mutually supportive partners to adviser and advisee. For one author writing for *Christianity Today*, Lear's leadership was indispensable to mainline leadership: "Many liberal churchmen, threatened by the rise of the Religious Right, are marching under his banner."[14] As such, I foreground Lear's programming in this chapter by first reviewing its theatrical tendencies in terms of both writing and production values. I then conclude the chapter with a close reading of select episodes from *All in the Family* in order to demonstrate the dimensions and characteristics of Lear's spiritual vision in prime time.

LEAR AS THEATRICAL WRITER AND PRODUCER: A THEMATIC OVERVIEW

Lear's programming dominated the 1970s with no less than six different sitcoms airing throughout the decade including *Maude, Sanford and Son, Mary Hartman Mary Hartman, Good Times*, and *The Jeffersons*. Such dominance spoke not only to the shifting programmatic tendencies of network executives at the time but also to Lear's commitment to entertaining and making people laugh through a dramatic interpretation of the situation comedy. What distinguished Lear from other entertainers and writers, however, was that he wanted to entertain and make people laugh *about something*. This "something" reflected Lear's own understanding of what role television should play in the education and entertainment of a national polity.

For Lear, "Comedy with something serious on its mind works as a kind of intravenous to the mind and spirit."[15] As a child of the radio, Lear understood the power of this medium and utilized its nearly ubiquitous reach to entertain and educate his American and international audiences about the challenges facing American families in the 1970s—bigotry, discrimination, and economic restructuring.[16] Lear's "something" was also a product of the tumultuous events of the 1960s—the details of which began reaching prime-time audiences during the same era when the shows of Norman Lear, James Brooks, and Larry Gelbart began dominating nightly ratings and awards shows, including *MASH* and *The Mary Tyler Moore Show*. These men left lasting legacies in the annals of television history and its study as a form of televisual literature, but it was Lear who forever altered the situation comedy genre in accordance with his spiritual vision of the nation.

Unfortunately for Lear, many laughed at what they saw not because of the satirical treatment of Archie Bunker but because of what he said—literally. Those who got it, got it. Those who didn't, still got it, but in an entirely different register. Lear's labor in and on behalf of the entertainment industry established what scholar of religion Jason Bivins has identified as a largely liberal "political culture of American religion," which encouraged civil religious remedies for the nation's socioeconomic ills—deliberation, argumentation, and civility.[17] Despite the high volume of most of his shows, Lear's writing did not single out the "correct" or "most legitimate" position or opinion concerning the topic of the week. Instead, it foregrounded the space itself, and the exchange of ideas that took place within, as the most valued aspect of American civic life. The content would vary from episode to episode and from week to week, but the format remained consistent: introduce controversial subjects to your viewership through the everyday interactions of an intergenerational American family that does its best to weather the throes of change and progress.

Reacting against the programming of his predecessors, Lear accomplished three goals by emphasizing real-world events in his scripts: he dealt with, reflected, and most important, *reported on* the times in which he wrote.[18] This journalistic impulse undergirded the relevancy programming that he and others became known for in the early 1970s with shows like *All in the Family* and *MASH*. Lear's dedication to cultivating programming relevant to his times and audience illustrates his instructional style of situation comedy writing, one that relied on satire for much of its moral and social critique. His programs were relevant because he and his team of writers made it a point to expose (and sometimes introduce) their audiences to the moment's most divisive social flashpoints including racism, bigotry, and sexual discrimination. Such topicality reflected the desires of a serious man interested in serious subjects, but it also spoke to the longer progressive tradition of ethical liberalism that sought a robust voice in public debates

For American religious historian Leigh Schmidt, the blending of "political progressivism, socioeconomic justice, and mystical interiority" grounded the development of a "Spiritual Left" in American religious life, a front of robust religiopolitical aspiration that found much to celebrate in Lear's programming and political activism in the name of tolerance and civility.[19] In this sense, Lear's work in television and nonprofit organizing falls squarely within the parameters of religious liberalism as one of its most significant contributors in the second half of the twentieth century. Despite the fact that Lear shared the same understanding of religion and spirituality as his religious liberal and liberal Protestant supporters, however, his emphasis on the ethical and moral dimensions of a given religious tradition was more a product of his liberalism than it was of a uniquely Protestant formulation. "Protestant liberalism altered the purpose of religion," argues Burnidge. "Religion centered on ethics and morals for liberal Protestants. According to most liberals, Christianity should improve society by bolstering ethical standards and improving social conditions."[20] As such, Lear's spiritual politics was equal parts religious and liberal, with the former emphasizing spiritual enlightenment and the latter encouraging ethical rigor and critical examination for their own sakes.

Like his unpublished and published writings, Lear's television programming narrated a vision for the nation through plot, character development, and dialogue. His desire to educate and illuminate through drama and satire found its realization in the topicality of *All in the Family* and the inevitable watercooler talk that followed in offices and living rooms across the country. The soundstage itself took on additional spiritual value for Lear as countless audiences throughout the decade laughed, cried, and gasped at the performances. For Lear and other theatrical liberals, the stage functioned as a sacred space where comedy and communal obligation came together in both writing and performance.

For scholar of religion Andrea Most, Lear's experiences speak to the intimate connection between word and spirit on the stage as experienced by countless Jewish playwrights and authors across the twentieth century. "These works reconstruct the theater as sacred space, a venue for religious expression, and the performance of acts of devotion, thereby turning theatricality into a respectable cultural mode."[21] In light of Lear's reliance on and deft utilization of media, Most's insight resonates well beyond the confines of the studio or theater stage—for it is this mode, the mode of culture, that emerged in the 1960s as the preferred medium of Lear and others for liberal politics. As such, Lear's writing can be understood as theatrically liberal because it emphasized public action over internal reflection and the human capacity to self-fashion despite external constraints.[22]

In addition, Lear's politics reflected the characteristics of the period's Jewish liberalism, which emphasized intellectual independence, social justice, and worldly engagement.[23] These largely Jewish values found much common cause with the tenets of ethical or mystical liberalism, which also emphasized public engagement and progressive social projects. For one scholar of American religion, "Mystical and ethical liberals typically championed a more progressive politics, including a robust social welfare state and, on occasion, pacifism."[24] Lear's ability to enact his concern for the spiritual health of the country through prime-time television in general and the situation comedy in particular added yet another chapter to a longer story about spiritual politics in a liberal key in late twentieth-century America.

Not unexpectedly, the varying familial relationships between the characters on *All in the Family* represented an amalgam of American social and cultural values in flux in the early 1970s—old and young, man and woman, conservative and liberal, all given voice in a span of twenty-three minutes. It is in these senses that we can call Lear's programming theatrically and religiously liberal based on its topicality and willingness to adapt to its social surroundings as an expression of his spiritual politics. "Theatrical liberalism represented for Jewish writers not only a spiritual calling but also a means by which to model a self, to integrate into American society, to gain the freedoms inherent in social and economic mobility, and to insure the widest possible application of these freedoms for all Americans."[25] Through careful study of these various techniques and narrative conventions, we are able to critically evaluate the greatest strengths and weaknesses of Lear's religious liberalism in serialized action throughout the decade under study.

Both Lear's chosen medium and genre, television and the situation comedy, respectively, embodied his commitment to a civil religious understanding of American public life that emphasized unity through and often at the expense of diversity in the name of understanding and toleration. As a result, television itself became a makeshift forum for debate and deliberation in the name of enlightening entertainment. "Theatrical liberalism guaranteed secular Jews the freedom to perform the self," argues Most, "a freedom cherished by a people so often denied the right to self-definition, whether by Christian dogma or racial science."[26] The threat to this freedom of expression posed first by Father Coughlin and then by the Christian Right were what most disturbed Lear. This especially became the case when Falwell, Robertson, and others began organizing "the electronic church" and the larger conservative movement around single-issue campaigns, Bible Scorecards, and claims concerning the legitimacy of Jewish prayers amid analogous Christian ones.[27]

In short, the "liberal vision" that historians, cultural critics, and journalists have associated with *All in the Family* resonated with Lear's own spiritual vision of America, one that was socially inclusive but largely religiously exclusive when it came to conservative Protestantism. This reality was a product of both Lear's individual biography and the longer tradition of liberal framing that had been ongoing since the Scopes trial of the early twentieth century.[28] Simply put, Lear's commitment to broadcasting material drawn directly from the news headlines of the day, in the sitcom format, facilitated numerous national conversations about sex, race, gender, and religion every week in prime time. This thematic emphasis linked Lear to other religious and spiritual liberals who championed freedom of expression, dialogue, and open debate regardless of the topic under discussion or medium of choice.

☞

In its heyday, Lear's *All in the Family* was the most watched show for five consecutive years by drawing upwards of 60 percent of the viewing public.[29] This translated into close to fifty million viewers nationwide each and every Saturday evening.[30] Once broadened to include all of Lear's shows broadcast throughout the 1970s, the numbers become even more extraordinary as close to 120 million Americans watched his programs weekly.[31] On set, Lear was the quintessential "bleeding-heart liberal" who was also a humanist, a pacifist, and a fierce defender of free speech.[32] Interviewer Barbara Cady said of him, "In the course of our many taping sessions, it became clear to me that Norman is a laboratory specimen of that all-but-vanished species, the bleeding-heart liberal. . . . His staff is a model of racial and sexual integration, [and] his shows are miniature morality plays for the social causes to which he devotes himself off-screen."[33] Both in front of the camera and behind it, Lear was an active participant in securing rights for his fellow writers in addition to battling and eventually suing the FCC and the networks for infringing on their free speech in prime time.[34] In this sense, Lear's status as one of Hollywood's earliest showrunners undergirded his larger religio-political agenda of defending the American Way and its civil public sphere through the medium of television and the genre of the situation comedy.

As an auteur, Lear possessed the rare power to define the social vision of his programming across his considerable televisual catalog. "At times, the differences over economic and creative interests result in programming fit for the widest possible audiences. However, for individuals like Lear, such conditions only encouraged him to push beyond what the network executives thought the country could handle as a 'voice of social commentary.'"[35] Considered within this analytical framework, Lear's entertaining appears as a much more complex process of statement making, entertaining, and comedic monitoring of social values and norms through television programming. As a result, Lear could not help but be concerned with how his artistic contributions participated in a larger conversation about civic life in America. "While concerned with the responses of his individual characters," historians Horace Newcomb and Robert Alley point out, "he is equally concerned that his presentations be considered as contributions to a wider social discourse. [Lear] injects his own ideas, via his television shows, into the national debates on general problems: racism, sexism, class conflict, and personal rights."[36]

Unlike his entrepreneurial media colleagues on the political and Christian Right, Lear did not intend to articulate a coherent position on a given set of issues of social or religious consequence while he was a producer. Instead, Lear vehemently supported the idea of the free exchange of ideas itself rather than advocating for a particular position on an issue in question. In this manner, Lear could be understood as simply "entertaining" and educating, not taking political stances in prime time (thus remaining in complete accordance with the federally created and maintained FCC fairness doctrine). On the other hand, Lear's insistence on free exchange also included sets of discursive rules for how such exchanges took place (civilly) and over what political issues (e.g., women's and First Amendment rights). Those who seemed overly divisive or combative on television or over the radio were more than likely left out of the ongoing conversation. In essence, social facilitators like Lear defined the parameters of televised public discussion by entertaining viewers and thereby monitoring the topics under discussion, the participants, and their collective values.[37]

In light of this evaluation, it is not surprising that by the late 1970s, Lear eventually admitted his concern for American society and culture beyond simply the network arena, which included everything from bigotry and sexual discrimination to religious intolerance. For Lear, "Television offers the excitement of having an idea on the fifth of September and seeing it dramatized and delivered to forty million people on the fourteenth of November. . . . The exciting thing in television is to pick up a headline on one day and have a story about it three months later on the air for a vast audience, much larger than ever imagined in the 1950s."[38] Lear's concern for the public resonance of his programming spoke to his civic desire to both entertain and educate viewers on the subjects of race, class, and gender while carving out a space in public for such a conversation to begin with. He also had much to say about the differences between his own sense of the religious or spiritual and the faith of the electronic church. It is at this intersection, one that was as much about contrast as it was about the coconstitution of opposing religio-political forces, that we find Lear's most articulate expressions of his spiritual politics in prime time.

Such analytical clarity does not stem from an ability to identify a particular "message" or, more important, a political position in a given episode but rather from the show's structure and form as well as its controversial subject matter. Despite the limitations of the situation comedy, Lear enthusiastically utilized its conventions in order to project an image of America that was conducive to both consensus and interfaith values of civility, public deliberation, and religious toleration. His programming sought a reinvigorated public life along the lines and regulations of liberal political theory, including bifurcations between public and private and a civil religious model of public reason.[39] Unfortunately, this model was only applied to the involvement of less than liberal constituencies in the country's political and social life, including Archie Bunker himself. As a result, Bunker became the paradigmatic character that reminded his viewers, through satire, why civic life required as many rules as it did protections of First Amendment rights.

It is in this sense that Lear's *All in the Family* can be understood as a product of religious liberal theorizing—it frames debates rather than ending them, it facilitates discussions rather than curtailing them, and it informs its audience rather than talking down to it (although this was certainly not an impossibility). The sheer dominance of Lear's situation comedies throughout the 1970s suggests that his position within the industry was not a politically or socially insignificant one. In fact, I argue that Lear's programming in general and *All in the Family* in particular contributed to the spiritual formation of an increasingly televisual culture according to the dictates of a theatrical and religious liberal.[40] This formation, however, did not unfold without its fair share of resistance and commentary. In fact, it possessed a moral context all its own, at once a reflection of and a contributor to the decade's cultural turmoil in a key of increasing polarization.

LEAR AND THE NEW MORALITY

Lear's relevance programming coincided with the emergence of "the New Morality," a heightened concern for the speed at which American society seemed to be progressing regarding its time-tested and religiously protected sexual, racial, and cultural norms.[41] Sitcoms were no longer populated exclusively by white or nuclear families like the programming of previous decades. In fact, it was this narrative vacuity that catalyzed Lear to formulate *All in the Family* as an explicit response to the lack of conflict or diversity depicted in the programs of the 1950s and 1960s in the first place. This experimentation and network-supported risk-taking reflected a larger social development at the time, namely a "New Morality" in both American culture and society.[42]

Predictably, both Norman Lear and fellow producer James L. Brooks (*Mary Tyler Moore Show*) were implicated in the emergence of this New Morality and its corrosive influence on American society. For one impassioned critic, television invited the backlash it helped to create due to the fact that it served as the gateway for less than desirable characters to enter into peoples' homes on a nightly basis. For one particular viewer, "That set is no longer a welcome guest in my home. I would no more plug it in today than I would invite a prostitute to dinner."[43] Much of this fervor found its characteristic expression in the activism of fundamentalist Billy James Hargis, who published a faulty report about a then recently purchased CBS movie archive of supposed "filth." Organizations such as Morality in Media and Stop Immorality on TV joined Hargis in criticizing network programming due to its pornographic and at times indecent content.[44]

Like other cultural conflicts during this period, the differences of opinion and taste over the appropriateness of television programming possessed their corresponding political expressions in the public sphere along liberal and conservative lines. "One polarized group feels America's moral backbone is decaying and is sure TV's new liberalization is both a cause and symptom of that decay. At the opposite pole are those who sneeringly dismiss the first group as far-right political nuts or religious fanatics."[45] Not only is this observation indispensable evidence of the burgeoning culture wars developing in America during the 1970s, it also points to how television in general, and prime-time TV in particular, was one of the many cultural entities under siege from various conservative and liberal political action and advocacy groups in the name of tolerance.

Lear directed his own criticisms toward televangelists Jerry Falwell and Pat Robertson for giving "simple answers to complex questions." For fellow producer and writer Ed Weinburger (*Mary Tyler Moore Show*), the New Morality reflected the changing times more than it did the nefarious machinations of Hollywood and intellectual elites as an expression of their freedom of speech.[46] Both Lear and Weinburger relied on a First Amendment argument to defend their respective programming against both the network-devised "Family Viewing Hour" and conservative attacks against the medium and its prime-time lineups.[47] For Weinburger, the most popular shows "deal with real issues. We can't hide from the real world." They also contributed something intangible, for better or for worse, to the American polity, "And I don't think this society is going to get any better by sticking to shows like Petticoat Junction."[48] Not only did Weinburger's conclusion assume that television could indeed influence its viewing public, it also held the implicit assumption that shows like *Petticoat Junction* did not pass intellectual muster in light of the shift to situational realism in the 1970s.

Despite the public antagonism directed at "permissive" sitcoms, numerous commentators identified Lear's programming as "moral" or "moralizing" relative to that of both his predecessors and his contemporaries. This characteristic marked his writing as a unique contribution to the history of the situation comedy and to the public debates at the time over economics, race, and culture. Writing in the pages of the periodical *American Film*, historian Robert Sklar described what he called "Electronic Americana" based on Lear's programming and his tendency to moralize in prime time.[49] "The Lear formula is like the Grand Canyon or the Mount Rushmore of contemporary television, one of the major landmarks of Prime-Time America."[50] But what exactly was the content of such a tradition? For Sklar, "Nearly all the [Lear] comedies are built around a gross caricature or stereotype, a kind of holy fool or lovable sinner, an errant egotist . . . who gives voice to forbidden, socially ostracized thoughts in a way that excites us without implicating us."[51] In addition, "The moral equation is always carefully balanced. The more aggressive, the more weakness, error, foolishness, . . . little lessons for the viewer on the right way to live."[52]

For fellow academic David Marc, these characteristics supported his argument that Lear was television's first auteur, an individual who single-handedly "turned the political philosophy of Hubert Humphrey into his own American commedia dell'arte."[53] Lear's very visibility as a mainstay of early 1970s network programming added to the impact his writing made on the entertainment landscape of the period. The novelty of his programming in its ability to spark both condemnation and admiration differentiated Lear from the rest of his left-leaning colleagues: "So clear were the Lear trademarks . . . that he emerged as the first sitcom maker identifiable to the public."[54] The fact that Lear was able to instill civil religious values through dramatic social analysis in a single situation comedy signaled his primary contribution to the history of the situation comedy and to the history of spiritual and theatrical liberalism: "The contribution of Norman Lear is certainly going to be less in the issues he aired or the way he confronted them than in his role establishing the genre as an appropriate vehicle for discussing social mores and concerns."[55]

In short, Lear and his fellow producers, including Garry Marshall, simply tried to "be useful" by including pressing social or serious concerns in their weekly table reads and episodes. This practicality, or "realism" as some critics described it, reinforced the show's most significant social dimension—the ability to encourage people to take a moment to think about what they were watching. "He has made almost everyone think," argued *Chicago Tribune* journalist Clarence Peterson. "*All in the Family* is the first television comedy ever to accomplish that. Some would say it's the first TV comedy that ever tried to make *anybody* think."[56] It certainly took some time for American audiences to adapt to Lear's social realism and theatrical style as an expression of the New Morality, but in short order, the show dominated headlines, Nielsen ratings, and Emmy award ceremonies because of its ability to balance self-reflexive programming and audience engagement with controversial story lines and Lear's oftentimes implicit social analysis.[57] This reception of Lear's programming, however, revealed only part of how the wider populace received the Lear-style sitcom. In reality, the show's broader reception said as much about American television as it did the American electorate, as Lear's programming found traction largely in conjunction with its ability to politicize prime time itself in the name of social relevance.

CRITICAL RECEPTION OF LEAR PROGRAMMING: THE NEW CLASS

Despite the overall positivity of its reception, however, *All in the Family* also possessed its fair share of critics on both racial and political terms.[58] One such critic composed a short piece for the *Chicago Tribune* titled, "Carroll O'Connor: A Tight-Lipped Type of Liberal." Quoting the likes of conservative commentator William F. Buckley in her own analysis of Lear's work, journalist Kay Gardella argued that *All in the Family* made "any right-wing ideas sound 'intrinsically looney, prejudiced, and anti-intellectual.'" In other words, Lear's situation comedy was guilty of capitalizing on the idea that "the hardhat conservative won't listen or discuss things intelligently, while the great, open-minded liberals are always willing to listen to all sides. This has to be one of the best promoted fallacies of all time."[59] This criticism echoed the analyses of other journalists and academics who saw rampant liberal bias throughout Lear's catalog during the 1970s. It also took advantage of a newly minted analytical category developed by the soon-to-be-named "neoconservatives" and their "New Class" analyses of American society and culture.[60] According to this school of thought, a particular socioeconomic class had begun to emerge in postwar America that accumulated power not by way of property, as traditionally had been done in industrialized societies, but rather by way of knowledge itself. Not unsurprisingly, the name of this New Class was the "knowledge industry," largely because it perpetuated itself culturally and politically through its influence in the federal government, think tanks, and most important, the entertainment industry.

Gardella deployed this type of analysis in her own criticisms of Lear and *All in the Family* by arguing that O'Connor the man was anything but the "open-minded liberal" who "believes in people's rights and the exchange of free ideas."[61] Archie, Edith, and the rest of the Bunker family visited countless American families weekly throughout the decade by helping the show's viewership recognize Archie's fallibility, yet this aspiration often came across as Hollywood all-knowing-ness and condescension. "It's a series that sets out to deliberately cause a false polarization, politically, socially, and intellectually," argued Gardella. "It suggested that liberals are the only people concerned about humanity, their country, women's rights, and those of the world of other colors, creeds, and allegiances. . . . When *All in the Family* gets off its political soapbox, and stops thinking it has a mission to fulfill on television, it has its amusing moments."[62] For individuals such as Garry Marshall, James Brooks, and Norman Lear, their attempts to "be useful" in giving voice to the serious issues of their times were nothing less than failed attempts to missionize their audiences on the topics of empathy and compassion in prime time. In short, the collective negativity of Gardella and others was the other side of the proverbial coin of the largely positive and liberal reception of Lear's prime-time programming as part of the New Morality. It also demonstrated the thoroughly liberal character of the Lear sitcom as a product of New Class interests and liberal religious sensibilities.[63]

The mixed reception to Lear's programming in *All in the Family* foreshadowed the cultural divides that were forcefully emerging during the 1970s—ones that Lear directly contributed to through his own prime-time offerings. Periodicals such as *Time* and *Esquire* published responses to Lear and his writing, hailing them as groundbreaking contributions to the history of American television. "[The] home screen is beginning to be a little less of a window on a void," commented *Time*. "It is becoming a little more of a mirror."[64] As early as 1972, a year after the show's official premiere, political pundits were already discussing a "Bunker Vote" that represented a volatile constituency on the verge of revolutionizing America's political landscape as part of "the silent majority." The urban hard hat in Archie found his political antithesis in another of Lear's characters, Edith's cousin Maude. Archie and Maude's interactions represented not only Lear's own political biography as a product of the social programming of FDR during the New Deal and the Great Depression but also the burgeoning strength of Nixon's silent majority.

Despite this political diversity, researchers argued that the show appealed to its audiences in two sociopolitical directions simultaneously. For one journalist at the time, "It is a cheap way for tolerant upper-middle-class liberals to escape their own prejudices while the bigots get their views reinforced."[65] These two concurrent receptions belied the sheer number of individuals who watched the show on a weekly basis, but they said a great deal about the thoroughly contested character of cultural production in the United States during a tumultuous time in American television history. Rather than remain on the social sidelines, Lear's writing foregrounded the contentious issues of the day through prime-time drama and situation comedy. For some, this was pure artistry.[66] For others, it was another indication of liberal moralizing over the airwaves. "It's as if Lear wanted to use television—*television!*—to make a personal statement. And maybe he does."[67]

Considered from an academic vantage, Lear's programming was also quite well received for the very same reasons—namely his tendency to moralize in prime time. In fact, one could argue that many of Lear's situation comedies gave the earliest scholars of American television their first subjects *as data* for analysis, both historical and contemporary.[68] For most of these authors, Lear's writing possessed a "liberal vision" that understood progress as measured and liberal in character by casting bigotry as identifiable and laughable once considered with the ironic distance of satire.[69] The Lear program was the first "media drama," a type of programming that united through a shared "contemporary consciousness of media" by way of television's ability to "propel . . . surface and political and social involvement through the national bloodstream."[70]

Lear's first prime-time family was as extended as it was nuclear—a reflection of both the postwar aspiration and interwar practicality of its author. The loudness of the show's arguments (or discussions, as Archie reminded his viewers) reflected Lear's own upbringing in a Jewish home with extended family in Hartford and New Haven, Connecticut. This notion of family, however, transcended the simple physicality of familial relations: "America, one of the founding myths holds, includes all peoples, all races, all religions, the young, the old, the Black and the White, Catholic and Jew. This is an article of faith in *All in the Family*, *all* of us are of the family."[71]

This notion served as both content and democratic form—an indication of Lear's investment in the idea of public deliberation and civility in the face of reactionary religious belief and unreflective bigotry. "Each character on the 'Family' is a counter in a larger reality of social conflict," argues cultural theorist Philip Wander. "White racist, Black racist, non-violent White saint, non-violent Black saint, young White liberal, young Black liberal, woman's liber, domestic slave, middle age reactionary, middle age liberal. . . . Symbolic worlds press in on one another in face-to-face conversation creating a space to explore the personal experience of social conflict."[72] These counters, or tropes, populated virtually every episode of *All in the Family* over the course of its eight-year run.

Despite the novel didactic aims of this type of programming, especially when understood as part of a spiritual vision of intellectual uplift, enlightenment, and relevancy, Lear's debate-centered program depended on particular forms of civic maintenance for both its own cultural logic and its contribution to American political discourse. Echoing his fellow commentators, Wander identified three characteristics of Lear's programming: (1) all conflict is nonviolent, (2) all political and social views are balanced, and (3) there is a sense of tolerance.[73] Each tenet works seamlessly with the next as part of a theory of liberal democracy within the longer orbit of American religious liberalism. The liberal religious defense of

First Amendment rights, including the freedom of worship and free speech, was portrayed dramatically by Lear through the interactions of characters and the negotiation of racial and political difference set at high volume.

In this sense, both content and form mattered to the execution of Lear's situation comedy, but they ultimately receded into the background as part of the show's larger cultural logic of civility. For Wander, "*All in the Family* raises social issues, but does not offer political solutions. Instead, it offers a frame within which to understand social conflict. . . . [It] has come to be a secular Sunday school, gently exhorting us to do the right thing, hinting at a better world if we will only lovingly persevere in what we are already doing."[74] For some, these narrative tendencies spoke to a humanistic understanding of the world and its inhabitants, one that bent toward optimism and idealism for the future.[75] Lear's trust in the American people to handle his programming without any televisual marginalia or commentary was the quintessential expression of this very idealism, yet in this instance, it was as much a product of humanistic thinking as it was Lear's own naivete concerning the manner in which his writing would be received. As one analyst remarked, Lear's satirical representation of bigotry and discriminatory behavior allowed for multiple interpretations simultaneously—ones that found humor in both Archie's racially charged tirades and his moments of enlightenment. In both instances, Lear's empathetic storytelling helped to amplify the topicality and thus the relevancy of his situation comedies, thereby establishing an identifiable prime-time tradition of liberal religious entertainment.

In essence, the Lear-style situation comedy raised the collective awareness of those watching at home, yet it did so through a process of cultural polarization. Those who picked up on the self-reflexive and satirical character of *All in the Family* felt better about their corresponding desire to inform and advocate for a social cause. They also viewed Archie's diatribes as evidence of a mindset destined for the dustbin of history, one located along a developmental schema that anthropologist Susan Harding has identified as a "storyline of liberal progress," which ultimately ended with enlightened, liberal forms of Christianity as most suited to democratic life.[76] Among the many responses to Lear's programming, *Life* magazine's John Leonard declared that it "demanded a moral response" for its audience, which conservatively numbered close to fifty million every Saturday night. The topicality of the Lear sitcom, along with his willingness to subject its content to liberal democratic form, reflected Lear's spiritual and religious predecessors' attempts to adapt their own spiritual or religious convictions to the conditions of time and space, a thoroughly modernist move that hearkened back to the Social Gospel movement of the interwar period and the civil rights movement only a decade before.[77] "It's very nice when you can say something about the structure of society and still get plenty of laughs," remarked fellow producer and writer Mel Brooks. "And the first one to do that was Norman."[78]

ALL IN THE FAMILY: CIVILITY AND SATIRE IN PRIME TIME

Situation comedies such as *All in the Family*, *The Mary Tyler Moore Show*, and *MASH* introduced America to television characters never before seen in prime time. This was largely the case because these particular shows possessed a different understanding of how prime-time TV could connect with its diversifying audiences and for what purposes. As alluded to, network executives were on to this slightly before the creative material reached their desks, anticipating the methods of niche-based programming that would come to dominate network programming in the 1980s, but in the end, it was the combination of corporate interests and creative story lines that led to the emergence of relevance programming, a tradition of storytelling that pulled much of its subject material from contemporaneous events and newspaper headlines as a form of topical story writing.

The humorous light and tone of Lear's relevance writing upset many, especially those who saw Archie Bunker as the domestication of bigotry rather than its corrective. In addition, the mature fashion called for an appreciation and understanding of self-reflexive comedy, which required a discerning audience that could pick up on the satirical presentation of Archie, beyond his epithets and one-liners, as a deeply flawed but human character. Many understood the satire in the name of tolerance and understanding despite the need for a fall character. Many others, however, interpreted the show according to their own dictates, which relied very little on Lear's own desires to educate through comedic reporting and satire.

In this way, the character of Archie Bunker signified two socioeconomic realities that continue to inform contemporary debates today—the disgruntled white ethnic worker seemingly left behind by societies both great and small amid a growing racial plurality and the working-class bigoted family man battling his inner prejudices through confrontations with his son-in-law and those around him. Despite the consistency of Lear's programming regarding his desire to report and to create conversation, the ultimate reception of his cultural productions was as diverse as his American viewership was.

This tactic created conversation and debate by naming the cultural fault lines of the period according to the dictates of a spiritual liberal, one who made common cause with various mainline communities of Protestants, Catholics, and Jews throughout the 1970s and 1980s. Lear's decision to write and produce *All in the Family* revolutionized prime-time situation comedy, and it did so at the expense of the televisual consensus so reviled by Lear and others who saw the programming of the 1960s as utterly vapid and devoid of substance. As a result, Lear was arguably as responsible for politicizing the American family through the culture and genre of the situation comedy as his conservative detractors were—especially those who would challenge his media supremacy from the televisual pulpits of the electronic church. While Lear's conservative counterparts criticized his programming as indecent and pornographic, it nevertheless projected a vision of human interrelation that depended on satire and satirical presentations for much of its social efficacy.

For historian Stephen Kercher, satire "deploys irony to criticize vice and raise awareness. Spurred often by anger or scorn and informed by serious moral concern, satire is humor with a social purpose—protest . . . couched in wit."[79] Defined in this manner, satire functioned as the ideal vehicle for Lear's vision in a business based largely on the bottom line of advertising dollars and viewership. The combination of the growing network preference for programming suited to upwardly mobile urban youth and Lear's brand of hard-hitting social commentary in the form of the situation comedy marked the beginning of not only niche or demographically specific television but also relevance programming itself. His writing and producing for *All in the Family* reflected the emphasis on topicality that the networks were beginning to monetize through programs like Lear's and *The Mary Tyler Moore Show*.

In fact, one could argue that relevancy programming itself developed out of Lear's commitment to a vigorous public sphere and the negative freedoms that theoretically protected minority communities from the religious tyranny of the majority. The narrative emphasis on the "here and now" reflected Lear's larger educational goals for both his programming and the medium itself. His at-times confrontational attitude relative to network tastes and narrative preferences stemmed largely from the realization that he could always write something else but also from his commitment to educating regardless of the venue. Even if the network canceled his show, Lear was content knowing that "we gave them plenty to think about." For actor Caroll O'Connor, Lear's sentiment meant everything to his own liberal commitments as a Hollywood actor: "But that, in the television industry, was a revolutionary and all but unattainable goal—the stimulation of serious social thought through comedy! I think, it must be Norman's greatest pride, in which we all share, that he achieved his goal."[80]

Lear's topical writing, combined with the developing attractiveness of being "hip" to current events, eventually found a supportive home on CBS after being passed over by the two other television networks, NBC and ABC. The idea for the show came from a British situation comedy called *Till Death Do Us Part*. Like *All in the Family*, it focused on the life and extended family of a working class, bigoted male, in this case Alfred Garnett, who lived in the East End of London. Not unlike Lear's sitcom, each character represented a certain kind of caricature. The husband of Garnett's daughter is a socialist-leaning "layabout," and Alfred's wife, Else, along with Alfred himself, characterizes the widening generational gap at the time between adult and youth. Both shows were written as satire, yet in each case, such storytelling left everything up to the viewer despite the best efforts of the respective writers. In this sense, each show was immensely popular, but for radically different reasons.

Due to the controversial nature of the shows' language and use of racially charged words and phrases, some viewers reveled in what Archie or Alfred said as a source of laughter or entertainment. In many cases, Archie *was* a member of the viewing public's family, like it or not. On the other hand, many other viewers "got" the satire of the show. This resulted in the realization of a "critical distance" between Archie's words, their social function, and the individual viewer, which, for both Lear and *Till Death*, was a product of their satirical take on working-class racial politics. The class-centered universe of *Till Death* assisted Lear's initial formulations about his own show. Instead of focusing solely on the class politics of Alfred's world, however, Lear decided to add sexual, racial, and religious dimensions to the conflicts on *All in the Family* in order to reflect the nature of the burgeoning American culture wars in the 1970s between hard hats like Archie (who worked as a foreman) and hippies like Mike ("Meathead"). Additionally, Lear drew heavily from his own biography in crafting the characters of Archie, Gloria, Edith, and Michael despite his reliance on *Till Death* for much of his program's narrative structure.

In many ways, Lear's world was Archie's world—that of the Great Depression and World Wars. Much of the look and feel of *All in the Family* can be directly related to the conditions of Lear's own upbringing, which were modest yet extremely loud.[81] The arguments that Edith would complain about between Archie and Michael in the show were simply "discussions" to Archie and to Lear, nothing more. In short, *All in the Family* could not have existed in the manner it did without the rich, autobiographical contributions of Lear himself. Countless Bunker diatribes were those of Lear's own father, who also commanded a great deal of authority from the cushioned seat of his living room chair.[82] This intimacy of narrative between biography and situation comedy may indeed be typical of all cultural artifacts. In the case of *All in the Family*, however, this connection is that much more important when examining the theatrical liberalism of its creator because of how thoroughly the show reflected the spiritual politics of its author.

⤫

The first season of *All in the Family* reads more like a syllabus than it does a prime-time lineup of network programming. Beginning with the pilot episode, appropriately titled "Meet the Bunkers," Lear's inaugural sitcom drenched its audience from the proverbial get-go in what could only be called high-volume entertainment with a didactic twist.[83] Titles such as "Writing the President," "Judging Books by Covers," "Lionel Moves into the Neighborhood," and "Gloria Discovers Women's Lib" give us a glimpse into the initial narrative arc of the show in both episodic and seasonal terms. In fact, "Meet the Bunkers" was the third of three titles for Lear's pilot. Earlier versions of the pilot possessed titles such as "Justice for All" and "Those Were the Days." While the second title resonated with the show's willingness to explore generational differences in uncertain social times through the character of Archie Bunker, "Justice for All" perhaps spoke better to Lear's spiritual sensibility as a theatrical and religious liberal—especially in light of his nonprofit future in the realms of school curricula, First Amendment rights, and the separation of church and state.[84]

As church historian Martin Marty would later argue, Lear's comedic vision was not solely determined by the conventions of entertainment, advocacy, or comedy exclusively, but rather by the terms of deliberative democracy itself—giving voice to the variety of political arguments and perspectives that were in the headlines at the time. Each episode possessed its own unique topic or theme, such as the racial integration of neighborhoods or the feminist analysis of Bunker-style patriarchy, but they all demonstrated a common form, or method, for delivering their content to the millions of viewers at home. This included largely theatrical performances in front of a live studio audience for the actors as part of a Lear-designed one-act play. This style turned the televised situation comedy into a makeshift radio experience since much of the comedy of the show could be heard as well as seen. My emphasis on Lear's form is a reminder that his spiritual politics, as understood through his theatrical tendencies, comes into clearest view less for its "messages" and more for how it structures ideas and debates from week to week about the nation's public life.

The pilot episode was purposely designed by Lear to thoroughly soak its audience in the conventions of the liberal morality play—topicality and controversy in the name of relevance. The notorious opening musical number of *All in the Family* established the temporal parameters of the situation comedy by situating it as a product of the interwar interreligious liberalism of the National Council of Christians and Jews (NCCJ), the social programming of Franklin Roosevelt, and the legislative agenda of Johnson's Great Society.[85] At the start of each episode, husband and wife came together at the family piano to celebrate the glory of past days when Herbert Hoover reigned supreme and the Depression forced everyone to appreciate what little they had.[86] The final two stanzas of the theme song reveal a great deal about the mindset of the central protagonist, Archie Bunker, and his political orientation:

> And you knew who you were then
> Girls were girls and men were men
> Mister we could use a man like Herbert Hoover again.

From the very first moments of the pilot, Lear orients us to the world of the Bunkers—which, not coincidentally, has much in common with Lear's own upbringing in Connecticut during tough economic times. The shrill character of Edith's singing prefigures the volume that the show's argumentation would assume each week between the central characters. The number's third and final stanza crystalizes the political sensibility of the show as a form of liberal satire:

> Didn't need no welfare state
> Everybody pulled his weight
> Gee our LaSalle ran great
> Those were the days.

Not only do we learn of one of the episode's scrapped titles, namely "Those Were the Days," we also begin to hear a clarion call that would rival those of the 1960s including "the personal is the political."

The myth of the lone individual pulling himself up by the proverbial bootstraps could be heard loud and clear in the words of the Bunker patriarch, yet it was not completely individual centered. Due to the actions of "the welfare state," fewer and fewer individuals were encouraged to pull their own weight, especially those on the racial and ethnic margins of American society—at least to Archie. These individuals were guilty of relying on the system without any recourse to their own agency in order to influence their surroundings. Bunker would rehash this argument multiple times during the show's run, typically in a key of white resentment of federal entitlements and protections for persons of color amid worsening occupational forecasts for the white working classes.[87]

These narrative statements were as much a reflection of Lear's upbringing as they were of Archie's own racial biases. In this sense, any portrayal of Lear's as depicted in one of his situation comedies, particularly *All in the Family*, was an intimate reflection of his own analysis of American society in the 1970s. "In many ways," argued writer A. Scott Berg, "Norman's progressive agenda is as accomplished and influential as those of Woodrow Wilson, LBJ, and Archie Bunker's bête noire, Franklin Delano Roosevelt himself."[88] In short, Lear's political sensibilities were forged in the crucibles of Depression and the New Deal in addition to the optimism of the Great Society and the civil rights movement for those on society's edges as part of the Religious Left.

As a result, Lear interpreted his sociopolitical surroundings according to the classically liberal Protestant tradition of FDR and the establishment Protestantism that backed his administration. "Social policies championed by the [Federal] Council became less controversial as they became more familiar, and many of them were implemented in the New Deal," argues scholar of religion Robert A. Schneider. "Council apologists were fond of quoting President Roosevelt's quip, when charged with radicalism, that he was 'as radical as the Federal Council of Churches.' "[89] This radicalism finds its voice in the disagreement between Archie and his wife, Edith, over the nature of the sermon they hear during the opening scenes of the pilot episode.

For Edith Bunker, forces too big to comprehend are at work in the transformations of American society during the late 1960s and early 1970s. "Why fight it? The world's changing. That's what the Reverend Felcher was sayin'. You two shoulda heard him. Of course, Mr. religion here wasn't seein' eye-to-eye with the sermon."[90] "What sermon?" Archie responds, contesting both Edith's description and categorical use of the term "sermon." "That was socialist propaganda, pure and simple. And don't give me that look." For Archie, the Reverend Felcher represents a growing Christian constituency in the United States that decided to back the various social movements of the period in the name of morality, ethics, and relevance.

These pastors, priests, and rabbis were on the frontlines of a newly formed spiritual movement that responded to the needs of those denied civil rights throughout the US South.[91] Compared to the writings of Jerry Falwell during the same period, which condemned the use of the Gospel for purely social causes, the actions of this interreligious (or ecumenical) front were radical beyond compare. In the hands of these able men and women, the Gospel became a mobile entity on behalf of a people still under the wrath of the pharaoh in a foreign land. For sociologist Jeffrey K. Hadden, this social allegiance between largely liberal

Protestants, Catholics, and Jews and their African American counterparts signaled a sea change in American Christianity—one that contemporary scholars continue to ignore at their own peril.[92] Reflecting on the shifting religious demographics of his existentially trying times, Hadden argues that a widening gap between pew and pulpit, not unlike the *cultural* gap between those in on the liberal satire and those looking in from the outside, threatened American Christianity itself from within: "The occupants of the pews continue to resist change, but those who occupy the pulpits have, to a considerable degree, experienced a deepening commitment to, and involvement in, the struggle for social justice. This is leading to the deepest schism in the churches since the Protestant Reformation."[93]

Lear's programming may not have explicitly contributed to this deepening schism in a religious register, but it most certainly provided the spiritual support for the very same social values defended by those on the front lines of the civil rights movement through the emphasis on relevancy. The argument, or discussion, between Mike and Archie locates this theological rift in real time in front of a live studio audience. Instead of identifying the "correct" side of the schism, Lear uses his sitcom to facilitate a *debate* over the limitations of "bleeding hearts" and Archie's silent-majority conservatism. No one voice is privileged over another, but the manner in which the characters discuss the issue reveals Lear's spiritual politics as understood by his commitment to civil deliberation under the right linguistic conditions.

Not only did Lear himself reflect such a commitment, his programming and weekly story lines also embodied the values of the Spiritual Left as an extension of civil rights activism, imagined or otherwise.[94] His cultural contributions to this widening gap mirrored those taking place in mainline and ecumenical congregations over issues like civil rights and the women's movement.[95] Lear used satire and dramatic comedy in order to challenge his audiences to think more reflexively about their daily interactions with others through the character of Lear's father, Archie Bunker. In short, Lear sought a raised awareness in his audiences through a theatrical didacticism executed through vigorous debate at high volume. All were heard regardless of political position. Unfortunately for Lear and his fellow "subversives," this vision of a deliberately balanced public square was largely the product of civil religious theorizing and interreligious aspiration, more the result of hypotheticals than of liberal democratic practice. The content of this vision left little in doubt to those on the frontlines of the welfare state, but its political application left much to be desired. In fact, Archie's dialogue conjured many a liberal stereotype that continues to haunt progressive social activism to this day.

Archie's comments about Felcher capture the religious tenor of a moment just completed. Airing in the wake of the civil rights movement, *All in the Family* features an explicit representation of the movement's goals and aspirations through the character of Mike, or "Meathead," Archie's son-in-law and sociologist in training. Mike's sole academic desire is to receive an education so he can "help people," a simple yet telling desire of the liberal constituencies that Mike represents as a sitcom character. After a brief exchange about the sermon, Archie names his true discomfort, "I ain't sittin' still for no preacher tellin' me that I'm to blame for all this breakdown in law and order that's goin' on."

Bunker's words express more than simply his own feelings about the racial strife building up around him. His concerns reflect a growing displeasure with what appears to be preferential treatment by the federal government for the country's racial and ethnic minorities and their fight for equal rights. Despite his frustration, Archie still manages a counterexplanation to the one authored by his son in law: "I'll tell you the cause of it—these sob sisters like your reverend Felcher and the bleedin' hearts and weepin' nellies like youse two." Not only does Lear point us to a moment of whiteness-as-guilty in the form of Bunker, he also addresses the pejorative term "bleeding heart" and its potential origins in the interactions between liberal and conservative Protestants during the 1960s. "I suppose the black man has had the same opportunity in this country as you?" Mike asks. "More," Archie responds. "He's had more. I didn't have no million people marchin' and protestin' to get me my job."

In typical Lear fashion, Archie's words function as a political statement within his dialogue as a sitcom character, yet they are balanced with other viewpoints according to the deliberative logic of the show itself and thus are all "equal." In this instance, Lear gives voice to a very real conservative concern at the time over rising crime rates and an expanding federal government. Archie's words have little time to ring, however, before such bluster is neutralized by the "Christ-like" Edith Bunker punchline, "No, his uncle got it for him." Conservatism finds its voice on *All in the Family* as one of many opinions on a given issue, but it ultimately loses some credibility in Lear's programming since its lone articulator is Bunker himself. "All that sociology and studyin' that welfare stuff, I don't call that no hard work," Archie argues. "Oh, Daddy, leave him alone," responds his daughter, Gloria. "I think it's beautiful that Michael wants to help the underprivileged." Archie retorts, "Listen, if he wants to help the underprivileged, let him start with himself."

Within this simple yet loud exchange, competing societal ideals meet head on—with one side largely dependent on the institutions and resources of the university and the other aligned with a burgeoning grassroots conservatism both populist and anti-intellectualist in its appeals to the beleaguered white majority. The decision to ground virtually every social conflict within the family unit itself reflects the growing rhetorical saliency and traction of "the family" as a political wedge issue. While groundbreaking in its own right, another "family" would ascend to highest prominence in direct opposition to the portrayal of family as seen on *All in the Family*. While the extended family tended to define Lear's comedies, it was the nuclear family, defended by the likes of televangelist Jerry Falwell, that would eventually reign supreme in the imaginations of those consuming Lear's programming. [96]

Lear's pilot episode exemplified the Lear sitcom in both content and form. Littered throughout were offhand comments about skirts being too short, *Cosmo* being too racy, and Mike's love for Gloria being too public for Archie's tastes. Each comment in itself, however insignificant, marked a generational consciousness of not quite being comfortable with the changing times of fashion and relational expression. This was both purposeful and designed. To encounter Archie's diatribes and subsequent reconciliatory moments was to experience a liberal ritual of race and racism. It assured erudite viewers that their once-powerful bigotry or discriminatory opinions were simply the residue of a gladly forgotten past. To these viewers, Archie's behavior also confirmed several liberal stereotypes and assumptions about conservatives and their less than sophisticated racial sensibilities.

Less than a decade later, Lear relied on this vision to build and organize a counteroffensive against a religious constituency that paid little heed to civic prerequisites like civility and public reason. "In the war for the American mind," argues historian Kathryn Montgomery, "entertainment programs have become political territory."[97] In this sense, it was Lear and his fellow Hollywood writers and producers in the Religious Left who counterintuitively first "politicized" television by bringing topicality and relevancy into prime time based largely on a moral imperative to speak out against social injustices. By doing so, spiritual imperatives to protect First Amendment rights to speech and religion contoured Lear's programming by mixing religion and politics in a manner conducive to largely liberal sensibilities of fairness and equal time.

⚘

Lear's engagement with his subjects every week generated its discursive power less from the specific topics and more from the framing of the discussion and the discussion itself. Many of the period's most divisive conflicts found their dramatic representation in Lear's *All in the Family* as an expression of his own desires to illuminate and educate on a mass scale through satire and topical writing. His presentations did not suggest one position over another regarding civil rights or the women's rights movement but rather foregrounded the conversation itself as the most important dimension of American liberal democracy. In other words, to understand the liberal character of Lear's situation comedy is to examine the *how* of debate and conversation in addition to the *what* of content and plot analysis.

"It would also be good for the country to have the dissonant variety inherent in our pluralistic society find its way to the tube," Lear remarked. "People of all races and religions and lifestyles—the 'hotheads, sybarites, ascetics, the poets, mockers and madmen.' "[98] As the product of both theatrical and religious liberalism, Lear's programming on *All in the Family* propagated a spiritual vision of the nation articulated through character dialogue and argumentation. This vision possessed a social dimension that found its clearest expression through the use of the "TV as classroom" model demonstrated by various social and advocacy groups of the period including Lear's own People for the American Way in the early 1980s. In particular, the show possessed its own theological assumptions about God, humanity, and their interconnected relationship, which found expression through plot and character development.

For example, Lear envisioned very specific roles for his characters, especially Archie's wife, Edith: "Now, there are two books written about Edith Bunker. . . . We knew she was a totally Christian lady by her every instinct—a Sermon on the Mount type of Christian, not a Pat Robertson type of Christian."[99] Lear's intent found common cause with local Presbyterian pastor Spencer Marsh, whose text *God, Man, and Archie Bunker* examined Edith's role in the show in a similar fashion. "Her understanding penetrates our moral darkness, and for this reason Edith is the 'Christ figure' in most of the episodes. Not only does she stand for what is good and right, but she is the humble lamb who goes to slaughter again and again."[100] For Lear and Marsh, Edith's character exuded the idealized characteristics of the figure of Jesus Christ as teacher rather than source of salvation. This point is significant because its representation of Jesus was heavily inflected with a religious liberal emphasis on Jesus as mediator, moderator, and medium of global communication rather than as personal savior.

In short, Lear revealed his own religious preferences and biases through both character development and satirical storytelling on *All in the Family*. Despite his desire for a diversity of religious and cultural expressions on television, Lear was nevertheless subject to his own critical analyses and observations of conservative religiosity dating back to his youth in New Haven, Connecticut, and the diatribes of Father Coughlin. Looking back on a long career in media as a "Born Again

American," Lear described the impact of Coughlin's speeches on his childhood according to the tenets of tolerance. He listened in secret because, he said, "I had already developed what turned out to be a lifelong sensitivity to religious intolerance and the intrusion of any one religion in the public square where all religions are welcome and no one of them favored."[101] This sensitivity was on full display during the writing and filming of *All in the Family* through Lear's empathetic examination of bigotry and its human face in prime time. In addition, Lear's future organizing on behalf of the American Way could be described as empathy incarnate in the public square—a religious liberal sentiment catalyzed into an institutionalizing movement in defense of the First Amendment in the names of pluralism and civility.

We see Lear's sensitivity to all subjects religious during the final episode of the first season, titled "The First and Last Supper." The episode opens with a debate over the origins of humanity, both sacred and profane. Archie is on the offensive: "We didn't crawl out from under no rocks. We didn't have no tails, and we didn't come from monkeys, you atheistic, pinko meathead!" Used to this sort of tirade, Mike responds calmly, "Archie, that's a fairy tale. The whole idea of taking a rib out of Adam and making a woman, it's Mandrake the Magician time." These are two antithetical interpretations doing battle within the confines of the American (sitcom) family. Unlike the public square, no one has to technically "lose" or "win" the exchange of ideas as encountered at the Bunker dinner table.

However, such interactions spoke to the headlines of the times—at least those read by Lear and his considerable team of writers. His ability to frame television plotlines within a larger religio-political vision of the nation spoke to Lear's cultural impact as a religious and theatrical liberal, one who used comedy and satire as vehicles for larger civic aspirations. This vision found its comedic voice through the mode of argumentation within *All in the Family* and the topicality of the show itself. "We don't have anything against God or the notion of God," argues Mike. "It's what people do in his name that we don't like. People hate in his name, people kill in his name. Look at Vietnam. 'We're there with his blessings, because God is on our side.'" Meathead's contention resonated with those of his generation—critical of institutional power without grasping fully the entirety of the combat. More important, this argument was eagerly supported by Lear and his fellow knowledge industry subversives who also used culture to enact their political inclinations and ambitions.

"Well?" Archie responds, chuckling. "You ain't gonna tell me he's on the side of them godless gooks." Archie's eloquence may come at the expense of racial sensitivity, yet it is a powerful indication of liberal storytelling, nonetheless. His swift analysis renders America on the side of cultural triumph and Southeast Asia on the losing end of civilization on both religious and racial terms. Instead of leaving the audience with these words, Mike responds in kind, "Why not? God created them gooks, too, didn't he?" The two verbal combatants fail to explore the point further, a narrative weakness on the part of Lear and his writers because the issue is never properly adjudicated. There is no "right" answer or response based solely on the character dialogue.

Ironically, this is perhaps the point. Lear's intention with *All in the Family* was never to identify the single best option when it came to politics and American religion but rather to expose his viewers to the diversity of a single issue in all its complications under the protection of the First Amendment. Such clarity of purpose would become a founding principle when Lear established People for the American Way in 1981 with the help of *Christian Century* editor Martin Marty. For both Marty and Lear, their principal mode of shaping public discourse was instructional rather than conversionary. The teleplays of *All in the Family* did not will viewers' adherence to an explicitly religious or Christian system of belief, but the show most certainly subjected its audience to a more subtle form of control—namely *influence* as both historical reality and categorical apparatus.

Considered historically, PFAW's mission represented the institutionalization of everything Lear and his writers attempted to convey through *All in the Family*, a serialized situation comedy, on network television, broadcast in prime time. The story lines may have varied from week to week, which was in itself a source of discomfort within a growing constituency of conservative Protestants, but the cultural logic of the show—the framework, if you will—remained consistent as the fundamental characteristic of liberal religious storytelling through the forms of satire and comedy.

All in the Family presented a family under siege from a variety of racial, economic, religious, and political vantages. The character of Archie Bunker served as the most significant part of the show in its attempts to educate and uplift, but he was only part of a larger portrayal of American family life, which at times grafted seamlessly onto contemporaneous events in American society due to the show's topicality. As a result, due to Lear's own spiritual and political idiosyncrasies, *All in the Family* represented a model of American civic life, one that depended on the classical (religious) liberal notions of civility, tolerance, and diversity. It was this vision of society, an expression of Lear's spiritual politics, that grounded the work of both Lear and Marty once the two began working together on behalf of a frustrated constituency of political and religious liberals who felt systematically excluded from politics due to two interrelated factors: the forcefulness of the nascent Christian Right and the inroads it was making into the largely liberal-controlled entertainment and knowledge industries.

In an interview with *Ebony* magazine in June 1972, actor Carroll O'Connor described how he played Archie when Lear wrote the character to educate and instruct in the name of tolerance and understanding: "You laugh as you watch him, but that man is in pain. You're laughing at a *loser*; a loser because of his misconceptions. . . . We show a man who is a racist and a bigot and who is digging his own grave on Earth." For O'Connor, this portrayal unfolded according to the didactic dictates of Lear himself and other sympathetic Hollywood liberals. "The lesson is—if you think this way, *change*. That's the lesson. But we don't come out and say so, because that is a very bad way to teach."[102] Influence instead of adjudication, exploration over certainty—these were two of the thematic and cultural tenets that guided Lear's scripts from week to week before almost one-quarter of the viewing country.

Unfortunately for O'Connor, Lear, and other Hollywood liberals, their interpretation of white progress, when it came to race, was presumptuous at best and naive at worst despite the show's adherence to civic and spiritual values such as tolerance and diversity. "He's a minority of white people. I think the rest of the whites are, as I said before, moving away from that," argued O'Connor. "They can still laugh at Archie because there is reminiscence involved. . . . Most of the white people I run into and who talk to me about the show tell me, 'Archie was my father; Archie was my uncle.' It's always *was, was, was*. It's not *now*."[103] O'Connor's confidence in identifying Archie with the "minority" of whites stemmed from the same idealistic optimism (or naivete) that held another set of whites to a more progressive trajectory of racial competency and understanding— namely the Hollywood community of political and religious liberals that O'Connor and Lear were themselves a part. Despite the fact that Lear denied the accusations made by political commentators, journalists, and religious figures that he intentionally inserted controversial subject matter into his programming in order to enlighten his audiences, O'Connor understood the show in exactly these liberal, didactic terms.

Much of this noble intention, however, ultimately depended upon the audience's' reception of Lear's and other's writing *as satire*, meaning that Lear's comedy depended upon the viewer possessing an awareness for how a television character can possess both content and form (or function): Archie's diatribes were full of offensive and never-before-heard-on-TV racial slurs, yet this content served the all-important secondary satirical purpose of moral instruction. In other words, *what* Archie said was not as significant as *why* he said it in Lear's attempts to expose his audience to divisive and controversial subject matter in prime time.

"Now our intention is not to make the racist laugh and enjoy himself. Our intention is to show him just what he is. . . . Whether he *does* laugh at that or whether he shrinks from it, we cannot foretell," O'Connor admitted. "We cannot plan for it. All we can do is show him honestly what he is doing and let the chips fall where they may. And I think the chips are going to fall on the right side."[104] Unfortunately, this prediction turned out to possess a great deal of truth that had very little to do with such attempts to enact progressive politics through culture. In this particular instance, O'Connor's "right side" resembled less the aspirations of his fellow laborers in the broadcast fields of the knowledge industry than it did the passions of those tilling the Sunbelt soils of entrepreneurial, antistatist, and evangelical conservatism in both word and grassroots deed.

In between the elections of Jimmy Carter and Ronald Reagan, Lear would begin to emerge from behind the camera in order to take his spiritual vision of civic life to the very audiences that he had entertained for nearly a decade in the name of civility and intellectual freedom.[105] His ability to do this was counter-intuitively made that much more difficult, however, due to his own successes at incorporating topicality into the sitcom narratives of prime-time television. Lear's contributions to and philosophy of American television set a structural precedent that did not require the same political concerns for its successful deployment in prime time. In other words, the Lear sitcom's success was based on its ability to remain and disseminate "relevancy" as both product and story line. As such, Lear's programming exemplified the "social issue group" usage of the medium as mostly an educational instrument within a larger "electronic classroom" model of communication. Unlike his more conservative counterparts in the American public square who deployed television in a conversionary effort to support their burgeoning ministries, Lear entertained in order to influence his audiences when it came to his weekly one-act plays of discussion, argumentation, and liberal deliberation.

The topicality of Lear's writing, his willingness to pull story lines from the daily headlines, represented yet another attempt to mobilize culture in the name of politics from a politically progressive vantage point. However, these narrative choices had consequences—namely the impact that Lear's writing had on the rhetoric and reality of the American family itself. In fact, one could argue that it was not Jerry Falwell or Pat Robertson who first politicized the American family over the airwaves or subjected it to the political interests of the American party system. Rather than portray the family as a refuge from an otherwise inhospitable world, Lear "portrayed the family as a political arena—as *the* political arena. . . . The Bunker household was, in short, a microcosm of America."[106] In this sense, Lear was arguably one of the first individuals to politicize "the family" over broadcast network television in the short history of American television media.

The willingness to adapt to one's cultural and social surroundings by making the American family the subject of his television writing locates Lear firmly in a modernist tradition of Protestants, Catholics, and Jews who viewed urban dilapidation and societal decay as communal sins committed against the nation and its citizenry. The theater was a sacred space for Lear and his fellow theatrical liberals dating back to the heyday of Broadway, but it was not exempt or removed from the contentious politics of the Vietnam War or the civil rights movement—quite the opposite, in fact. Lear's programming functioned as an application of the activist clergy tradition of the same decade to network television during prime-time hours.[107]

Like his fellow activists, Lear's interests and concerns were firmly those of the present—systemic racism, sexual discrimination, and bottom-line thinking were to be examined and researched for the betterment of the country's minority communities. The counterintuitive results of these thematic emphases, however, ultimately overshadowed the liberation-based aspirations of the various freedom movements of the period. This was so because of the cultural gap that formed between those who were on the frontlines of the movement, either in physical or televisual manifestation, and those who saw such activism as detrimental to both their local congregations and American Christianity itself.

In light of this, Lear's involvement in the entertainment industry as a liberally minded prime-time entertainer is significant because he challenged seemingly self-evident distinctions between comedy and entertainment, politics and popular culture, religion and the naked public square that he himself was invested in maintaining. This was especially the case when he was confronted by a vocal and vociferous grassroots effort to mobilize conservative voters across the religious and political spectrum around the clarion calls against government overreach and increasing secularization at the hands of the nation's highest court and its prime-time programming. As a result, the debates surrounding the increasing imbrication of religion and politics with Reagan's election included Lear more often than not as a voice of authority in the nation's public life.

Unbeknownst to Lear, this televisual tendency stretched back to the earliest days of the FCC and the federal regulation of the airwaves in relation to ecumenical and mainline Protestantism. As a variety of historians have observed, federal policy concerning who received broadcasting licenses and who did not throughout the 1930s revealed the government's preference for more liberal forms of Christianity over and against conservative evangelicals or fundamentalists who were also clamoring for airtime. "The purpose of network programming for the religious groups was not to convert, and they did little direct preaching *a la* today's electronic church," argues former director of communications for the National Council of Catholic Men Richard Walsh. "The point was to foster dialogue."[108]

Beginning with the premiere of *All in the Family* on CBS in 1971, in addition to programs such as *MASH* and *The Mary Tyler Moore Show*, religious liberals like Lear enacted their own political aspirations, and those that defined the previous decade's social tumultuousness, through their television writing instead of more formal articles, treatises, or position papers authored by a nonprofit or think tank.[109] This reality, however, was not far off as both liberals and conservatives battled one another over the primary means of cultural production in the 1980s—the television.

3

Norman Lear, the FCC, and the Holy War Over American Television

L ear's relevance programming set the tone for prime-time lineups across the three networks throughout the 1970s.[1] Along with programs like *MASH* and *The Mary Tyler Moore Show*, *All in the Family* established a type of realism-based situation comedy that entertained according to a set of civic principles based on contemporaneous events—namely those that Lear supported himself, such as unfettered debate and civility in public life. However, Lear's depiction of family life was radically different from that of his predecessors.[2] This was not only a thematic observation by Lear himself but also a vocational charge to write "about something" in prime time. Despite the controversy that surrounded many of his individual episodes, including those that explored the feminist movement and male impotence, it was an episode from one of Lear's many spin-offs that generated the most controversy and mobilization against entertainment television—a first in the medium's short history. *All in the Family* certainly received its fair share of negative mail, including a death threat directed at Lear himself, but it was the organizing that followed a controversial two-part episode of *Maude* that foreshadowed the contentious decade to come in media and American public life.

This decade witnessed a radical retuning of American political life according to the dictates of culture and those who evaluated its efficacy based on the "public interest," a tried and tested concept originating slightly before the establishment of the Federal Communications Commission in 1934.[3] Unfortunately for Lear and others in the "middling mainline," the nation's public interest was anything but public, especially in times of mature programming and its subsequent vociferous criticism.[4] "How could they beam a program such as *Maude* into the American living room?" asked Dorothy Stone, a concerned citizen, in a *Los*

Angeles Times editorial. "Pregnancy, vasectomy, abortion, 'don't pat me below the wasteland, that's how this all got started!' What a show for 8 p.m.! And to think they are taking Bonanza off in favor of this trash . . . the vast tasteless TV sea."[5] Compared to something like Alistair Cooke's *America*, Lear's program offended as much as it entertained.

Featured directly below a picture of actress Beatrice Arthur, an indication perhaps of the linkage in the public eye between Arthur, Lear, and the subject matter of his shows, the editorial relied on a particular vocabulary that not only established the author's authority but also defined the deficiencies of Lear's programming according to what can only be described as taste in both descriptive and categorical terms.[6] The author's anxiousness grew in proportion to the nature of the programming she perceived as either tasteful or, in this case, tasteless. Although Stone was clear about the difference between better and worse programming in prime time, the viewing public was anything but as it witnessed the tense negotiations between the networks, Lear, and his conservative opposition. The fact that the author used the word "beam" was also indicative of a discomfort with the ease at which television found a voice in homes across the country, a fear shared by Lear and others when it came to conservative religiosity in general and, later in the decade, to the electronic church in particular.

This largely taste-based dynamic shaped the directions of public debate in the 1970s over the relationship between politics, entertainment, and the American family.[7] Perhaps better known as "the culture wars," these disagreements over what was "mature" and what was "tasteless" reflected the broader social and cultural shift toward a cultural register of politics that surrounded the broadcast of *Maude*, the ensuing protest that followed, and numerous other instances of cultural skirmishes over reproductive rights, pornography, or free speech during the decade.[8] Although one might think that this discursive migration of politics toward the cultural favored those who deployed culture on their own behalf in the name of politics, namely the Religious Left, it in fact assisted the political and Christian Right even more in their formulation of a "family values" politics.[9] This religio-political agenda took advantage of the growing gap between cultural and religious authority figures and those in the pew according to a claim to a superior "morality."[10] For historian Kathryn Montgomery, these debates represented a new front in the ongoing negotiation of the idea of America and its representation in public life in late twentieth-century America. "In the war for the American mind," she remarks, "entertainment programs have become political territory."[11]

This chapter explores further the relationship between prime-time television *as* political territory and various federal regulatory institutions in light of Lear's programming and its cultural impact during the mid-1970s. Lear's concerns about conservative religiosity were initially a reflection of his deeply felt commitment to minority rights and the First Amendment regardless of the social setting, including Hollywood. In fact, an emphasis on free speech was a direct outgrowth of his childhood memories of Catholic radio preacher Father Charles Coughlin and his awareness of the blacklisting that took place in Hollywood during the 1950s.[12]

Lear made a point to speak out for creative freedom when it came to television writers and producers who were slowly realizing that their programs were no longer seen simply as forms of prime-time entertainment. Not only did this have cultural and political implications, it would also have legal repercussions when it came to federal regulatory policy of the airwaves executed in the "public interest."[13] In light of this, I argue that the historical difference between those religious groups that received sustaining time, ones that possessed public interest programming, and those that had to pay for their airtime commercially (usually conservative Protestant groups) plays a significant role in this story. This is the case because Lear's religious liberalism found much in common with the goals of sustaining programming and public television more generally, which were largely educational and didactic in nature.[14]

Additionally, various advocacy groups began forming at this time in both liberal and conservative guises, largely in response to what the three networks were broadcasting over the airwaves. Lear's worries over conservative Protestantism had first been expressed in a key of civil liberties; however, a more accurate description highlights Lear's cognizance of how conservative programming threatened to consume the airwaves themselves in the form of a hostile takeover, something akin to what would unfold in the collective minds of liberals following the Iranian Revolution of 1979.[15] This was especially disturbing for liberals at the time because they tended to read domestic events through analogous events abroad. Sociologist Peter Berger perhaps demonstrated this tendency best when he wrote, "The fanatical mullahs have been let loose in the land, *this* land. They travel all across America in the flesh; even more alarmingly, they fill the air with the electronic projections of their presence."[16] At the very least, these words demonstrate Berger's concern for presence, both physical and spectral. Not only are "they" here "in the flesh," namely televangelists and conservative entrepreneurs, they are also present as "electronic projections" of presence. For academic commentators like Berger and Marty, this presence represented a serious threat not only to civic life but also to institutional church life itself as television relativized physical space and the various mainline notions of community forged within.

Set against this historical backdrop, I argue that Lear's programming benefited explicitly from the historic tendency of the federal government to privilege certain forms of religion over others in the public square and over the airwaves. I rely on three case studies to demonstrate how his situation comedy writing shaped network policy and the federal adjudication of taste differences in determining what was explicitly "political" and what was "entertainment" before the law. These case studies, which include the Family Viewing Hour controversy, the abortion episodes of *Maude*, and a Hollywood retreat to Ojai, California, demonstrate the breadth of Lear's impact not only on the prime-time shows themselves and on their relevance content but also on the very structure of prime time itself in addition to the laws and regulations that governed it.

Following previous chapters' investigations of Lear's theatrical liberalism and his prime-time programming in *All in the Family*, this chapter explores the deep unease that coursed through the entertainment industry during this period as burgeoning advocacy groups aimed their politically inflected sights at Lear and others for their inaccurate portrayal of minority groups and their pornographic content, depending on the viewer in question. I argue that Lear's involvement in these various moments in the recent past further illustrates both the scope of his cultural impact through his programming and, perhaps more important, his religio-political involvement in the public square in the name of such liberal tenets as civil liberty, tolerance, and religious pluralism over and against his conservative adversaries. In this sense, Lear's spiritual politics was the product not only of a rich tradition of theatrical and religious liberalisms but also of a contemporaneous encounter with its civic antithesis in the public square—namely "the Christian Right." In fact, one could even argue that such metonyms for conservative religiosity were the direct product of both the spiritual politics of the Religious Left during this period and Lear's own biographical particularity. Unfortunately for Lear, much of his own complicity in these events remained unexamined or obscured from introspective view until pressed for explanation in a court of law in defense of the "public interest."

These liberal religious tenets experienced their first examination in the mid-1970s in the form of a federally mandated policy known simply, as the Family Viewing Hour. For Lear and his fellow Hollywood supporters, this act was the first instance of federally authored "censorship" in prime time due to their programs' at-times explicit material. Despite the cultural continuity that existed between Lear's writing and the federally defined "public interest," a rhetorical move not lost on his lawyers, Lear and others still feared a conservative takeover of the airwaves due to the expanding televangelist presence of Falwell and Robertson. I argue that widespread concern for violence on television at the time served as the perfect opportunity to question not only Lear's usage of "public interest" in defending his programming but also his deployment of federal policies as defensive measures against his conservative opponents. It also encouraged a reexamination of just how the federal government adjudicated scarce broadcast time among a variety of religious communities, both conservative and liberal, that viewed broadcast television as the next frontier for their respective religio-political and electoral agendas. For some, this usage meant new opportunities for prose-lytization. For others, it meant the equally important desire to influence and raise awareness about the pressing issues of the day presented in dramatic fashion and at high volume.

REGULATING TELEVISION: HISTORY, RELIGION, AND THE PUBLIC INTEREST

In 1974, NBC broadcast a television movie in prime time titled, *Born Innocent*. Starring actress Linda Blair in her first role beyond *The Exorcist*, the movie explored a number of controversial themes including childhood trauma, domes-tic abuse, and violence against women and children. One of many realist programs offered to audiences in the wake of Lear's *All in the Family*, the movie focused on the story of Blair's character, which involved her living in an all-girls deten-tion center at the age of fourteen due to her criminal indiscretions. During her stay at the center, Blair's character was subjected to countless beatings and vio-lent acts by her fellow inmates. One particular instance of a violent attack would catch the attention of not only the viewing public but also network censors and the Federal Communications Commission regarding what was appropriate or not for prime-time viewing.

The scene in question was the first of its kind. It featured Blair and her attack-ers in a graphic scene of a group of children gang-raping another child in the com-munal showers with a plunger handle. Despite the fact that numerous individu-als and organizations had been organizing against violence on television since the early 1970s, this singular event catalyzed public debate and, as such, demanded a federal response. Not only was prime-time TV fast becoming a significant front in the culture wars, it was also becoming a "contested zone" due to the organizing of both liberal and conservative advocacy groups against their respective televi-sual transgressions.

The first such TV reform groups to emerge in the 1970s were largely liberal in aspiration and composition. A product of the civil rights movement of the previ-ous decade and its strategic justice-oriented goals, various liberal activists orga-nized against two offenses in particular as part of a newly emergent "media reform movement"—the misrepresentation of minority communities on television and segregation writ large in US society. Liberal Protestant denominations such as the United Church of Christ (UCC) and organizations like the National Organization for Women (NOW) and the NAACP found common cause against racism and discrimination, televisual or not, during the early 1970s. Such organizing began much earlier, however, with the actions of the Office of Communications in the United Church of Christ against Jackson, Mississippi, television station WLBT in 1964. Organizers succeeded in denying the station its license through the filing of a "petition to deny" with the FCC regarding the station's broadcast license and its habit of discriminating against black employment and programming. The end result of this encounter between liberal advocacy groups and the federal government resulted in the eventual denial of the station's license because of its racial discrimination, the evidence of which had been reported by UCC operatives through careful monitoring and reporting of anomalies in the WLBT broadcasts.[17]

This was a landmark decision in the history of television and its regulation because it allowed citizens to take part in license hearing protocols for the first time. Not only did this mirror Lear's own preference for "the people" to make their own decisions when it came to television programming, more important, it set a precedent for groups and individuals to articulate and protect their interests as part of the community that television served in the name of the "public interest."[18] In this sense, Lear found common religio-political ground with individuals within the Religious Left such as William F. Fore, who became the executive director of the Broadcasting and Film Commission of the National Council of Churches (NCC) during the same year.[19] Fore was also concerned about the relationship between programming in the "public interest" and programming in the "partisan interest" once stations received their federally mandated licenses. In light of the ongoing postwar conservative mobilization of funds that would eventually culminate in the formation of the electronic church during the late 1970s, Fore argued that federal regulation did not inherently challenge First Amendment rights to speech that was broadcast over the airwaves. "The freedom of religious expression is not threatened," he argued. "What may be threatened is the 'freedom' with which some religion stations have operated a *public* facility in the interest of *private* sectarian causes."[20]

For some commentators at the time, however, the FCC was in violation of the separation of church and state by default because it required its license holders to include religious programming in their respective schedules. This resulted in the FCC essentially determining what was and was not "religion" according to its own stipulations. Due to the FCC's historic preference for mainline traditions when it came to radio and television broadcasts, other less well known or less recognized traditions could not attain a similarly powerful platform due to the perceived incongruity between programs that served the "public interest" and those that did not. As a result, the FCC, "through its licensing process, has in effect graded religions by the standards of what a few people have defined as the 'public interest.'"[21] Luckily for Lear, his programming was understood largely as contributing to the "public interest" due to the topicality and seriousness of his story lines told through situation comedy. In this sense, Lear can be understood as benefitting from such federal dynamics in the name of "the public interest."

Fore's words, however, foreshadowed the upcoming decade's religio-political challenges that Lear and others would face in the public square—namely whose interests reflected publicly agreed upon principles and whose did not. In other words, who agreed to the terms of public reason when entering political deliberation and who did not? For Lear, this question had been answered during the 1930s through the diatribes of Father Charles Coughlin, an individual who represented anything *but* the public interest due to his anti-Semitism. After giving a particularly explicit speech pertaining to the Treaty of Versailles in 1932, CBS decided to stop selling airtime at commercial prices for religious broadcasts like Coughlin's. This policy followed the same one executed by NBC less than ten years before.

Coughlin's rhetoric reached fever pitch when he began identifying wealthy Jewish businessmen with the most sinister machinations *as Jews*. In response, the National Association of Broadcasters altered its own radio code in 1939 in order to ban attacks against others made on the basis of race or religion.[22] Such a change, however, did not stop the networks from broadcasting programs on "sustaining," or free, time as part of their collective service to the "public interest" in the name of balance. In 1944, the Joint Religious Radio Committee of the Congregational, Methodist, and Presbyterian US churches and the United Church of Canada formed the first nationally syndicated religious programs in addition to awarding individual ministers funds to attend radio institutes.[23]

With titles such as *Church in the Air*, these radio programs represented a variety of denominational interests in spirit, yet they were ultimately most reflective of the mainline and the NCC. In addition, such programs purposefully did not solicit funds from their audiences—the classic tenet of commercial programming usually associated with conservative viewpoints. "We feel that religious broadcasting is a public service," argued CBS founder William S. Paley, "which should be administered as far as possible under the guidance of persons closely associated with the religious endeavor and definitely capable of handling such broadcasting in the public interest."[24] For Paley and countless others, first in radio and later in television, the "most capable" individuals were those organizations and individuals who also sought balance and service in the public interest, namely mainline and liberal Protestants.

This network preference would continue throughout the course of the twentieth century, especially when it came to Lear's programming and later his nonprofit organizing on behalf of the American Way. The events and decisions of the 1930s pertaining to the media and its federal regulation would be felt during the 1960s and 1970s in the courts and in the general political discourse of the period, which grew more dependent on newly emergent yet all too familiar rhetorical binaries such as public/private and partisan/public interest. These terms, including the public interest itself, influenced the next decade of church/state debates and political confrontations in the public square between individuals such as Lear, televangelist Jerry Falwell, and even President Ronald Reagan himself.

For former FCC chairman Frederick W. Ford, the act of defining "the public interest" was best left to the words of an early twentieth-century congressman who argued that the public interest is "service to the public; service of the highest order reasonably and practically possible. This means, first of all, the availability of programming of an acceptable signal quality, and secondly it means content designed to serve a *useful social purpose*."[25] Despite the amount of time that separated Ford's words from those of his example, there existed, in between and beyond these years, a remarkable level of epistemic consistency when it came to "the public interest" and its execution over the airwaves—an expression of an institutional form of "common sense."[26] The FCC itself admitted to the less than clear consensus that existed concerning questions of definition, but its members could nevertheless agree on one thing—the public interest called for a definition and thus an understanding of religion and appropriate religious programming according to the dictates of political and religious liberals, an established federal tradition arguably dating back to the likes of FDR, the NCC, and the New Deal.

Lear took advantage of this history because his spiritual politics aligned perfectly with the liberal common sense that undergirded the federal notion of programming in the public interest. For scholar of religion John Modern, "common sense" refers to the socioeconomic conditions that normalize particular understandings of the religious and the secular in a given moment in time. Based on this definition, I would argue that Lear's secular formation was more conducive to the state's in light of their common emphasis on public reason and its public/ private binary. Lear's understanding of relevancy as demonstrated in his television writing and behind-the-camera activism reflected the very same assumptions that undergirded the public interest in its pursuit of balance, tolerance, and fair representation across the scarce resource that was the federally regulated airwaves.

As previously mentioned, the days and nights Lear spent listening to his crystal radio as a child were certainly filled with the vitriol and condemnation of Coughlin, but there were also moments of encouragement and positivity expressed in the key of a *Social* Gospel, a New Deal for a depressed people. "The liberal theologians of the Social Gospel movement tried to derive from the Christian message a motive for social reforms in the factories, tenement slums, and streets of urban America," argues scholar of religion David Chidester. "Christianity was to become *relevant* to the problems of the modern world by forming a base for social action by which the social welfare . . . of all people in America might be improved."[27] For those following Lear's moves beyond the formal stages of *All in the Family*, *Maude*, and *Sanford and Son*, his story lines arguably retained much of their didactic and dramatic character as understood through social relevance. They were, however, articulated in a slightly different register—one suited to both the conditions and the timbre of American politics. In short, Lear identified his own programming as contributing to and a product of "the public interest."

We are able to identify and thus describe the religious investments of the public interest as uniquely liberal and religious based on what can be understood as a custodial imperative of social uplift. "According to most liberals," argues Cara Brundidge, "Christianity should improve society by bolstering ethical standards and improving social conditions."[28] Unlike their conservative counterparts, religious and political liberals in the Religious Left benefited greatly from this notion of the public interest because it was conducive to particular formations of the religious and the secular—namely those authored by religious liberals like Lear, Moyers, and Marty along a trajectory of liberal progress and enlightenment. This argument found its paradigmatic application and expression in the Family Viewing Hour controversy of the 1970s, one in which Lear was a focal point as one of Hollywood's leading proponents of the freedom of creative speech.

CONTESTING THE FAMILY VIEWING HOUR

"There have been notable changes in the activities of religious groups as well as in the character of the public utterances made by their leaders," observed scholar of communications Robert R. Smith. "In speaking of contemporary religious activity, commentators frequently find that they are not speaking of religious activity as a special realm of experience, but that they are discussing foreign policy (peace movement), civil rights, urban renewal or the distribution of the school budget."[29] In addition to taking part in this religious trend, Lear's commitment to defending the Hollywood community's First Amendment rights in the face of possible censorship grew out of his discomfort with the manner in which the blacklist silenced (yet again) a largely Jewish community of writers and directors. In this sense, Lear interpreted the calls for a mandatory Family Viewing Hour (FVH) as a product of federally administered discriminatory policies. The policy was simple, yet its interpretation was anything but: "Entertainment programming inappropriate for viewing by a general family audience should not be broadcast during the first hour of network entertainment programming in primetime and in the immediately preceding hour."

No longer a vast wasteland of programming, television had instead become the stuff of politics, of policies, and (thus) of power. Even those who continued to bemoan the networks acknowledged the medium's newly discovered power: "So the apocalyptic struggle between darkness and light will, finally, be waged not on the heavenly fields of cosmic space but, perhaps more aptly, in the dismal swamp of network television."[30] The Family Viewing Hour was a singular yet powerful reaction to the public outcry over "sex and violence" on television as seen in TV movies such as *Born Innocent*. More important for Lear, it was also an attempt to reestablish control over a medium whose tragicomic faculties had been unleashed in the name of relevance and realism as witnessed in the one-act plays of Lear and others in prime time. Through pressure from the FCC and meetings between its chairman and the presidents of the three networks, the Family Viewing Hour became institutional practice beginning in February 1975. Lear's reaction was equally swift and well organized.

"We want American families to be able to watch television in that time period without ever being embarrassed," argued CBS president Arthur Taylor, a strong proponent of the Family Viewing Hour. For Lear, this statement implied that there was a single "American family" that reacted uniformly and negatively to the same televised content. Not only did this remind him of the 1960s network content policy of "least offensive programming possible," it also suggested a depoliticization of television airspace itself—the very same space politicized originally by Lear earlier in the decade with programs such as *All in the Family*.

"I said there was no way I was going to—or would have any idea how to—change America's most popular show to meet the vague standards of *decency* that the Family Hour demanded," observes Lear in his autobiography, *Even This I Get to Experience*. "*All in the Family* was virtually devoid of sex and violence, but its propensity for dealing with topical subjects was evidently deemed equally unfit for children. . . . The creative climate was becoming increasingly oppressive."[31] Lear's identification of the policy's concern with notions of taste and decency is yet another indication of the terms of cultural warfare that were gaining rhetorical and political traction during this period. If Lear and Holly-wood stood on one side of this religio-political divide, then conservative sena-tors and the FCC chairman stood on the other, at least in this particular instance. In short, Lear argued that the Family Viewing Hour implicitly targeted his pro-gramming because of its topical and socially relevant nature.

When challenged by the networks, or in this case the federal government, Lear acted with focused abandon because it concerned matters of social significance, principled questions of serious concern. In this instance, the Family Viewing Hour was a veiled attempt to censor the creative agenda of Hollywood's best and brightest in the name of social responsibility. Not only was this a move to scape-goat Lear and his supporters for the violence in the industry, it also infringed on their First Amendment rights regardless of time of viewing. The reception of this case, then, becomes paramount to understanding Lear's spiritual agenda in front of and behind the camera during this period leading up to the formation of Peo-ple for the American Way. Not only was the Family Viewing Hour a violation of free speech for Lear, it was also a direct intervention into a realm of culture dom-inated largely by political and religious liberals and their tales of diversity and racial tolerance.

By 1975, all three networks had signed onto implementing the Family View-ing Hour for their upcoming programming schedules. The subsequent lawsuits filed against the FCC, and CBS in particular, by Lear, his production company, and various Hollywood guilds such as the Writers Guild of America questioned the legality of the networks' decision to approve such a regulated segment of pro-gramming in prime time. More important for Lear, the outcome of these filings had the potential of affecting his and others' access to the airwaves themselves. "The question before the court was not the desirability of the family viewing pol-icy, but 'who should have the right to decide what shall and shall not be broad-cast and how and on what basis should these decisions be made.'"[32] Lear had been used to acting without constraint, without editorial marginalia. The network's office of standards and practices was impeding enough, but this incident was one of many to come, played out across stages both political and entertaining, which shaped Lear's ability to maintain his position of authority within the knowledge industry as one of its primary religio-political representatives. The rise of the elec-tronic church would serve as another moment of pause for Lear and his support-ers as they realized that they were no longer the only game in town in prime time.

The terms of Lear's rhetorical defense in court against the FCC's federally mandated act of censorship tell us much about how he understood his own pro-gramming and its relationship to the nation's civic life. They also assist us in iden-tifying the characteristics of his spiritual politics as understood through the genre of the situation comedy. "*Writers Guild* plaintiffs considered the FVH to be a threat to television's move toward realistic and socially important themes," observed one commentator in 1977. "*Tandem* plaintiffs also asserted that the FVH deprives the public of *diversity* in entertainment programming." With respect to *All in the Family*, the FVH "excluded a program that often deals with issues of serious concern and significance to the American people."[33] These arguments were made by numerous individuals on the plaintiff side of the case, which included not only Lear but also Larry Gelbart, Susan Harris, Ed Weinberger, and Paul Witt, who were responsible for various television programs at the time including *MASH*, *The Mary Tyler Moore Show*, *Rhoda*, and *Barney Miller*.

The arguments above stated that Lear's and others' programming was guilty not only of using too much "sex and violence" in the story lines but also of tackling subject matter unsuited for family viewing. In other words, *because* of the nature of Lear's relevance writing style, his and others' programs were being singled out by Congress and the FCC as evidence of a faulty regulatory system regarding the country's scarce airwaves. The court concluded, however, that the dealings between the FCC and the networks that resulted in the FVH altering prime-time scheduling and content compromised licensee independence, including Lear's. Testifying in front of the Communications Subcommittee of the House of Representatives in 1976, producer Larry Gelbart and others stated their case simply as supporters of the First Amendment: "We want the right, not just in our own interest, but in the country's, to be able to discuss mature themes on television, to illuminate our concerns and yours. We think more freedom, freedom with responsibility, is the answer, instead of more censorship."[34] Reflecting the liberal mainline tendency of reading individual interest as communal interest due to the custodial nature of the religious liberalism, Gelbart argued that Hollywood possessed a unique opportunity to engage serious topics in a "mature" fashion in prime time for the betterment of not only the individuals writing and producing the shows but also the viewing audience—understood *as* the country itself.[35]

The fact that Lear was Jewish did not affect his ability to participate in the custodial politics of the Spiritual Left through his own writing of theatrically liberal productions such as *All in the Family*.[36] In fact, the two idioms of social responsibility articulated by Gelbart and Lear functioned as part of a larger Hollywood ethic of illumination, a project stemming largely from the public interest itself and its own national logic. "It is the right of the public to be informed, rather than any right on the part of the Government, any broadcast licensee or any individual member of the public to broadcast his own particular views on any matter, which is the foundation stone of the American system of broadcasting."[37] In short, Lear produced, wrote, and performed *All in the Family* on a weekly basis to a quarter of the country as part of his own understanding of the public interest as defined by the FCC and the Supreme Court in cases such as *Red Lion Broadcasting Co. v. FCC*. As a result, he was able to defend the content and purpose of his programming in the name of the public interest since his writing was both *public* and *of interest* to American viewers because of its topical, relevance-driven subject matter.

Unlike his conservative counterparts, who appeared to him as "Stop Immorality on TV people," Lear was able to rhetorically align his interests with those of "the public interest" because he and his Hollywood supporters ultimately saw them as one in the same.[38] "Those of us who create the shows you see on television feel that *the public interest* will not be served so long as the decisions about everything on television continue to be made monopolistically by a handful of dollar-oriented network executives," argued Lear. "We think that what goes on the air should be determined by the personal judgment, good taste, and creative imagination of professional showmen."[39] This quotation speaks particularly well to the nature of cultural and spiritual conflict in the 1970s as understood from the Religious Left: Since Lear and his supporters possessed a superior sense of taste when it came to entertainment (exemplified by comments such as "the great unwashed get what they deserve"), their collective New Class opinion inherently outweighed that of their executive "business-class" counterparts in the networks.[40]

The differences in *taste* between these two sets of class interests reflected the larger cultural cleavages of the time, resulting in the New Class assuming more "liberal" concerns over and against the "conservative" interests of network executives. Examples of liberal organizing in the name of less violent television included public contributions from the National Parent Teacher Association, the American Medical Association, the United States Conference of Catholic Bishops, the National Council of Churches, and the Southern Baptist Convention.[41]

This collective effort exemplified the congruence between political and religious liberalism(s) in the 1970s led largely by Lear's Hollywood-based activism. Additionally, this movement of the Spiritual Left mirrored another burgeoning organization of conservative yet ecumenical Protestants that would play significant roles in both the 1976 and 1980 elections. Once again, Lear's programming served as the cultural litmus test of televisual decency for both the Spiritual Left and the Christian Right—one defending its maturity, the other bewailing its controversial content. "His shows are miniature *morality plays* for the social causes to which he devotes himself offscreen as well as on," observed journalist Barbara Cady. "And he champions the right of his writers to speak their minds with an

intransigent high-mindedness that has become legendary."[42] A most unlikely figure would take center stage in another public skirmish involving Lear's situation
comedy over the content of prime-time airspace—Beatrice Arthur, better known
as Maude.

MAUDE AND THE FIGHT OVER ABORTION

"Why did the Maude people do it? What were they trying to prove? That they
are honest and brave and can joke about any subject?" asked editorial writer Joan
Hoyt. "Abortion isn't funny. Vasectomy isn't funny. They are subjects of deep
moral concern to many people."[43] Like her fellow letter writer, who yearned for
the simplicity of *Bonanza*, Hoyt could not understand how television could
address a topic of "deep moral concern," especially since the *Maude* story line in
question ended not in life but rather in death. Instead of supporting what Hoyt
and Stone contended about Lear's programming, the editor of this particular section of the *Los Angeles Times* offered his own response to the *Maude* two-part
episode (titled "Maude's Dilemma" and "Walter's Dilemma," respectively) arguing that its writers handled the subject of abortion with care and maturity as an
appropriate subject for television. "Whether you agree with Maude's decision (and
I'm not sure I do), it is a subject which I believe television has every right to discuss even within the limitations of popular programming."[44]

This brief disagreement between editor and letter writer was a microcosm for
the more serious disagreements taking place over the role and place of culture
(high and low) in American society. To what extent could it accurately and appropriately explore topics of "serious moral concern?" Was there something transcendent about the subject, set apart from typical discussion and debate, or was
it purely a matter of immanence, fit for all mediums and methods? This was not
the first time that such questions had been asked by religious Americans, especially those who identified as Christian, but it did mark a novel moment in the
recent past when traditionally religious questions of translation and communication were asked of largely cultural and social agents and materials. Unlike Hoyt,
Lear answered these questions in the affirmative not only because he relied on
culture to enact his politics in public but also because to address a different
set of subjects, ones of less moral concern, would be anathema to his spiritual
vocation—to reflect and thus *to report on* the times.

From one newspaper headline to another, each author seemed to have his or
her own opinion about Lear and his television programs. "The extraordinary

success of all three of Lear's shows (*All in the Family*, *Maude*, and *Sanford and Son*) comes in part, I think, from the fact that all three more or less, deal with impolite subjects that haunt us, including illness, aging and the abrasiveness of private relationships, and death."[45] For Lear, there were no subjects that were beyond the creative pale—assuming they contributed to his larger project of raising awareness through entertaining, relevant programming in prime time. CBS initially said that it would not fund the shooting of Lear's "abortion" episodes of *Maude* due to their content, which also included discussions of birth control and sexual embarrassment. "My fight is to get a funny script on a subject that is adult and meaningful," Lear observed. "I enjoy stirring feelings, even negative feelings, because I think that is what theater is about." Once the shooting was complete, Lear's flair for the dramatic led him to hide the two-part episodes' true subject matter from advertisements in sources such as *TV Guide*.[46]

The two episodes brought in almost half the share of the New York–Los Angeles television audience combined upon its initial airing. This was especially noteworthy since *Maude* had previously only captured only 38 percent of the collective audience. These subjects stretched the medium's capacity to capture the social tenor and unrest of its cultural surroundings. Would a flood of angry mail and calls *actually* follow the showing of such material? When it came to the pilot of *All in the Family*, the answer had been a definitive no. When it came to these episodes, the jury was slightly more mixed. For some, however, there was no question about Lear's entertainment. "Lear is, of course, correct. The honorable vulgarity of *All in the Family* has opened the door to Maude's abortion. If we're lucky, it's a door that will never shut properly again."[47] For those who continue to think that most of the cultural conflict during this period lacked any concrete "physical warfare," Lear did in fact receive a number of letters in response to the *Maude* episodes in question. Along with letters of support, he also received death threats and a collection of glossy photographs documenting the graphic signs of a fallen country—aborted fetuses.

For Lear, the very conception of the Beatrice Arthur sitcom made little sense outside of a liberatory context.[48] "*Maude* was lauded or loathed depending on how the reviewers, and viewers as well, felt about the then relatively new feminist movement," Lear observed. "The character was a role model and hero to all who cheered on the movement, and was reviled by those who held fast to the idea that 'a woman's place is in the home.'"[49] The medium and programming of television had certainly come a long way since the days of fathers knowing best and hillbillies staking their claim in Southern California. The feminist declaration that the personal was the political had come full circle and then some in the writing of Lear and others. What had been a largely private affair, women's birth control and reproductive rights, had become the stuff of prime-time network television. The personal had become public in these story lines, but the extent that it was "political," and how, was not yet clear.

The escapism of the preceding decades' prime-time lineups motivated Lear to write about what he thought was meaningful, significant, and most important, relevant—a level of topicality never before seen on television yet supported by the equally topical Protestant mainline. The editorial discussion concerning subjects of "deep moral concern" that took place in the pages of the *Los Angeles Times* could not have been a more appropriate result following the viewing of a single episode of *Maude*. Two episodes in particular, the "abortion episodes," captured Lear and his writing at the most controversial, at least to those who fought to "Stop Immorality on TV" from within the rhetorical and organizational confines known as the nascent Christian Right.

"Maude's abortion story, written by Susan Harris, took two episodes and went on the air early in the first season," Lear explained. "Two Illinois affiliates, in Champaign and Peoria, refused to air the shows—the first time that any CBS station had rejected any episode of a continuing series."[50] Not only had the network balked at paying for the production of these episodes, two local channels had also refused to broadcast them due to their controversial nature. More likely, however, was the fact that those who made the programming decisions for the local affiliates disagreed with the content of the programs—a difference in cultural taste and decency. For the manager of the Champaign office, it was a simple question of subject matter. "We don't think abortion is a proper subject for treatment in a frivolous way in a comedy program."[51] In response to these actions against Lear's program, the National Organization for Women filed a class-action suit demanding that the stations show the episodes in question.

While most scholars are familiar with conservative *counter*mobilization movements during this period, Lear's programming and its effects on the regulation of American broadcasting illustrate as much about his liberal supporters as it does his conservative detractors—perhaps even more so. This would not be the last time that a left leaning organization would come to Lear's aid in the name of fairness and the public interest regarding his relevance programming. Far from it. In fact, one could argue that were it not for the encouragement and support from organizations such as the Population Institute, the abortion episodes would never have come to pass.[52] "Although the Population Institute had provided the incentive for the two episodes, it had not served as a technical consultant on the script. That role was played by the Los Angeles chapter of Planned Parenthood.... As a result," argues historian Kathryn Montgomery, "Planned Parenthood leaders were in a good position to anticipate opposition from antiabortion groups and to plan a counter-strategy."[53] Such support should come as no surprise in light of the show's explicit grounding in the women's movement in general and Maude's rights in particular.

Relative to Archie, Maude possessed an undeniable presence as "the flip side of Archie, . . . a Roosevelt liberal who has her feet firmly planted in the forties."[54] Of all the shows Lear composed during the 1970s and 1980s, *Maude*, with its strong female lead, was the closest representation of Lear himself and his politics—an individual shaped by the notions of a New Deal and Jewish conspiracies. It certainly was a continuation of the relevance programming that originated with Lear's *All in the Family*, but it was also an amplified iteration of the original in the genre. In light of the popular and critical successes of *All in the Family*, the two abortion episodes of *Maude* brought a newfound attention to the medium of television as both an agent of transmission and a medium for storytelling and theater. "It tested, as never before, the boundaries of acceptability for program content; it pushed into the public arena a debate about the proper role of television in dealing with controversial political issues," or as Lear would articulate it, issues of "deep moral concern."[55] Once the tune of such mass media appeal began to change, however, with the ascendancy of the Christian Right and its electronic church, the allure of the medium's scale began to morph into a portentous threat.

In the wrong hands, the television would supplant the radio in its ability to reach the greatest number of listeners at one time. The newfound pressure applied to the networks and their shows' sponsors by both impassioned individuals and organizations known as "advocacy groups" from both sides of the political spectrum further bifurcated the cultural landscape between those who approved of Lear's programming and those who did not. The various reactions to the *Maude* episodes and their subsequent reruns tell us much about liberal and conservative mobilization during this period as a *coconstitutive* process. For each conservative reaction, there was a liberal anticipation of the very same reaction. This was arguably the case because the liberal builders of single-issue advocacy as deployed during the civil rights movement recognized their own handiwork in the conservative organizing of conservative ministers, businesspeople, and television evangelists against immorality and indecency on television. The media reform movement may have stemmed from the largely liberatory project of the New Left, civil rights activism, and the NCC, but those who achieved its culminating application in public were conservative in political and religious philosophy.

Despite these successes, we are still able to locate liberal religious mobilization in the name of the First Amendment during this period against the local stations that refused to broadcast the episodes. The Population Institute's David

Poindexter described his response in a letter to Lear in light of a Detroit station's refusal to broadcast the episodes: "A small task force of us from our Center, from Planned Parenthood–World Population and from some of the Protestant churches got on the long distance phone and stirred up a considerable bit of protest in Detroit." Like his conservative counterparts, Lear also possessed an extensive network of supportive organizations and individuals who came to his defense on both the legislative and grassroots levels in the name of free speech. Lear would have to wait until the early 1980s, however, before he could begin institutionalizing this support against the Christian Right through his nonprofit advocacy group People for the American Way. His detractors would become more organized as well over the course of the 1970s as they began reacting to and organizing against the broad national subjects of conservative criticism and scorn, including the controversy surrounding *Roe v. Wade*.

Like the larger antiabortion movement itself, Catholics were the first ones to organize against the abortion story lines of *Maude*. On November 21, 1972, a group representing the Archdiocese of Rockville Centre marched to CBS headquarters in New York "and proceeded to blockade the limousine belonging to CBS vice Chairman Dr. Frank Stanton."[56] Catholics also challenged the legitimacy and (at times) legality of Lear's programming through the application of the federally mandated fairness doctrine, which called for a "balanced" presentation of differing points of view about a particular subject of public importance.[57] In fact, the National Council of Catholic Bishops responded to the second of two *Maude* episodes by filing an official complaint first with CBS in 1973 and later with the FCC once it realized the network was not going to cooperate with its demands.

In response to these objections, CBS categorized its prime-time programming as solely "entertainment," even when particular programs explored topics seemingly of public importance. In a network-authored statement, the *Maude* episodes were "intended for entertainment and not for the discussion of viewpoints on controversial issues of public importance."[58] The network defense of Lear-style programming took advantage of the fact that shows like *All in the Family* and *Maude* walked a fine line between comedy and commentary, entertainment and social analysis. Despite the fact that Lear himself defended his programming in the name of relevance, topicality, and subjects of "deep moral concern," the networks and the federal government could not deploy the same defense because they could be seen as supporting a *partisan* perspective on a given issue instead of providing quality programming in the public interest.

These Catholics found a supportive voice in the organizing of the Stop Immorality in TV group based out of Warrenton, Virginia, whose advisory board included individuals such as Phyllis Schlafly, Fred Schwartz, baseball player Phil Rizzuto, and comedian Red Skelton. Like other nonprofits during this period, this group conducted mass mailings in order to alert Americans of television that was destroying "Judeo-Christian principles . . . through programs that defy the standards we hold sacred." Such programs included *All in the Family*, *Maude*, and *MASH*.[59] For one writer for the *Village Voice*, shame rather than praise fit the descriptive bill for Lear's abortion episodes. "Thanks to the vigilance of an organization called Stop Immorality on TV—a project of the Society for the Christian Commonwealth—we can all sleep better in front of our video sets," observed Helen Kruger. "The Virginia-based group has awarded its first 'Shield of Shame' to Norman Lear, producer of 'Maude,' for his 'tasteless intrusion into American homes . . . whereby he assaults the family's basic sense of decency by advancing coarseness, crudity, and a system of moral values which debase the religious principles of millions.'"[60] For Executive Director Paul A. Fisher, shows like *Maude* possessed a "low moral tone" compared to the "deep moral concern" of editorial writers and Lear, himself. Typical of disagreements within the culture wars, the personal had not only been exposed to the public, figures like Fisher and Lear had made it the stuff of *politics* and public policy itself. In short, one person's indecency was another's in-depth exploration of teenage sexuality, racism, or adult impotency.

Expanding on the notion that Lear's programming represented a "system of moral values," Fisher argued that "morality, decency, devotion to God, family, duty and country, are held up to mockery and laughter with the suggestion that they are 'old fashioned,' dirty and sick jokes about religion [because] decency and family life are far from humorous for American families."[61] Despite his commitment to journalistic objectivity, the author himself responded to Fisher's words, arguing that Lear's work marked the medium's maturity rather than its juvenility. In fact, Lear could not have defended his work any better. "And here TV thought it was finally coming of age, growing up to a point of accepting realities of life, and not the kind of fantasies or low intelligence baiters of the 'Green Acres' or apple-pie 'Ozzie and Harriet' era," journalist Dan Lewis declared. "It seems strange, too, that the shows that have become the target of the Stop Immorality on TV all are forms of comedy and variety, which now slice their humor from real life, and not the plastic world of make-believe. . . . [Are] violence and shoot-'em ups okay, just as long as they don't get sexy?"[62]

What is clear from these exchanges between Lear, the media, and his detractors is that while editorials tended to be more critical of his work, the voices of those on staff at various magazines and newspapers were largely supportive.

They also suggest that Lear possessed his own "system of moral value" in the public square as understood through his various cultural productions in prime time. While the vitriol of these debates continued to build, Lear and CBS began exploring the inherent dangers in showing the episodes in their traditional rerun schedule during the summer of 1973. The timing could not have been more significant. "The 1972–1973 year had become a critical test year for determining just how far entertainment television could venture into controversial territory."[63]

On January 22, 1973, abortion officially became legal across the country, encouraging Lear and CBS to go ahead with the reruns in traditional, clandestine fashion. Relying on the deft public relations skills of newly hired executive Virginia Carter, Lear anticipated antiabortion counterattacks with his own preemptive campaign, which drew on the letter-writing support of the National Organization for Women, the National Association for the Repeal of Abortion Laws, and the American Civil Liberties Union. When the United States Catholic Conference learned of CBS and Lear's rebroadcasting plans, they charged the network with "undeniable malice and a calculated intent to offend the sensibilities and deeply held beliefs of a substantial portion of the American public." A few days before airing part two, "Walter's Dilemma," the conference distributed instructions to their 163 dioceses to campaign against *Maude* during the next Sunday's sermons.[64]

Like the pilot of its prime-time progenitor, *All in the Family*, the summertime reruns of the *Maude* episodes were broadcast with a network-composed advisory to those watching at home. It would be a couple of years before the Family Viewing Hour would take hold of prime-time lineups nationwide, but this editorial aside was an indication of the developing cultural tensions between television's commercial and creative interests—those on the floor during the table reads and those making notes on the very same scripts thirty floors up. These divisions arguably reflected the larger societal restructuring that was taking place at the time between the interests of the New Class, or knowledge class, and the business class.[65]

The disclaimer that preceded the *Maude* episodes on August 14 and 21, however, highlighted the stark differences between those who supported relevance programming and its oppositional detractors: "Tonight's episode of *Maude* was originally broadcast in November of 1972. Since it deals with Maude's dilemma as she contemplates the possibility of abortion, you may wish to refrain from watching it if you believe the broadcast may disturb you or others in your family." In comparison to the *All in the Family* disclaimer, this one named the option of opting out of the episodes altogether. No longer did Lear's program shed a humorous light on human absurdity; instead, it named the disturbance of "the family" before it even took place.

The difference in tone between the two statements reveals the extent to which American citizens had learned to organize against their most beloved medium—the television. CBS anticipated this type of blowback by including an out for offended viewers in their statement, yet these preemptive measures echoed the support shown to CBS in its decision to air the controversial episodes. The ACLU, along with the Freedom to Read Committee of the Association of American Publishers, the National Council of Churches, the Union of American Hebrew Congregations, and the Young Women's Christian Association, issued a public statement congratulating CBS "for their courageous decision to proceed with the re-run . . . despite pressure to withdraw it." For Lear's supporters, who were as diverse as the characters in his programs, as well as for Lear himself, shows like *All in the Family* and *Maude* were not the narrow, partisan programming that Fisher and others described. In fact, it was just the opposite: "The public interest is not served when a station's program decision is made on the basis of fear of controversy, or when an advertiser's sponsorship is determined by fear of economic reprisal."[66]

Lear's commitment to exploring serious subjects in a mature fashion through his television programming, regardless of the content, upset many in light of the relative nature of decency and taste. These differences reflected the widening divisions at the time between conservatives and liberals across the political spectrum and oftentimes across the religious spectrum as well. In short, Lear understood his programming as contributing explicitly to the federally administered "public interest" precisely because of its subject matter as relevance programming, which included subjects such as diversity, civility, tolerance, and bigotry.

All but defeated, the Catholics who had originally protested against the *Maude* episodes had the final word when it came to Lear's usage of "the public interest" in defense of his relevance programming. For authors Robert B. Beusse and Russell Shaw, the Lear case was anything but decided: "There is something strange in the fact that protests and pressure against the *Maude* shows on abortion evoked outcries in some quarters; while the pressure that helped bring Maude's pro-abortion decision into millions of living rooms is passed over in silence." In closing, Beusse and Shaw name arguably the single most important narrative device when it comes to renarrating postwar conservative mobilization in the United States since the 1960s: "Perhaps the strongest lesson in all this for pro-life people, is to 'go and do likewise.' "[67] Like their civil religious counterparts, conservative Protestants were also realizing that they, too, could make their collective presence felt through the very same mediated channels of dissemination and communication—the airwaves.

For many, the election of Jimmy Carter was the last bit of encouragement needed to convince conservative Protestants of the importance of mobilizing politically on behalf of the unborn. In the 1960s, evangelist and future televangelist Jerry Falwell first argued against applying the Gospel to society and its politics in his sermon "Ministers and Marches." Less than two decades later, Falwell founded his own advocacy group to organize conservative interests under the banner of the Moral Majority. Despite the fact that there is little to no scholarly consensus as to why Falwell changed his mind by the late 1970s, careful study of Lear and his career in media may give us a clue as to Falwell's change of heart. At the very least, we are able to understand better how and why Falwell identified Lear as "the number one enemy of the American family" and why fellow televangelist Pat Robertson warned Lear that his arms were "too short to box with God."

THE TELEVISION SUMMIT: OJAI, CALIFORNIA

As Lear documented this religio-political ascendancy with increasing attention, he and others in Hollywood began to feel the pinch of a radically altered sociopolitical landscape—one that was increasingly bending under the growing power of the single-issue advocacy group as seen during the civil rights and media reform movements of the late 1960s. Largely in response to the intensifying pressures on the networks from both liberal and conservative media groups, Lear and others organized a private summit in Ojai, California, titled the Proliferation of Pressure Groups in Primetime Symposium in 1981 in order to better address the changing media landscape.[68]

The meeting's attendance list reflects the diversity of opinions surrounding the issues in question—namely advertising interests, controversial subject matter, and network interests broadcast in prime time. Included in the lineup, besides Lear and all three network heads, were Tyrone Brown (former FCC chairman), Geoffrey Cowan (PBS), Betty Friedan, Robert Goldstein (Proctor & Gamble), Mark Goode (TV consultant to President Reagan), Rev. M. William Howard Jr. (president of NCC), F. Kent Mitchell (General Foods), William Rusher (publisher of *National Review*), Gail Smith (General Motors), and Grant Tinker (president of Mary Tyler Moore Productions) along with Lear's Tandem Productions partner, Bud Yorkin.

Despite its largely bipartisan composition, the meeting's lineup still leaned to the political and Religious Left when it came to the issues under discussion. Echoing Lear, chairman of the Academy of Television Arts and Sciences David L. Wolper stated outright that "pressure groups that push for their values and views to be reflected by the addition of programs with more *diversity* to television are desirable. What is not," Wolper argued, were "pressure groups that demand the values and points of view they disagree with be totally excluded from television are unacceptable." In addition, Wolper acknowledged the legality of organized boycotts of commercial products according to particular television programs, but they were ultimately not, as Lear would say, in the spirit of the law. "An organized boycott . . . is constitutionally legal but, in the opinion of the symposium, morally wrong and damaging to the free flow of ideas."[69] In light of this observation, one could argue that that if conservatives claimed a more economic reading of "the market" at the time as an organizing logic of postindustrial America, then liberals appropriated their own usage of "the market" as well, one of ideas and creativity that would not (and could not) bend to any form of censorship whatsoever.

For both Wolper and Lear, the public interest was best represented by programs that engaged themes like diversity within a free-flowing marketplace of ideas. Those groups and individuals that did not sign onto the same set of religio-political values fell outside of the public interest due to their partisanship. Wolper mentioned specifically both the National Coalition for Better Television and the Moral Majority as the primary dangers threatening an otherwise unregulated marketplace. For all intents and purposes, the summit appeared to simply echo Lear's own priorities when it came to the freedom of speech within an industry increasingly regulated by the federal government, advocacy groups, and the FCC. The opening plenary address, however, said otherwise.

The symposium's first afternoon plenary session was given by William Rusher, publisher of the *National Review*, one of the foremost conservative periodicals in the United States at the time. Rusher's opening statement expressed his gratitude for the opportunity to speak to such an esteemed group of industry leaders. Well aware of his audience's political predilections toward conservatives, he differentiated himself from any and all associations with "the rural." "Since we are going to be talking about the religious right and the Moral Majority and things like that," Rusher stated, "let me assure you that I am not a redneck—I am a New Yorker."[70] For someone like Norman Lear, who also dedicated serious attention to the differences between "the old Religious Right" of the Scopes trial and "the new Religious Right" of the Moral Majority, this distinction spelled trouble for those seeking to limit the exposure of the electronic church over the highly contested airwaves through the use of "the public interest" or the fairness doctrine. Broadly considered, the conservatism of Rusher's arguments was closer to that of fellow conservative William F. Buckley than conservative evangelist Pat Robertson. In fact, Rusher's rendering of the Religious Right possessed an admirable level of descriptive clarity in light of the proximity to his subject and the ever-expanding contemporary literature on the Christian Right.[71]

Rusher knew that his audience tended to see the Christian or Religious Right as a cohesive entity seeking to establish a theocratic government in the United States. "Let's first of all clean up our terminology a little bit," Rusher suggested. "If you want to talk about it [Moral Majority], talk about it. But do not confuse it with that larger entity that is called the religious right, which is all the groups that are interested in that kind of thing these days." The New Right, including Richard Viguerie and Howard Phillips, was yet another component of the Religious Right, but for Rusher, they were also removed from it philosophically due to their libertarian sensibilities. "And just to make matters still clearer and worse, don't confuse any of them with neoconservatives, Irving Kristol and Norman Podhoretz and that crowd."[72]

Rusher's words set the descriptive bar for any and all discussions of the Religious Right that followed his plenary address during the symposium. They also represented some of the most well-reasoned criticisms of Lear's spiritual vision of civic life in light of the rise of the Christian Right and the subsequent formation of People for the American Way by Lear and others in the interfaith and ecumenical mainline. "As a matter of principle," argued Rusher, "a person ought to be allowed to deploy . . . his dollars where he wants to. I didn't hear any great objections from the liberals when Caesar Chavez urged us all to boycott lettuce."[73] As Falwell and others were beginning to do in light of Lear's public visibility, Rusher identified the double standard that tended to shape how public spaces were religiously understood and consequently governed by the federal government, the FCC, and Norman Lear himself. "When we speak of fairness," argued Rusher, "let us be certain the same standards of fairness apply to *all* broadcast content. . . . Is it not fair that situation comedies and other entertainment-type programs that cover controversial issues be measured by the same standards of fairness as are the *Old-Time Gospel Hour* and *700 Club*?"[74] Despite the fact that Lear often answered this question with a definitive no, Rusher identified a crucial weakness within Lear's understanding of American public life in particular and liberal democracy in general. This question was that much more important in light of the technological advances at the time in television broadcasting.

Echoing some of the observations by television critics of the 1970s regarding Lear's programming, Rusher argued, "In terms of television, it has become a national community.... Jerry Falwell wasn't trying in these last 20 years to impose his views on anybody. The aggression was all coming from the other direction."[75] The early 1980s was certainly a moment defined by conservative ascendancy both on the television and in the Oval Office, but it also witnessed its fair share of liberal mobilization—often in more vociferous terms than its conservative counterparts. For Rusher, television was beginning to function within and contribute to a set of cultural conditions that made its programming that much more significant. Due to the increasing influence of media such as television and its prime-time programming on politics and the political process itself, discussion and analysis of Lear's politics and programs of the 1970s assumed a greater degree of social saliency for advocacy groups on both sides of the aisle. "It is a public morality we are talking about here," Rusher observed, identifying the most important category under dispute during the culture wars.[76] "I think the 1980s are going to see a great deal of hammering out of things. It may be that the whole decade will turn out to be primarily, at least in its domestic aspects, a decade in which we slug out this question."[77]

Rusher's predictive powers proved eerily accurate as the 1980s unfolded not along the lines set out by contemporary liberalism but rather by its conservative antagonists, both religious and political, new and old. Producer Richard Levinson captured the less than admirable place prime-time programming occupied amid countless claims to voices left unheard: "We are in the dilemma of having people wish us to be propagandists, rather than dramatists, providing we propagandize in their interest."[78] Perhaps the public interest—the very same interest that guided FCC regulation and network philosophy concerning prime-time TV licenses—was not so public after all. For former FCC chairman Tyrone Brown, the issue was a straightforward one—Lear and others needed to start seeing themselves as religio-political actors and not simply as entertainers. "As far as television is concerned many of you are not accustomed to seeing yourselves as representatives of pressure groups. But that is what you are ... which make[s] you the gatekeepers of the airwaves."[79]

The most stringent defense of the airwaves, over and against organizations like the Moral Majority, came from vice president of ABC Al Schneider. Unlike the measured accounts offered by Lear and others in the symposium, Schneider specifically targeted the Christian Right in its attempts to interrupt or otherwise interfere with the "marketplace of ideas" that those in Hollywood and elsewhere depended on for both livelihood and political platform.[80] "The television industry is now under assault from 'moral' crusaders who want to dictate the programming content offered to the American public," argued Schneider. "You have all heard the rhetoric from both sides. You are all aware of the potential dangers to our system, to individual creativity, to the way we conduct business and the way we direct our lives in a free society."[81] Like lawyer Alan Dershowitz, who was also in attendance, Schneider focused on the threat of possible censorship as a subject related to both the market and maintenance of the public interest.

Based on his own definition of "the public interest" and understanding of its purpose, Schneider's argument closely resembled Lear's in the emphasis on achieving an informed citizenry through a diverse array of programming. "Serving the public interest involves the public's right to know." This task, however, involved limits. "The commitment is to offer a variety of opinions and ideas to the total public. It is not a requirement to grant access to the medium to any one individual or group."[82] The terms of this debate, namely the rhetorical binaries private/public and public/partisan, were as much a product of their own times as they were of American history writ large. For producer Grant Tinker of *The Mary Tyler Moore Show*, Lear represented one of many possible ways of addressing the Religious Right and its advances in the public square. Despite Lear's energy, Tinker was not completely on board despite having the same goal: "Our group spent very little time thinking about or talking about People for the American Way (PFAW), the organization put together by Norman Lear and others. There was no disapproval of this sort of activity; we just seemed to be trying to find an easier way than all-out war."[83]

Lear's motivation for gathering the funds and support necessary to start a civil liberties–oriented nonprofit during the early 1980s stemmed from the very same concerns—namely how one view could become the only view when it came to a particular issue or subject in the news at the time. This was especially the case when it came to subjects of "public importance," those topics that both Lear and the Christian Right built their respective careers upon in media, but in dramatically different ways. Yet such subjects were ultimately bound by the "taste" and conception of "decency" of the viewers themselves amid the culture warfare of the 1970s and 1980s. Schneider closed with an insight seemingly borrowed from Lear himself: "But no individual, no group has a right to impose its values and beliefs on others. That is the issue at stake with groups like the Moral Majority. . . . This effort to impose their values on others through television is antithetical to the principles governing a free society. . . . The television industry must protect the most pervasive medium of communications from any assault that reduces the choices available to viewers."[84] The entertainment industry survived America's midcentury blacklisting, but it left an indelible mark on how Hollywood collectively responded to instances where its creativity or freedom of expression was challenged from the outside.

The rise of the Moral Majority and the Coalition for Better TV (CBTV) was a familiar challenge, but one that possessed a danger all its own. For Lear and those at the symposium, televangelists like Falwell succeeded with the American people by limiting their political horizons of possibility instead of expanding them. In this sense, the fate of television and its programming arguably lay with those who perhaps knew the least about it—the American people themselves. "I think that one of the problems we're having is that the elite people are all thinking in the same terms," argued general counsel for Planned Parenthood Harriet Pilpel. "We can come to an excellent consensus here, but the question is whether the millions and millions of Americans who are not on this level would even understand what we're talking about, much less agree with it."[85] For Lear and others in Hollywood, this varied audience was both salvific and condemnatory—it reflected the best of what America could be, but it also represented the worst, as evidenced by the growing number of audiences watching the programming of the emergent electronic church. Despite the fact that these numbers were more than likely overblown, they still presented a cross-section of the country to Hollywood's best and brightest that seemingly cared little for what was going on in New York or in Los Angeles. Lear's willingness to bring so many individuals together from within the creative community spoke to his position within the Hollywood community and the Religious Left as a leader when it came to his fellow writers' freedom of speech and the American people's freedom of expression in the public square.

LEAR VS. FALWELL: THE CONSERVATIVE RESPONSE

Another Lear-related effort to articulate Hollywood-specific concerns amid boycotts, show cancellations, and the Moral Majority came from the journal *American Film*. In its October 1981 special edition, titled "Special Report: Pressure Groups and the Media," three authors examine the changing media landscape in the age of the advocacy group and the subsequent First Amendment challenges that followed. Despite the fact that groups like Donald Wildmon's Coalition for Better Television received much scorn from the Hollywood elite, including Lear himself, the broader concern for these authors was how the advocacy group itself challenged how the networks and federal government regulated programming content in its most prized time slot—prime time. This was especially difficult in light of the developing media narrative that placed Norman Lear in direct opposition to Jerry Falwell. Because of each man's respective nonprofit work, their disagreements arguably became that much more public as both People for the American Way and the Moral Majority gained strength in the newspaper headlines and with the American people.

In February 1981 and 1982, the *Saturday Review* and *Vogue*, respectively, featured articles examining the antagonistic relationship between the two men and their ideas of "decency." For conservative analyst Ben Stein, Lear and Falwell were two combatants in the "War to Clean Up TV." On one side stood Lear's Hollywood infidels, while Falwell's crusaders stood on the other—the entirety of the battlefield was encompassed by the color television screen and its promise of programming carried out in the public interest.[86] The following year, journalist Maureen Orth argued something similar, observing, "The true battlefield in the fight for the hearts and minds of America is the TV screen."[87] Eight months later, *Newsweek* published an article that explored similar material without mentioning Lear explicitly. The headline read, "TV's Latest Listing: Archie vs. Jerry."[88]

Donald Wildmon, a third figure in what were often stories of conservative religious triangulation (Falwell, Wildmon, and Lear), also received his fair share of newspaper headlines and editorials during this period. His Mississippi-based ministry, the National Coalition for Television (NCTV), eventually caught the attention of Falwell and his organization the Moral Majority in 1980. Like Lear, Wildmon had had his own encounter with less than hospitable programming four years prior. Unable to find anything suitable for him and his family to watch, Wildmon had taken it upon himself to address the profanity that he witnessed in the form of a personal crusade in the name of decency—a cornerstone of his larger organization the National Federation for Decency (NFD).[89] Lear and his programming scored quite poorly according to Wildmon's periodic network monitoring campaigns. In fact, Wildmon often referred to Lear by name. "The CBTV was a protest against the networks' perceived arrogance and indifference," argues Robert Mendenhall. "Clear-TV continues as a protest against those who, like Norman Lear, Wildmon perceives as functioning essentially as secular preachers—'evangelists' of television entertainment."[90]

The various campaigns and boycotts that Wildmon orchestrated over the course of the 1980s with the help of Jerry Falwell, Phyllis Schlafly, and others led many in the media industry and Hollywood to refer to him as "the ayatollah of the airwaves," yet, more significantly, Wildmon was seen as instituting covert forms of censorship not unlike those of the McCarthy era. The holy war that appeared to be raging between these men in the media found its network representation in NBC president Fred Silverman, who described Wildman's work as "a sneak attack on the foundation of democracy."[91] Despite the lack of consistent physical violence, these rhetorical exchanges were no less martial in their own right—a form of cultural skirmish soon to be documented by sociologists in the name of cultural warfare.[92] Various advertisers and news outlets, including Proctor & Gamble and *Newsweek*, acknowledged the divisive state of affairs. In short, the images of both hit lists and holy wars helped define how the media reported on the conflict, which it was largely responsible for, to the American people.[93]

The fact that Falwell, Wildmon, and others were perceived by the political and Spiritual Left as challenging the First Amendment protections of free speech and freedom of the press through censorship was a reality not without its own effects on the journalists who were composing the stories about Falwell and Lear during this period—including those in the *American Film* special issue.[94] "Feeling defensive, journalists have responded the best way they know: by writing stories," observed Tina Rosenberg. "Most of them leave the careful reader or viewer with little doubt as to the reporters' sentiments. Sometimes the criticisms are explicit, usually they're more subtle. There's an obvious sneer behind such phrases as 'Bible-thumping, polyester-clad fundamentalists.' "[95] Compared to these rather incendiary pieces, other journalists wrote more balanced studies that sought to investigate both liberal and conservative accounts when it came to issues of censorship and minority representation. In fact, many even pointed out the hypocrisy that lay at the heart of liberal-authored arguments against conservative outcries over TV. "One man's 'compensation' is another's 'quality control,' but when the Religious Right adopts the tactics of the Left, leftists are among the first to accuse it of 'intimidation,' " argues film critic Carrie Rickey. "If the Left gathers to protest, it's a demonstration. When the Right does it, it's a mob."[96]

Despite the contemporary resonances of these words, they were first authored in the early 1980s, a sign of the developing partisanship that would course through the body politic throughout the decade and into the 1990s and 2000s.[97] This was arguably the case because, unlike previous American conflicts in the twentieth century, those between Lear, Falwell, and the viewing public were dependent solely on the ammunition of culture itself to name and identify the most dangerous aspects of US society. The theaters of conflict that at one time spanned the Atlantic and the Pacific seemed to have found a home within the continent of North America itself, particularly within its continental states. Only this time, the terrain would be virtual—the airwaves themselves. "We must make it clear," argued NBC chairman Thomas Wyman, "that what is at stake is not the prosperity of the networks, but the freedom of the airwaves."[98] Lear's activism throughout the 1970s on behalf of this very principle continued rather unabated into the early 1980s, enough so that his work was the subject of its own analysis titled "Rallying Round the Flag: Norman Lear and the American Way" in the special issue of *American Film*.

CONCLUSION: REFRAMING THE CHRISTIAN RIGHT

Like her fellow journalists, Leslie Ward acknowledged the state of American public life in terms of its primary form of entertainment, referring to "Lear the
writer, worshipper of words, . . . thinker, social activist, idealist. Optimism, and
a master's touch for the medium, since television is the battlefield where modern-
day ideological wars are waged, Lear's got the touch, even the most *ultra* of conservatives agrees, in spades."[99] Lear's analysis of the Christian or Religious Right
revealed a different picture than most at the time or, arguably, in the contemporary literature. Rather than a bottom-up, populist, grassroots movement of mid-
dle- to lower-class Americans, Lear instead saw a highly sophisticated, pragmatic
organizational logic that sought national headlines through the appropriation of
local stories involving school boards or their curricula.

For Lear, the Christian Right was a thoroughly top-down movement funded
by wealthy businesspeople. It achieved many of its political successes by turning
conservative Protestants like Falwell and fellow televangelist Pat Robertson into
"'pawns' of ultraconservative politicos and direct-mail wizards such as Terry
Dolan, Paul Weyrich, and Richard Viguerie."[100] Despite this argument's reliance
on a form of manipulation, a common theme in Lear's and others' analyses of conservative religiosity in general and the Christian Right in particular, it nevertheless reorients our attention productively as commentators and scholars of American religion toward the highest rungs of corporate ladders, to the deep fryers of
fast-food restaurants, and to the massive floors of twenty-four-hour-a-day retail
stores.[101] We have learned a great deal about the employees of these facilities to
significant acclaim, but as this evidence and current historiographic trends
indicate, the top has remained relatively obscured from view in favor of the popular, the grassroots of the Christian Right.[102] An analysis of Lear's writing reveals
someone political at both an elite and a popular level simultaneously—one who
occupied a New Class position of symbolic influence in Hollywood yet programmed to the masses each and every week throughout the 1970s as part of the
Religious Left.

Like the previous decade's spiritual activism, Lear described his disagreements
with and criticisms of the Christian Right in the 1980s as a problem of religious
intolerance. "As a Jew, it troubles me when I watch these preachers tell their large
congregations that Buddhists, Confucianists, Muslims, Jews, and others, who
cannot by reason of their own religion accept Jesus as their Savior, will roast for
an eternity in hell," Lear explained. As he would describe later during the formation of his nonprofit organization People for the American Way, Lear could not

stand by while bigotry continued to fill the airwaves and "scripture was being tormented."[103] As a "spiritual leader" to both his television crews and his mainline and ecumenical Protestant supporters during this period, Lear stood out among many liberal voices as one of liberalism's most ardent and successful defenders, particularly when it came to religious pluralism and freedom of expression.[104] For onetime personal assistant Sonia Johnson, Lear's career in media could be summed up rather succinctly in light of the Moral Majority's advances into the airwaves and onto countless television screens around the country. In short, his movies "are about the same things as People for the American Way stands for. They reaffirm values of love, hope, questioning, and freedom of thought."[105]

The consistency of Lear's message from the beginning of the 1970s through the early 1980s regarding First Amendment rights, civility in public life, and constitutional protections for religious minorities in the public square grounded much of the liberal activism during this period when it came to mainline and ecumenical Protestantism as well as interfaith Catholicism and Judaism. His spiritual vision of American civic life, first explored through the dramatic interactions of Archie, Edith, and Meathead on *All in the Family*, began to find numerous supporters, including the likes of Notre Dame president Theodore Hesburgh, University of Chicago professor Martin Marty, and journalist Bill Moyers.

Despite the fact that Lear arguably contributed to the very phenomenon he was fighting against in his confrontations with the nascent Christian Right, namely censorship in the name of publicly accessible arguments, he also set the spiritual agenda not only for Hollywood and its politics but also for much of mainline Protestantism itself as understood through the activities of the National Council of Churches and its flagship periodical, the *Christian Century*. Lear's actions during the latter half of the 1970s and into the early 1980s on behalf of countless Hollywood writers' and producers' intellectual freedom significantly altered the televisual landscape and the manner in which the federal government regulated the airwaves in the name of the public interest. In essence, his activism defined the parameters of a politically informed spiritual liberalism that was aware of its antagonists yet was built exactly for such encounters. It was mobile, active, and organized—and well funded.

The culmination of this spiritual politics would not be long in coming for Lear and his ardent supporters. In fact, for journalist Tina Rosenberg, Lear's actions were part of something larger yet still relatively unknown and unrealized. "The press likely will discover yet another phenomenon," she explained. "For example, a resurgence of liberal Christians demanding such things as nuclear disarmament and an expansion of social programs."[106] If People for the American Way stood for anything, it was the ability to choose a given political agenda without feeling excluded from the conversation due to one's reasons. One might not agree with the content of a given argument, but one still possessed the right to articulate that argument without duress or evaluation based on an arbitrarily defined system of taste and decency—liberal or conservative.

An extension of activism rather than an isolated incident, the establishment of People of the American Way by Lear and others reflected the belief in the effectiveness of the advocacy group to accomplish religio-political goals during this period and the contention that public discourse, as part of the marketplace of ideas, should have little to no censorship in the name of decency. As such, Lear's leadership position within the Religious Left during this period should not be seen as an aberration in the history of religions liberalism but rather its culminating public expression in the formation of People for the American Way, an interfaith organization that reflected both the goodwill movement of the early twentieth century and the activism of Lear and others in the recent American past. In short, Lear was a significant contributor to the formation of a "spiritual front" in American politics during one of the most contentious periods in American history—the culture wars.

4

People for the American Way and Spiritual Politics in Late Twentieth-Century America

The scene opens simply enough. A white man wearing a yellow hard hat steps off a forklift in order to tell his audience that he has a problem. "I'm religious, we're a religious family, but that don't mean we see things the same politically. Now here come certain preachers on radio, TV, and in the mail telling us on a bunch of political issues that there's just one Christian position and implying that if we don't agree we're not good Christians." Despite the message's clarity, the man tells us that his wife and son are bad Christians on some issues and good Christians on others depending upon the particular issue in question. Unlike his family, however, the man is lucky enough to be "one hundred percent Christian" because he agrees with the preachers wholeheartedly on all the issues. His problem, nonetheless, persists.

"My problem," he says, "is I know my boy is as good a Christian as me. My wife, she's better. So maybe there's something wrong when people, even preachers, suggest that other people are good Christians or bad Christians depending on their political views." Looking intently at the camera, which by this time has zoomed in on his weathered yet kind face, the man concludes his argument with the simplicity that the television spot opened with: "That's not the American way." The clip lasted less than a minute's time, yet its impact on the formation of what would become one of the most influential interfaith nonprofit organizations since America's midcentury could not have been greater. In fact, without the hard hat, forklift, and message of political toleration and difference, the "People" would never have found the "American Way."

This particular television spot was the creation of none other than Norman Lear himself. It aired in 1980, followed shortly thereafter by four others starring Hollywood celebrities Goldie Hawn, Carol Burnett, and Muhammed Ali, who spoke on behalf of the American Way in a comical, lighthearted manner. In collaboration with countless liberal Protestants and Catholics, including Martin Marty and Theodore Hesburgh, Lear traversed the country "showing the PSA, pitching my heart out in countless homes and hotel ballrooms across America to raise money and awareness" for the soon-to-be-realized People for the American Way.[1] Known for his critically acclaimed situation comedies such as *All in the Family* and *Maude*, Lear made the transition from television production to nonprofit activism largely in response to the very same radio and television preachers mentioned in the first ad spot, or, as it came to be known later, public service announcement (PSA). Lear's writing left nothing to chance. His decision to use a hard-hat-wearing blue-collar worker for his message of religious and political tolerance was meant to appeal to the audience most network executives patronized as a conservative "middle American" who inhabited the "fly-over states" of the country. In addition, his emphasis on the man's working-class attire and occupation echoed another one of his similarly positioned characters in the American economy in the 1970s—Archie Bunker.

Originally played by Carroll O'Connor, who possessed a deep ambivalence concerning Bunker's politics and frequent usage of racial slurs, Archie was meant to convey the difficulties that assembly-line workers faced in a period of unprecedented economic restructuring, one that seemed to privilege the emerging knowledge industry and its reliance on higher education for much of its economic efficacy.[2] Lear's attention to socioeconomic detail in both instances spoke to his upbringing as a child of the Depression and his desire to understand the economic plight of the working man. His message was simple: political parochialism should have no bearing on one's status as a Christian, good or bad.

Despite the fact that individuals like Archie began migrating to the political right in the form of "the silent majority," Lear foregrounded the working class because he thought he *knew* them—just as he had known that the country was ready for his style of relevance programming in spite of the networks' reluctance to engage topical subject matter in prime time. Lear's nonprofit organizing defended liberal religious principles of First Amendment rights, civility, and the separation of church and state over and against those who provided their viewers with the Christian position on any particular political issue. As previously mentioned, Lear had worked ceaselessly throughout the 1970s to entertain his audience *about something* by reporting on the times through his various television programs.[3]

His decision to apply this focus on relevance to American public life through nonprofit organizing was anything but an aberration in his long career in entertainment, which included testifying in front of congressional boards, protesting federal attempts to censor prime-time programming, and establishing caucuses for greater creative control in Hollywood. The media-based programming, activism, and politics of People for the American Way captured Lear's own attention to and concern with the threats posed by a growing community of conservative Protestants. In this sense, People for the American Way served as the institutional culmination of Lear's spiritual liberalism in public on behalf of political consensus in the names of civility and the religio-political vision of the Religious Left.

This chapter explores the history, composition, and cultural productions of People for the American Way as an "interest group" within the "third sector" of American society.[4] Lear's entrance into American politics had to be handled delicately and with thought. His biography as one of Hollywood's elite producers qualified him to speak as an entertainer, yet his vision by the early 1980s had expanded beyond the realm of prime-time programming exclusively. In addition, Lear's Jewishness worked against his political credibility despite the fact that his programming had revolutionized American situation comedy through its engagement with bigotry and discrimination. Lear recounts these challenges himself when asked about the history of PFAW. He thought that his wealth and association with Hollywood as a Jewish person disqualified him permanently from speaking about religion and politics publicly. This was particularly the case when he decided to take on what he understood as the Christian Right through his television spots and nonprofit organizing.[5]

In light of this, I argue that the manner in which Lear positioned himself publicly was essential if he was to have any career as a political activist as part of the Religious Left. This also included how journalists and television hosts reported on the emergence of PFAW as a confrontation between Lear and televangelists such as Jerry Falwell and Pat Robertson. Lear's decision to seek the counsel of numerous political and religious leaders of the Protestant mainline regarding the formation of PFAW, which also included Catholic and Jewish leaders, buttressed his public image against possible criticisms of his political relevancy or accusations of "secular humanism." Despite the fact that People for the American Way became much bigger than the actions of a lone individual, we cannot lose sight of the fact that none of its successes would have been possible without Lear's enthusiasm and commitment to a robust yet civil public life as witnessed in his defense of the free exercise of religion, the separation of church and state, and civil deliberation.[6]

Like Lear himself, People for the American Way based most of its claims to a more civil public on an interwar formulation of religious diversity and civility championed by the likes of the National Council of Christians and Jews and the National Council of Churches. When associated with "public" or "religion," as in "civil religion," my usage of the word "civil" implies the realm within which politics traditionally takes place as part of a liberal democracy and a behavioral expectation by those (like Lear) who saw civil religion as an antidote to the nation's divisiveness and discord. In this sense, "civil" means acting, speaking, and behaving in a manner conducive to a harmonious polity. In particular, this chapter argues that PFAW grounded its social vision for the country on the American Way tradition, which found much of its own initial salience in the collective advocacy of advertisers, government officials, and private citizens in midcentury America.[7]

People for the American Way's internal structure also spoke to what I have identified as its interfaith concerns. Its board of directors and advisory committees reflected the values of the larger nonprofit institution by including Protestants, Catholics, and Jews in its composition in addition to prominent members of the business community. Despite Lear's reasoning for organizing PFAW as a strategic response to the electronic church and its televangelist contributors, the nonprofit organization itself championed broader civic values of education, equality, and fairness in politics and American public life.[8] In addition, this chapter also explores a number of the cultural productions of PFAW, including television spots, printed publications, and position papers on the time's most pressing concerns, such as prayer in public schools, regulation of the airwaves, and the teaching of creation science alongside evolution. Lastly, I consider PFAW as an advocacy group in the third sector of American public life and what this meant to American religion and the future of American politics.

Considered in the broadest sense, the purpose behind much of PFAW's literature both in print and on television was educational. This was part of a larger effort to raise awareness of the social and political challenges that the organization felt were most pressing and thus most threatening to American civil liberties. In light of this civic concentration, I argue that the formation of PFAW was a direct response to emergence of the Christian Right based largely on the growing political influence of televangelism as witnessed in the activities of the electronic church. Lear's encounter with televangelists such as Jerry Falwell and Pat Robertson through his beloved medium of television transformed his distanced amusement into righteous indignation once Falwell and others emerged into the public sphere as a direct affront to the American Way. Despite the notoriety of PFAW within Religious Left circles, it ultimately succumbed to its own internal contradictions and philosophical limitations by the time Reagan occupied the White House.

ROOTS OF THE AMERICAN WAY

The formation of People for the American Way could not have come at a better time for liberally minded political actors both in Hollywood and in the larger Protestant mainline.[9] The transition from the 1970s to the 1980s signaled a profound shift in US society toward a religio-political culture of conservatism. Despite the fact that Jimmy Carter had been elected president as a Democrat, his ascent to the oval office depended upon his popularity in the increasingly Republican South as well as his testimony as a born-again Christian. In this sense, Carter's successes as well as his failures laid the groundwork for conservative voices to take advantage of his born-again politics in support of their own concerns over America's moral state with the help of the newest arrival to the airwaves—the electronic church. Despite the ambivalence of many within the New Right over the inclusion of conservative Protestant ministers within their ranks, the social influence of individuals such as Jerry Falwell and Pat Robertson could not be ignored.

This influence encouraged ministers such as Falwell, who had taken a stand against applying the Christian Gospel to politics during the civil rights movement, to rethink their approach to engaging politics in light of their growing successes in the media. This internal negotiation that was taking place within what was referred to as "the Christian Right," "the new Christian Right," or "the new Religious Right" worried those on the opposite end of the religious and political spectrum—namely Lear and his Protestant, Jewish, and Catholic supporters. In fact, the emergence of a seemingly united front of conservative Protestants in American public life in the late 1970s—which included Pentecostals, evangelicals, and fundamentalists—struck a discordant note in PFAW's otherwise harmonious rendering of the American public as tolerant, civil, and diverse.[10]

The fact that a number of ministers within the electronic church had taken firm stances against politically liberal interests such as civil rights, gender equality, and discrimination suggested to Lear and others a shift in political sensibilities at best and a hostile takeover at worst. This fear was periodically reinforced by the not-so-subtle usage of anti-Semitic language by conservative televangelists and ministers who targeted Lear based on his ethnicity.[11] The formation of People for the American Way was not only a direct response to such anti-Semitism, it was also a corrective to what Lear and others saw as a fundamental violation of the separation of church and state by the electronic church based on its explicitly political appeals to its congregants. PFAW sought to address the rhetorical iniquities committed by the televangelist wing of the Christian Right by stressing educational freedom, awareness, First Amendment rights, and civility in the public sphere. By "awareness" I mean PFAW's intent to expose its constituencies and others to potential challenges to the First Amendment and civil rights. Awareness also included PFAW's tendency to circulate what it thought to be politically damaging information regarding politicians and preachers in a manner reminiscent of "rights watch" groups. However, despite Lear's and others' best intentions, the aspirations of PFAW regarding tolerance and religious diversity were largely unrealized since much of its civic energy depended on rendering Falwell and others as *aberrations* within a longer narrative of liberal progress.

The formation of People for the American Way in the early 1980s was a direct outgrowth of a single man's experience of economic depression, world war, and nascent culture wars.[12] Like much of his prime-time programming, Lear's non-profit activism was intimately connected to his own biography as someone who benefitted from the constitutional freedoms granted to minority citizens of the United States. At the same time, Lear encountered memorable instances of virulent discrimination against his ethnic, racial, or sexual difference. This backstory cultivated a defensive stance within Lear's social vision that heightened his sense of fairness and equality in American society in addition to the manner in which such a civil state of affairs could best be established and maintained. The emergence of televangelism on a mass-mediated scale in the late 1970s immediately alerted Lear to possible moments of social exclusion or, in his case, anti-Semitism. Not only was this type of speech a violation of the nation's commitment to racial and religious tolerance, it was also broadcast to millions of homes on a weekly basis for much of the calendar year. Lear's experience of the ubiquity of entertainment on television gave him an appreciation for how influential such a group of conservative Protestants could be in swaying the country away from its largely consensus politics of the New Deal toward a fundamentally restructured society based on the principles of the free market and deregulatory federal policies.[13]

His first reaction to witnessing televangelists in their newly minted pulpits was a familiar one—to use the means and medium he knew best to identify the disjuncture between the politics of the Christian Right and the American Way of doing politics, namely civilly, tolerantly, and respectfully. In foregrounding these values in his initial attempt at political mobilization, Lear drew on a longer tradition of interfaith or Tri-Faith cooperation that found much of its own sources of support in both the Judeo-Christian formulation of the early twentieth century and the goodwill movement of the interwar period.[14] In addition, Lear's participation in World War II as a gunner also contributed to his appreciation for interfaith coalitions in light of the war's significance as a transitional moment in the history of Jewish acculturation through the Judeo-Christian formula of

"Protestant-Catholic-Jew."[15] "In this context," argues historian Wendy Wall, "ecumenical religion could serve simultaneously as a symbol of American pluralism and American consensus."[16] Despite the support that this particular political project received from individuals in the entertainment industry, the federal government, and the private sector, its dependence on "diversity" signaled its primary strength and its principal weakness.

Diversity, both religious and political, was a value that many in interfaith circles saw as instrumental to a harmonious public sphere, Lear included. Yet within its own expansive possibilities lay the very seeds of its undoing. If a feeling of optimism characterized much of this activism in the name of understanding and cooperation in opposition to totalitarian regimes around the globe, then an equally powerful fear of unbridled and unrestrained diversity also suffused these efforts at societal progress. Diversity suited the nation-state by demonstrating its ability to forge a consensus amid a dizzying array of religious options. This consensus, however, required an epistemological split between behavior in public and the same behavior in private.[17] As a result, unity in public came at the expense of unbridled religious expression because its expression depended upon "a private arena of diversity and tolerance and a public arena of unity and consensus."[18] In this sense, a notion of diversity, regardless of its ecumenical origins, signified both an appreciation for what it claimed and an attempt to restrain what it most feared by reinforcing political consensus.

Lear's nonprofit organizing took advantage of this particular history by emphasizing consensus through religious and political diversity in his attempts to combat the Christian Right and its seemingly absolutist method of engaging politics. Despite the fact that this community of conservative Protestants represented a particular facet of the diversity that Lear and others defended rhetorically, it ultimately functioned as a discursive "other" against which religious liberals could leverage their oppositional political identities as defenders of the American Way. "By marginalizing dissenters," argues Wall, "by casting out those who disrupted unity as somehow un-American, they shored up the social, economic, and political status quo."[19] In short, Lear's attempt to provide support for this type of consensus politics depended on disciplining his own collection of religious outliers.

Lear's efforts were met with an equal amount of passion and dedication from televangelists and politicians alike, primarily because they possessed their own formula for public deliberation and expression that did not rely on Lear's consensus for its discursive successes. Moreover, the fact that the Christian Right wielded any power whatsoever in American politics suggested a breakdown to Lear and others in what had largely determined the tenor and content of the nation's deliberative processes. For Lear and People for the American Way, the extremism of the Christian Right posed a threat to democracy itself and to First Amendment rights. To the Christian and political Right, efforts by conservative ministers symbolized the growing power of a constituency that had been largely shut out from the media arenas of influence since the interwar period. Although People for the American Way was a product of a longer, established history of interfaith cooperation and Judeo-Christian values, it was also guilty of the same consensus-driven assumptions about how best to conduct oneself in public.

Despite these shortcomings, PFAW proved to be the best option in an increasingly conservative and mediated political environment that had both religious and political liberals scrambling for stable ground. Lear's bid for political relevance in an age of advocacy projected the strongest future for those mainline Protestants in the Religious Left who had been eclipsed by their more conservative colleagues in Christ. In particular, PFAW's self-conception and media campaigns further demonstrated the organization's dependence on an interfaith advocacy model of adjudicating pluralism in the public sphere and its method of organizing in the face of an increasingly insistent community of conservative Protestants, Catholics, and Jews.[20]

BUILDING A PEOPLE FOR THE AMERICAN WAY

Lear's relevance programming in the early 1970s, along with his participation in congressional hearings over the issue of censorship during the Family Viewing Hour debates, demonstrated his commitment to the First Amendment and its guarantees of free speech and religious practice in both the entertainment industry and the larger American society. His decision to leave television producing by the decade's end certainly signaled a professional transition to new opportunities and experiences, yet his decision unfolded according to the very same set of concerns for relevance he had brought with him into prime-time programming in the first place.

By the late 1970s, Lear had grown increasingly alarmed at the power and influence of conservative politics as evidenced by the various communications of the electronic church to audiences across the country. This was largely the case because of his own encounters with a similar religio-political constituency while he was a network producer due to the perceived immorality of his television programs, which resulted in boycotts, public demonstrations, and mobilization led by the Reverend Donald Wildmon through his Campaign for Public Decency. Regardless of whether such efforts to curb the freedom of expression came from the federal government through the FCC or conservative advocacy groups, Lear remained committed to the idea of the free exchange of ideas in entertainment and politics.

The emergence of the Christian Right as witnessed through its televangelist supporters troubled Lear not only due to its developing political platform but, more significantly, because of its method of political engagement. To Lear and later People for the American Way, the Christian Right relied on an exclusionary and incendiary method of politics that claimed its positions to be beyond rhetorical reproach regardless of the interlocutor. In addition, the Christian Right also argued that their political agenda represented *the* position on a political issue, rendering those who disagreed misinformed at best and delusional at worst. Perhaps the most disturbing aspect of this mobilization for Lear was the fact that conservative ministers and televangelists proclaimed their arguments to be the Christian position on a given subject regardless of the particular policy under debate, including prayer in school, the women's movement, and the economy. In short, Lear was appalled by the social agenda of the Christian Right and its primary means of dissemination by absolutist claims to political and religious legitimacy.[21]

Despite Lear's extensive background in television, his preliminary response to the proliferation of conservative televangelists was to first research his subject and then compose a treatment for the silver screen. This approach set the agenda for much of what would become People for the American Way and its nonprofit purpose of educating and raising awareness of potential threats to First Amendment rights. Lear spent hours in front of television screens with VCRs, recording, watching, and commenting on a variety of televised ministries and their diverse array of programming. "My first experience [of watching television ministers] had been Jerry Falwell, catching a glimpse of him here and there and laughing as most of us did, not taking it seriously," Lear admitted. "But then I watched fifty, sixty hours of Pat Robertson, Jimmy Swaggart, and others, and I became deeply concerned at the way they were mixing politics and religion and suggesting that a person was a good Christian or a bad Christian depending on their political point of view."[22] Not only did this observation serve as the foundation for People for the American Way's theory of deliberative politics, it also served as the primary source material for his soon-to-be-completed screenplay titled *Religion*.

Along with other films of the period that examined the phenomenon of televangelism with a critical edge, *Religion* explores the journeys of two friends (played by actors Fred Willard and Martin Mull) who become ordained through the mail as part of a larger institutional body called the Universal Life Church.[23]

One friend takes advantage of the nonprofit tax benefits of the institution in order to achieve wealth and fame while the other works on behalf of the impoverished.[24] In the end, the duplicitous friend falls victim to his own successes only to be saved by his friend who stayed true to his convictions as a Christian.[25] Lear's intentions were blatantly obvious—to question the veracity of conservative Protestant churches regarding their tax-exempt status and to make a point about the nature of the Christian faith in its commitment to the poor. In particular, his focus on finances grew out of his concern that the electronic church regularly violated its nonprofit and tax-exempt status by making overtly political statements from the pulpit while raking in unheard of amounts of money from its distant congregations.

Lear's commitment to the film project remained steady until he witnessed the unthinkable in his research. During one particular televised service, Jimmy Swaggart asked his congregation to pray for the removal of a Supreme Court justice over the airwaves. To Lear, this was a profound violation of the separation of church and state because televangelists like Swaggart were prohibited from making explicitly political claims as part of their tax exemption. Considering his response, Lear decided against pursuing a claim to equal time through the federally regulated fairness doctrine and instead explored alternative means of getting his message out to the public beyond the confines of a feature film. Swaggart's words catalyzed Lear's transition into American politics by shifting his attention from the prolonged experience of making a movie to the more efficient medium of short television spots in the form of the public service announcement. Drawing on his experience as a television writer and producer, Lear composed a number of spots designed to introduce a counteractive voice against those who questioned the validity of the nation's public servants based on their own idiosyncratic formulations of what was required of a Christian citizen.

Lear's first and most significant spot centered on the words of a blue-collar worker in a warehouse driving a forklift. His main contention, one that Lear had been developing throughout the 1970s, was not only that preachers on television were telling Americans how to vote but also that their very vote functioned as a résumé of sorts in determining the validity of one's Christian faith. As we learned earlier, the spot ended as elegantly as it began with a reminder that such divisive politics was not "the American way." The spot gained traction initially on local affiliate television channels including those connected to the three major networks as part of a grassroots effort to draw attention to the iniquities committed by the electronic church—real or imagined.[26] The PSAs that followed the success of Lear's first included A-list directors and actors from Hollywood including Goldie Hawn and boxer Muhammad Ali, but they would not have been as impactful without the words of the man in the forklift. The spots were light-hearted, but they were also quite serious about the importance of valuing the diversity of opinions. In this case, Lear's understanding of diversity may have focused on trivial matters such as how people liked their eggs, but the spots' larger message foregrounded the efficacy of debate, differences of opinion, and respect for that difference. His claim to a political voice through his minute-long spots would not have been possible, however, without the guidance and direction provided by what would become one of Lear's and PFAW's most passionate supporters—the liberal Protestant and Catholic mainline.

Even before Lear composed his television spots, he knew that his entrance into the nation's public life as a political actor would not be accomplished smoothly. In fact, Lear saw three strikes against his credibility as an outspoken critic of the Christian Right—he was from Hollywood, he was Jewish, and he was wealthy.[27] In order to offset these perceived limitations, Lear decided to reach out to some-one he thought could assist him in establishing his credibility as a political actor in public by way of his short public service announcements. He first contacted Father Theodore Hesburgh, who was then president of Notre Dame and a for-mer board member of the United States Civil Rights Commission. Lear consulted with Hesburgh about how best to address the impending confrontation with the Christian Right by way of its televangelist presence in the media. After playing the original television spot, Hesburgh gave Lear his full-fledged support and sug-gested contacting other like-minded religious figures who could assist his cause. "Let me help you," Hesburgh said. "You need to get as many mainline church lead-ers involved as you can."[28]

After making a number of calls and appointments, Hesburgh encouraged Lear to seek counsel from as many individuals as he could in order to forge a united front against those who "torture scripture." Hesburgh's assistance set Lear on a course that took him around the country in hopes of establishing a supportive network of religious and spiritual liberals for his nascent organizing. Not only were Hesburgh's actions instrumental in the formation of People for the Ameri-can Way, his words also gave Lear a guiding image to take with him on the road as a reminder of why he was traveling in the first place—conservative religious figures torturing scripture for political gain. To Lear and his interfaith support-ers, the fact that the Christian Right lacked any considerable attention to pov-erty, the environment, or the disenfranchised in their political agenda was offen-sive at best and sinful at worst.[29]

Lear's travels were nothing less than formative to his future as a political orga-nizer. "I toured the country visiting these mainline church leaders, all of whom said, 'This is terrific, and you should do more of them [spots],'" Lear recalls. "One of them said, 'institutionalize it.' Because the guy on the commercial wound up saying, 'That's not the American Way,' somebody suggested the name, 'People for the American Way.' And an organization was formed."[30] The individuals whom Lear met with were some of the most significant figures in the interfaith community in the early 1980s, which, as we saw with Hesburgh, included liberal Catholics and Protestants as well as secular humanists.[31] The fact that Lear was Jewish completed the interfaith composition that would define PFAW's numerous advisory boards and committees in a manner that hearkened back to the goodwill movement of the interwar period. Although he did not realize it at the time, his meetings laid the groundwork for the very institutionalizing that had encouraged Lear to continue his journey in the first place. In other words, the individuals Lear initially met with felt so strongly about his cause that they decided to lend their support on an organizational level as a response to the conservative Protestant ascendancy that was just cause for much mainline concern and trepidation.

Stopping in cities such as Chicago, New York, San Antonio, Austin, and Washington, DC, Lear met with the likes of Rev. Jimmy Allen (then president of the Southern Baptist Convention), Rev. James Dunn (the Southern Baptist Convention's national spokesman), Charles Bergstrom (spokesman for the Lutheran Church), William Sloane Coffin (senior minister at Riverside Church), Colin Williams (dean of Yale Divinity School), Congressman John Buchanan (who was also a minister), Congresswoman Barbara Jordan, and Martin E. Marty (church historian at the University of Chicago).[32] Not only did the members of this group lend their names and time to Lear's cause, they also served as a sounding board for his conception of the American Way itself. In fact, Lear relied on the public status and historical knowledge of church historian Martin Marty for much of his own theorizing about the place of religion in American public life.

After a final consultation session with Los Angeles–based civil and human rights attorneys and interfaith activists, Lear made his final decision, " 'That's not the American way,' our hard hat said of the mixture of politics and religion in the PSA, and so People for the American Way was established as a 501(c)(3) nonprofit organization."[33] With this pronouncement, television writer and producer Norman Lear arguably became the unofficial spokesperson for interfaith and mainline communities in the early 1980s as a representative of spiritual liberalism in public and a defender of the First Amendment, the separation of church and state, and the freedom of religious practice in a civil society.

Despite the fact that PFAW's first offices were built in Washington, DC, they eventually found homes in Los Angeles and New York as well beginning in April 1981. At its organizational core stood three men who not only supported

Lear in his political endeavors but also epitomized Lear's reliance on and expansion of prewar interfaith formulations such as "Protestant-Catholic-Jew" and postwar articulations like "Tri-Faith" to include secular humanists for his own interfaith organizing: Catholic Theodore Hesburgh, Rev. James M. Dunn, and Rabbi Marc Tanenbaum. Lear's initial investment of $200,000 soon grew to $2 million as he continued to labor and fund-raise on behalf of the American Way.

RECEIVING AND MANUFACTURING PFAW

Lear moved quickly in order to spread awareness about People for the American Way as an organization devoted to the protection of civil liberties in the face of an impending political force of imposed religiosity in public. From ballrooms to hotels rooms to living rooms, Lear traversed the country in hopes of garnering enough support and finances to get his nonprofit off the ground successfully and efficiently. The selection of lawyer Tony Podesta—a veteran of political campaigning for the likes of Eugene McCarthy, George McGovern, and Ted Kennedy—as PFAW's first president spoke to both the political orientation of the nascent organization and its future as a watchdog of threats to civic harmony and consensus. The broadcast of Lear's original public service announcement in Washington, DC, assisted his project of public exposure greatly through coverage in the national press, the nightly news, and an interview with news anchor Tom Brokaw on the *Today* show. "A single impression on a network news broadcast back when there were only three of them was a very big deal," Lear observed. "In a single eight-minute interview . . . People for the American Way gained recognition by the establishment and more media attention followed."[34]

The support for Lear's ads not only reminded him of his time in television production, it also helped him raise money to buy more airtime for his additional PSAs, which included the likes of Hollywood actors Carol Burnett and Ned Beatty. People for the American Way marked the materialization of Lear's own brand of religious liberalism and also signaled a significant moment in the history of Hollywood-based activism in American politics. In fact, the election of President Reagan itself, based on the multifaceted support system of conservative religious and political strategists and ministers, signaled Hollywood's official arrival onto the political scene on Republican terms. It took little time for Hollywood's liberals to organize themselves in kind, largely through Lear's programming, institutional organizing, and political stances in public.[35]

The beginning of the 1980s marked a significant increase in organizations and nonprofits designed to resist the Christian Right's influence on American public life despite the fact that one of its key supporters, Ronald Reagan, had just become president of the United States. One could argue that these organizations were equally committed to combating both political and religious manifestations of conservative politics regardless of the particular guilty party—individual or organizational. Norman Lear's PFAW was certainly a part of this liberal religious activism against a seemingly hostile foe, but his connection to this moment was weighted differently in relation to groups such as theologian Daniel Maguire's Moral Alternatives in Politics, politician George McGovern's Americans for Common Sense, or Virginians Organized for Informed Community Expression. In short, Lear's nonprofit organizing contributed to and served as inspiration for further civic activism in the name of the American Way.[36]

These preliminary interactions with the media laid the groundwork for how news organizations, newspapers, journals, and the spokespersons of the Christian Right framed Lear's relevancy as a political activist on a national scale. His short television spots may have inaugurated Lear's activism, but his reception by the media determined its significance. In this sense, Lear and PFAW were discursively manufactured in much the same way as the Christian Right was as a social movement through countless reports, articles, interviews, and television spots.[37] Beginning with his interview with Tom Brokaw, Lear's narrative of television producer turned nonprofit activist hinged on his seemingly evident confrontation with the Christian Right. In fact, as Lear recounts in his autobiography, *Even This I Get to Experience*, Brokaw's producers advertised the interview as, "Hollywood Coming After the Christian Right."[38] The news media—at the time comprising print sources such as *Time, Newsweek*, the *New York Times, Vanity Fair*, and the *Los Angeles Times* in addition to visual sources like the *Today* show, *Firing Line*, and the *Phil Donahue* show—circulated taglines similar to the one formed by Brokaw's producers about the Christian Right in general and Lear's activism in particular. Once Lear began to assemble more support and attract more media attention, his activism through PFAW came to be understood as a confrontation with particular televangelists including Jerry Falwell and Pat Robertson in the most martial of terms.

A brief search for Lear-versus-Falwell headlines from print sources of the early 1980s reveals a narrative designed to take advantage of the two public figures in order to tell a larger story about the confrontation between largely conservative and liberal political forces in the public sphere. Periodicals and newspapers such as the ones listed above dedicated numerous pages to outlining the public confrontation between Lear and Falwell despite the fact that neither of the religious combatants viewed their interactions in the same oppositional manner.[39] The two men had certainly exchanged words throughout the 1970s and into the 1980s, including Falwell's labeling of Lear as "the number one enemy of the family in this generation," but neither Lear nor Falwell saw the other as his enemy outright.

This particular narrative emerged from the pages of a variety of magazines and periodicals including *Time*, *Saturday Review*, and *Vanity Fair*. Between the years of 1980 and 1982, newspapers and magazines across the country documented Lear and his engagement with televangelists and the Christian Right by way of his nonprofit organization People for the American Way. In November 1980, *Time* published a short piece titled "Smiting the Mighty Right: PAW [*sic*] vs. Political Preachers," which examined the grassroots methods Lear used to get PFAW off the ground through the televised PSA format. "Beyond the new TV spots," the article says, "PAW is working on educational programs with leaflets and articles on 'the nature of our pluralistic society,' for distribution in schools, churches, and libraries." Largely educational in nature, this was how PFAW meant to disseminate its message of pluralism and understanding and what exactly it found wrong with Falwell and the electronic church.[40]

Based on the nonprofit's inaugural statement, PFAW argued that the "Religious New Right" attacked any and all who disagreed with its political positions in public. Taken a step further, former Yale Divinity School dean Colin Williams argued in a PFAW position paper that the "Protestant Right" threatened the most instrumental of civic values including pluralism, democracy, and the American Way. Williams's words were supported by a list of notable public figures including former FCC chairman Newton Minow, President M. William Howard of the National Council of Churches, and editor Norman Cousins. Those who supported People for the American Way's educational programming did not intend to deny the right of Falwell or others to speak in public. Instead, their grievances concerned the form or method that the Christian Right relied on for many of its political successes. "The problem, they say, lies in the *methods* used by the religious right, especially widespread lists of the supported Christian positions, and attacks on legislators who disagree."[41]

In this sense, the Christian Right and its televangelist representatives were guilty of two interrelated linguistic indiscretions: first, for consistently attacking those who disagreed with them over political positions and, second, for enumerating and thus determining the moral or "Godly" argument on an individual or series of individual policy questions. Not only did individuals like Lear disagree with the methods of the Right, periodicals from within the Christian Right's orbit such as *Christianity Today* were also concerned about the lack of a social justice agenda amid calls for a greater "pro-family" politics. The same *Time* article closed with a quote from Falwell himself, who questioned Lear's commitment to the interests of women when his programming was principally pornographic. "He's just playing games again," Falwell stated, "and using some liberal theologians for his own devices." This article represented one of many that documented PFAW's rise to political prominence by naming Lear's PSAs, exploring People for the American Way's composition, delineating its educational agenda, and closing with the words of Falwell as an example of his seemingly uniform attention on Lear and PFAW. Magazines such as *Newsweek* and *Vogue* would follow suit in describing one of the most visible political confrontations over what President Reagan called the "orderly society" in America's recent history.

In "Norman Lear vs. the Moral Majority: The War to Clean Up TV," journalist Ben Stein observed that Lear and others represented the "television establishment of networks" over and against the newly ascendant "Christian militia."[42] "A battle is raging for control of network television. Storming the citadel of imperial TV power is the new Christian Right, allied with the new political right, and its spearhead political-action commando group, the Moral Majority." Stein named Lear as the establishment's leader, arguing that "two warring parochialisms" went head-to-head over the precious advertising real estate of prime-time programming. After documenting the conflicting interests between Lear and Falwell, Stein broadened the terms of the media engagement by connecting Lear's television catalog and creation of PFAW to his history of supporting the American Civil Liberties Union and political candidates such as Ralph Nader and John Anderson. Not only does this information give us a sense of how Lear and Falwell conducted themselves politically, it also contributed to Lear's own political persona through his allegiances as a nonprofit organizer. Against the backdrop of "special-interest groups" and "pressure groups" of various sorts, Stein concluded by naming the two sides of the debate as "Falwell's crusaders" and "Lear's Hollywood infidels."[43]

While hyperbolic, these terms tell us much about the tenor of these interactions and their terms of conflict—namely prime-time programming, the educational outreach of PFAW, and Lear's seemingly bipartisan involvement as the country's newest public defender of the American Way.[44] Perhaps *Vogue* writer Maureen Orth captured the conflict best in the opening line to her piece titled "Religion on TV: Norman Lear Tackles the New Hot Issue." For Orth, "The true battlefield in the fight for the hearts and minds of America is the TV screen. . . . Their views [Lear's and Falwell's] are diametrically opposed and television has become their electronic dueling ground."[45] Despite his best attempts, Lear could not augment the media-based narrative of his entrance into American politics as one inseparable from Jerry Falwell and the Christian Right. This was partly his own doing since Lear and PFAW targeted the actions of the electronic church largely through the agendas of individuals like Falwell and Robertson. Lear had also first established himself as an influential opinion maker through his television producing in the 1970s, which, for many in the media, defined Lear's potential impact as one heavily dependent on various forms of media. As a result, his nonprofit organizing was most often interpreted in the press in these terms in spite of PFAW's educational and awareness-based agenda. In no uncertain terms, Lear had most certainly arrived.[46]

Lear's public organizing did not simply capture the attention of mainstream periodicals and newspapers. It also grabbed a number of headlines in broadly Protestant publications including the *Christian Century*, *Christianity Today*, and the *New Oxford Review*. In fact, by the time Lear and PFAW reached the mid-1980s, a defense of Lear's politics and spiritual vision had already been authored by one of mainline Protestantism's most well-known spokespersons, Martin Marty. Numerous reporters also included details concerning Lear's support system of Protestants, Catholics, and Jews who eventually served in prominent roles within People for the American Way as part of committees and advisory boards. In an anonymously written two-part article in *Christianity Today*, we can discern that the National Council of Churches had lost its prophetic way and was searching eagerly for a new direction.[47] Religious figures such as Richard John Neuhaus and Edmund Robb were brought in to advise at a luncheon sponsored by the NCC at Riverside Drive.[48] Both Neuhaus and Robb accused the mainline of "leftist political leanings" that resulted in alienated congregations. James Armstrong, then president of the NCC, accused Neuhaus of offering a plan fit for the Reagan administration's foreign policy agenda. Despite the name recognition of these mainline Protestant men, it was another attendee who had the honor of being featured speaker that day.

In a subsection of the article titled "Meanwhile: Norman Lear on Spirituality," we learn that Lear was featured prominently in a meeting convened by the National Council of Churches on the heels of People for the American Way's successful formation in 1981. Not only was Lear's voice a valuable one amid the mainline's most seminal figures in the Religious Left, it also stood out against the maelstrom that was the NCC's political agenda with a singular quality of guidance. "He was the day's featured speaker," the article stated. "Many liberal churchmen, threatened by the rise of Religious Right, are marching under his banner."[49] Rendered in this manner, Lear's nonprofit organizing in the early 1980s took on a significance that resonated far beyond his own concerns as an

American citizen on behalf of the American Way. The simultaneous unfolding of mainline confusion, Lear's activism, and the electronic church's growing influence left the NCC with few options for a liberal politics of civility.

The coherence of PFAW's agenda grounded mainline interests without relying on their own troubled internal support structure. Reflecting back on his time in television in order to present something useful to his audience in a spiritual key, Lear argued that through the "spiritual nature of laughter" experienced from his writing, people were fed an idea—most notably empathy or compassion for the differing point of view. The stasis that defined the NCC's future was assuaged slightly by Lear's emphasis on his notion of the spiritual that pushed past the bottom-line thinking that to him defined the age. The intricate connections evidenced by the NCC's meeting steered the mainline away from the rocky unease of its political future toward the safer harbor of a people dedicated to vigorous deliberative politics—within limits.

PFAW'S COMPOSITION

People for the American Way's formation was a product of its organizational time. Relying on the very methods that would catapult the Christian Right into political dominance, including direct mailings, church-basement meetings, and informational flyer and bumper sticker campaigns, Lear and his dedicated staff organized their own advocacy group around a collective concern for the nation's democratic life and its flourishing public square. For PFAW, the best way to protect this space from an overly imposed politics of singularity as part of a broader interfaith coalition of religious diversity was to champion the separation of church and state and First Amendment rights of free religious expression.

When asked, the American Way comprised these elements and more as the most cherished components of American civic life, including "pluralism, individuality, freedom of thought and religion, . . . [and] tolerance and compassion for others." Overseen by the likes of Father Theodore Hesburgh, Rev. James M. Dunn, and Rabbi Marc Tanenbaum, PFAW took its message of freedom of thought to the viewing public through PSAs, local informational meetings, and fund-raisers, including an inaugural meeting in Lear's own home. One line in particular from a *Los Angeles Times* article revealed a great deal about PFAW's original aspirations as an educational nonprofit seeking to engage the public on a number of pressing issues, "For months the group has been holding meetings in church basements and private homes throughout the Southeast and Midwest.

The people who attend are given information packets and asked to contribute money so the group can send out speakers to debate members of the Moral Majority and other conservative organizations around the country."[50]

The organization's dedication to combating the political and Christian Right not only called for a coherent set of principles disseminated widely through TV and Hollywood, it also included a mobile collection of voices willing to travel and debate its political antitheses in public. PFAW possessed both a disciplined plan for distributing its educational material and a commitment to raising awareness about the plurality of views on a given issue. The living embodiment of the federally executed fairness doctrine, those who went out from People for the American Way into boardrooms and living rooms did so out of a desire to present the discussion surrounding an issue as an alternative to the singular answer provided by the Christian Right and its Bible Scorecards.[51] A closer look at PFAW's founding mission statement and its literature reveals an organizational apparatus designed to uphold freedom of thought, yet there were stipulations. Assuming that the content of one's utterance was not beyond the pluralist pale—a tendency that was most evident with speakers such as Falwell, Robertson, and historically Father Charles Coughlin—then PFAW was there to help.

However, if a particular statement or declaration relied on exclusion or division for its unifying content, then PFAW had to make a decision—protect the space of free exchange, which possessed its own PFAW-authored rules, or defend the content, whatever it may be. When it came to the electronic church and its many conservative televangelists, PFAW simply decided to reinforce the parameters of public deliberation rather than the content of the church's message. This decision proved costly for all those involved, including Lear and the NCC, since it was Lear himself and his spiritual agenda that PFAW most closely represented in its public encounters with the Christian Right.

"Evangelists of the electronic pulpit who imply that God is a conservative Republican who hates the ERA, abortion, Panama Canal treaties and 55-mph speed limits and will condemn to eternal hell all who vote otherwise aren't the only ones who can wage a political holy war," reporter Kenneth R. Clark wrote in October 1980 for the *Pittsburgh Press*. "A coalition of clergy and laymen, led by Norman Lear, the king of sitcoms, has formed a jihad of their own."[52] Numerous articles from this period relied on the trope of the extremist power from the Middle East for their persuasiveness, since the events of 1979 were not too far behind in the nation's collective rearview mirror. Additionally, those in the media who utilized such images in sources such as the *New York Times* or the *Christian Century* often tended to lean toward the political left in their politics. This meant that a newspaper article was at once a source of "news" and also an iteration of ignorance about the very individuals or groups under media scrutiny.

Much of this subtlety was lost, however, amid outcries from both Left and Right that were *less* over particular policy arguments or concerns and *more* over the means of political deliberation themselves, or the lack thereof. This media-saturated environment led to the production of PFAW's founding mission statement in addition to numerous pamphlets, leaflets, and short PSAs as part of its foundational organizing moment. Former dean of Yale Divinity School Colin Williams composed one of PFAW's earliest position papers that articulated the nonprofit's intent and aspirations for American public life in light of the Christian Right.[53] "People for the American Way has as its initial aim the encouragement of participation in the political process and reaffirmation of commitment to the American Way: a commitment marked not by polarization or demon hunting, but by a mutual search for consensus in an atmosphere of mutual respect." Williams writes, "The problem is not that the evangelical right takes political positions." Rather, "The problem lies in their refusal to respect those who differ. Branded as enemies of God, those they oppose are judged to be subversive of America's true interests."[54]

Williams's source of disquiet, like those of Lear and his Christian supporters, concerned the means and method of conservative Protestant participation in American public life rather than the explicit content of such participation. For PFAW, divisive measures that excluded in order to identify coherent constituencies as targets of direct mailing campaigns reduced the political complexity of a particular policy concern down to a singular "Christian position" despite the myriad of ways one could interpret it. For Williams, Hesburgh, and Lear, this type of politics mirrored the "torturing of scripture" that took place in the electronic pulpits of Falwell and others, yet, in this instance, the political process itself, along with its sacred documents, served as the source material for such torturing. In other words, the scriptural concerns of Hesburgh and Lear found their mirror image in the American public sphere in the Christian Right's tendency to simplify the diversity of opinions surrounding a given issue down to a single perspective.

The "atmosphere of mutual respect" that Williams foregrounded was an essential component in PFAW's remedy for "demon hunting" and the polarization that it saw emanating from conservative Protestantism. The mutuality of behavior that Williams's claims depended on, which for PFAW was indispensable to a harmonious public, was arguably a product of what each side mutually sought—consensus. Williams's notion of an atmosphere of respect depended on his notion of consensus instead of functioning as a precedent for such a consensus's successful formulation. In other words, political actors had to buy into the very terms of public deliberation themselves, those of a consensus-supported atmosphere of respect, before stepping into the public discussion as citizens. The simplicity of this arrangement made its logic appear coherent and widely accessible to a variety of organizations and individuals.

Unfortunately, the fact that every move made by Falwell, Robertson, or the electronic church in general functioned as an affront to Williams's and Lear's calls for greater understanding and pluralism in American public life made PFAW's media campaigns that much more significant. In this sense, PFAW contributed to the very polarization it sought to rectify through its own forms of rhetorical stridency on behalf of the American Way and its expression through consensus. For Lear, his organization encouraged participation, not further division: "People for the American Way allows citizens to enlist and be active. Everything's a theatre to me," Lear stated. "We had a broad canvas five nights a week when we were dealing with television. Now, with the organization, we have an even broader canvas, one that allows all Americans to be a part."[55] Despite the participatory tenor of Lear's assertion, it arguably could not be realized without first adhering to its broader assumptions about how best to "mix" religion and politics. In short, Falwell mixed while Lear and others campaigned for fairness in American public life. This irony, while acknowledged at times in op-ed pieces and short articles, was lost on Lear and his considerable support system of religious and business leaders.

Further evidence of PFAW's expansive yet limited vision of democratic harmony can be found in the organization's mission statement and a selection of its publications, which were considerable throughout the 1980s. As primarily an education-based nonprofit organization, People for the American Way sought to address both the political iniquities committed in public by the Christian Right and the reasons that such a constituency could prove to be so compelling in transitional times in the first place. A number of pamphlets, leaflets, and meetings helped to disseminate the information Lear and others thought was needed in order to confront a divisive, exclusionary politics of certitude. In this way, PFAW sought to educate by raising awareness about a number of key issues including the separation of church and state, the rights of women in the workplace, and the dangers of the Christian Right. The organization accomplished these goals by sending representatives out to correct politically and religiously conservative statements and producing primers and question/answer guides for those with unsure political footing.

MISSION STATEMENT: CIVILITY IN ACTION

If left to its own devices, the American public would witness "a rise in 'demonology' and hostility, a breakdown in community and social spirit, a deterioration of free and open dialogue, and the temptation to grasp at simplistic solutions for complex problems."[56] Not only do these words take advantage of what one scholar of religion has called "chaos rhetoric" for much of its saliency and relevancy, it also assumes a great deal about the nature of educating oneself on the pressing issues of the day.[57] For Lear, challenging times called for discerning answers that surveyed the complexity of a given political challenge. His public addresses about the Christian Right also depended upon a similar assumption about how best to address the social controversies confronting the country. In short, the conservative and Christian Right provided its audience with what to Lear appeared to be anything but complexity, which called for an equal and opposite response of awareness in a key of consensus. More specifically, a response based on the American Way was exactly what such political discord called for.

For those who composed the mission statement, which included Norman Lear, Theodore Hesburgh, politician Barbara Jordan, and former CEO of *Time* Andrew Heiskell, the American Way consisted of value statements and empathy: "By this [the American Way], we mean pluralism, individuality, freedom of thought, expression, and religion, a sense of community, and tolerance and compassion for others." The first four characteristics addressed the Christian Right specifically in terms of its inability to appreciate certain elements of the American Way embodied in a diversity of opinions. The latter calls for tolerance and compassion highlighted the religious liberal commitment to empathy materialized in public that PFAW hoped to demonstrate to its supporters.

They also gestured to another essential characteristic of a harmonious public that was deeply indebted to the consensus ideals PFAW hoped to build its mobilization on—civility.[58] The long-term agenda of PFAW included "reducing social tension and polarization, fostering understanding among different segments of our society, and increasing the level and quality of public dialogue.... We shall communicate with the American people through printed materials, radio, television, public lectures, and discussions."[59] By way of the printed word and the latest in communications technology, PFAW sought a more robust and informed public through its own awareness campaigns as a relatively unencumbered space within which citizens could voice their opinions without any threat of political apostasy.

A second component to PFAW's approach to public consensus required information gathering and the subsequent exposure of its findings in line with its awareness objectives. "We will gather information, analyze it, and distribute our findings to the public in a manner that provides for full and fair exposition on the issues," according to the PFAW mission statement. "Our highest purpose is to nurture a national climate that encourages and enhances the human spirit rather than one which divides people into hostile camps."[60] There is arguably no better synopsis of PFAW's approach to the Christian Right as a reflection of Lear's own spiritual agenda than these sentences.

Under Lear's and others' leadership, People for the American Way strove for a deliberative space where each citizen had the requisite information on hand in order to make an informed political decision. Individuals within PFAW gathered, analyzed, and distributed crucial information about what they considered to be a threat in itself or under threat by conservative Protestant politics. This process did not involve Lear directly, but he most certainly saw a given day's reports and findings through internal office memos and communications.[61] In fact, Lear's own research for his unrealized movie *Religion* led to a similar conclusion—Christian Right politics created more divisions than it addressed. This approach to cultivating awareness helps explain why the organization thought it was important to send rhetorical counterweights out into the fractious world of politics—namely in order to level the epistemic playing field by exposing the voting public to the same edifying information.

The program also helps to contextualize how and why PFAW came to possess thousands of hours of recorded tape and hundreds of pages of transcribed text in its archives documenting who, when, and what an individual or organization stated that qualified as a potential danger to American civil liberties or served as an example of Christian Right–authored bigotry or religious discrimination. Such examples were not only archived by PFAW itself; if they served a particular need in real time, then sound bites or the printed text of what was said would be distributed to the proper authorities in order to "distribute our findings to the public" as a "fair exposition of the issues." In light of these concerns, we are able to understand PFAW's mission statement and its stated goals as a product of what I identify as a form of *civic vigilance*, a relentless monitoring of public spaces in the name of the First Amendment and its constitutional protections: "By educating the American people and raising their level of understanding about the basic tenets by which our society is sustained, People for the American Way will fulfill its mission."[62]

Unfortunately for PFAW and its allies, the arguments that defined the relationship between religion and American politics in the 1980s concerned the very tenets that PFAW took for granted as uniformly accepted across the country. In fact, the contests between liberal and conservative actors like Norman Lear and

President Ronald Reagan explored the means and manner through which one engaged politics itself in addition to particular policy debates themselves.[63] In this way, the Religious Left and PFAW attempted to remind the American citizenry, over and against the Christian Right, of the proper way of conducting oneself politically through civility, respect, and well-informed claims. For Lear and his fellow cofounders, because they articulated this message through the apparatus of an interfaith organization, their claims against an intrusive Protestant force were made that much stronger since they could be seen as embodying PFAW's own set of civic and spiritual values. In a war of words played out across countless television screens and newspaper headlines around the country, PFAW represented itself as consistently adhering to its values of mutual respect and understanding. Despite this consistency, an organization promoting tolerance inevitably became intolerant of another form of intolerance—the Christian Right.

CULTURAL PRODUCTIONS OF PFAW

In addition to numerous PSAs, fact sheets, and pamphlets, PFAW also authored a number of texts for public distribution that served as both an argument for a civil public and a resource for fellow defenders of the American Way. Looking back on an otherwise fractious decade of discord and disagreement, author Jim Castelli composed a text entitled *A Plea for Common Sense: Resolving the Clash Between Religion and Politics* in 1988 that attempted to delineate the differences between proper and improper engagements with politics from religious positions in public.[64] In fact, the text's entire first chapter, appropriately titled "How to Mix Religion and Politics," establishes five distinct rules for mixing the two that emphasize common sense, civil religion, and the American Way.[65] For Lear, who wrote the book's foreword, Castelli's words establish a civic baseline for engaged citizens to make their individual claims in public without infringing upon others' rights to do the same.

As part of a "focused response to the Christian Right" in defense of America's constitutional liberties, PFAW made raising awareness central to its various media campaigns by educating the public about the inconsistencies and iniquities committed by the Christian Right in general and individual televangelists in particular. "The Religious Right myth holds that if its values are not codified, then all values and all religion have been driven out of the public arena," argues Lear. "While the Religious Right offers the wrong way to 'mix religion and politics,' there is a right and proper way to do so, while respecting our national heritage and the spirit of liberty."[66] If those on the right were guilty of improperly mixing religion and politics, then where could citizens look for examples of how to mix religion and politics properly?[67] For Lear, a majority of Americans already shared a common framework for understanding human flourishing. "Most Protestants, Catholics, Jews, Muslims, and 'secular humanists' share a set of beliefs on how we should live here on earth, even as we differ over questions that may never be settled in this life."[68] The form of Lear's expression perhaps said more than his content ever could—"Most Protestants, Catholics, and Jews." In this sense, civil-minded interfaith groups, along with the Protestant mainline, exemplified what Lear and PFAW supported as the American Way of doing politics. Despite the appeals to common sense, Lear and PFAW's educational productions were anything but common.

Castelli follows Lear's lead from the foreword by laying the groundwork for a common-sense approach to religion and politics. His intentions for the text are clear: "This book is an effort to present . . . a framework within which to understand the relationship between religion and politics." Unlike PFAW policy primers, which addressed the most contested issues of the day by discussing them in question-and-answer format for readers to follow, *A Plea for Common Sense* identifies potential threats to the free exchange of ideas while also prescribing an antidote to the civic and constitutional challenges still causing trouble in the eyes of Lear and others. This prescription comes in the form of a normative proscription from any and all political behavior that was beyond the pale of the American Way as defined by the organization and its attentive monitors of televised public speech. Like much of the literature produced by PFAW at the time, this document also contributes to raising awareness about potentially dangerous individuals or social movements. In this text's case, Pat Robertson's campaign for president disturbed many at PFAW, including Castelli, who titled his Robertson chapter, "Pat Robertson: Extremist with a Baby Face."

Castelli argues that PFAW's common-sense approach is far superior to the Christian Right's because it does not depend on parochial claims or absolutist arguments: "Civil religion makes no claim that its values will get you into heaven; it only claims that they will make you a good citizen."[69] A good citizen is also a civil citizen as part of civil religion's claim to a "public religion" and to civility itself in American public life. "The Religious Right rejects civility as a sign of a lack of commitment to 'biblical values,'" argues Castelli, "but the Founders rightly saw that civility was essential to the maintenance of the republic." Not only does this quote speak to the dependence of PFAW on the notion of civil religion for much of its theorizing about American religion and politics, it also demonstrates the Religious Left's own tendency to wax nostalgic about a past authority on all issues of church and state. In other words, a reference to "the Founding Fathers" functions very similarly, in a discursive sense, to the Christian Right's tendency to refer back either to the biblical text or to Jesus himself as arbiter all of things good and contemporary.

Castelli further argues for a five-rule system for mixing religion and politics that focuses on *how* the two should come together instead of *whether* they should in the first place. Most of these rules follow the basic outlines of the First Amendment, arguing that the federal government can neither single out any one religion specifically for special treatment nor subject candidates for public office to a religious test. They also reflect Lear's understanding of civic engagement to the letter. Where PFAW differed in relation to the amendments was its emphasis on how to claim a political position in public. Rule number two demonstrates this point succinctly: "In entering the political arena, religious leaders may not rely on doctrine, appeals to religious authority, or claims to speak for God to advance their case; they must play by the same rules as everyone else and argue their case on its merits."[70]

Students and theorists of liberal democracy will recognize this formulation of the relationship between religion and politics as an outgrowth of the writings of philosopher John Rawls, who famously coined the notion of "public reason" as a way of describing how differing claims within a pluralistic democracy are adjudicated by both the listening parties and the rules of the public itself. For Rawls, and arguably Lear and PFAW, the ideal of public reason is realized when "judges, legislators, chief executives, and other government officials, as well as candidates for public office, act from and follow the idea of public reason and explain to other citizens their reasons for supporting fundamental political positions. . . . In this way, they fulfill what I call their duty of civility to one another and to other citizens."[71]

The confluence between Rawls and PFAW can be seen most clearly in the notion of "the rules of the game," which in this case refers to the manner and methods through which individuals defend their political positions in public. Not only do one's reasons have to be equally accessible to one's adjudicators, as PFAW argued, they also have to contribute to the overarching civility that determines how differing opinions encounter one another as products of potentially antithetical knowledge systems.[72] In light of such systems, Castelli concludes his text by stating outright how religion itself is either good or bad for the American political system. On the one hand, "Religion is good . . . when it supports the civil religion: when it speaks out with civility and respect; when it accepts the principles of tolerance and pluralism; when it appeals to a shared sense of morality and not to religious authority or doctrine."

On the other hand, "Religion is bad . . . when it undermines the civil religion; when it speaks of political matters with the certitude of faith in a pluralistic society in which faith cannot be used as apolitical standard; when it treats opponents as agents of Satan; when it violates the precept of the Virginia Statute for Religious Freedom which formed the basis for the First Amendment."[73] Based on these words alone, it is not difficult to infer which tendency describes which constituency—PFAW or the Moral Majority. Those willing to adhere to the civility of religion in public, such as People for the American Way or other similarly themed advocacy groups, conducted themselves properly in public. It was this standard of political behavior that defined much of PFAW's nonprofit work and media campaigns on behalf of Lear's spiritual vision and the American Way. In addition, the emphasis on "tolerance and pluralism" within "good religion" is a direct product of Lear's own concerns for the position of the religious minority in the United States—one that experienced a sense of precarity when confronted with the possibility of a religious majority or a strident voice that spoke to majority interests of morality and decency. In this sense, *A Plea for Common Sense* embodied PFAW's educational aspirations by distinguishing positive and negative uses of religion in addition to composing rules for the mixing of religion in politics.[74]

Along with this type of publication, PFAW also authored guidebooks and primers for citizens and interested parties that presented the most important debates in an easily understood format: question and answer. This type of text also listed organizational and institutional details about PFAW including its advisory boards, governing committees, and directors at the time of its founding. In 1982, People for the American Way published author David Bollier's *Liberty and Justice for Some: Defending a Free Society from the Radical Right's Holy War on Democracy*.[75] With a cover featuring an image of the statue of liberty holding the torch of liberty in one hand and a heart in the other, *Liberty and Justice for Some* explores the most pressing concerns that PFAW attempted to address through its awareness campaigns and PSAs. Issues such as book censorship, church-state separation, mandatory school prayer, creationism, and the role of religion in public policy outlined the political terrain upon which PFAW would define itself as an advocacy group fighting on behalf of Americans' First Amendment rights. In particular, this text functioned as primer, resource guide, and document of public record simultaneously.

As a primer, the text utilizes the question-and-answer format to investigate the historical relationship between church and state and the manner in which the Christian Right attempted to erode the wall of separation that stood between them. As a resource guide, *Liberty and Justice for Some* provides its readers with countless citations and bibliographies for further reading and research in the areas of tolerance, civility, and conservative politics. As a document of public record, Bollier gives his readers unadulterated exposure to some of the most virulent quotations from individuals such as Jerry Falwell, Phyllis Schlafly, and Pat Robertson. As part of PFAW's commitment to raising awareness by distributing information to the public that it considered essential to the *public interest*, the text emphasizes the less than charitable opinion that many in the Christian Right had for Lear and others who worked for PFAW. Lastly, Bollier viewed his primer as a catalyst for political mobilization.

The book was nothing if not a reason to get involved in American politics on behalf of the American Way against those who would violate its principal values of tolerance, pluralism, and civility. Lear and others at PFAW depended on the assumption that if exposed to the horrors of the Christian Right's political aspirations as heard by its primary spokespersons, citizens would respond in kind in defense of the very rights that made such utterances possible in the first place. In other words, PFAW hoped that the right combination of shocking quotation and bibliographic data would catalyze Americans into defending the only sensible politics in American public life—one drawn from common sense itself. The composition of PFAW's leadership said as much about this goal as Lear's leadership did in establishing PFAW as the Religious Left's awareness-raising nonprofit.

PFAW'S ORGANIZATIONAL CONTEXT: THE NONPROFIT GOES TO BATTLE

Clearly, People for the American Way was the product of multiple individuals and instances of institutional support beyond, yet inclusive of, Lear's own spiritual idiosyncrasies. It was also, however, thoroughly a product of its socioeconomic and religio-political times. Recent monographs by historians Robert O. Self and Daniel Rodgers have attempted to grapple with our contemporary moment by foregrounding "the family" and fracture as central narrative motifs of the last half century of American history.[76] The gradual displacement of political and economic causes for social and cultural concerns as an outgrowth of the move toward "identity politics" following the freedom movements of the 1960s made what happened to American families that much more important to some and dire to others.[77] As a result, "the family" emerged as one of the most (if not *the* most) powerful organizing tropes for political and religious mobilization in the second half of the twentieth century.[78] The once-powerful welfare state of midcentury

America, one that initially provided for families through social programming and economic safety nets, had gradually begun to weaken under the relentless criticisms authored by the nation's racial, gender, and ethnic minorities as the nation experienced one traumatic event after another.

In addition, various religious constituencies, including those within conservative Protestantism, viewed such assistance as an overextension of federal power that resembled other instances of government overreach such as the Supreme Court's 1962 *Engel v. Vitale* school prayer decision.[79] As a result, the notion of the family became something to defend out of a sense of protection instead of provision. This distinction contributed to the ongoing fracturing of public life as new organizational bodies arose, including think tanks, national magazines, and special interest groups, which were dedicated to a particular religio-political view of the world over and against its perceived opposition. New religious and political allegiances that seemingly ignored more traditional alliances along denominational lines aided the organizing of protection- and provisions-based constituencies and organizations, further dividing the country along a number of culturally determined lines of fracture.

The establishment of People for the American Way as an educationally minded nonprofit organization by Lear and his supporters exemplified these socioeconomic shifts in American public life in the lead-up to the 1980s. The public association of candidate Ronald Reagan with the electronic church forecast an uncertain political future for Lear and those he gathered behind him as one of America's most beloved television producers *and* as the country's most vocal proponent of civility and tolerance in American politics. If interfaith coalition building described PFAW's claim to religious leverage in opposition to the perceived absolutist and exclusionary politics of the Christian Right, then the advocacy group operated as the elemental form of social cohesion for both the political Right and Left/center as a form of demographic mobilization, public building, and resistance.[80] In other words, the currency of politics in this period depended upon utilizing the most recent means of communication and organization in order to compete for media exposure and narrative traction over and against the manifest opposition—both political and religious.

Sociologist of religion Robert Wuthnow identifies this space of activism as the "third sector" of American politics.[81] This term does not describe the actions of the state or individuals themselves but rather the collective action of nonprofit organizations like PFAW or the Moral Majority that unfolds in the space between the federal and the individual. "It functions as a *public sphere*," Wuthnow argues. "That is, the third sector is of interest primarily as a locus of public discourse about the collective values of the society. It provides an arena in which fundamental values...can be discussed, experimented with, symbolized, and ritually enacted."[82] In this sense, debates and concerns that had once tended to remain local or regional came into view in national terms through disagreement with other similarly designed organizations within their respective media environments. As such, visibility itself became a significant source of religious capital in the exceedingly public confrontations between Left and Right over foreign policy in Central America and social policy on the domestic front. In fact, the names of many of these organizations themselves, including People for the American Way, the Christian Voice, and the Moral Majority, said as much about their intentions and aspirations as their media campaigns did regarding the country they wanted to reclaim for their respective constituencies.

This style of politics depended on the single-issue organizing that had been commonplace throughout the 1960s as civil rights movement participants attempted to draw the nation's attention to the various socioeconomic injustices experienced on a daily basis. By the 1980s, coalitions had broadened to include a more diverse collection of individuals and vested interests, yet they came together around an equally partisan claim to be the best "America" possible in contentious times. In this sense, individuals like Lear and Falwell played instrumental roles in the formation of various publics as an outgrowth of the organizing that took place on behalf of an internally besieged nation.[83] Unlike previous periods of activism, however, the one that confronted Lear and Reagan possessed its own unique communicative possibilities: "Movements, political actions committees, direct-mail campaigns, and lobbying provided the framework in which participation in the public sphere was described."[84] Not only did this visibility hold more promise for the respective interested parties, it also was a potent source of division and discord as one organizational absolute went against another in an age of fracture; political certainty clashed with civic toleration as the separation of church and state itself came into question through the claims of Lear, Falwell, and others on behalf of their concerned constituencies.

"Special interest groups give explicit identity to religious and religio-moral issues," argues Wuthnow. "They provide a way in which individuals can reinforce one another . . . as persons with common religious convictions. In so doing, they also make religious convictions more visible in the public arena."[85] PFAW and the Moral Majority demonstrate this aptly through their activities and organizing tactics both in print and over the airwaves. Lear's organization acted on behalf of an imagined polity that was otherwise free from internal discord since it functioned on largely shared concerns for mutual respect and toleration of political difference. This public functioned smoothly according to the guidelines of a pluralist consensus model within which diversity served as both a unifying concept and evidence of unity forged out of multiplicity.[86] The Moral Majority not only contested the politics of PFAW, it also questioned the very *terms* upon which its notion of public deliberation took place. Its political statements were neither careful nor civil according to the descriptive measure of PFAW since it did not respect the rules governing religion's appearance or usage in public life.[87]

This disjuncture between the two groups was largely a product of People for the American Way's notion of "the public," which served as "a safe space for pluralism, a zone wherein citizenship trumps sectarian desires to legislate morality."[88] Although Lear and others may not have realized it at the time, the formation of PFAW was one attempt among many to establish a reasoned, religiously informed voice in the face of global movements of intolerance that threatened to establish themselves on US shores through the means of the electronic church and the voices of those who populated its virtual pulpits.[89] It operated as a form of special interest activism as understood through the advocacy group in defense of interfaith values of religious pluralism and separation of church and state. Ironically enough, religious leaders during this period, including Falwell and Lear, arguably encouraged their constituencies with the same mantra despite their vehement differences: "awareness is the watchword, freedom the slogan, and action the mandate."[90]

If we can understand the third-sector mobilization of this period as a collective reaction to the state and its growth in postwar America in both supportive (PFAW) and critical (Moral Majority) modes, then Lear and Falwell have much more in common than initially realized.[91] Instead of particular policies or politics serving as the focal point of religious activism, the state itself became the oppositional force against which various communities of protest mobilized. As a result, the terms of debate for this particular period took place on a discursive level that certainly encompassed individual claims about federal policy made public, yet they centered on the apparatus of deliberation itself and its preservation in American public life—a task supported ardently by Lear and those at PFAW. Considered separately, each organization furthered its cause through similar means, including the use of print and television, charismatic leadership, and chaos rhetoric.[92] Each group was also reactive in its own way—one responding to the other in kind. When considered together, however, a different picture emerges.

The formation of PFAW in the early 1980s pointed to the fracturing of American public life that had been ongoing since the 1960s over the role of the federal government in the lives of American citizens as it attempted to "legislate morality" through its various governing bodies. For Lear, the religious integrity of these structures, namely their ability to withstand appropriation by the Christian Right, was dubious at best in light of Reagan's election to the Oval Office and Jimmy

Swaggart's requests to pray for the removal of Supreme Court justices. These examples proved to Lear that the nation's founding documents, including the First Amendment, would not be enough to stave off the civic nightmare that grew more ominous on the distant horizon of the country's political future.

What made these debates unique in the recent religious history of the United States was that the content of morality itself, as well as its public and private applications, seemed to encompass many of the debates between liberals and conservatives, including those between Lear and Reagan themselves.[93] "What had once been a sharp symbolic boundary between private morality and collective life," argues Wuthnow, "had become so ambiguous that writers and public figures began openly challenging the earlier privatistic notions."[94] Although initially supported and understood in a completely different social register, one goal of the liberal movement seemed to have been realized in the public sparring between People for the American Way and the Christian Right—the private had indeed become the political.

PFAW AND CIVILITY IN THE PUBLIC SQUARE

The programming and policy concerns of PFAW remained educationally focused throughout the course of the 1980s. Debates ranging from what should be taught and read in school classrooms to the selection of Supreme Court justices drew much of PFAW's attention as it continued to find its footing in politically uneven times. For all their concern for individual instances of discrimination, legislative injustices, or religious suppression, those who occupied the advisory board of PFAW, including Lear himself, typically relied on a broader set of values that reinforced the nonprofit's platform of First Amendment rights and the separation of church and state. Capacious yet no less instructive of PFAW's politics, these values included the free exchange of ideas, tolerance, diversity, liberty, dialogue, and perhaps most important, civility. If the spirit of liberty was under siege from the rhetorical onslaughts of the electronic church, then civility was not far behind in experiencing its own forms of civic abuse.

The liberal response or reaction to such challenges assumed a level of finality rarely before seen in public: "To be sure, there are few if any issues in the past century which have evoked such unilateral and resolute reaction on the part of such a broad coalition of liberal groups."[95] This coalition was certainly indebted to its liberal forebears who had taken up similar causes during the various freedom movements of the 1960s, but it also came together in hopes of addressing a disturbing force in American public life that grabbed newspaper headlines the globe over—conservative religiosity. Despite the fact that both PFAW and the Moral Majority committed the antidemocratic act—one not completely unrelated to how scholars describe American wars of culture—of "deliberately attempting to monopolize the symbols of legitimacy (patriotism, Americanism, family, First Amendment, etc.)," it was PFAW that blended prescription with description in the face of consistent evangelical accomplishments in politics.[96] This epistemic blending found its bearings in PFAW's application of civility to the country's many sources of political discord.[97]

Tolerance of difference, a diversity of opinions, a robust exchange of ideas— these broadly construed themes capture much of Lear and PFAW's activism and awareness campaigns in the early part of the 1980s. These particular values also mapped seamlessly onto previous interwar and midcentury efforts by activists who defended the US tradition of interfaith cooperation in the face of totalitarian inroads or the Lear-authored "moral McCarthyism" of the Christian Right epitomized in the Bible Scorecard.[98] In one historical moment, this pluralist configuration manifested as "Protestant, Catholic, and Jew." In another, a "Tri-Faith America" rang clearest on behalf of America's rich history of religious diversity.[99] By the time Lear established PFAW, this notion had transformed yet again into simply, "the American Way."[100] People for the American Way's confidence in these ideals stemmed from its commitment to education and awareness since it contributed to a healthy democratic exchange of deliberation and debate— one ideally suited to the discord and division it confronted in the wake of Reagan's election to the presidency.

The attention PFAW paid to sites of learning, instruction, and idea formation functioned as a transitional moment in the recent history of the United States as the martial legacy of the Cold War, a conflict between competing ideas within the mind itself, resurfaced with a vengeance in the publications of PFAW and numerous leaders of the Christian Right, including Jerry Falwell, Timothy LaHaye, and Francis Schaeffer.[101] This concentration on ideational production was expertly deployed by PFAW in its consistent surveillance of the Christian Right's media usage, its substantial archive of right-wing movements in the United States, and its creation of various informational fact sheets for concerned constituencies. PFAW echoed the emphasis on ideology as witnessed during the Cold War, yet it also prefigured the terms of public debate in the age of fracture as defined by the wars of culture that would engulf the United States in the early 1990s. Recalling the history of interfaith exchange across denominations and cultures assisted PFAW in staking its claim for tolerance in the American public over and against the Christian Right, but it needed additional ideological support in order to establish its political efficacy as an alternative to an abrasive and divisive politics of absolute certainty.

The calls for civility and tolerance authored by People for the American Way in both their printed material and formative PSAs assumed a great deal about the American nation-state and its civic organization. Drawing on postulations usually associated with consensus models of American governance, PFAW argued that the United States operated as a civil society replete with publics and counterpublics along with their requisite claims to political maneuverability. Politics served as the backdrop for much of this public exchange as one individual after another jockeyed for position in public. Over time, spaces linked to *the* public came to be associated with particular sexes, races, and, for my purposes, religiosities that were conducive to its various operations. As a result, the public/private binary came to define much of what could be understood as the "architecture of consensus" regarding who tended to be privileged or discriminated against within the rules of civil politics.

Civic ideals such as toleration and civility aided the purpose of consensus itself, which was to cultivate harmony out of a dizzying array of cultures, practices, and traditions. This social formation, however, also required a particular understanding of religion that did not venture beyond the home or local community organization due to its potential divisiveness.[102] It is in this sense that diversity functions as both consensus's primary accomplishment and its most susceptible ideal. Assuming such diversity could be kept in check, regardless of its cultural or religious valence, the larger civil society would continue functioning. If, on the other hand, this particular rendering of pluralism was left to its own devices, especially that of the Christian Right, then there was no telling what the repercussions could be. As a result, different communities interpreted civility differently depending on their position within American civil society.

Civility sounded, and perhaps felt, very different for the religious actors explored thus far. For PFAW, it was an indispensable component of their overall approach to maintaining (and thus monitoring) a robust public life through the unencumbered exchange of ideas. In this sense, the "civil" in "civil society" was more than simply an adjective; it was a prescriptive antidote for political strife. For Falwell and the Christian Right, the promises of civility rang hollow in an environment that was bent against their political claims due to the framing of conservative religiosity as the "repugnant cultural other" by the media writ large.[103] As a result, notions such as civility and the separation of church and state, which possessed institutional backing from PFAW and others, functioned less as a maintenance mechanism and more as a curtailment of religious possibility.[104]

"Persistent calls for civility in the present mythological contest by representatives of the center will not resonate with those who feel that the center is itself a liberal construct which is being used normatively," argues scholar of religion Donald Heinz. "If that is so, civility is a centrist virtue espoused by those who regularly find that the system, or currently dominant cultural definitions, works for them."[105] Rendered in this manner, the cultural productions of People for the American Way on behalf of the public's awareness for right-wing movements reminded their readers that the delicate balance within civil society between universality and particularity was precarious at best. This was especially the case when it came to religion and its proper role in public as understood by Lear, PFAW, and the Religious Left.

Due to Lear's own investments in religious liberal ways of thought that tended to see the universal in religious particulars, he and PFAW saw little at issue when speaking of a common vision for the country when articulated by the members of his interfaith advisory board. Once circulated within the media, however, such suggestions took on a defensive quality in an attempt to name their most visceral enemy—the Christian Right. For Falwell and others in the electronic church, PFAW represented anything but the liberty-centered nonprofit it claimed to be. In fact, for many on the Christian and political right, "the separation of church and state came to be, by and large, the *isolation* of religion from politics." Lear and PFAW expected citizens of the United States to behave civilly when conducting themselves politically, yet with the arrival of Falwell, Swaggart, and the electronic church, each of the tenets espoused and defended by the nonprofit came into view in the less than flattering light of intolerance. As a result, the tolerant gradually became intolerant of intolerance itself, as witnessed in the speeches and writings of the Christian Right.[106]

For Lear and PFAW, the diagnosis was a simple one—the Right did not follow the "ethic of civility" in its political activities.[107] As perceived "peddlers" of divisiveness and belligerency, Falwell and others left little to moderation or gentility. Theirs was a politics of offense rather than "no-fense." Their voices were to be heard no matter what in a manner fitting to an increasingly mediated age. As sociologist James Davison Hunter fittingly describes it, "The 'New Christian Right' has violated the moral strictures of civility by crossing over the barriers separating public and private spheres and attempting to retain, through political means, traditional moral standards. With the relatively forceful reintroduction of conservative Protestant symbols into the public realm, political decorum was besmirched."[108] In light of this particular description, the accusations of PFAW were not only designed to draw attention to the dangers of conservative religiosity, they were also part of a larger strategy of maintenance and protection of public space itself from the likes of Falwell and his generous congregations.

Lear's and PFAW's desire to raise the nation's collective awareness concerning these threats stemmed from its commitment to defending free speech as a First Amendment right, yet the nonprofit's cultural productions accomplished a great deal more once uttered to eager audiences and journalists the country over. The numerous publications and addresses of PFAW, in addition to the writings and productions of Lear himself, "set the discursive terms of civil society by naming and locating the sacred *and* the profane, while simultaneously prescribing the rules of engagement for the ritual interaction of both in public space . . . under the name of civic protection."[109] It is in this sense that we can name such acts of discursive fashioning as part of the *religious mechanics of civility*. These processes were intimately related to the interfaith politics of consensus on which Lear and PFAW grounded many of their arguments for a more civil space of American politics. Scholar of religion Chad Seales's analyses of Southern white usages of "civility" on their own behalf illuminates PFAW's own deployments of "civility," only in a different register—namely the religious rather than the racial. His narrative depiction of the on-the-ground effects of such civility captures the manner in which PFAW employed civility in an attempt to cleanse the American polity of all exclamations and behaviors that reflected badly on the American Way tradition of mixing religion and politics properly according to the dictates of a broadly defined civil religion. It is in this analytical spirit that I quote Seales at length:

> White officials in New South towns and cities drained secular spaces of an exuberant emotion that they associated with those primitive outbursts. They filled that emptied space with refined etiquette, which they associated with a modern disposition. . . . Citizens could still bring pious feelings into the secular chambers of government and law, but they had to remake them as modern. Public prayers had to be offered in accordance with the rules of civility. They must be conciliatory, given in the name of transcendent virtues, of love and peace, common to all Christians regardless of race [or religion]. . . . Ultimately, they leveraged civility to enforce a religious justification of [religious] hierarchy.[110]

The varied results of PFAW's social programming as a response to the threat of an "evangelical America" had much in common with this description of how civility could be utilized to buttress local, state, and federal authority in circumscribing public space according to certain epistemological assumptions about the relationship between American religion and politics.[111] Distinctions such as these, including those that separated the sacred from the profane and the civil from the uncivil, did nothing if not establish the discursive power of consensus to monitor and regulate religious expression in the public sphere through civility, tolerance, and diversity. People for the American Way reacted to the Christian Right in kind through an equally divisive rhetoric of chaos that helped mobilize its supporters against the constitutional threats of Christian Right politics. This is not to say that PFAW did not accomplish its own self-defined goals because, on this account, it most certainly did.

Despite their best intentions, however, Lear and his advisory board launched a counteroffensive against the electronic church and its representatives that ultimately resulted in an equally divided citizenry in an effort to remind this polity of the country's consensus ideals enshrined in both print and television special. To say, as Falwell did, that PFAW literature was largely the product of "Norman Lear's Way" would be an overstatement, yet it nevertheless pointed to the receptivity of American public spaces to a specific formation of spiritual liberalism that found its catalytic mechanism in the appearance of its discursive opposite—the Christian Right. In this sense, Lear provided religious and political liberals in this period with a new set of rhetorical tools with which to defend their interfaith interests as understood through a civilly organized society by rendering their pluralist project as part of a "new modern mainstream." Thus, the social and political polarization of our contemporary moment is indebted not simply to a Falwell or a Robertson but also to Lear and PFAW's politics of consensus as a remedy for the spiritual ills that confronted them. This was nowhere more evident than in the space understood best by the likes of Norman Lear, Larry Gelbart, and others: the prime-time soundstage.

5

Liberalism as Variety Show

I Love Liberty *and the Decline*
of the Religious Left

Despite the initial momentum in the lead-up to and following the founding of Lear's nonprofit People for the American Way, the organization had a great deal to achieve politically if it was to respond convincingly to the electoral victories of the GOP and the subsequent rise of not only "the electronic church" but also "the Christian Right." Resembling his approach to other sociopolitical challenges of the day, Lear decided to deploy what he knew best—the soundstage as understood through the nearly ubiquitous medium of television on behalf of a largely liberal conception of citizenship in the public square.

"As well as PFAW was doing two years in, it didn't assuage my frustration over the still unfinished script for [the feature] *Religion*," Lear admitted.

> God, the Bible, and love of country were still, as I saw it, the sole province of the Right. On the Left we were behaving as though we didn't care, and I simply had to do something about that. One morning I awoke with an idea . . . a two-hour, star-studded, nonpartisan salute to America on the occasion of the 250th anniversary of George Washington's birth. I would produce it under the People for the American Way banner "to show that God and the flag belong to all of us, no matter where we stand politically."[1]

Lear's notoriety as a television producer, based on sitcoms such as *All in the Family* and *The Jeffersons*, allowed him to begin composing the then fictitious show alongside his longtime partner, Bud Yorkin. By the time Lear finished shopping the idea around to the major television networks as well as to various Hollywood actors in the industry, he had settled upon a title as well as the prime-time venue—both of which spoke to Lear's pragmatic spiritual predilections: *I Love Liberty* was to be coproduced and broadcast by PFAW and ABC. Due to the political discrepancy between ABC and Lear's very public nonprofit organization, a civil common denomination had to be established first in order to avoid accusations of spiritual collusion between the two religio-political entities.

"ABC, the network most attracted to it, held back the order until I could offer what they considered proof of its nonpartisan origin," Lear described. " 'Get two ex-presidents, one Republican and one Democrat, to cosponsor the show' I thought, . . . so I asked ABC if they would be satisfied with a president and a first lady, Gerald Ford and Lady Bird Johnson, as co-chairs of *I Love Liberty*. They said yes."[2] Like many of his more conservative Protestant counterparts, Lear also had to worry about running afoul of the fairness doctrine, which virtually forced television networks at the time to broadcast a diversity of opinions regarding controversial subject matter whenever addressed in prime time. As we have already seen, Lear's typical defense of his unique brand of entertainment programming drew on the notion of the "public interest" in order to illustrate the civic significance of a television character like Archie Bunker to the nation.

In other words, Lear was not simply giving airtime to a bigoted racist for its own sake; he was also trying to address the rampant racism he saw coursing through the body politic by encouraging viewers to question their own views on the issues presented to them each and every week. "President Ford believed firmly that the government must not favor any one religion over others and that each man's love of God was unique to the individual. The same held true for love of country," Lear argued, "so religion and patriotism, as symbolized by the Bible and flag, belonged equally to people of all faiths and beliefs. This was the credo our show would seek extravagantly to celebrate."[3] Perhaps for the first time in his storied career in American media, Lear was neither joking nor intending to make a joke—far from it. In fact, Lear could not have been *more serious* about the ills that plagued not only the nation but also the very constitutional liberties that he had defended abroad in the European theater of the Second World War.

This chapter foregrounds Lear's *I Love Liberty* for historical, analytical, and ideological reasons. Lear's variety show serves as a chronological bookend to a largely thematic story of one individual's efforts to remake the public square in his own image. While the show may have appeared on a major network in prime time, it seemed to have found its true inspiration in the less televised "I Love America" rallies of conservative evangelist Jerry Falwell that took place over the course of the previous decade in various public spaces.[4] I have decided to identify this image of the variety show, and its respective contents, as part of the spiritual politics of the Religious Left because it ritualizes much of what has already been explored and described as Lear's civil religious vision of the nation's manifold religions—especially those labeled "conservative" or "fundamentalist."[5] In this sense, Lear's *I Love Liberty* is illustrative of how liberal religious actors constructed themselves theatrically as political subjects through the stories, routines, and jokes found in the genre of the Lear-authored variety show.[6]

To state the case in slightly different terms: the various sketches composed for *I Love Liberty*, some of which were cowritten by close confidant Martin Marty, embody a longer historical tradition of engaging the public square based on explicitly social grounds. Despite the nearly ten years that had passed between the premiere of *All in the Family* and the founding of People for the American Way, Lear still had many unresolved concerns to address when it came to the threat of dogmatic Christianity in both the Oval Office and the public square. Like many of his mainline Protestant and interfaith supporters, Lear saw himself as someone who not only contributed to the creation of such a public, and thus the public interest itself, but also as someone who would come to its defense whenever under spiritual siege.

Similarly, many contemporary liberals, including Lear and his various supporters, have since understood themselves as stewards or protectors of a uniquely constructed sociopolitical space.[7] As such, Lear's *I Love Liberty* was certainly made possible by way of federal and network assistance, yet, more important, it helped to inculcate the terms, agendas, and frames of thought that Lear had been exposed to since he was a child sitting before his grandfather and the crystal radio. In many ways, I have in mind what historian Daniel Rodgers has described as the creation a liberal *tradition* for what Lear authored in prime time for his various viewing audiences:

> Ideologies need arenas of practice in which their core assumptions are acted and reenacted, learned and internalized. They need places and occasions for repeating their key verities, their already scripted slogans, their creeds and catechisms. They need rituals and institutions. They need all this not only for the purposes of social mobilization. They need this, no less critically, to reproduce themselves over time, so that the young not only know how to speak the symbolic language of their parents but they actually see the world of experience in their elders' way.[8]

There is no better example of this type of liberal tradition creation than Lear's prime-time special *I Love Liberty*. While this chapter's primary focus will be on the composition, history, and execution of Lear's variety show in three acts, it will also compare it to similarly produced conservative "I Love America" rallies during the same period. In other words, in order to properly understand Lear's uniquely liberal theatrics in an age of Reagan, we must attend to its antithetical other across the televisual landscape: "the electronic church" as represented by Jerry Falwell. In fact, Falwell's failed attempts to become part of the programming of *I Love Liberty* spoke powerfully not only to the limits of Lear's understanding of First Amendment rights and freedom of speech but also to the limits of American religious liberalism itself following the defeat of Jimmy Carter and the rise of the Sunbelt as personified by former governor of California and actor Ronald Reagan.[9] In short, the following analysis will make use of the variety show *I Love Liberty* in order to demonstrate the most significant strengths and weaknesses of Lear's spiritual politics as a religious liberal, including appeals to racial diversity, religious toleration, and constitutionally protected liberty.

BACKGROUND AND CONTENTS: JERRY FALWELL MEETS *I LOVE LIBERTY*

Despite the novelty of the Lear-produced variety show, it was far from an original theatrical production.[10] In fact, soon-to-be televangelist Jerry Falwell had presented his own version of an entertainment special across America throughout the 1970s entitled "I Love America." Not unlike Lear, Falwell had also been galvanized to act in the public arena on behalf of a beleaguered constituency based largely on something that he saw performed, only this time it was on a soundstage instead of a television screen. "After seeing a musical titled *I Love America*, Falwell decided to stage musical rallies around the country, the nation's bicentennial providing a way to tie nationalism with traditional morality," historian J. Brooks Flippen describes. "Falwell selected seventy students from his college and purchased buses to carry them. Behind the buses came tractor trailers carrying stage equipment and costumes. The evangelist himself flew to each city. . . . In all, Falwell's I Love America rallies visited 141 cities, including 44 of the state capitals."[11]

Falwell had been known to reject arguments that attempted to apply the Christian Gospel and its varied messages to explicitly social challenges, including civil rights during the 1960s with his notorious sermon "Ministers and Marches."[12] By the time the early 1970s had come and gone, Falwell had not only begun his long publishing career as an evangelist and author with titles such as *Church Flame*, he had also begun strategizing about how best to address America's moral ills through concepts gleaned from the worlds of advertising and marketing.[13] In fact, by the early 1980s Falwell had begun including short summaries of his sermons and major talking points in his publications for easy dissemination and consumption in hopes of saturating the proverbial market. The title of one of these summaries, published in the last pages of *Listen America!*, read, "Seven Principles That Made America Great."[14]

These rallies were not simply exercises in misdirected religio-political enthusiasm as described by Lear, Marty, and a variety of Protestant print media throughout the 1970s.[15] For one observer, the Falwell-led occasion was nothing short of dramatic. "The brisk wind snapped the row of American flags to attention as Dr. Jerry Falwell exhorted the crowd to oppose pornography, abortion, the Equal Rights Amendment, and the call to draft of women. . . . The occasion was an 'I Love America' rally sponsored by Falwell's Moral Majority Inc., a political group he hopes will put America back on the right track on lobbying against so-called 'liberal' issues."[16] The purview of Falwell's vision was limited exclusively to what conservative strategists at the time referred to as "the social issue." Relative to Falwell's previous public stances concerning the proper relationship between religion and politics, this more sophisticated set of claims gestured to two interrelated sources of production: Jerry Falwell himself and individuals such as Richard Viguerie and Howard Phillips, both of whom began consulting with and advising Falwell concerning any and all nonprofit aspirations following the success of his national rallies.

Lear's variety show had a national exposure that dwarfed that of Falwell's sketches and songs, but Falwell's production made up for the lack in their unique brand of conservative grassroots theatrics: "The rallies addressed large fundamentalist audiences with a combination of music, songs, and oratory. Weeks in advance of each rally, representatives of the 'Old Time Gospel Hour' alerted Christian schools in the region of the upcoming rally and offered to help provide the logistical support necessary to transport large numbers of people to the rally site."[17] Acting upon some of his earlier writings on market saturation and the Christian Gospel, Falwell often preceded his events with a local PR campaign of his own making: "In the weeks before the rally, quarter- to full-page advertisements appeared in local newspapers; the ads typically featured a large photograph of the Reverend Falwell and an invitation to attend a rally in support of America."[18]

Despite the obvious gap in viewership, each instance of religio-political artistry made an equally powerful impact on American public life—one associated with the Protestant mainline, the other connected to various fringe organizations of "the Radical Right."[19] In other words, Falwell's work as an individual pastor went far beyond his individual acts—mighty as they were, either in print or over the airwaves. Like Lear did for PFAW on *I Love Liberty*, Falwell helped generate what Michael Warner and others have referred to as "a public." On the one hand, a public can be understood as a type of "social totality," one that shapes the conditions of its own production. In this sense, a public "is as much notional as it is empirical." On the other hand, a public can be understood as "a concrete audience, a crowd witnessing itself in visible space, as with a theatrical public. Such a public also has a sense of totality, bounded by the event or by the shared physical space."[20]

Unlike Falwell, Lear's organization had already been formed by the time ABC broadcast his variety show in prime time, so in this sense, *I Love Liberty* was not instrumental to the formation of People for the American Way or its programming. Nevertheless, the variety show functioned as an interfaith public by gathering the "middling mainline" together within a theatrically bounded space under the banner of Lear-led pluralism, political cooperation, and religious toleration. Compared to Lear, then, Falwell's decision to organize, conduct, and preach the Gospel for "I Love America" rallies throughout the 1970s had a much more substantive impact on the ultimate formation of the Moral Majority than did Lear's show with PFAW.[21] "The rallies of 1979 were one-shot affairs that helped to establish the structures of the Moral Majority, but did not provide the detailed and ongoing education necessary to sustain grassroots involvement. . . . The Moral Majority's initial audience was the members of Falwell's church, the viewers of the 'Old-Time Gospel Hour,' and the people contacted during the 'I Love America' rallies."[22]

Over the course of the 1970s, Falwell's travels connected the country in a manner that Lear could only have dreamed of. To Lear, *broad*casting one's message about the nation's ills was most important of all; the broader the message, the bigger the audience, the better. While Falwell was well within his constitutional rights to not only challenge Lear's variety show but also request an appearance on a program that was otherwise bipartisan, he also possessed a different set of means to enact his message and mobilize his various audiences in the public square. Falwell may indeed have chosen theatrics and music in order to make his own arguments about the fallen state of the nation and its people, but he also knew how to position his performances in public venues for his respective rallies, including the stone steps of countless state capitals across the country. For anthropologist Susan Harding, the social force of Falwell's "Bible-based language" deserved its own ethnographic excavations. Exploring what she called Falwell's "cultural politics," Harding identified not only the circulatory density that soon came to define much of the electoral power of conservative Protestantism but also the very process through which a new political subject was born:

In effect, Jerry Falwell turned his empire of ministries, including the Moral Majority, his church and university, the Old-Time Gospel Hour, and a half dozen other outreaches, into one large, long consciousness-raising meeting. This "meeting" was political in a broad sense of rearranging cultural power relations, but not in the narrow sense of conventional politicking. The agenda was to convert his people from "fundamentalists," whose only mission in American society was evangelism, into "conservative Christians" who would fight worldly battles and who sought worldly power and influence in the name of "Christian values."[23]

In this sense, the social impact of Falwell's words went far beyond their literal meaning or political conveyance to a particular audience—made present either physically by their own action or televisually through Falwell's later command of "the electronic church." As Harding implies, Falwell's presentation helped cultivate a renewed, or perhaps reborn, political consciousness, one that had not been entirely unfamiliar with the ways and means of mass media and the public sphere but was nevertheless conducive to numerous political aspirations—either of its own making or by others. This is not to say that the public square had always been an utterly desolate place for the likes of conservative fundamentalists, Pentecostals, and evangelicals.[24] Far from it. What Falwell made possible and what Lear reinforced with his prime-time variety show special was an epistemic grounding for political mobilization itself, as articulated from the proverbial Left and/ or Right.

In other words, Falwell and Lear gave their respective supporters a modus operandi for either engaging or protecting a political space dominated largely by a liberal democratic rationale that bifurcated American citizens according to their "public" actions and their "private" beliefs and motivations.[25] This cultural assumption led many academics and those in the media to criticize Falwell and his actions for "mixing" religion and politics in an unholy manner, a manner that literally seemed to threaten the very foundation upon which American democracy rested. "At the time, most of us did not recognize these sensations, let alone see them as the classic signs of lost hegemony, of our having lost the easy and apparently (but not really) effortless assumption of political and cultural dominance," Harding describes. "Instead, we—or, more precisely, the public intellectuals (journalists, pundits, scientists, scholars, policy experts) who represented us—set about trying to explain how this breakdown of public order had occurred, so that we might get things back to normal."[26] By placing commentary on Falwell's theatrics alongside the commentary that accompanied Lear's variety show, we are able to understand both as attempts to raise the political consciousness of various political constituencies that are otherwise alienated from the political process or dependent on it for their collective source of religio-political power.

If Lear's leadership functioned as a clarion call to other mainline and inter-faith progressives to *continue* their work in the electoral process, then Falwell's work in theatrical form achieved something even greater; it cultivated an entirely new political subject while still demonstrating "Christian values" in the political arena. "It was preachers, evangelists, teachers, and writers—men and women whom God had anointed to speak for him—who helped Protestant fundamen-talists discern their new calling in the 1980s," concludes Harding. "Above all, preachers, the master-speakers of Bible-based dialects, enabled fundamentalists to know God's updated will for them."[27] As stated from the outset, Lear could only have dreamed of having such an influence in the sort of public-creation that Falwell was up to in his jet-fueled travels around the country.

In time, conservative strategists would take advantage of this intimate rela-tionship between pastor and congregation to further their own electoral ends through Falwell, both as a man and as a figure, namely that of a reconstituted GOP along the lines of the New Right, the Moral Majority, and the increas-ingly emergent Sunbelt. "As conservative Protestants commingled their reli-gious and political imaginations in the Moral Majority, on the Nation's Mall, and on the airwaves of television or radio, they tore up a tacit contract with modern America, . . . the social contract of American secular modernity."[28] In no uncertain terms, Lear would come to this contract's defense on behalf of the American Way and the public interest. And in like kind to Falwell, Lear was ready for war.[29]

RECEPTION: PATRIOTISM OF A DIFFERENT KIND

It was originally referred to as "America's first left-wing patriotic rally." On March 20, 1982, the *Washington Post* published an article titled "Miss Liberty's Left Hand." Authored by noted television critic Tom Shales, the piece described the contents of the show as the product of a Capitol Hill screening conducted by Lear himself in Washington, DC. "Norman Lear is trying to steal back some of the patriotism that he feels has been co-opted by the so-called New Right," Shales observed. "He says liberals and moderates can get just as emotional about their country as super-conservatives and endeavors to prove it with this enor-mous and dazzlingly well-staged whiz-bang."[30] Lear's approach to combating the conservative appropriation of America's most iconic symbols for political ends fought fire with proverbial fire.

Instead of arguing that conservatives had misunderstood or misread American patriotism, he argued that conservatives had co-opted it, implying that there was an original and thus "truer" meaning than the one disseminated by individuals like Falwell and Robertson. Echoing Lear's aspirations, Shales's description of the show not only included criticisms of its staged execution, it was also illustrative of a pervasive liberal assumption about conservative religiosity in the public square: namely that it is unruly and utterly dominated by emotion. Thus, by arguing that the show's success depended entirely on it equaling the religio-political fervor found on the political right, Lear had *implicitly* accepted the rhetorical terrain of an *explicitly* conservative argument. After all, what was a "super-conservative" if not a fundamentalist masquerading as a legitimate political subject as seen through the eyes of Lear, Shales, and the *Washington Post*?

"The program, meant as a celebration of American diversity of opinion and the First Amendment that protects it, was produced by Lear's People for the American Way, a group formed to counter the influence of the Moral Majority and other such outfits." When pushed, Lear defended his program according to the above description by arguing that the presence of individuals such as John Wayne and Barry Goldwater made up for the fact that both ABC and PFAW contributed financially to the making of Lear's *I Love Liberty* extravaganza. As such, the show could both *entertain* and *provoke* audiences at home through its constitutionally protected yet somewhat veiled didactic intent—a characteristic common to most Lear-authored prime-time products of popular consumption.

Despite the conceptual clarity that seemed to accompany Lear's defenses of his own programming, Shales was already onto the less than clear line between politics, entertainment, and the public interest that Lear's programs seemed to negotiate so effectively. "At one point . . . actor Martin Sheen says how wonderful freedom in the USA is and exhorts the audience, 'Come on, let's hear it for us!' Why," Shales asks, "does Norman Lear think we should come on and hear it for us at this particular time?" The spirit of Shales's question is one that historians, scholars of religion, and political scientists continue to wrestle with, yet in my estimation, Sheen's exhortation is less a reflection of an individual assessment and more indicative of a constellation of mainline and liberal progressive thought that foregrounded racial and ethnic diversity as an indispensable component of a larger spiritual politics of the public square.

Lear makes this point quite clearly in the subsequent paragraphs, which take the form of an interview. Responding to a question about what a "right-wing" produced TV special would sound like, Lear replied, "It would not have a sense of humor, for one thing. It would take itself 100 percent seriously. And"—most important it seems—"it wouldn't have a group of five minorities talking about their grievances with society."[31] While this may be a slight mischaracterization by Lear of the actual sketch in question in *I Love Liberty*, it nevertheless illustrates elegantly the conceptual disjuncture that resided at the heart of liberal progressive understandings of race, religion, and American public life. For many who supported Lear at the time, critique of the country's misgivings was what constituted the patriotic act itself. As such, giving space to various racial and ethnic minorities to voice their misgivings and complaints about America in prime time served two purposes simultaneously: it demonstrated a commitment to diversity and its representation as a form of patriotism while reinforcing the need for such attention in the first place.

In this sense, diversity itself became less about establishing a pluralistic environment in *I Love Liberty* and more about how best to represent it to supportive audiences in reminding them why they were committed to issues of diversity and racial inclusion as liberal progressive actors in politically hostile times. Seen in this contextual light, Shales's apt question concerning the timing of the Lear-authored exhortation speaks for itself. Sheen's celebratory request to his various viewing publics served as a rallying cry for Lear and others in the mainline in the wake of Reagan's election, which was made possible by their worst nightmare: Jerry Falwell and "the electronic church." Some may have loved America, but Lear wanted to make sure that America knew that he loved liberty. After all, *he* had what *they* did not—"stars like his."

Despite the impressive level of star power that *I Love Liberty* possessed, including the likes of Robin Williams, Gregory Hines, and the aforementioned Sheen, it could not reconcile the apparent contradiction in programming terms evident in the Lear-composed TV special. Shales was one of the first to identify the literal mixed messages of the variety show, but he was far from the only commentator to do so—liberal or conservative. In the pages of the *New York Times*, future *Time* writer Richard Zoglin titled his analysis of *I Love Liberty* "Is This Entertainment Special Promoting a Special Interest?" More pointed than Shales, Zoglin focused his attention on the support given to Lear by television network ABC, which totaled $1.8 million for production costs. "Is ABC, for instance, unfairly giving exposure to a controversial organization by running an 'entertainment' special it has produced? What are the chances that a man without the show-business clout . . . would have been able to command prime time for a two-hour special espousing the views of his organization? Perhaps most important, is the show setting a dangerous precedent, opening the door for networks to tele-vise other specials produced by more overtly political groups?"[32]

Unlike Shales and others, Zoglin saw past the individual political indiscretions of *I Love Liberty* in order to identify the most damaging dimension of Lear's politics-through-entertainment formula. While the show's association with Lear's nonprofit People for the American Way as well as ABC came off as a potential conflict of constitutional interests, especially to conservative viewers, the more pressing concern was whether the show's form (as opposed to its largely liberal mainline content) would set the stage for others to take advantage of Lear's clever rhetorical hedging for conservative causes.[33] "In effect," explained journalist John O'Connor, "he has tried to reclaim for all Americans those symbols and values that sometimes have seemed to be monopolized by groups with various narrow interests. This star-packed production is an exuberant celebration of the flag and patriotic songs and, most significantly, diversity of opinion."[34] The *Christian Science Monitor* echoed these sentiments, arguing that Lear's *I Love Liberty* "invests the love of freedom, liberty, and the flag symbol itself with a kind of natural and refreshing sophistication in which all Americans can join unashamedly."[35]

Despite these respective authors' support of *I Love Liberty* and its value as a civically minded composition, they also unknowingly gave voice to its convoluted commitment to diversity and its representation in American mass media. People for the American Way certainly claimed that it defended the First Amendment in the public square against those who would monopolize its application, but *I Love Liberty* was not solely a PFAW-authored product; instead, it was authored by none other than Norman Lear and others on behalf of the public interest. In this sense, the diversity of which Lear spoke through the cacophonous complaints of America's minority communities was perhaps not as diverse as it proclaimed to be, despite Sheen's passionate encouragements.

According to Shales, "The Rev. Jerry Falwell, head of the Moral Majority—and an enemy of Lear's group—wired Lear asking that he be allowed to speak on the program. Lear says he rejected the notion not because he didn't want Falwell, but because he didn't want speeches."[36] Again, Lear was able to categorize a particular debate based on the terms that fit him and his interests best. There is no question that *I Love Liberty* possessed any number of acts that could be defined or interpreted as "speeches," yet for Lear the particular word in question was almost superfluous if not for its ambiguity. Literally speaking, Falwell more than likely would have given a sermon or exhortation due to this professional training. As a master of connotation, Lear more than likely meant "speech" to imply that Falwell's delivery would have been irrelevant for his particular audience regardless. In this sense, Lear's rejection had *less* to do with Falwell's literal words, and *more* to do with Falwell as the very symbol of unadulterated political conservatism and religious fervor that PFAW attempted to curtail.

"Why should people in our business have to forfeit their right to speak out?" Lear asked as a form of retort. "Nobody says anything when Joe Coors, a head of a brewery, speaks out, or when J. Willard Marriott, the head of a big hotel chain, speaks out. Just because I made my achievements in show business, must I forfeit my rights, my values, as a citizen?[37] Lear's question is most certainly a valuable one. Those questioning the political intentions of both his programming (*All in the Family*) and his variety shows (*I Love Liberty*) did so because the content of Lear's writing and the manner in which he presented it often ran afoul of federal regulations that dictated the manner in which controversial issues were engaged in public venues—especially televised ones. No one at the time was saying that Lear could not "take a stand," including Jerry Falwell. Instead, what many of Lear's conservative detractors argued was that Lear voiced his opinion through means and venues that were otherwise beyond the pale of controversy as federally stipulated. After all, Lear himself, along with Larry Gelbart and others, had argued vehemently in federal court that shows like *MASH* and *All in the Family* served the public interest because they were *not* beholden to a particular political persuasion. Unlike the private businesses of Coors and Marriott, Lear used explicitly public funds and platforms in order to get his message out. This meant that he, unlike Coors, could not make similar arguments or take similar stands. Since Lear's activism depended on a publicly regulated entity, namely the airwaves, he, unlike Marriott, could not make explicitly political claims without violating the very credibility that allowed him to speak in the first place.

For one contemporary commentator on events past, Lear's experience in media gave him insight into how best to manipulate the regulatory system to protect his own interests while rejecting those that did not fit the religio-political protocols of the liberal public sphere. "Of course everyone has the right to free speech. Except one of the first things Norman Lear did as a political activist was to take legal action to apply the antiquated 'Fairness Doctrine' to limit the airtime and influence of televangelists," argues commentator Mark Hemingway. "Maybe Lear didn't have to beg for money like the televangelists he so despises, but he too profited handsomely from his demagoguery. And no one threatened him with the Fairness Doctrine . . . nor was it applied when ABC paid Lear and People for the American Way almost two million dollars to produce a primetime network special called *I Love Liberty*."[38]

All this is not to say that Lear's actions in any way negated or compromised his religious liberalism. He was relentless when it came to issues of religious diversity and tolerance; as such, Lear understood the Christian Right and its electronic church to be the greatest threats to American democracy because they theoretically compromised one of America's most cherished liberties—religious freedom itself. What I am saying, in short, is that Lear's spiritual politics were guided by two coconstitutive forces: a fierce commitment to First Amendment rights and a realist understanding of cultural politics. Lear knew he was walking a fine line with the law and with public opinion when it came to his unique brand of didactic entertainment television. Maybe the journalists had a point; maybe cultural clout counted for something after all—especially for the one responsible for the manifestation of "the Bunker Vote" less than ten years before.

Perhaps the clearest explanation of *I Love Liberty* and its creative vision came from coauthor and writer Martin Marty of the University of Chicago Divinity School. There, Marty served as professor of American church history as one of the most prolific and well-respected members of and contributors to the field of American religious history.[39] "Some of us bystanders felt that People for the American Way was being forced to be a mere respondent. Was it not time to set some terms?"[40] Like the organizational impetus of PFAW itself, *I Love Liberty* also attempted to reclaim a particular public vocabulary while protecting the rights of others to do the same. As a result, *I Love Liberty* was designed "not to take a stand on the great issues of the day (Panama Canal, Department of Education), but should provide a framework for debate about them."[41] When compared to Lear's descriptions of the same subject, Marty's seemed to be slightly askew. Lear defended his right to take stands as a loyal American citizen, yet his organization's "party ideologue," Marty, advised against the very same suggestion.

In this sense, shows like *All in the Family* and *Maude* were great not because Lear "took a stand," they were groundbreaking because they created space for their respective audiences to discuss the contents of the shows *alongside* Lear-generated frameworks. For Marty, Lear, and others, the work of putting the show together was about more than the production itself; it was a matter of effectively counterorganizing against a newly invigorated religio-political foe in the public square. "When the religious right grimly emerged, it was mad and it made other people mad," Marty remarked. "Let's play the game they play, it was said; let's get organized. How to do this without grimness? Among the counter organizers was television and cinema pathfinder Norman Lear. . . . We were making our statement."[42]

As previously argued, Lear's interfaith organizing on behalf of the American Way helped galvanize an entire religio-political community in responding to the establishment of a new conservative order. In addition to the ongoing work of People for the American Way at the time, Lear's decision to compose his form of resistance and organization through the variety show *I Love Liberty* with the help of countless Hollywood actors and activists further defined his contribution to larger debates surrounding religious freedom and conservative Protestantism in the public square. However, Lear rarely acted without the valuable counsel of his closest confidants, Marty included. In fact, Marty largely approved of what was eventually televised that night in the Los Angeles Sports Arena for the better part of two hours.

"I urged, as an historian, that such a show deal with history, however lightly," Marty encouraged. "The Muppets, doing the Constitutional Convention, made their point and more than satisfied mine. Judd Hirsch does an almost too optimistic celebration of a Jewish theory of American liberties. . . . Only one scene gave me pause, a slightly grim and then too partly affirmative 'Frustrated Americans' episode. It was the only one that had a tinge of 'knee-jerk liberalism' to it, but some whose knees don't jerk did find it among the more moving segments."[43] Like other contemporaneous commentators, Marty had similar reservations about the sketch where each "minority" complained about the state of American public life yet nevertheless acknowledged the country's unique contributions to the history of human liberty and freedom. Despite these thematic shortcomings, Marty was a firm supporter of the show, but less for its content as a prime-time television special and more for its cultural resonance that reverberated well beyond the confines of Southern California.

"The show sets out to display and quicken a sense of the contagion of liberty," Marty argued, "especially for a new generation that has no memories of 'before Vietnam and Watergate' and the angry, sullen times. . . . More must be done to restore the larger American community of public discourse. Who expects a two-hour television special to do that for them?. . . Some days civil people can become unlocked through celebration, in order to make their arguments more civil. *I Love Liberty* is a stab at that."[44] While the night itself was seemingly one of theatrics and entertainment, Marty's emphases told a completely different story. Each sketch possessed its own purpose and intended audience as part of a broader vision of civic life that I have described as the spiritual politics of religious liberalism.

The prime-time broadcast of *I Love Liberty* embodied Lear's style of religio-political engagement, which foregrounded popular culture and the sitcom as the primary arenas within which cultural warfare would unfold in the name of the American Way. Each sketch also possessed its own authors and actors, many of whom came from Hollywood or, in Marty's case, the storied yet sequestered halls of academia. As scholar of religion Andrea Most has argued more broadly, Lear's theatrics can be understood as a form of "theatrical liberalism" whereby Lear attempted to harmonize explicitly Jewish notions of self and citizenship with the broader contours of public Protestantism and/or the Protestant secular.[45] "The power of this popular culture resides not in its secular neutrality," argues Most, "but in its specific *spiritual vision*, one that makes use of secular cultural modes to express a morally coherent and passionately felt worldview."[46]

In light of this analytical context, perhaps Marty was onto something in his description of liberty-as-contagion. Maybe the show *did* unlock those otherwise locked in debate in order to begin the work of deliberation anew. Despite these possibilities, by utilizing prime-time programming as a venue for politics making, Lear opened himself up to valid critique from both sides of the aisle because he used public means for private purposes, namely those of his nonprofit organization and the network executives at ABC. This is not to say that Lear's claims or intentions were invalid or categorically wrong; it is to say that while the "complaint" sketch attempted to address systemic challenges of racial discrimination in America, it did so by reinscribing the unequal conditions and assumptions that produced such complaints to begin with by having a white character play the butt of the joke—not unlike the character of Archie Bunker on *All in the Family*. When considered aspirationally, the various sketches fulfilled their intended purposes as Marty described, to reinvigorate public life according to the dictates of religious liberalism, liberal democracy, and public reason. When examined critically, a different show rises to the interpretive surface for us to consider in light of the criticisms of Falwell, Wildmon, and others.

PATRIOTISM IN PRIME TIME: RACE, RELIGIOUS TOLERATION, AND THE PENDULUM OF LIBERTY

Upon the formation of People for the American Way, Marty gave Lear a very clear and concise list of suggestions concerning the composition and direction of the nonprofit in the public sphere. Surprisingly nonpartisan in its execution, Marty's list also served as an example of the initial conceptual framework that outlined *I Love Liberty* as a reflection of the spiritual politics of religious liberalism. More wishful than pragmatic, the six items spoke to what religious liberals like Lear and Marty aspired to for the American viewing public through their respective cultural productions. Directed at the New Right as both demographic and discursive reality, Marty advised the following: "*Never say* (1) that they have no right to speak up and organize, or (2) that they have a patent on single-issue politics, or (3) that religion and politics dare not mix, since all six of us were mixers." Marty then added, "(5) stress and demonstrate that a pluralist society has generated and can generate common stories, symbols, values, and hopes, and (6) have a good time doing so."[47]

While all of Marty's advice applies to *I Love Liberty* and its creative generation, only the final two items reflect the actual execution of the variety show itself.[48] In an attempt to create the common stories, symbols, values, and hopes that pluralist societies depended on for their survival, which included the likes of Martin Sheen, the Muppets, and Big Bird, Marty and others had to assume a conservative conceptual other in order to complete their theorizing of public space. This made the unlocking process of which Marty spoke that much more challenging to establish since freely articulated deliberation seemed to depend on monitoring, or at least addressing, the presence of individuals like Falwell and Robertson as potentially threatening forces.

As such, sketches that foregrounded racially specific complaint and exhortation may have made sense to those on the creative side of the camera, but to many at home, the thought of actors voicing criticisms of the country and thus the commercial industry that made their lives possible was the height of arrogance and condescension. Regardless of which side you were on, *I Love Liberty* was not simply a variety show like any other. Due to the timing of Lear's move from producer to activist, he was able to leverage network television against conservative political interests in a manner that few could hope to match due to his media notoriety and developing visibility as a "countermobilizer" from the civil religious mainline. To writer and editor Leslie Ward, the timing could not have been any better "since television is the battlefield where modern-day ideological wars are waged."[49] Lear could not have agreed more, if only he would admit it.

"Bringing *I Love Liberty* to fruition—before some ten thousand in person and millions on TV—was the headiest experience of my life," Lear admits. "On what other occasion might you see Robin Williams, as touching as we was hilarious, playing the American flag? Or Senator Barry Goldwater—likely the most conservative candidate to run for the presidency—introduce the most fantabulous opening this liberal could imagine?"[50] Despite Lear's humility, he was not simply "this liberal" when it came to how he applied his spiritual politics to the genre of the variety show, which was replete with dance numbers, singing routines, measured recitation, and passionate argumentation. Surrounded by some of the best and brightest of the writing and acting worlds, including writers Richard Alfieri, Rita Mae Brown, and Rick Mitz, Lear composed most of the sketches for *I Love Liberty* alongside his consultants Martin Marty and acclaimed writer and producer Norman Corwin. In fact, Corwin's work on *I Love Liberty* received particular attention from the *Christian Science Monitor* due to his radio work during World War II.[51]

I Love Liberty consisted of an opening song from a chorus of children followed by a variety of sketches, reenactments, and monologues by some of Hollywood's most recognizable faces. Once he appeased the network when it came to the bipartisan nature of the variety show, which was tenuous at best, Lear called upon the services of Jim Henson, Mary Tyler Moore, John Wayne, Gregory Hines, and others in hopes of not only entertaining America but also cultivating water-cooler talk about the issues of the day, which for Lear were obvious and clear.

The following analysis focuses on those sketches and numbers that illustrated the most significant dimensions of Lear's religio-political activism as an expression of the Religious Left's spiritual politics. Regardless of the form, from the first episode of *All in the Family* to his guerilla PSAs on behalf of People for the American Way, the content of Lear's civic engagement was often quite consistent. While the "complaint" sketch was criticized by Marty and various journalists for being the product of a "bleeding heart," it nevertheless attempted to demonstrate the importance of prophetic critique to the liberal religious imagination when it came to race and potential threats to American religious freedom. In particular, I focus my analytical attention on a recitation, a sketch, and a sermon in order to demonstrate how *I Love Liberty* theatrically enacted Lear's civil religious vision of American public life and its pluralistic constituents.

☙

I Love Liberty was just over two hours long and broadcast on ABC in prime time from the Los Angeles Sports Arena in the heart of Los Angeles, California. Following the show's stirring opening, which featured a stunning chorus of children's voices, the audience's attention was directed to a man dressed in a three-piece suit who strode confidently toward the stage. Many in the viewing audience already knew the man as actor Burt Lancaster, but his task that evening was to read a midcentury speech by Justice Learned Hand entitled "The Spirit of Liberty." Lear was quite fond of citing writings on liberty by Hand, one of America's most well-known circuit judges and judicial philosophers when it came to religious liberty and First Amendment rights. As previously argued, Lear relied a great deal philosophically on Hand's insights to outline much of his own thought (and, arguably, post–World War II religious liberalism in general) when it came to American public life and how it should be conducted. *I Love Liberty* was no different. Hand's words, read verbatim by Lancaster, set the conceptual stage for the rest of the show in its attention to issues of race, tolerance, and religious freedom.

"What then is the spirit of liberty?" Lancaster inquired of his audience. "I cannot define it, I can only tell you my own faith." A testimony of the spirit soon followed, yet in this instance, it was anything but one authored by the likes of a Pentecostal witness:

> The spirit of liberty is the spirit which is not too sure that it is right; the spirit of liberty is the spirit which seeks to understand the minds of other men and women; the spirit of liberty is the spirit which weighs their interest alongside its own without bias; the spirit of liberty remembers that not even a sparrow falls to earth unheeded; the spirit of liberty is the spirit of him who, near two thousand years ago, taught mankind that lesson it has never learned, but has never quite forgotten—that there may be a kingdom where the least shall be heard and considered side-by-side with the greatest.[52]

The words were powerful in themselves, but when delivered with Lancaster's rhythm and cadence, they took on a power all their own. Religious liberals like Lear and Marty valued deeply the empathetic imagination of Justice Hand in his emphasis on doubt, humility, and social equity in both the kingdom and in the courtroom. What is especially surprising, however, is how Christ-centered this rendering of spirit is despite its less than Christian admirer—Lear. Instead of turning to the writings of James, Frost, or Thoreau, Lear turned to the reflections of a constitutional judge who, at America's midcentury, followed the example of Christ in both word and deed in the name of the First Amendment. The decision to place this particular recitation at the beginning of the variety show, which was ultimately only one of many, suggests that it was also meant to define a common rhetorical agenda for the various performances of dance and speech. As long as the least would be first, as understood according to Lear's spiritual calculus, then all would be well in time. More important, Lancaster helped introduce Martin Sheen as one of the evening's most important characters as well as its emcee. "Congratulations, Americans," Sheen said with a wry smile, hands tucked into the side pockets of his dark-blue pants. "And welcome to *I Love Liberty*."

A number of sketches, dances, and performances followed Sheen's introductory remarks, including a conversation between the master of that evening's ceremonies and Jim Henson's Big Bird in full costume. The two discussed the nation's turbulent origins and the historical significance of the first meeting of the Continental Congress in 1774. Once again, the reenactment of the Congress that followed included additional members from Henson's catalog such as Miss Piggy, Kermit, Fozzie Bear, and Gonzo. After a rousing rendition of "When the Saints Go Marching In" sung over the top of "A Benevolent Brotherhood of Man," a disheveled-looking man dressed in a suit and tie walked onto the stage.[53] His stride was short, and his hands clasped his hat nervously, as if he was about to step into such a space for the very first time. Once the man reached his spot, he began to address the audience in what only can be described as a thick Eastern European Jewish accent. The man was Judd Hirsch, yet in this particular sketch, he went by the name of Kaminski.

After telling the viewing audience about his arrival in America in 1898 in the belly of an overcrowded ship, Kaminski went on to speak about an upbringing during the Great Depression of the 1930s. His family had found Kaminski's brother, Harry, dead, because of "the great crash." Undeterred, Kaminski assured his listeners that America always bounces back, and that Harry had given in too early. "America always bounces back!" Kaminski exclaimed from his theatrical stage. He then described how he liked to go to Union Square Park (more than likely in New York City) on Sundays in order to talk to the people about his ideas. As such, Kaminsky proceeded to address the audience as if it were his own park-hosted audience. "People of the park!" Kaminski yelled.

"Yoo-hoo! Yoo-hoo! Look at him," a woman from the crowd yelled back, interrupting him. "Listen to him—mister public speaker." It was none other than Kaminski's wife, Ethel, played by Valerie Harper, who proceeded to lambast her husband, Morris, about his incessant speeches and boring talks on the seventh day.

"You cannot have daily democracy without daily citizenship," Kaminski replied, amplifying the volume of his voice to match his wife's. "They are here, looking at a citizen, doing his daily."

"Then why do they throw things at you, Morris?" Ethel yelled back.

"Maybe an orange, maybe an apple," Kaminski admitted, "but at least it shows that they're listening!!

"There's a lot that we've got to understand here," Kaminski insisted. "And what we've got here is liberty." For Kaminski, American liberty resembled the motion of a pendulum. The more people worked on behalf of liberty, the less often people would go without it. In other words, the higher the swing up, the more liberty there is in the world. "More up, less back! The citizens . . . you have to make it swing! More up!" In short order, Kaminski gave his philosophy a name: the Kaminski Pendulum Theory.

Nothing about Hirsch's character was left to chance from his clothing and message to this accent and theatrical style. Kaminski was both immigrant *and* American, one who possessed memories of waves and seas and a shining Lady Liberty on the horizon. He also was directly impacted by the stock market collapse and the Great Depression that followed, not unlike Lear himself. While the manner in which liberty is manufactured or produced by the people was left undescribed by Kaminski, his message was understood loud and clear by the viewing audience that night—democracy is made possible through citizen action. For coauthor and reviewer Martin Marty, Hirsch's portrayal of Kaminski spoke to a "Jewish theory of American liberties, one that moves with a pendulum that swings ever higher after setbacks."[54]

For Andrea Most, this idea was exactly the type of cultural production that could be understood as theatrically liberal in both content and argumentative agenda—it constructed a particular notion of self that was at once traditional and modern, secular and religious, civil and uncivil. It may have sounded like the old world, not unlike Kaminsky himself, but it was familiar with the modern rhythms and sensibilities of the soundstage and the television camera by the 1970s. More important, theatrical liberalism spoke through the language of rights and religion instead of the language of action and obligation. This signaled a fundamental transition into a modern subject who thereby occupied a similarly modern liberal democracy according to the schema of the lone, bifurcated individual situated under the canopy of the Protestant secular.[55]

In this sense, *I Love Liberty* served as an illustrative example of how Lear at once adapted and contributed to a larger secular Jewish culture, one that was identifiable largely by its spiritual content or theatrical vision of public social action over private interiorized virtue. This personal-as-political approach to addressing social challenges not only reflected the literal philosophical fallout from the similarly articulated clarion call of the previous decade, it also spoke to Lear's tendency to write himself and his own spiritual vision into his compositions for both stage and screen. For Yiddish scholar Jeremy Dauber, the show demonstrated how Lear and his varied cultural productions "Americanized the Jewish milieu of his upbringing" for hundreds of millions of viewers for more than a decade's time. As a result, "If Jews were becoming Americans, then Americans," concludes Dauber, "were also, in their own disguised way, Jewish."[56] Kaminski was the paradigmatic example for this argument, evidence of an assimilated and then reproduced subject willing to teach others on behalf of the spirit of liberty and the First Amendment—with a thick accent for comedic effect. The pendulum's animating spirit was certainly evident that night in Los Angeles for Lear and company, but it was only one dimension of his religious liberal sensibilities as witnessed in prime time. Another was religious freedom.

In this sense, *I Love Liberty* functioned not only as a partially subsidized PSA for People for the American Way and ABC programming, it was also the theatrical expression of Lear's larger spiritual politics as understood on racial, religious, and First Amendment terms as a form of obligation, or *mitzvot*.[57] To Lear and his supporters, action was called for because foreign forces threatened the very cultural vitality that *I Love Liberty* spoke of and sought to defend.[58] This custodial impulse to protect the contents and designs of the public square is not only uniquely characteristic of religious liberal thought, it also reflects a specifically Jewish notion of obligation that tends to place individual impetus below communal knowledge—especially when it comes to the stage and the theater.

Lear was invested in such a project largely due to his own experiences with religious discrimination, yet he was also responding to what he saw as an act of spiritual tyranny in how the American Right had claimed exclusive rights to American patriotism and the nation's flag. In order to accomplish this feat, however, Lear had to ground his claims in the broader American Way tradition, one that tended to downplay religious difference and particularity in the name of interreligious cooperation. As a result, the religious difference of a given individual could be empathized with, but that same person's political difference could present the religious liberal with a serious dilemma—especially if it was fundamentalist in any way.

In her own study of some of America's midcentury Jewish authors, Andrea Most writes, "Although these writers and artists come from a wide variety of Jewish backgrounds, they are united by a liberal Jewish perspective that insists on the potential compatibility of Judaism with American liberalism." As such, "they created a new form of secular Judaism, expressed in a hybrid and enormously successful popular culture, which tapped into the theatricality of American democracy and spoke (and continues to speak) to a broad American public."[59] *I Love Liberty* was no different, especially when it featured civil disagreement between conservatives and liberals for its own didactic sake. Because it was Lear at the narrative helm, the actors called upon to satisfy both reluctant ABC executives and the federal government were John Wayne and Jane Fonda. "Naturally, I think she's a little bit messed up with her thinking, and I guess she feels the same way about me," Wayne admitted. "That's our right as Americans." Fonda concluded the piece by reading the First Amendment verbatim, pausing briefly on the freedoms of assembly and religion. To emphasize the point, the sketch that followed would leave no one confused about how best to negotiate religious difference.

"I am the Reverend Timothy Newport. The year is 1782. George Washington is now fifty years old." The man who uttered these words was tall and slender, dressed in the long black formal robes of the church, yet he commanded the small stage with a strength fitting a superhero. "Oh," he explained hurriedly, "I'm the pastor at First Congregational Church in Todbridge, Massachusetts. But I've been told that I'm not needed." Taking his position atop a formidable lectern, actor Christopher Reeve began his sermon confidently as pastor-in-residence of *I Love Liberty*. "My dear brothers and sisters, I would like to use this, my final sermon, to discuss what I believe to be the Lord's wish for all of us." Yet before Newport could continue, a stern voice bellowed from somewhere in the crowd. "THE LORD'S WISH!?!? Or your wish, Reverend Newport?" The man who addressed the reverend was dressed in a somewhat equally disheveled suit, his collared shirt unbuttoned under a wrinkled suit jacket. His face was as weathered as it was stern in its questioning. "Tell me please," actor Walter Matthau implored. "The Lord's wish? Or your wish?"

The question was as timely as it was representational for its moment. For many on both sides of the aisle, both Lear and Falwell could appear to be misguided at best and delusional at worst. Even their respective supporters could disagree with either one of them on definitional grounds—including *The Mary Tyler Moore Show* producer Grant Tinker. How was one to know who was right in the age of the think tank, direct mail, and the electronic church? The man who spoke for the mainline, the given majority of American Christianity? Or perhaps Kaminski himself, the one with the steady cadence who seemed to speak on behalf of both a minority and a majority population at the same time? Whose wish, indeed? Newport's? Lear's? Or Falwell's?

Newport responded in kind. "Well, I'm not trying to speak to change your mind, Mathew Stone. But the war for independence is over. And in that war, we died side by side with Catholics and with Baptists. And it is time now to learn to live side by side."

"I don't have much book learnin'," the man admitted in response, "but I know what's right for me and mine. And I can't see livin' cheek-to-jowl with no Catholic."

Another voice echoed from the crowd in support, "We have just fought a war to ensure our own religious freedoms, and we will not have that threatened now by a papist conspiracy!"

"Card playin', dancin'," Stone yelled. "Drunkenness!"

"Those ways may not be your ways Mathew Stone," Newport responded wearily. "And their ways are not my ways either. But it is time now to decide for every family how it is going to be for them, as long as what they do does not impinge on others."

"Matthew Stone," Newport said, turning his attention once more back to the lectern and its superior position relative to his interlocutors, "there is indeed one truth for you, and one truth for your neighbor. You use the word heresy. Heresy! Well . . . do you think it is really heresy to believe that all people can seek happiness as individuals and still share a common future as Americans? I ask you urgently to ponder that question." Closing his eyes, Reeve as Newport brought the conversation to a close with a prayer. "May the Lord grant that however different our sentiments may be, that one day we will be united in love and that this church and that this nation will live under his grace."

The exchange between Superman turned New England minister and what appeared to be a slightly dense farmer played by Matthau may have confused the crowd slightly, but its overall message was anything but opaque. While the sketch borrowed many turns of phrase from more contemporary understandings of the "conservative" voice as a Pentecostal voice, here represented by the colonial farmer and his inability to cope with Catholic neighbors and dancing, it nevertheless spoke to a theme that ran throughout much of the history of American religion that coauthor Martin Marty taught to countless students over the course of his storied career at the University of Chicago Divinity School: to be American is to dissent. It is distinctly *un*-American, however, to discriminate against one's own neighbor in the name of the Lord. Or, in the case of *I Love Liberty*, it is utterly un-American to discriminate in the name of someone's race.

As alluded to earlier, the initial reviews of *I Love Liberty* focused their critical attention on one sketch in particular: "The Angry Fill-in-the-Blank" sketch.[60] In fact, words like "preachy" and "bland" cascaded across the pages of reviews from coast to coast. Even consultant and cowriter Martin Marty acknowledged the sketch's less than desired composition. Regardless of its less than perfect execution, the sketch remains incredibly valuable in identifying both the strengths and limitations of religious liberalism in general and political liberalism in particular when it comes to understanding race and racial difference. The fact that the characters were typically referred to as "an angry black" and "an angry Hispanic" by both Lear and his respective writers did not immediately inspire confidence in reviewers in newspapers or at home watching. In short, the group onstage included an "angry" black man, a Hispanic man, an Indian (Native American) man, a gay white man, and a white woman. Each member of the group voiced his or her respective dissent in the land otherwise known for its opportunities— except for one.

His voice was heard, but usually because it served a larger comedic purpose as comic relief at his own expense. Only, in this case, his expense was not simply his own individual expense but the expense of all of those people who looked and sounded like him. Those who complained about high property taxes amid increasing racial diversity. Those who understood themselves as rule followers and hard workers only to have their places in the proverbial line compromised by those who were less deserving in their eyes.[61] Once again, in the name of fairness, equality, and didactic improvement, another working-class white had to be instrumentalized for the sake of Lear's comedic sensibilities on behalf of the

American Way. "My name...just call me angry. You know, America could work for these folks if they just called themselves Americans. Not blacks, not Hispanics, but just Americans. I've worked hard all of my life, and a good part of my tax money has gone to help them. But now I'm hurting. I need some help. But that's not the same thing as saying that America doesn't work for me, because it does."

Here, a heartfelt plea was heard on behalf of working-class whites played by actor Dick Van Patten. Even though the character was not able to articulate himself racially like the others, or at least chose not to do so, he most certainly represented a Bunker-like character to the audience and in comparison to the other racially and ethnically specific groups represented onstage. What Archie was not able to do, however, Patten as the "angry white" was able to do flawlessly—he asked for help. Despite the tone of this request, the working-class white slowly began to turn into a prop as the sketch neared its end. Each character in turn stood up to remind the audience of his or her argument—in other words, why they were angry collectively yet still appreciative of American civil liberties—and Patten responded in kind.[62] "They lower my property values, and they don't stop complaining!" "They take away our jobs, and they don't stop complaining!" And last, following the line of "the angry woman," "We let them out of the house, and they don't stop complaining!"

Here, a matter of minutes after the previous plea, the heterosexual white male goes from one among many to comedy punchline. The pleas that had earlier been heard clearly from "the angry white" were no longer credible because his purpose onstage had been reduced to a form of comic relief.[63] Despite these seemingly insurmountable differences in race, gender, and class, the group was able to close the sketch on a note of agreement. Articulated in unison, with an air of confident trepidation, the performers came to their conclusion collectively through the words of Lincoln: "America is the last, best hope of this earth." In other words, despite the challenges that the actors spoke of at length, America itself and those who called themselves Americans were very much worth celebrating—even if Lear and his supporters were still coming to terms with a Reagan White House that had been made possible by an ascendant evangelical age.[64] In fact, the forlorn nature of the above statement about America arguably reflected the less than settled organizing of religious liberals over and against Christian conservatism through venues such as network television and the Lear-authored variety show.

As such, the at-times self-congratulatory tone of *I Love Liberty*, first identified by the show's initial reviewers, spoke to a community that was somewhat lost for words—sure of itself in terms of what it valued but utterly unsure of how to best convince others, namely "the angry white," of its cultural and spiritual salience *for them*.[65] We heard a similarly pitched claim earlier in the variety show from emcee Martin Sheen, yet it was expressed slightly differently, in hopes of achieving the same effect relative to its audience. "Let's hear it for us!" Sheen had yelled over and over, reminding those in the audience and at home of how special America was not only due to its diverse inhabitants but, more important, due to those who fought on their behalf. Why else celebrate American liberty if not to identify those who understood it best in the public square and those who seemingly meant to destroy it?

By the sketch's end, the idea of America being the last, best hope had done its job; where there had once been a collection of individual voices, each spoken in turn, there was now a singular chorus of voices, thereby subsuming the angry white within a canopy of pluralist consensus. This act of consensus creation interpellated lower-class white voices as either bigoted or simply ignorant for the sake of a joke. Unfortunately for Lear, such stereotypes would come back to haunt him and other religious liberals as not one but two Republican candidates from the worlds of movies and television would become American presidents due in large part to "Bunker-like" working-class support from individuals like the angry white.

CONCLUSION: BARRY GOLDWATER AND THE GREAT COMPROMISE

In the end, many of the reviewers' comments were right. *I Love Liberty* was a throwback to a prewar America, one that was defined either by the interfaith optimism of America's interwar period through the actions of the NCCJ or by the midcentury notion of a "Tri-Faith America," of traveling priests, pastors, and rabbis, that held the country to its Protestant promise of religious liberty and freedom of speech.[66] While the notion of nostalgia has typically been associated with conservative forms of political mobilization in the twentieth century, it could just as easily be applied to the spiritual politics of Norman Lear and other religious liberals in the Religious Left who sought to enact their own vision of the public square and its diverse inhabitants. But what cost would much of this organizing exact from the very same public arena and those who defended it? In other words, did Lear open the proverbial door for others to walk through by composing a prime-time variety show that was partly subsidized by ABC? Was Lear's refusal to let Falwell onto *I Love Liberty* his implicit recognition of the implications of his own brand of Hollywood-based activism? And last, what made Lear's politics more conducive to television and its broadcasting when compared to

Falwell's? Both men occupied positions of influence relative to their respective constituencies, yet it was Lear who was worried that Falwell would give a "speech," and thus disqualify himself from the festivities.

In reality, both Lear and Falwell helped generate a particular religio-political consciousness for their respective supporters when it came to "framing" either "the Left" or "the Right," yet it was Lear who feared tyranny from America's right wing when it was Lear himself who had exclusive access to an otherwise publicly disseminated resource—the airwaves.[67] As already identified, Lear negotiated this somewhat nonsensical notion by arguing that his programming was "bipartisan" and as such was not simply a platform for his newly formed nonprofit organization People for the American Way but rather a momentous occasion for celebrating America's First Amendment rights and George Washington's birthday. He accomplished this by stating that multiple conservative or nonpartisan voices were part of the show's design and programming, including the aforementioned John Wayne, Lady Bird Johnson, and former president Gerald Ford.

While this may have been a smart move on Lear's part at the time, what arguably was not smart was including someone like former Arizona senator Barry Goldwater in one of the show's opening numbers. For, if anything, Lear's inclusion of Goldwater spoke to a continued and enduring misunderstanding of or lack of respect for conservative voices—regardless of social class. Lear's agenda had been to confront a rampant conservatism that had appropriated the American flag in an exclusive manner, yet he arguably ended up giving it further leverage by placing Goldwater front and center—the man responsible for singlehandedly setting the GOP on a new, more unruly course with the help of the Sunbelt and its various inhabitants.[68]

As it happened, Goldwater's appearance followed Sheen's robust celebration of America's ethnic and racial diversity. Sheen had brought the audience to its feet by seemingly shouting out each and every race or ethnicity in attendance, and the crowd responded as if on cue. If following the rules of comedy, this moment would have been followed by a more subdued delivery or performance within the variety show—an exhortation or perhaps a historical reenactment of nineteenth-century slave life. In this instance, Goldwater walked purposefully onto the stage from behind the curtain, black-rimmed glasses shining brightly against the ever-brightening lights of Hollywood. After waiting for the applause to die down, Goldwater greeted his audience in his characteristically measured voice.

"They wanted me to introduce the next musical number, and I suggested something patriotic—very patriotic, that's my style. What's wrong with a little flag waving?" Goldwater remarked. "Well, not everyone agreed with me. When it came to staging this next musical number, we argued those two points among ourselves. Half of us, my side, wanted to make this number really big, super patriotic. And the rest, you know, wanted to be subtle about it. So we did what all Americans do when they are in absolute disagreement: we compromised." As the sketch unfolded, the audience quickly caught on to the fact that Goldwater was overselling the compromise. The performance ended up using multiple marching bands and countless balloons and dancers—so many, in fact, that the larger joke would not have worked without it. "And that," Goldwater declared, "was our compromise."

Not unlike Archie Bunker or "the angry white," Goldwater's purpose that night was an instrumental one—namely to allow Lear to make a broader point about American civic life and how it should be conducted at the expense of the conservative. The audience heard nothing about the *content* of Goldwater's presence; it only knew him as a precategorized entity, one that was ultimately not suitable to the type of public square Lear himself envisioned. Not only was Goldwater's failed campaign in Arizona responsible for introducing direct mail to conservative mobilization efforts in the post–World War II period, it also incorporated new political actors and groups in the electoral process, including the likes of Robert Welch and the John Birch Society. Goldwater's election documentary, titled *Choice*, also helped introduce the image of "two Americas" into American political life as it deftly utilized images of crime and black violence to galvanize its viewers into action.[69]

In other words, when comparing the content of Lear's spiritual politics to that of Goldwater's, the two could not have been more different. In fact, the idea of "the masses" that many liberal religious actors feared from the Right was embodied in the very communities that were drawn to Goldwater and his message within the burgeoning Sunbelt.[70] Without hearing Goldwater speak, however, the audience would know nothing about this message or longer history besides what they already knew of Goldwater himself. As such, Goldwater's presence functioned less as a conservative voice within a chorus of voices and more as a prop used to make a larger didactic point about the value of compromise in American public life.[71]

☙

While Lear certainly championed the civic values he spoke of, including religious toleration, deliberation, and compromise, each value only made sense within the larger constellation of ideas and concepts that I have thus far identified as a spiritual politics. Lear's usage of the writings of Justice Learned Hand to ground much of his public philosophy concerning religion's proper relationship to politics spoke to this passion and commitment to First Amendment rights, yet the notion of liberty on display in *I Love Liberty* was not as expansive as Sheen, Lear, and even Marty had hoped it would be. Combined with the fact that Falwell was not allowed to speak due to his potential speechmaking, Goldwater's largely ceremonial and thus instrumental role within *I Love Liberty* spoke to a fundamental flaw in Lear's and the Religious Left's broader understanding of conservatism and its varied history of political engagement.

One could conclude that the apparent successes of Lear's television programming in both the variety and sitcom forms came at the expense of the very religiopolitical aspirations foregrounded in *I Love Liberty*. "Paradoxically," argues historian Jennifer Burns, "when they turned to culture, liberals lost the ability to understand how conservatives connected with a larger audience for they stopped taking conservative arguments seriously."[72] Relative to other sources of liberal religious action in the public square, this sentiment elegantly explains how and why television programming in general, and late-night commentary in particular, tends to be so disconnected from the conservative subjects it appears to know something about. As such, network television shows continue to have a direct effect on how conservatism is perceived and thus consumed by their various viewing audiences and political constituencies.

Not only did Lear rely on the tools of culture exclusively for his various civil religious projects, his strong resistance to Falwell's involvement also spoke to his understanding of religion itself as always and already conducive to civility and public deliberation. In many ways, this characteristic of American religious liberal thought perfectly encapsulated broader Enlightenment notions of religion as reasonable and guided most strongly by critical thought, deliberation, and public debate. "This was religion prescribed for the mind where in effect the public disciplined the private, where standards of conduct drawn from social experience and rational argumentation, and not from dogma, ordered and admonished the conscience."[73]

Defined within such a public, the category of religion itself functioned less as a tool of liberation as it often has, and more as an example of categorical and thus practical *constraint* relative to conservative Protestant religious practice and political mobilization in the public square. The category of race functioned similarly as each "angry minority" spoke to the enduring challenges of American race relations through his or her respective truth—except one. He was known simply as "angry," but why? Why had Lear chosen to write this character in such a manner? Purely for comedic effect? Or perhaps because he himself did not know *how* to write such a character outside of its liberally authored interpellated image of "the conservative" and thus the retrograde political subject.

In this sense, Lear pushed the genre of satire to its logical conclusion—it had backfired upon its own author, revealing the somewhat compromised inner thoughts of one of America's most beloved figures in television history. Only, in this instance, the laughter that followed tended to divide more often than it united. More precisely, it was a form of unity forged out of a tacit agreement concerning who could be properly political and on what grounds. In short, the nature of the political subject itself was on the line as Lear and Falwell established their respective corners of an increasingly mediated public sphere in the name of the First Amendment.

Conclusion

Religion, Politics, and the Public Square—2019

On October 8, 2015, former CEO of Columbia Pictures and chairman of Coca-Cola Fay Vincent authored a piece for the *Treasure Coast Palm* entitled "Examining the Role of Religion in 'the American Way.'" Vincent's tale was one of a common yet complicated genealogical ancestry. Not only did Lear and Vincent share a geographical upbringing on the East Coast in New Haven, Connecticut, Lear also consulted Vincent during the seminal organizational moment for Lear's nonprofit People for the American Way. In his piece, Vincent reminded Lear of his many objections to PFAW's original religio-political agenda made at the time, including the argument that defended the application of religion to politics in the name of the Jews during the Second World War.

To Vincent, Lear's organization represented a hostile critic of explicitly religious claims in the political square. "Is it not the American way," Vincent asked, "to find in religion the light to illuminate moral teachings?" On some level, Lear could agree with Vincent—to the extent that the conversation never made it to the "*which* moral teachings" part. Rehearsing a familiar argument in favor of de facto religious tests when running for the American presidency, Vincent argued that Americans have a "right and duty" to "judge a person on any aspect of that person's total personal, and religious beliefs."[1] Less than three weeks later, Lear authored his own response to Vincent's claims in an equally public forum—the Huffington Post.

"People for the American Way has never argued that people should not bring their religious and moral perspectives into public life," responded Lear in his October 21 piece entitled "Ben Carson and the American Way." "What troubled me about the political televangelists of the day was not that they were encouraging fellow conservative Christians to get involved in politics, but that they disparaged the faith and patriotism of people who didn't share their religious beliefs and right-wing political views."[2] Vincent had come to Carson's defense when Carson admitted that he would not support a Muslim presidential candidate who practiced Sharia law. These arguments caught Lear's attention because they were exclusionary and thus counter to the American Way tradition he had so vigorously defended for the past half century. Unlike Vincent, however, Lear argued that civic life did not necessarily depend on the shared illumination of seemingly universal moral teachings despite his own commitments to many of them as a religious liberal. "As Kennedy made clear," Lear argued, "what unites us as Americans is not a set of religious beliefs, but the US constitution, which guarantees freedom of religion for all peoples and prohibits any religious test for public office."

Not only do these particular arguments continue to characterize much of our contemporary political debate, they also eerily resemble the exchange that Lear initially had with President Ronald Reagan in the pages of *Harper's* magazine. Despite the nearly three decades that separated the two debates, parallel issues continued to be at stake for the respective combatants. Over and against Reagan's association with the "Christian Nation movement," Lear argued in negative terms against Vincent's defense of America's *positive* freedoms of religion since it supported exclusionary evaluations of presidential candidates. Additionally, Lear argued that the nation's constitutional protections of freedom *from* religion were more significant than those that encouraged freedom *for* religion. The fact that both men were discussing the appropriateness of right belief and religious tests in American public life only fortified Lear's defense of the separation of church and state and its subsequent negative freedoms and liberal principles of public reason and civil deliberation.

What Lear did not necessarily realize at the time of PFAW's formation, however, was that his own thinking tended to take on a similarly exclusionary and thus a classically liberal tone when confronted with conservative religiosity in the public sphere—both at home and abroad. This connection in the liberal imagination between "homegrown Ayatollahs" in the United States and Iranian "fundamentalists" in the Middle East, one on full display in the Vincent-Lear conversation over Sharia law, helped make possible the invention of both the Christian Right and a newly invigorated rendering of fundamentalism as uniquely liberal conceptions of unruly public religion within a liberal democratic polity.[3] Said in slightly different terms, fundamentalists like Falwell and others became known or subject to what could be understood as a larger secular calculus of American public life once they began organizing against the various "social issues" of the day.[4] As one of the most public defenders of the American public square within the Religious or Spiritual Left, Lear helped reinvigorate related notions of "the fundamentalist" through his own programming and publications as well as his theatrical productions in prime time in the name of the American Way.

In this sense, Lear's understanding of "religion" as a largely circumscribed public entity could not have been farther away from Falwell's conception as always and already Bible-believing and emboldened to remake the world in its image. As a result, individuals like Falwell possessed "a religion" in so far as it could be understood on the terms established theoretically by Lear and practically by the liberal state. Not unlike depictions of nineteenth-century Mormonism's encounter with similar liberal norms and expectations, notions of the Christian Right arguably emerged when they did because they took part in a similar process of state-sponsored interpellation highlighted elegantly by a form of secular knowledge articulated and disseminated by Lear and his supporters on behalf of the public interest. Like the fundamentalists of which Lear and other religious liberals spoke in both print and televised form, "Mormonism does not cease being a 'religion,'" argues literary critic Peter Coviello. "It *becomes*, rather, a religion by the lights of secularism."[5] Read in this manner, we can hold Lear and the Religious Left accountable for their not-so-inconsiderable role in helping to generate the very form of fanatical religion that Lear fought so hard *against* over the course of his storied career in the public eye.

⟨☙⟩

This study has argued that since the beginning of the 1960s, the United States and its citizens have engaged one another in prolonged cultural warfare over the most fundamental assumptions about the relationship between religion, the state, and the protection of the public good.[6] On the one hand, Lear's upbringing in the 1930s introduced him to a commitment to the public interest in the form of the New Deal and its social programming. On the other, the same moment introduced him to the theoretical need to curtail a given citizen's freedom of speech if not articulated in the terms of the public interest. In this sense, both FDR and Father Charles Coughlin influenced Lear's understanding of the proper relationship between religion and liberal democracy as a spiritual liberal, which called for tolerance, empathy, and diversity in public life in equally accessible terms. As such, the spiritual politics of the Religious Left were most evident as a theory of religion and liberal democracy in two contradictory yet inextricable ways: abhorrence of the Christian Right's exclusionary politics *and* the commitment to the separation of church and state. As such, Lear made his own contributions to the history of liberal framing of conservative religiosity dating back at least to the writings of H. L. Mencken in the 1920s and later midcentury studies of conservative anxiety and anti-intellectualism.[7] In short, one could argue that this contradiction between antipathy and empathy lies at the very heart of liberal secular governance—the assumption that religious exuberance is best practiced in the privacy of one's own home, especially if it is conservative in content or practice.

Lear's spiritual liberalism found a supportive yet divided audience in his situation comedies *All in the Family* and *Maude*. I have argued that one of the most understudied ways in which religious and spiritual liberals have enacted their politics in public, for better and for worse, is through various artistic and cultural productions—especially on prime-time television. Lear's programming, however, did not emerge in a vacuum. Instead, Lear and others relied on a sophisticated form of comedic satire to establish "relevance programming" as part of the 1970s television network landscape. While shows such as *MASH* and *The Mary Tyler Moore Show* contributed significantly to this new type of topical programming, it was Lear's catalog in particular that established this specific form of didactic comedy as understood through the virtual classroom of the situation comedy, or sitcom. As such, Lear's shows presented an idealized form of American civic life based on the fundamental principles of deliberation, civility, and public reason that left little room for conservative forms of religiosity and politics making.

Additionally, Lear's characters, including Archie and Meathead, said much about the increasingly antagonistic relationship between the country's working class and its emergent student-worker population. Meathead's interests in sociology identified him with the emerging New Class while Archie's resentment of his son-in-law's socioeconomic interests identified him with the not-so-silent majority. Little did Lear know that it would be this constituency that would go on to redefine the GOP according to more Western and Southern regional interests—including those of conservative Protestants in the Sunbelt that stretched from Southern California to Arizona to North Carolina to Florida.[8] In short, these realignments arguably laid the groundwork for the religio-political climate that continues to define American public life today in a key of polarization—the culture wars.

Lear's defense of the airwaves unfolded according to the public interest, a hotly debated concept dating back to the origins of the FCC and its exclusionary stipulations concerning Father Coughlin's radio addresses—the very same ones that had shaped Lear's own sense of personhood as an ethnic outsider to the American melting pot. These debates are significant because they identified prime-time television as the next battleground of the culture wars in late twentieth-century

America. In this sense, Lear can be understood as one of America's earliest culture warriors as part of the Religious Left, one who went on to oppose more well-known warriors from the Right such as Jerry Falwell and Pat Robertson. This type of reception certainly did more to reify the differences between individuals like Lear and Falwell, but it was also how the public at large understood the conflict between television producer and televangelist. Either way, the point of contention during these debates was arguably over the power of the prefix and its disseminatory powers: *tele*-vision.

Lear's decision to leave television for nonprofit activism by way of People for the American Way and its star-studded variety show *I Love Liberty* helped institutionalize the spiritual politics of the Religious Left in a public setting—the third sector of American public life. Reflecting his spiritual politics and religious liberal commitment to civility and the separation of church and state, Lear toured the country in order to address the inroads that conservative politicians and evangelists had made into the political process. For many at the time, such inroads were understood as the "emergence" of the Christian Right, an observation that spoke to liberal understandings of conservative religion as always ever maturing and developing.

Lear was instrumental in this instructional process, one that relied on journalists, politicians, entertainers, and writers in the formation of the Christian Right as both rhetorical tool and metonym for conservative Protestantism in late twentieth-century America. His variety show, appropriately titled *I Love Liberty*, explored similar themes of religious and racial toleration for one's fellow citizen as an instance of a left-wing patriotic rally. It also served as an instance of theatrical liberalism, a uniquely Jewish way of understanding the sacrality of the stage and the subsequent obligation to it and those who stood upon it.[9] In addition, it spoke to Lear's attempts to calibrate a form of American Judaism according to the dictates of a liberal democracy. As a result, Lear's sketches illustrated how Jews assimilated into a foreign culture by voicing a largely *secular* vision of public life that was conducive to both tradition and personal invention before the bright lights of Hollywood.

Following its official formation, Lear's People for the American Way went on to play a significant leadership role within a larger mobilizing front that included liberal progressive Protestants, Catholics, and Jews from New York to Hollywood. Such organizational fervor reflected the liberal antagonism directed toward the conservative policies and constituencies of then President Reagan and his supporters in the Christian Right. Lear assumed a predominant leadership position within multiple progressive religious communities throughout the 1970s, including the ecumenical mainline, the Protestant mainline, and interfaith groups as well as more secular organizations such as the American Civil Liberties Union. Rather than an aberration in the long history of religious liberal organizing, this moment was, in fact, a culminating one as liberal religious sentiment continued its migration beyond institutional church walls and onto the front pages of the *New York Times* and *Los Angeles Times*—only this time, it was in the key of Lear's spiritual politics.[10]

❧

Lear's visionary position within ecumenical, interfaith, and mainline Protestant circles speaks to one of the many myths in the study of American religions addressed and challenged by this monograph. Rather than contribute to a story of American secularization during the twentieth century, Lear and his diverse supporters created their own forms of religious liberal mobilization in response to their conservative counterparts.[11] In fact, one could argue that both Lear and his detractors possessed their own understandings of secularism and the duties of the secular state regarding charismatic spiritual or religious outbursts in public.[12] However, Lear and PFAW were not acting as a vanguard force within religious liberalism during the 1980s but rather functioned as a rearguard faction of concerned citizens who feared the shifting grounds of religious claims in American public life spurred on by the electronic church and its conservative supporters. In this sense, Lear's nonprofit certainly gave the Religious Left a voice to address both public policy and the moral fiber of the nation, but it nevertheless embodied the same philosophical and theoretical shortcomings that plagued Lear and others throughout the 1970s—cultural *influence* meant more than political *power* with conservatives "hijacking religion" for their own insidious purposes.

Lear's role as the founder of the nonprofit People for the American Way speaks to the need for more study of the religious, spiritual, and economic interests of corporate entities and their employees in the study of American religion. Studies such as Kathryn Lofton's *Oprah: Gospel of an Icon*, Darren Grem's *The Blessings of Business: How Corporations Shaped Conservative Christianity*, and Kevin Kruse's *One Nation Under God: How Corporate America Invented Christian America* demonstrate the efficacy of research and analysis based on the top floors of corporations as supplementary studies to those still attuned to the proverbial grassroots. Such a change in academic vantage would be especially productive for those studying the history of the Christian Right since much of its study has assumed the importance of the grass roots, and for good reason. At this moment, however, there is arguably a need for more top-down studies of the same subjects due simply to the influence that marketers and business executives have had and continue to have on the formation of conservative religious constituencies in the United States. In many ways, the work of such marketers contributed to the fall of the Religious Left in their clever appropriations of single-issue advocacy and direct mail on behalf of a Christian nation—real or imagined.

For my purposes, a Hollywood community of largely liberal Jewish writers and directors during the early 1970s served a larger descriptive and categorical agenda of naming a *politics of spiritual liberalism* in late twentieth-century America. This attention to corporate power, particularly in the form of liberal political and cultural influence, would be enhanced if focused on liberal religious actors like Norman Lear, Martin Marty, and journalist Bill Moyers. Due to the power that various historians, sociologists, and scholars of religion have given conservative religiosity in American religious history since the country's midcentury, liberal culture warriors like Lear have been largely ignored either as part of the mainstream or due to their cultural ubiquity. These types of studies have arguably defined the field since the 1980s, but if we foreground Lear and his interests in the public square, we are better able to understand how terms like "the Christian Right" and "the Religious Left" are part of longer active histories of liberal interpellation and conservative authorship. My attempt in this study has been to open up some of these wider connections in the study of American religious liberalism through Lear, his programming, and his supporters as well as through his conservative detractors from within the Religious Left.

This work has also attempted to blend histories of the Christian Right with the Spiritual Left in order to demonstrate their intimate and coconstitutive relationship in the recent past.[13] Figures such as Jerry Falwell, Pat Robertson, and Donald Wildmon make appearances in this work because they contributed to the formation of both the electronic church and the Christian Right. They were also the primary foils of Lear and his liberal supporters. In this sense, Lear ironically helped these figures achieve the religio-political prominence that they did during this period by drawing attention to their respective televised actions and messages through his own organizing and activism. Lear shadowed Falwell's actions as the head of a tax-exempt nonprofit organization while Falwell's presence shadowed Lear by echoing the religious intolerance of his youth. As such, these debates between Lear and various representatives of the electronic church fundamentally altered the landscape of American religion and politics by reimagining a new public life beyond yet inclusive of pluralism and its adjudication by the largely liberal state. This is why Lear defended his programming in the name of the public interest to begin with, thereby reflecting the custodial impulse of the Religious Left itself as empathy incarnate in public.

The analytical complexity of Lear's articulations, ones that both curtailed and protected freedom of religious expression, speaks to both lived religion approaches to the study of religion and contemporary studies that examine the socioeconomic and epistemic conditions that make certain conceptions of the human possible.[14] Scholars of American religion have recently begun asking questions about many of the field's practices and common-sense tendencies, including the archival impulse to catalog as the primary form of knowledge production about the past. "In the study of American religions," argues Finbarr Curtis, "suspicion of technical scholarly discourse mirrors a popular preference for common-sense realism and a belief in individual freedom." For Curtis, "The common-sense tradition holds that conceptual complexity detracts from good storytelling. . . . One prominent example of the coupling of individual freedom and religious diversity in the study of American religion can be found in the accumulation of mircohistories of previously excluded groups in the hope of recovering their subjects' agency."[15]

In other words, the scholarly assumption that has guided much of this spirit of accumulation since the 1970s is not only the image of the freely choosing religious subject but also the analytical maxim "What we study, what we want, is *more*."[16] I have attempted a blended approach to my subject as a product of critical and historical study—one interested in both synchronic and diachronic analyses of religion and its formation in the recent American past. It has also been an analysis and evaluation of pluralism as both civic ideal and discursive formation across the twentieth century. In fact, the analytical impulse to catalog and archive through microhistory and thick description reflects the very same pluralist values that help produce the subject material for and serve as a demonstration of a thriving "American religious landscape."

Put in another way, these assumptions are the product of what sociologist Courtney Bender has called "the power of pluralist thinking" in the sociological study of American religion, a train of thought that Lear and others were intimately familiar with.[17] "Much as the 'positive thinking' espoused by Norman Vincent Peale hid the mechanics of social institutions that shape human lives and their many contingencies," argues Bender, "contemporary pluralist thinking hides the mechanisms through which we recognize religions as free and many, or why we even find these tallies and their evaluations useful or necessary."[18] In light of this analysis, we are able to better understand and describe pluralism as both an engine of analytical insight and a disciplining mechanism of scholarly description. In the case of the Religious Left, pluralism functioned multivalently as both the content of its own spiritual politics and a rhetorical weapon in the defense of the public square over and against the largely imagined Christian Right.

❧

In light of these analytical and methodological choices, I sense that the study of American religion currently sits at an analytical crossroads. Those trained in history and religion departments dating back to the 1970s have grounded the study of American religion in the systematic exploration of the archive and its myriad sources of epistemic illumination. This intellectual expectation continues to define the quality of historical work in the study of American religion based on the scholar's ability to narrate a story of human improvisation and contingency. Such observations have been made possible largely through the work of scholars who have begun identifying some of the field's fundamental analytical assumptions, including its own depiction of human agents and their ability to choose their religious futures within the marketplace of rational choice. If previous generations of historians and scholars of religion established the parameters of the study of US American religions, then contemporary analysts continue to investigate these stories in a self-reflexive manner that not only asks narrative-driven questions but also questions how such narratives have become naturalized to begin with. In this sense, what I call the "conditions of religious possibility," not simply the possibility itself, have become the latest multiform subject of our collective labors in the critical study of American religious history.

It is in this spirit that I have conducted my own study of Lear's spiritual politics during the American culture wars of the 1970s and 1980s. Focusing our collective attention on the careers of individuals such as Lear speaks to the narrative and analytical concerns of both historians and scholars of religion. This story is at once uniform and historically contingent because it speaks to change over time *and* its contemporary resonance as a genealogical investigation of our collective political present. My study of Lear and the Religious Left is significant because it contributes a new, compelling subject to the field while also questioning the means by which we evaluate proper subjects of American religious study to begin with.

Despite the analytical differences that exist between such disciplinary registers, historical subjects like Lear demonstrate how the interdisciplinary study of media can reconcile individual and systemic analyses of American public life by turning our attention to the conditions of religious possibility that our subjects navigate on a continuous basis. In this sense, understanding Lear and the Religious Left as a collective archive for scholars of American religion allows us to chart the last half century of American religion and politics according to the predilections of a spiritual liberal, one who contributed to the cause of religious freedom, oftentimes at the expense of religious expression.

Lear's story also speaks to the struggle of liberalism itself as it confronts its greatest challenge to date: neoliberal economic policy and populist counterreaction as the new form of American common sense. What was once a collective task of determining the public good has now evolved into a largely private enterprise driven by deregulatory agendas and "bottom-line thinking," as Lear himself observed. As a result, American public life itself has fractured beyond recognition into its constitutive cultural, social, and racial parts. Both sides of the proverbial aisle have played a role in this vicious state of affairs whereby citizen is pitted against fellow citizen according to one's "Democrat" or "Republican" cup at convenience stores during the election season. In fact, stores like 7-Eleven have been keeping their own polling data since 2000 with surprisingly prescient results.

While political candidates themselves have not literally endorsed or condoned such business practices, they nevertheless speak to the overly saturated and exposed character of American public life in the twenty-first century. Combined with social media apps such as Twitter and Facebook, the personal has truly become the political in all its reality-scripted glory. For those who thrive on such conditions of spectacle and hyperreality, there has not been a better time for politics making in the name of "the people" and their respective interests. Those who do not, namely the Religious Left, have struggled to articulate a cohesive message or vision of the country to match many of their prophetic claims in the name of justice and the kingdom on earth.

The various counterintuitive ironies pointed out over the course of this story by way of Norman Lear's career in media speak to both the rise and fall of the Religious Left: with cultural influence came a means of speaking directly to the people about the public square, yet at the same time, it reinforced a sense of cultural superiority over conservative actors that is still very much with us today. As a result, television in general, along with its late-night and premium-channel programming, came to be understood as a more political space than the streets and marches that defined liberal religious activism on behalf of a reinvigorated Social Gospel only a decade before. As one of the Religious Left's most vocal representatives, Lear serves as an ideal type for such a line of argumentation because his religio-political vision found the most traction with the voting public through the genre of the situation comedy versus through his own nonprofit and its educational programming and awareness campaigns. Such disjuncture speaks to the strengths of a *prophetic* vision, but it also points to the lack of equally powerful *political* vision of the nation and its inhabitants. Those who see themselves as bridge builders and meditators in the prophetic tradition must also come to see and understand themselves as pragmatic political actors in the public square who are willing and able to hone a coherent message for an otherwise distracted populace. Otherwise, clumsy references to "deplorables," as well as to those who "cling to guns or religion or antipathy," will continue to plague progressive politics making, due largely to self-inflicted wounds.

Within these extremely tumultuous socioeconomic conditions, American religious liberals may continue to remain content in their cultural victories, but at what cost to our shared conceptions of the public good and those who work on their behalf? In order to better understand the nature of the Religious Left's rise and fall since the 1970s, I have argued that the soundstage and its deployment in wars of culture tell us a great deal about how the Religious Left has operated in the name of the American Way and American civil religion over and against the Christian Right. Unlike the Right, however, the Left is still in search of an explicitly *political* platform that translates *prophetic utterance* into *pragmatic activism*. Combined with accusations of conservatives "hijacking religion," religious liberals like Lear have avoided asking themselves how they have contributed to their own irrelevancy in American public life. In this sense, the Left has to begin to accept some responsibility and accountability for its own estrangement from American public life.

As sad as it may be, there is nothing inherently valuable about any of the prophetic proclamations periodically made from the Religious Left in the name of the public good once they reach the realm of politics. While something like civil religion is supposed to keep the nation in check by subjecting it to a divine standard, the very same tradition saw itself in opposition to conservative forms of religiosity as first described by sociologist Robert Bellah himself. For Bellah, an "American-Legion type of ideology that fuses God, country, and flag has been used to attack non-conformist and liberal ideas and groups of all kinds. . . . For all of the overt religiosity of the radical right today, their relation to the civil religious consensus is tenuous."[19] If there is a story to tell about the Religious Left's departure from the public square, it has to include these early assessments of conservative politics and their limitations, which date back at least to Bellah's published article.[20]

In many respects, the Religious Left has lost its way, wondering how it could have abandoned one of its clearest principles: a custodial vision of the public and its defense from any and all dangers. For scholars and historians of American liberalism, including the likes of sociologist Daniel Bell, progressive actors gradually lost the ability to speak to the people as they transitioned from a socioeconomic emphasis on *class* to emphases on *culture* and *identity*. While this was partly engineered by the Right as part of a larger plan to remake politics around "the social issue," it was also the product of liberal religious notions of religion itself. Religion and power suffused everyday life; the personal was indeed the political, but at what cost to those who valued privacy? Religious liberals must think harder and more closely about their understanding of politics and what it calls for in the public square. If at one time conservative evangelicals and Pentecostals were the ones faced with a similar series of questions, it is because the two examples are more than coincidentally aligned.

For too long, excuses such as the "hijacking" of religion by the Right have stood in for actual analysis of conservative methods of cultural appropriation. Such accusations are more than simply played out; they prevent their authors from examining themselves and their own political priorities, or lack thereof, in tumultuous times. If the Religious Left is not going to be results oriented when it comes to American politics, then it is going to need to find an alternative means for measuring success in American public life on behalf of various liberal religious communities. For the New Right, anything and everything was up for grabs in the pursuit of power. The Religious Left may like to think of itself as possessing the ability to speak truth to power, but what if no one is listening to or cares about such truths? Then what? The Left may not need to mimic the ruthless tactics of the Right, but it does need to figure out what it wants through politics, and why, and to what ends.

For many on the Right, government is there to be seized and thus deployed on behalf of a given truth. In many ways, the future of the Religious Left depends on its ability to translate its moral vision into a context largely defined by its antitheses: mindless entertainment and a resentment of those with more. Any and all attempts to minimize the Trump phenomenon thus far authored by the Religious Left have largely failed. Not unlike former Alabama governor George Wallace's campaigns during the 1960s, such attempts have tended to backfire because Trump became an underdog in the eyes of many. In this sense, such strategizing "was wishful thinking, as they sought to deny a reality that they must have felt they could not control."[21] Cultural victory may indeed be a significant indicator of social and spiritual influence in a given historical moment, especially for those who think they know the truth and its power, but for all intents and purposes, it will never equate with the actual power and influence established through presidential elections, congressional races, or mayoral campaigns. To those who see themselves as part of an emerging Religious Left in an age of Trump, I ask you this: What are you willing to lose, or give up, for the sake of the kingdom on earth? Nothing, or everything? The choice is yours.

Notes

INTRODUCTION

1. Norman Lear and Ronald Reagan, "A Debate on Religious Freedom," *Harper's*, October 1984, 15–20. For more on political religions, see Jason Bivins, *Religion of Fear: The Politics of Horror in Conservative Evangelicalism* (New York: Oxford University Press, 2008).

2. See Jeffrey K. Hadden, "Clergy Involvement in Civil Rights," *Annals of the American Academy of Political and Social Science* 387 (January 1970): 119.

3. See Hortense Powdermaker, *Hollywood, the Dream Factory: An Anthropologist Looks at the Movie-Makers* (1950; New York: Martino, 2013). For more on California's liberal religious cultures, see Eileen Luhr, "Seeker, Surfer, Yogi: The Progressive Religious Imagination and the Cultural Politics of Place in Encinitas, California," *American Quarterly* 67, no. 4 (December 2015): 1169–93.

4. Wendy Wall, *Inventing the "American Way": The Politics of Consensus from the New Deal to the Civil Rights Movement* (New York: Oxford University Press, 2008). For Wall, the American Way can be best described as a consensus-based model of political deliberation that foregrounds individual freedom, rights, and liberties as the most significant components of American democracy. Much of this tradition begins in opposition to "totalitarian regimes" during America's midcentury involvement in the Cold War.

5. William F. Buckley Jr. , "The Nightmare of Norman Lear," *National Review*, November 27, 1981, 1441.

6. For the standard work in this field, see Andrew Hartman, *A War for the Soul of America: A History of the Culture Wars* (Chicago: University of Chicago Press, 2015).

7. For the latest account of the Religious Left, see Doug Rossinow, Marian Mollin, and Leilah Danielson, eds., *The Religious Left in Modern America: Doorkeepers of a Radical Faith* (New York: Palgrave, 2018). For a broader collection on the same topic, see Rebecca Alpert, ed., *Voices of the Religious Left: A Contemporary Sourcebook* (Philadelphia: Temple University Press, 2000). For a more historical account of liberal religion generally considered, see Matthew Hedstrom, *The Rise of Liberal Religion: Book Culture and American Spirituality in the Twentieth Century* (New York: Oxford University Press, 2013); Leigh E. Schmidt, *Restless Souls: The Making of American Spirituality* (Berkeley: University of California Press, 2012). For more on the Religious Left in real time and its definition, see Nadia Marzouki, "Does the United States Need a Religious Left?," *Social*

Science Research Council, January 23, 2019, accessed February 22, 2019, https://tif.ssrc.org/2019/01/23/does-the-united-states-need-a-religious-left/.

For historian Rebecca Alpert, the "religious left" describes "many different groups that advocate a range of issues with common themes of peace, justice, and support for the disenfranchised and speak from a religious perspective. The religious left is composed today of groups and individuals with progressive political values that are undergirded by their religious beliefs in justice, freedom, and peace. But these groups and individuals do not agree about all of the issues that comprise a progressive political agenda. . . . The religious left is multifaceted rather than cohesive. The absence of theological or political consensus contributes to the inability of the religious left to have a unified voice or a stronger public presence today" (2). "Any study of the religious left," argues Alpert, "must include the voices of Muslims, Buddhists, and Native Americans, as well as Protestants, Catholics, and Jews."

Since the term "Religious Left" is arguably as ephemeral as "the Religious Right," my usage of the term is more out of necessity than it is out of convenience. In short, Lear's career in media is representative of a Religious Left understanding of American religion and politics as illustrated from outside the confines of traditionally institutional settings, such as churches or synagogues. As such, Lear's work illustrates why liberal religious activism in the name of the First Amendment and religious freedom finds many of its most effective tools of organizing and argumentation outside "religious" settings and vocabularies. This tactic has arguably been American religious liberalism's greatest strength and its greatest weakness. As it gains power and influence in culture, it loses its ability to speak to a religio-political vision of the nation and its inhabitants. As a result, liberals of various sorts may be able to influence and shape culture—or even win wars of culture—but largely at the expense of political power itself. Lear's career in media is the paradigmatic example of American liberalism's overreliance on culture for its politics making. Counterintuitively, such influence has resulted in a form of cultural revolution by way of popular culture at the expense of a political one via an emphasis on class. For more on this sociological argument, see Daniel Bell, "Afterword (2001): From Class to Culture," in *The Radical Right*, ed. Daniel Bell, 3rd ed. (New Brunswick, NJ: Transaction, 2002), 447–503. For more on "halfway houses" within American religious liberalism and the Religious Left, see David Hollinger, *After Cloven Tongues of Fire: Protestant Liberalism in Modern American History* (Princeton, NJ: Princeton University Press, 2013).

8. My understanding of conservative Protestantism follows the lead of historian Timothy E. W. Gloege, who argues that the term describes evangelicals who "emphasize that their individualistic relationship to God is with a person, generally a 'he.' Their individualistic, 'plain' interpretation of the Bible is superintended by dispensational assumptions that keep the most radical implications of the Bible in check, . . . and generally, they consider social reform a fruit secondary to evangelism." I support Gloege's notion that evangelicals have made themselves "the public face of conservative Protestantism." While this has been a remarkable "rhetorical achievement, . . . it was precisely that." See Timothy E. W. Gloege, *Guaranteed Pure: The Moody Bible Institute, Business, and the Making of Modern Evangelicalism* (Chapel Hill: University of North Carolina Press, 2015), 13.

9. My usage of quotation marks around "the Christian Right" and the "electronic church" here are intended to suggest that such terms are largely fictitious ones, inventions of a collection of liberal and conservative actors in the public square during the 1970s designed to capture a particular religio-political sentiment in the name of electoral politics.

10. These stereotypes were arguably the product of what literary theorists identify as (political) *metonymy* and *synecdoche*, specifically liberal ones. In each instance, a linguistic "part" stood in for a larger social "whole," whereby "the new Christian Right" functioned as a metonym for conservative Protestant Christianity within the United States by representing the social whole through the rhetorical part. These arguments, and their application to the study of religio-political discourse since the 1960s, are in the preliminary stages of development.

11.   Martin Marty, "A Profile of Norman Lear: Another Pilgrim's Progress," *Christian Century*, January 21, 1987, 56–60. "Like the proverbial elephant investigated by blind men," argues American religious historian Elesha Coffman, "the mainline is all of these things: a set of denominations, a mode of religiosity, a social network, and an attempted religious establishment. . . . A study of the mainline as a tradition reveals the ways in which personal and organizational history, social location, and the interplay of ideas created not just a network of linked institutions but also the presumption that they were central and powerful." For more, see Elesha Coffman, *The Christian Century and the Rise of the Protestant Mainline* (New York: Oxford University Press, 2013), 6.

12.   My emphasis on conservative Protestant "method" resonates with Gloege's analyses, which contend, "The lasting significance of *The Fundamentals* project laid in its methods, not its contents. It pioneered a *means* of creating an evangelical 'orthodoxy' out of an ever-shifting bricolage of beliefs and practices, each varying historical significance and some entirely novel. . . . *The Fundamentals* thus pointed the way forward for modern conservative evangelicalism by modeling the methodology for creating, and constantly recreating, whatever 'orthodoxy' the present moment required." There is no better evidence for this argument during the period under study than the actions and cultural productions of evangelist Jerry Falwell and his advocacy group, the Moral Majority. The creation of the Bible Scorecard, a document that evaluated the Christian character of a politician or person in office based on a predetermined conservative policy agenda, was arguably part of evangelicalism's ability to carry out and successfully execute instances of improvisational orthodoxy. For Gloege, *The Fundamentals* "replaced doctrine with the *performance* of orthodoxy facilitated by modern promotional techniques." Perhaps most important, "the work created an imagined community of Protestants united in their opposition to theological modernism" (*Guaranteed Pure*, 11, 163, 181).

13.   Norman Lear, *Even This I Get to Experience,* (New York: Penguin, 2015), 330.

14.   Jay Demerath III, "Cultural Victory and Organizational Defeat in the Paradoxical Decline of Liberal Protestantism," *Journal for the Scientific Study of Religion* 34, no. 4 (December 1995): 458–69.

15.   My articulation may seem like a binary one, but I am not arguing that there were *literally* only two religio-political perspectives at the time. Instead, I contend that thanks to the influence of the media and documents like Bible Scorecards, there *appeared* to be only two choices due to the developing polarization of American public discourse in a key of cultural warfare by the early 1980s.

16.   For more on this history, see Schmidt, *Restless Souls*. In his study of antebellum American religion, scholar of religion John Modern argues that spirituality was "recognizable as a formation of secularism, a liberal style of piety in which religion, politics, and epistemology congealed at the level of affect." In addition, "It was among liberals and their institutions that spirituality became increasingly associated with the human capacity for religion. . . . This capacious concept of spirituality bubbled up, through, and with various cognates of 'spirit.' The grammatical vectors included spirit-filled, spiritual religion, spiritual discernment, spiritual activity, spiritual perception." See John Modern, *Secularism in Antebellum America* (Chicago: University of Chicago Press, 2011), 121. See also Courtney Bender, *The New Metaphysicals: Spirituality and the American Religious Imagination* (New York: Columbia University Press, 2010).

17.   For Lear and his fellow religious liberals, "Our highest purpose is to nurture a national climate that encourages and enhances the human spirit rather than one which divides people into hostile camps." For more, see "People For's Founding Mission Statement," People for the American Way, accessed May 9, 2015, http://www.pfaw.org/about-us/founding-mission-statement/.

18.   For scholar of religion David Chidester, the term "religio-political power" attempts "to capture the inevitable interrelation between religious and political power within any social system." As such, "a religio-political system generates a legal force field which defines the public order within which religion may legitimately emerge." I argue that like Falwell, Lear attempted to create his own

liberal religious "legal force field" in order to eliminate any and all forms of conservatism from American public life. See David Chidester, *Patterns of Power: Religion & Politics in American Culture* (New York: Prentice Hall, 1988), 5–10.

19. My understanding of "consensus" has been informed by both historical and cultural studies. My usage of the term certainly refers to histories of midcentury America, but it is ultimately more concerned with the ways in which both the term and its deployment attempt to maintain particular religio-political arrangements—in this case, the civil public sphere as Lear understood it. "Indeed," argues literary scholar Sacvan Bercovitch, "its function was partly to mystify or mask social realities. Nonetheless it denoted something equally real: a coherent system of symbols, values, and beliefs, and a series of rituals designed to keep the system going." Sacvan Bercovitch, *The Rites of Assent: Transformations in the Symbolic Construction of America* (New York: Routledge, 1993), 30.

20. Based on the recent work of scholar of religion Isaac Weiner, Lear can be understood as both a "privatist" and a "pluralist." Despite the fact that Lear argued for a clear distinction between public and private so that "religion" could be safely contained, he also called for greater understanding of religious difference. "Although the pluralists sought to celebrate and bridge religious differences," Weiner argues, "their arguments ran the risk of effacing differences altogether by diminishing their significance." See Isaac Weiner, "Calling Everyone to Pray: Pluralism, Secularism, and the Adhan in Hamtramck, Michigan," *Anthropological Quarterly* 87, no. 4 (Fall 2014): 1049–78.

21. The *I Love Liberty* prime-time television special authored by Lear and PFAW aired on March 21, 1982, on ABC. It was written primarily by Lear and featured a "nonpartisan" board of directors and cast including Barry Goldwater, Jane Fonda, Robin Williams, Judd Hirsch, Valerie Harper, and many others. Aesthetically, it very much resembled the televised rallies of the Christian Right, yet Lear disagreed with this notion vehemently. In essence, *I Love Liberty* served as the definitive example of how spiritual progressives attempted to mobilize according to their own notions of patriotism and religious freedom. It also demonstrated Lear's reliance on Hollywood resources in communicating his message of humility and civility over and against the divisiveness he saw operating on the Christian Right. The last chapter delves more deeply into these issues.

22. For more, see Andrea Most, *Theatrical Liberalism: Jews and Popular Entertainment in America* (New York: New York University Press, 2013).

23. Most, 9–10.

24. He also self-identifies as spiritual in addition to naming his religious autobiography *Life of the Spirit*. I argue that "spirit," as both category and descriptor, assumes a much greater role in American public life during this period (1960s–1980s). Both conservative and liberal Protestants as well as liberal Jews relied on a language of the *spirit* to detract from their political opponents.

25. This type of spiritual activism is intimately connected to what historian Leigh Schmidt has identified as "the Spiritual Left" in American history. See Schmidt, *Restless Souls*.

26. In this manner, we can understand spiritual liberalism as equally dependent on epistemic forms of "common sense" as its political opposition, namely conservative evangelicalism. For John Modern, talk of spirituality assisted nineteenth-century Unitarians who were "drawn to Common Sense because they could legitimate the empirical reality of spirit." Like Lear and other spiritual liberals, "The exercise of human reason became a pious end unto itself, the surest method to discover its divine source." See Modern, *Secularism in Antebellum America*, 141.

27. See Peggy Shriver, *The Bible Vote: Religion and the New Right* (New York: Pilgrim, 1981).

28. "Because social justice provides the vital framework for balancing individual rights and the common good," argues scholar of religion Brantley Gasaway, "leaders regarded it as the highest ideal of public life." See Brantley W. Gasaway, *Progressive Evangelicals and the Pursuit of Social Justice* (Chapel Hill: University of North Carolina Press, 2015), 54–55.

29. Unlike their conservative colleagues in Christ, these progressive evangelicals saw the state as playing an essential role in fostering social justice by "promoting politics of distributive justice." See Gasaway, 54.

30. See Arlie Russell Hochschild, *Strangers in Their Own Land: Anger and Mourning on the American Right* (New York: New, 2017).

31. Schmidt, *Restless Souls*, 287. Schmidt's name could also be listed alongside Lear's in light of the fact that both individuals celebrate and analyze the tradition of which they are a part, namely American religious liberalism *and* the Spiritual Left. For scholar of religion Kerry A. Mitchell, much of this work (and the scholarship on "spirituality") "has been heavily informed by the discourse of liberalism, even to the point of celebrating this politico-intellectual tradition." This has led to the academic tendency to reproduce the discourse under study rather than subject it to critical explication. See Kerry A. Mitchell, "The Politics of Spirituality: Liberalizing the Definition of Religion," in *Secularism and Religion-Making*, ed. Markus Dressler and Arvind Mandair (New York: Oxford University Press, 2011), 126. See also "Managing Spirituality: Public Religion and National Parks," *Journal for the Study of Religion, Nature, and Culture* 1, no. 4 (2007): 431–49. For historian Eileen Luhr, this tendency is part of the "pluralist thesis," which "fails to account for the ideological work that religious pluralism does in an uneven global economic structure of exchange that valorizes individual spiritual and secular expression through choice while masking, continuing, and often deepening histories of expropriation, colonialism, and conquest." See Luhr, "Seeker, Surfer, Yogi," 1172.

32. For more on the American form of liberalism examined in the subsequent analysis, see the following titles: Neil Jumonville and Kevin Mattson, eds., *Liberalism for a New Century* (Berkeley: University of California Press, 2007); Harvard Sitkoff, ed., *Perspectives on Modern America: Making Sense of the Twentieth Century* (New York: Oxford University Press, 2001); Mark Lilla, *The Once and Future Liberal: After Identity Politics* (New York: Harper, 2018); Alan Brinkley, *Liberalism and Its Discontents* (Cambridge, MA: Harvard University Press, 1998); James Kloppenberg, *The Virtues of Liberalism* (New York: Oxford University Press, 1998); Steve Fraser and Gary Gerstle, eds., *The Rise and Fall of the New Deal Order* (Princeton, NJ: Princeton University Press, 1989); Jonathan Rieder, *Canarsie: The Jews and Italians of Brooklyn Against Liberalism* (Cambridge, MA: Harvard University Press, 1985); Paul Gottfried, *After Liberalism: Mass Democracy in the Managerial State* (Princeton, NJ: Princeton University Press, 2001); Patrick J. Deneen, *Why Liberalism Failed* (New Haven, CT: Yale University Press, 2018).

33. Cheryl Greenberg, "Twentieth-Century Liberalisms," in *Perspectives on Modern America: Making Sense of the Twentieth Century*, ed. Harvard Sitkoff (New York: Oxford University Press, 2001), 57.

34. Jennifer Burns, "Liberalism and the Conservative Imagination," in Jumonville and Mattson, *Liberalism for a New Century*, 70–71.

35. Greenberg, "Twentieth-Century Liberalisms," 75.

36. Introduction to Jumonville and Mattson, *Liberalism for a New Century*, 7.

37. Alan Brinkley, "Liberalism and Belief," in Jumonville and Mattson, *Liberalism for a New Century*, 89.

38. Most, *Theatrical Liberalism*, 9.

39. See Wade Clark Roof (presentation, Religion Session, Civility & Democracy in America Conference, Spokane, WA, March 4, 2011), available at Thomas Foley Institute, video, YouTube, November 18, 2014, accessed January 10, 2016, https://youtu.be/CByykqALjdo.

40. For more on the relationship between sitcoms and liberal religious politics, see L. Benjamin Rolsky, "Confessions of a Hollywood Liberal: American Sitcoms and the Culture Wars, from Norman Lear to *Parks and Recreation*," Marginalia, March 31, 2015, accessed November 16, 2015,

http://marginalia.lareviewofbooks.org/confessions-of-a-hollywood-liberal-american-sitcoms
-and-the-culture-wars-from-norman-lear-to-parks-and-recreation-by-l-benjamin-rolsky/.

41. For more, see Mary Douglas and Steven M. Tipton, eds. *Religion and America: Spirituality in a Secular Age* (Boston: Beacon, 1982), v.

42. Heather White, *Reforming Sodom: Protestants and the Rise of Gay Rights* (Chapel Hill: University of North Carolina Press, 2015), 7. White's analysis of progressive Protestantism is worthy of emulation. For White, liberal Protestants adhere to what scholar of religion Webb Keane calls "the moral narrative of modernity," which posits religion as an obstacle to human development. "This way of telling religion and modern change," argues White, "is the constitutive tale of secularism, and it obscures the particularities of liberal Protestant influence" (7).

43. This work has already begun in Lily Geismer, *Don't Blame Us: Suburban Liberals and the Transformation of the Democratic Party* (Princeton, NJ: Princeton University Press, 2015). See also Lily Geismer, "More than Megachurches: Liberal Religion and Politics in the Suburbs," in *Faithful Republic: Religion and Politics in Modern America*, ed. Andrew Preston, Bruce Schulman, and Julian Zelizer (Philadelphia: University of Pennsylvania Press, 2015), 117–30.

44. For historian Matthew Hedstrom, religious liberals can be identified in two ways: laissez-faire and mystical/ethical. I argue that Lear is part of this latter group in his emphasis on "social activism and moral sophistication." See Hedstrom, *The Rise of Liberal Religion*.

45. For more on liberal religious mobilization in postwar suburban America, see Geismer, *Don't Blame Us*. For Geismer, such suburban spaces cultivated shared concerns among Jewish, Protestant, and Catholic neighbors, respectively. "These activities revealed not only the common values of these various congregations, but also the ways in which their commitment to principles of anti-prejudice, equality, and community aligned with many of the core tenets of postwar liberalism." For more, see Geismer, "More than Megachurches," 122.

46. Many of the questions I (and others) bring to the study of the Christian Right have already been explored in Linda Kintz and Julia Lesage, eds. *Media, Culture, and the Religious Right* (Minneapolis: University of Minnesota Press, 1998). For additional examples, see Axel R. Schäfer, *Countercultural Conservatives: American Evangelicalism from the Postwar Revival to the New Christian Right* (Madison: University of Wisconsin Press, 2011); Schäfer, *Piety and Public Funding: Evangelicals and the State in Modern America* (Philadelphia: University of Pennsylvania Press, 2012); Schäfer, ed., *American Evangelicals and the 1960s* (Madison: University of Wisconsin Press, 2013). Additionally, see Kevin Kruse, *One Nation Under God: How Corporate America Invented Christian America* (New York: Basic, 2015); Bethany Moreton, *To Serve God and Wal-Mart: The Making of Christian Free Enterprise* (Cambridge, MA: Harvard University Press, 2009); Bivins, *Religion of Fear*; Tracy Fessenden, *Culture and Redemption: Religion, the Secular, and American Literature* (Princeton, NJ: Princeton University Press, 2011); Darren Grem, "The Marketplace Missions of S. Truett Cathy, Chick Fil-A, and the Sunbelt South," in *Sunbelt Rising: The Politics of Space, Place, and Region*, ed. Darren Dochuk and Michelle Nickerson (Philadelphia: University of Pennsylvania Press, 2011); William Connolly, "The Evangelical-Capitalist Resonance Machine," *Political Theory* 33, no. 6 (December 2005): 869–86; Matthew Sutton, *American Apocalypse: A History of Modern Evangelicalism* (Cambridge, MA: Harvard University Press, 2014); Sarah Hammond, "God's Business Men: Entrepreneurial Evangelicals in Depression and War" (PhD diss., Yale University, 2010); Molly Worthen, *Apostles of Reason: The Crisis of Authority in American Evangelicalism* (New York: Oxford University Press, 2015); Neil J. Young, *We Gather Together: The Religious Right and the Problem of Interfaith Politics* (New York: Oxford University Press, 2015); Emily Johnson, *This Is Our Message: Women's Leadership in the New Christian Right* (New York: Oxford University Press, 2019).

47. As argued by historian Darren Grem, the recent attention to historical and theoretical studies of the relationship between capitalism and American religion(s) calls for more top-down approaches

to the study of corporate religion and corporate influence on religious practice. My work can be understood as contributing to the study of corporate power and influence within largely liberal or "New Class" communities including those in Hollywood and academia. See Darren Grem, *The Blessings of Business: How Corporations Shaped Conservative Christianity* (New York: Oxford University Press, 2017). See also Kim Phillips-Fein, *Invisible Hands: The Making of the Conservative Movement from the New Deal to Reagan* (New York: W. W. Norton, 2009); Phillips-Fein, *Fear City: New York's Fiscal Crisis and the Rise of Austerity Politics* (New York: Henry Holt, 2017).

48. Young, *We Gather Together*, 169. For more on Goldwater's legacy in the contemporary conservative movement and Republican party, see E. J. Dionne, *Why the Right Went Wrong: From Goldwater to the Tea Party and Beyond* (New York: Simon and Schuster, 2016).

49. For a similarly themed study of conservatism, see Phillips-Fein, *Invisible Hands*.

50. Gloege, *Guaranteed Pure*, 192.

51. Methodologically speaking, my approach to the study of history in general, and the Christian Right in particular, reflects the interests of two distinct but interrelated methodologies: the scholarly empathy of Walter Capps and the genealogical work of critical theorists such as Theodor Adorno and religious studies scholars Kathryn Lofton and John Modern. For Modern, "If historians focus on change over time, genealogists seek to name continuity—or family resemblances—through comparative analysis of documents pertaining to a common theme. Genealogy is a kind of grey documentation, an effort to disabuse oneself of particular presumptions through examining how presumptions come to be. Genealogy, then, is a mode of analysis that addresses concepts that have become naturalized." For Capps, see Walter H. Capps, *The New Religious Right: Piety, Patriotism, and Politics* (Columbia: University of South Carolina Press, 1990); Capps, "Contemporary Socio-Political Change and the Work of Religious Studies," *Council on the Study of Religion Bulletin* 12, no. 4 (October 1981): 93–95. See also John Modern, "Did Someone Say 'Evangelical Surge?'" *Church History* 84, no. 3 (September 2015): 630–36. For more on genealogy, see Mark Poster, "Foucault and History," *Social Research* 49, no. 1 (Spring 1982): 116–42. The scholarly reception of the recent application of genealogical method to the study of American religion arguably mirrors Foucault's work in the 1960s: "Professional historians recognized it as being a work of history, and many others, who have an antiquated and no doubt completely obsolete idea of history, clamored that history was being murdered." For more, see Michel Foucault, "On the Ways of Writing History," in *Aesthetics, Method, and Epistemology*, ed. James D. Faubion (New York: New, 1998), 279–96.

52. Steven Miller, *The Age of Evangelicalism: America's Born-Again Years* (New York: Oxford University Press, 2014).

53. For more, see Whitney Strub, *Perversion for Profit: The Politics of Pornography and the Rise of the New Right* (New York: Columbia University Press, 2011).

54. Matthew Lassiter, "Inventing Family Values," in *Rightward Bound: Making America Conservative in the 1970s*, ed. Bruce J. Schulman and Julian E. Zelizer (Cambridge, MA: Harvard University Press, 2008), 16–17.

55. Scholar of religion Stephen Prothero takes these issues head on in his book, *Why Liberals Win the Culture Wars (Even when They Lose Elections): The Battles That Define America from Jefferson's Heresies to Gay Marriage* (New York: Harper Collins, 2016), arguing that it has been conservatives who have tended to set the terms of cultural debate in the recent past. One could argue, however, that Prothero not only reads "culture wars" back into American history in favor of a synthetic narrative but also rehearses liberal arguments that assume conservative manipulation of its supporters due to a form of "status anxiety" or deprivation. As Prothero argues, "Culture wars are often seen as these battles between liberals and conservatives over cultural questions. But I see them more as dramas that are produced and acted in by conservatives. They are conservative projects whose purpose is to drum up support from traditionalists in society who perceive that something precious is being lost to them . . . *in order to activate that anxiety*, which is an important part of my

book, which is going to create a political upsurge for your party, you need to find an issue that will agitate peoples' emotions" (my emphasis). For a more balanced treatment on virtually the same period, see Dionne, *Why the Right Went Wrong*.

56. For more on taste, see Raymond Williams, *Keywords: A Vocabulary of Culture and Society* (New York: Oxford University Press, 1983), 314–15.

57. For more on how secularism shapes political expressions in the public sphere, see Finbarr Curtis, *The Production of Religious Freedom* (New York: New York University Press, 2017). For more on the burgeoning relationship between a rebirth of studies of secularism/secularity/secular and American religious history, see Joseph Blankholm, "The Political Advantages of a Polysemous Secular," *Journal for the Scientific Study of Religion* 53, no. 4 (December 2014): 775–90; Modern, *Secularism in Antebellum America*; Janet R. Jakobsen and Ann Pellegrini, eds. *Secularisms* (Durham, NC: Duke University Press, 2008); Talal Asad, *Formations of the Secular: Christianity, Islam, Modernity* (Stanford, CA: Stanford University Press, 2003); Tisa Wenger, *We Have a Religion: The 1920s Indian Dance Controversy and American Religious Freedom* (Chapel Hill: University of North Carolina Press, 2009); Rosemary Hicks, "Between Lived and the Law: Power, Empire, and Expansion in Studies of North American Religions," *Religion* 42, no. 3 (2012): 409–24; Kathryn Lofton, *Oprah: The Gospel of an Icon* (Berkeley: University of California Press, 2011); Linell E. Cady and Elizabeth Shakman Hurd, eds. *Comparative Secularisms in a Global Age* (New York: Palgrave Macmillan, 2010); Fessenden, *Culture and Redemption*; Elizabeth Shakman Hurd, *Beyond Religious Freedom: The New Global Politics of Religion* (Princeton, NJ: Princeton University Press, 2015); Winnifred F. Sullivan, Elizabeth Shakman Hurd, Saba Mahmood, and Peter G. Danchin, *Politics of Religious Freedom* (Chicago: University of Chicago Press, 2015); Mayanthi L. Fernando, *The Republic Unsettled: Muslim French and the Contradictions of Secularism* (Durham, NC: Duke University Press, 2014).

58. Lear, *Even This I Get to Experience*, 350. For more on being "one step removed" as a formal liberal religious stance relative to "religion," see Hollinger, *After Cloven Tongues of Fire*. Lear's activism seems to prove Hollinger's argument that liberal Protestantism often functioned as a "halfway house" for those interested in pursuing politics as a religious liberal, Protestant or Jewish.

59. For analyses of the illiberal tendencies within liberalism and its representation within the academy, see Mitchell, "The Politics of Spirituality."

60. For more on "framing," see Jon A. Shields, "Framing the Christian Right: How Progressives and Post-war Liberals Constructed the Religious Right," *Journal of Church and State* 53, no. 4 (Autumn 2011): 635–55.

61. For an example of this type of mindset as understood in an editorial comment, see James M. Wall, "The New Right Comes of Age," *Christian Century*, October 22, 1980, 995–96.

62. This description was inspired by Robert Wuthnow, *The Restructuring of American Religion: Society and Faith Since World War II* (Princeton, NJ: Princeton University Press, 1989).

63. Hadden, "Clergy Involvement in Civil Rights," 118.

64. Jason Bivins, "*Embattled Majority*: Part II of Jason Bivins on His Work *Embattled Majority*," *Religion in American History* (blog), November 7, 2012, accessed June 10, 2015, http://usreligion .blogspot.com/2012/11/embattled-majority-part-ii-of-jason.html.

65. For scholar of religion David Chidester, the Christian Right and its supporters combined two usually distinct Protestant positions in order to forge a renewed political agenda for the 1980s and beyond. "The political crusaders of the religious right combined a *premillennial* separatism in theology with a *postmillennial* religio-political vision of God's kingdom unfolding in America." See Chidester, *Patterns of Power*, 275.

66. In this sense, I follow the exemplary work of political scientist Michael Lienesch, who argues that for many liberal academics and journalists, including Lear himself, "conservative movements are the meteors of our political atmosphere. Awesome and unpredictable, they streak across our skies

in a blaze of right-wing frenzy, only to fall to earth cold and exhausted, consumed by their own passionate heat." For more, see Michael Lienesch, "Right-Wing Religion: Christian Conservatism as a Political Movement," *Political Science Quarterly* 97, no. 3 (Autumn 1982): 403–25.

67.   For more on this period's economic history as intellectual history, see Imre Szeman, "Entrepreneurship as the New Common Sense," *South Atlantic Quarterly* 114, no. 3 (2015): 471–90.

68.   For more on America's fault lines, see Kevin Kruse and Julian Zelizer, *Fault Lines: A History of the United States Since 1974* (New York: W. W. Norton, 2019).

69.   This book relies on scholar of religion David Chidester's writings on *power* for its analyses of religion and American politics. For Chidester, "*political power* is generated out of a conflict of interests, and it may be exercised to enforce one set of social interests over another, to set the terms within which social interests might be realized, and even to instill certain interests in those who find themselves under the control of a particular domain of power." In addition, "*power* pervades social relations; it produces the very strategies through which individuals participate in society; and it generates powerful symbols, myths, and ideologies through which contending individuals and social groups are defined and define themselves. *Power* is the dynamic energy that infuses a social system" (my emphasis). For more, see Chidester, *Patterns of Power*, 8.

70.   For Chidester, civil religion is best understood as a form of consensus, one that has "achieved a relatively unified consensus by excluding others from full participation" (107). I would argue that conservative Protestants have been on the losing side of this formulation more often than not. It is productive methodologically to refer to civil religion as a formation of power in order to emphasize its consensus-generating capacities.

71.   For more on this particular approach to historical analysis, epitomized by the publications of the academic journal *History of the Present*, refer to the pamphlet authored by historians Joan Scott, Ethan Kleinberg, and Gary Wilder, *Theses on Theory and History*, Wild On Collective, May 2018, accessed January 4, 2019, http://theoryrevolt.com.

72.   White, *Reforming Sodom*, 1–16.

73.   Marty, "A Profile on Norman Lear," 1986.

74.   Robert J. Thompson, *Adventures on Prime Time: The Television Programs of Stephen J. Cannell* (New York: Greenwood, 1999), 1–25.

75.   For more, see Robert C. Allen, ed., *Channels of Discourse, Reassembled: Television and Contemporary Criticism* (Chapel Hill: University of North Carolina Press, 1987).

1. NORMAN LEAR, THE CHRISTIAN RIGHT, AND THE POLITICS OF THE RELIGIOUS LEFT

1.   Martin Marty, "A Profile of Norman Lear: Another Pilgrim's Progress," *Christian Century*, January 21, 1987, 56.

2.   Marty, 58, my emphasis.

3.   See Jay Demerath III, "Cultural Victory and Organizational Defeat in the Paradoxical Decline of Liberal Protestantism," *Journal for the Scientific Study of Religion* 34, no. 4 (December 1995): 458–69.

4.   See David A. Hollinger, "After Cloven Tongues of Fire: Ecumenical Protestantism and the Modern American Encounter with Diversity," *Journal of American History* 98, no. 1 (June 2011): 21–48. For Hollinger, "The leadership of ecumenical Protestantism, as it engaged the diversity of the modern world, enabled its community of faith to serve, among its other roles, as a commodious *halfway house* to what for lack of a better term we can call post-Protestant secularism" (my emphasis, 46).

5. The significance of Lear's leadership relative to the ecumenical mainline comes into sharper focus when understood as part of what Hollinger calls "the loss by the old Protestant establishment to secular enterprises of some of the energies that had made it a formidable presence in American life" (29).

6. Leigh Eric Schmidt, *Restless Souls: The Making of American Spirituality* (New York: HarperOne, 2005). Schmidt has suggested a similar formulation for his own purposes, a "doubled perspective" that is at once open yet critical (xi). For historian David Hollinger, this characteristic of ecumenical Protestant analysis is best understood as "self-interrogation" or "self-critique." For Hollinger, this practice gave Protestants and others the confidence to explore outside their own traditions and church structures for perhaps better means of achieving their respective religio-political goals. See David Hollinger, "Afterword and Commentary: Religious Liberalism and Ecumenical Self-Interrogation," in *American Religious Liberalism*, ed. Leigh Schmidt and Sally Promey (Bloomington: Indiana University Press, 2012), 374–87.

7. John Lardas Modern, *Secularism in Antebellum America* (Chicago: University of Chicago Press, 2011), 128n20. For Modern, "Religious liberals tended to define social justice as a religious issue because the object of such justice was the whole of humanity."

8. As a result, the academic tendency to equate "backlash" with purely reactionary and thus conservative actors has to be seriously reevaluated in both scholarly and public venues.

9. I am following Schmidt's terminological lead in two ways: describing Lear as a religious liberal with a spiritual politics of tolerance and civility and identifying Lear as a significant actor in the history of the Spiritual Left in the recent American past. In fact, Lear's spiritual politics manifested in both public and private settings. For example, he established his own version of a retreat community where each Columbus Day, Lear and others would set out on a pilgrimage to poet Robert Frost's former estate (now owned by Lear) as part of a gathering that has gone on since the early 1980s. Marty himself mentions this retreat by name in his *Christian Century* piece and recalls fondly how Lear responded to the notion of worship as gratitude. These yearly meetings cultivated multiple characteristics of religious liberalism identified by Schmidt, including an emphasis on solitary contemplation, seeking, and mystical experience. In this way, Lear became part of (and thus representative of) the ecumenical mainline within American religious liberalism.

10. Norman Lear, *Even This I Get to Experience* (New York: Penguin, 2015), 20.

11. Lear, 34.

12. Lear, 51. Lear was aware of both domestic and global instances of anti-Semitism, which in turn influenced his spiritual politics. His hometown of New Haven, Connecticut, featured a university (Yale) that had a quota system for its Jewish applicants. Combined with Coughlin's broadcasts and news of Mussolini's anti-Jewish legislation in Italy, Lear began to feel out of place relative to the rest of the American melting pot.

13. Lear had participated in his Bar Mitzvah only seven years before his decision to enroll. The ceremony took place in Shaari Zedek synagogue in New York City.

14. For American religious historian Elesha Coffman, "the mainline" as both category and narrative descriptor is a retroactive one. "A coalition of highly educated, theologically and politically liberal Protestants" emerged during the first quarter of the twentieth century to establish themselves as the nation's moral and cultural guardians through their flagship periodical, the *Christian Century*. "The rise of the mainline coincided with a long reign of liberal politics, which began fitfully with the Progressives and gathered strength with the New Deal." See Elesha J. Coffman, *The Christian Century and the Rise of the Protestant Mainline* (New York: Oxford University Press, 2013).

15. By the time Marty's *Christian Century* piece was published, he and Lear had been friends for the better part of a decade, dating back to their work in and around Lear's ABC-broadcast variety show *I Love Liberty*.

16. For an example of how Marty could serve as *data* for journalists and scholars alike, see Margaret O'Brien-Steinfels and Peter Steinfels, "The New Awakening: Getting Religion in the Video Age," *Channels of Communication* 5, no. 2 (January/February 1983): 24–27, 62.

17. My usage of "liberal" and "progressive" is interchangeable in this work. These terms refer to individuals and organizations (such as Lear and People for the American Way) that set themselves against the politics and policies of Ronald Reagan in the 1980s. I rely on a document titled "The 'Remaking of America': A Message to the Churches" published in *Christianity and Crisis* for the content of this political and religious liberalism. For more on this historical context, see Christian Smith, *Resisting Reagan: The US Central America Peace Movement* (Chicago: University of Chicago Press, 1996); Hilary Cunningham, *God and Caesar at the Rio Grande: Sanctuary and the Politics of Religion* (Minneapolis: University of Minnesota Press, 1995).

18. For an example of this type of analysis, see Charles P. Lutz, "Middle America: Theologically Formed," *Christian Century*, March 18, 1970, 324.

19. For more, see Tina Rosenberg, "How the Media Made the Moral Majority," *Washington Monthly*, May 1982, 26–34. Original citation found in Steven P. Miller, *Age of Evangelicalism: America's Born-Again Years* (New York: Oxford University Press, 2014).

20. For historian Thomas Borstelmann, "An unexpected and little noticed result of this peculiar confluence of egalitarianism and market values in the 1970s was a striking reversal in the contents of the public and private spheres of American society." See Thomas Borstelmann, *The 1970s: A New Global History from Civil Rights to Economic Inequality* (Princeton, NJ: Princeton University Press, 2012), 17.

21. Wendy Wall, *Inventing the American Way: The Politics of Consensus from the New Deal to the Civil Rights Movement* (New York: Oxford University Press, 2008). Like Wall, I am also interested in "the ways in which Americans' common language and iconography both divided them and drew them together." This was especially the case with a phrase such as "the American Way," which was supported in both the private and public sectors by businesses, the federal government, and interfaith organizations such as the National Council of Christians and Jews. This common language emphasized a "shared public vocabulary" that established a "framework in which many social and economic issues were ultimately addressed. That framework privileged individual freedom, national unity, and a shared faith in God above all else" (10–11).

22. The term "relevance programming" describes a transitional period in American television history marking the ascendancy of a new type of prime-time programming. It was controversial because it addressed the most divisive issues of the period, including women's rights, racism, sexism, and religious intolerance, in front of hundreds of millions of viewers weekly. This approach differed radically from the previous network policy of "least offensive programming." See Gary Edgerton, *The Columbia History of American Television* (New York: Columbia University Press, 2007). See also Ella Taylor, *Prime-Time Families: Television Culture in Postwar America* (Berkeley: University of California Press, 1989).

23. Lear's activism can be connected historically to two separate but related liberal responses to religious diversity. For historian David Mislin, these two traditions were those of the Social Gospel, which included "the effort to link religion and popular culture [which] also inspired churches to make better use of the nascent advertising industry and growing mass media" and an approach that embraced religious pluralism as a spiritual value. See David Mislin, *Saving Faith: Making Religious Pluralism an American Value at the Dawn of the Secular Age* (Ithaca, NY: Cornell University Press, 2015), 8.

24. For more, see Daniel Callahan, "The Quest for Social Relevance," *Daedalus* 96, no. 1 (Winter 1967): 151–79.

25. Mislin, *Saving Faith*, 65.

26. Norman Lear, "Liberty and Its Responsibilities," in *Broadcast Journalism, 1979–1981: The Eighth Alfred I. Dupont Columbia University Survey*, ed. Marvin Barrett (New York: Everest, 1982).

27. I refer back to this phrasing throughout because it defines the relevance thrust that lay behind each and every show Lear wrote during this period, not to mention those composed for Mary Tyler Moore and Alan Alda by individuals such as James Brooks and Larry Gelbart.

28. For more, see Tona J. Hangen, *Redeeming the Dial: Radio, Religion, and Popular Culture in America* (Chapel Hill: University of North Carolina Press, 2002), 153. See also Heather Hendershot, "God's Angriest Man: Carl McIntire, Cold War Fundamentalism, and Right-Wing Broadcasting," *American Quarterly* 59, no. 2 (June 2007): 373–96.

29. Based on the work of Courtney Bender and others, one could also argue that Lear demonstrates a "politics of spiritual pluralism" in his activism and organizing. See Courtney Bender and Omar McRoberts, "Mapping a Field: Why and How to Study Spirituality" (New York: SSRC Working Paper, 2012).

30. Lear, "Liberty and Its Responsibilities," 236.

31. Lear was not the only spiritual liberal who referred to the writings of Justice Hand. Mainline supporters including Donald and Peggy Shriver also refer to his writings as a way of addressing the divisiveness that characterized much of the religious politics during the 1970s and 1980s. See Peggy Shriver, *The Bible Vote: Religion and the New Right* (New York: Pilgrim, 1981).

32. Lear, "Liberty and Its Responsibilities," 237.

33. Lear, 237.

34. Lear's claim here is debatable. I would argue that he had as much to disagree with the Christian Right about in terms of their claims as he did with their specific stances on social issues.

35. For more, see the special issue of *Annals of the American Academy of Political and Social Science* published in 1970 titled "The Sixties: Radical Change in American Religion."

36. For examples of these, see *Pray TV* (1980) and *In God We Tru$t* (1980). If Lear had gone on to produce a movie instead of going with thirty-second spots for his initial People for the American Way organizing, he, too, could be added to this list based on the title, *Religion*.

37. "Framing" describes the manner in which a group or community of people come to be understood according to the values and social conditioning of another group or community of individuals primarily through linguistic and discursive formations. Such formations do not have to include stereotypes, but in Lear's case, they very much did according to preceding patterns first established by journalists who reported on the events of the Scopes trial to a national audience. For anthropologist Susan Harding, this discursive tradition emerged in order to better represent "the repugnant cultural other." For more, see Susan Harding, "Representing Fundamentalism: The Problem of the Repugnant Cultural Other," *Social Research* 58, no. 2 (Summer 1991): 373–93.

38. For Shields, this type of analysis was all too common even in the most academic of sources. In fact, this particular quotation comes from an issue of *Annals of the American Academy of Political and Social Science* published in 1948.

39. Regarding the relationship between Catholics and Protestants, Shields argues, "It is remarkable that Progressive and postwar liberals were able to see deep affinities between Catholics and evangelicals, especially given the sharp tensions between them. It is even more remarkable that they articulated what some regard as the major fault lines in today's culture wars." For more, see Jon A. Shields, "Framing the Christian Right: How Progressives and Post-war Liberals Constructed the Religious Right," *Journal of Church and State* 53, no. 4 (Autumn 2011): 650.

40. Shields, 650.

41. Lear, "Liberty and Its Responsibilities," 238.

42. Harding, "Representing Fundamentalism," 374. Also see Harding, "American Protestant Moralism and the Secular Imagination: From Temperance to the Moral Majority," *Social Research* 76, no. 4 (Winter 2009): 1277–306.

43. This statement comes from a talk titled "America Has Not Yet Awakened to the Threat" that Lear gave at the Beverly Hills Bar Association in June 1986. In it, he reached back to what historian Leigh Schmidt has documented as "priestcraft" by calling such entrepreneurs of the spirit "talented manipulators" who are out to give simple answers to not-so-simple questions.

44. Norman Lear, "Our Political Leaders Mustn't Be Evangelists," *USA Today*, August 17, 1984.

45. For more from the production side as well as the media side of the culture wars, see James Davison Hunter, *The Culture Wars: The Struggle to Define America* (New York: Basic, 1991).

46. One could argue that this appreciation for the spiritual character of one's surroundings was a transcendentalist one that had been appropriated by Lear (and other religious/spiritual liberals) in his understanding of spirituality. For scholar of religion Cara Burnidge, "From nature walks to reading, transcendentalists expanded acceptable forms of religious practice for liberal Protestants." I would also add for Jews, like Lear, who were interested in interfaith cooperation. See Cara Burnidge, "Protestant Liberalism," in *Encyclopedia of Religion in America*, ed. Charles H. Lippy and Peter W. Williams (Washington, DC: CQ, 2010), 1783–91, http://dx.doi.org/10.4135/978 1608712427.n301.

47. Both of these citations come from Molly Worthen, "Faithless," review of *The Twilight of the American Enlightenment: The 1950s and the Crisis of Liberal Belief*, by George Marsden, *Democracy: A Journal of Ideas* 32 (Spring 2014), 77–85. The latter quotation is Marsden while the former is Worthen.

48. Schmidt has suggested a similar formulation for his own purposes, a "doubled perspective" that is at once open yet critical (*Restless Souls*, xi).

49. Amanda Anderson, "The Liberal Aesthetic," in *Theory after Theory*, ed. Jane Elliott and Derek Attridge (New York: Routledge, 2011), 249–61. For more, see Amanda Anderson, "Aesthetics: The Case of Trilling and Adorno," *Critical Inquiry* 40, no. 4 (Summer 2014): 418–38.

50. Anderson, "Liberal Aesthetic," 251.

51. Burnidge, "Protestant Liberalism."

52. Another important element of religious liberalism to consider in light of Norman Lear's biography is its self-interrogative impulse relative to its own truth claims and those of others. For historian David Hollinger, ecumenical self-interrogation is one of the most important aspects of liberal Protestant thought because it has encouraged its practitioners to venture beyond the borders of their own traditions as part of a larger seeking culture that has characterized US religious life since its midcentury. For more, see Hollinger, "Afterword and Commentary," in Schmidt and Promey, *American Religious Liberalism*, 374–87.

53. Anderson, "Liberal Aesthetic," 251.

54. One such address took place at Harvard Divinity School in 2002. The title, "Power and Principles: Leaders in Media and Finance," conveyed Lear's interest in harmonizing spiritual values with ethical business practices. This impulse lead Lear and James Burke, former chairman of Johnson and Johnson, to found the Business Enterprise Trust in 1989 with help of many of America's most prominent figures in business, including Warren Buffett, Katharine Graham, and Henry B. Schacht. Lear and others focused their attention on business leaders who set positive examples in times of what Lear identified as "bottom line thinking." In their words, the Business Enterprise Trust "identifies and honors acts of courage, integrity, and social vision in business" by way of a strong, "constructive business ethic." This is but one manifestation of Lear's influence in the corporate world. For more, see David Bollier, ed., *Aiming Higher: 25 Stories of How Companies Prosper by Combining Sound Management and Social Vision* (New York: Amacom, 1996).

55. This document, like others in my Lear archive, does not possess page numbers. The particular words in this citation are arguably as important as their location within the speech itself. The longer Press Club speech has, in fact, been broken down into subsections including this excerpt's section, "Confessions of an Unaffiliated Groper." The subsection's title says a great deal about how Lear

conceives of his own spiritual journey of discovery in addition to his notion of affiliation regarding a religious or spiritual tradition.

56. Hollinger, "Afterword and Commentary," in Schmidt and Promey, *American Religious Liberalism*, 374–87. For Hollinger, "If the field of religious history were to be understood not so much as the history of various religions, but rather as the history of *engagements* with religious issues, . . . [we] could direct attention to the ways in which religious communities sustain themselves, transform themselves, or decline, in relation to intellectual critique as well as in response to social conditions" (385).

57. These names compose a short selection of authors Lear cites in public. One could argue that these sources also serve as influences on Lear and his writings as part of a broader reading list.

58. Both Lear's wife and historian Martin Marty suggested to Lear that he read James's *Varieties* according to Lear's presentation.

59. For historian Matthew Hedstrom, "The Jamesian emphasis on religious experience permeated American religious liberalism in the twentieth century and branched in a variety of directions." For more, see Matthew Hedstrom, *The Rise of Liberal Religion: Book Culture and American Spirituality in the Twentieth Century* (New York: Oxford University Press, 2013), 8.

60. See Hedstrom.

61. Schmidt, *Restless Souls*, 57.

62. Lear is particularly drawn to Bellah's writings on "civil religion" and its prophetic qualities. In fact, Lear favors civil religion as a way of thinking about religious diversity and free speech in the United States.

63. This sentiment comes from private correspondence from Lear written to a Mr. Kohl, thanking him for making Lear part of the Woodland Historical Document Collection. I have not been able to determine which society Kohl represents or who Kohl himself is. The title given to this letter is "Packing for the Spiritual Journey."

64. This citation comes from Lear's "The Search for E Pluribus Unum" speech given at the National Press Club on December 9, 1993. For Lear, *mama-loshen* is "a Yiddish word describing the understanding that comes when one's common sense derives as much from the soul as the mind. The Sermon on the Mount is simple mama-loshen. And anything that ain't mama-loshen doesn't square with my religious sensibilities." More of this can be found at Norman Lear, "A Church for People Like Us," HuffPost, May 1, 2010, accessed December 10, 2015, https://www.huffpost.com/entry/mamaloshen-a-church-for-p_b_480896.

65. Despite the anti-Catholicism that coursed through James's writings in *Varieties of Religious Experience*, Hedstrom argues that it helped "twentieth-century moderns retain spiritual vitality." The text was also important "because of its applicability to those seeking meaning, happiness, and wholeness in a modern, consumerist, psychologically oriented culture." For more, see Hedstrom, *The Rise of Liberal Religion*, 8, 93.

66. For more on this slippage and its relationship to Jewish theatricality, see Andrea Most, *Theatrical Liberalism: Jews and Popular Entertainment in America* (New York: New York University Press, 2013). I will draw on Most's writings in the next chapter on television and spiritual liberalism in order to highlight the particularly *Jewish* aspects of Lear's programming regarding liberal democracy and its defense of free speech and separation of church and state.

67. Lear, "The Search for E Pluribus Unum."

68. Lear.

69. Schmidt, *Restless Souls*, 114, 138.

70. My use of "seeker" here reflects both analytical and popular usages. In a 2008 address to his fellow PFAW supporters, Lear observed that "groper" may not have been the best term to describe his journey. "In light of recent headlines, friends have advised me to change groper to seeker. . . . To some extent, it would seem we are all seekers." These words come from Lear's "Why I Am a Born

Again American" speech given March 19, 2008. The title alone suggests that Lear has attempted to challenge normative applications of terms such as "spirit" and "born-again" with his own unique understanding.

71. The fact that Lear spoke at all at a gathering such as this speaks volumes about how scholars conceive of Lear's significance in conversations about values and religion. It also further supports Martin Marty's original *Christian Century* contention that Lear deserves to be a part of discussions concerning human well-being in a late-modern age regardless of the setting.

72. These topics will be explored in depth in subsequent chapters. For more, see Norman Lear, "Rewriting the Bottom Line: Hollywood, Profits, and the Life of the Spirit," *Image: A Journal of the Arts and Religion* 27 (Summer 2000): 117–23.

73. Norman Lear, "Nurturing Spirituality and Religion in an Age of Science and Technology," *Religion and Public Education* 16, no. 3 (Fall 1989): 395–408.

74. Lear.

75. Thomas M. Landy, "What's Missing from This Picture: Norman Lear Explains," *Commonweal* 119, no. 17 (October 1992): 17–20.

76. My interview with Norman Lear was conducted on April 28, 2014, at his home in Brentwood, California. This took place after I fulfilled all of Drew University's Institutional Review Board protocols.

77. For more on how I understand the relationship between popular culture and religion and its effective study, see R. Laurence Moore, "Religion, Secularization and the Shaping of the Culture Industry in Antebellum America," *American Quarterly* 41 (1989): 216–42.

78. Jason Bivins, *Religion of Fear: The Politics of Horror in Conservative Evangelicalism* (New York: Oxford University Press, 2008), 214.

79. Lear, "Rewriting the Bottom Line," 121.

80. For more, see Demerath, "Cultural Victory and Organizational Defeat in the Paradoxical Decline of Liberal Protestantism."

81. Jim McKairnes, "The Meaning of Lear," *American Way*, 1991.

82. Gerry Nadel, "All in His Family," *New Times*, July 9, 1977, accessed March 5, 2014, http://www .normanlear.com/backstory/press/all-in-his-family/.

2. *ALL IN THE FAMILY* AND THE SPIRITUAL POLITICIZATION OF THE AMERICAN SITCOM

1. For competing views, see Lynn Spigel and Michael Curtin, eds. *The Revolution Wasn't Televised: Sixties Television and Social Conflict* (New York: Routledge, 1997); Christine Acham, *Revolution Televised: Prime Time and the Struggle for Black Power* (Minneapolis: University of Minnesota Press, 2004).

2. Horace Newcomb and Robert S. Alley, *The Producer's Medium: Conversations with Creators of American TV* (New York: Oxford University Press, 1983), 177.

3. "It was largely as a new marketing device," argues historian Ella Taylor, "that the turbulence of the middle to late 1960s and the adversarial spirit of the generation coming of age during this period found their way into the genres of television entertainment." See Ella Taylor, *Prime-Time Families: Television Culture in Postwar America* (Berkeley: University of California Press, 1989), 42. While I agree with the economic origins of the term, it is also thoroughly a product of Lear's own spiritual orientation toward the social and raising awareness of how best to address its shortcomings.

4.   James Wall, "Norman Lear in His Pulpit: Editorial Correspondence," *Christian Century*, November 12, 1975, 1019–20.

5.   Wall, 1020.

6.   As argued in a previous note, "the mainline" as both category and narrative descriptor is a retroactive one. "A coalition of highly educated, theologically and politically liberal Protestants" emerged during the first quarter of the twentieth century to establish themselves as the nation's moral and cultural guardians through their flagship periodical, the *Christian Century*. "The rise of the mainline coincided with a long reign of liberal politics, which began fitfully with the Progressives and gathered strength with the New Deal." See Elesha J. Coffman, *The Christian Century and the Rise of the Protestant Mainline* (New York: Oxford University Press, 2013).

7.   These were the words before the official premier of *All in the Family* in 1971 on CBS. The show had gone through three different pilots and two networks before it landed, rather slowly, on CBS. The full disclaimer read as follows: "The program you are about to see is *All in the Family*. It seeks to throw a humorous spotlight on our frailties, prejudices, and concerns. By making them a source of laughter, we hope to show—in a mature fashion—just how absurd they are."

8.   Contemporary authors continue to describe Lear's impact in glowing terms. See Emily Nussbaum, "The Great Divide: Norman Lear, Archie Bunker, and the Rise of the Bad Fan," *New Yorker*, April 7, 2014.

9.   For more, see Daniel Callahan, "The Quest for Social Relevance," *Daedalus* 96, no. 1 (Winter 1967): 151–79.

10.   Besides his fellow religious liberals, Lear also found inspiration for his programming in the writings of renowned journalist Edward R. Murrow. For Lear, "Murrow said that television could and should illuminate, inspire, and educate, or it would be just wires and lights in a box." For more, see Norman Lear, "Television: Its Culture, Its Impact, Its Ethics, Its Future," Norman Lear Seminars at the Museum of Broadcasting: The Mark Goodson Seminar Series (June 1986), accessed March 20, 2014, http://www.normanlear.com/backstory/interviews/television-its-culture-its-impact-its -ethics-its-future/.

11.   "Theatrical liberalism" comes from Andrea Most, *Theatrical Liberalism: Jews and Popular Entertainment in America* (New York: New York University Press, 2013).

12.   For more, see Cara Burnidge, "Protestant Liberalism," in *Encyclopedia of Religion in America*, ed. Charles H. Lippy and Peter W. Williams (Washington, DC: CQ, 2010), 1783–91, http://dx.doi.org /10.4135/9781608712427.n301. See also Cara Burnidge, "U.S. Foreign Relations and American Religious Liberalism," *Oxford Research Encyclopedia of Religion*, accessed March 2, 2018, http:// religion.oxfordre.com/view/10.1093/acrefore/9780199340378.001.0001/acrefore-9780199340 378-e-410.

13.   This is one of the foundational arguments in Andrew Hartman, *A War for the Soul of America: A History of the Culture Wars* (Chicago: University of Chicago Press, 2015).

14.   See "Meanwhile: Norman Lear and Spirituality," *Christianity Today*, April 23, 1982, 42.

15.   Norman Lear, *Even This I Get to Experience* (New York: Penguin, 2015), 235. Lear's use of "spirit" prefigures much of his spiritual politics that would later surface through his nonprofit organization People for the American Way in the early 1980s.

16.   Lear's childhood experiences of Father Charles Coughlin mirrored those of critical theorist Theodor Adorno, who made arguments similar to Lear's in terms of the social theory of conservative religiosity. For more, see Theodor Adorno, *The Psychological Technique of Martin Luther Thomas' Radio Addresses* (Palo Alto, CA: Stanford University Press, 2000); Paul Apostolidis, *Stations of the Cross: Adorno and Christian Right Radio* (Durham, NC: Duke University Press, 2000).

17.   Jason Bivins, *Religion of Fear: The Politics of Horror in Conservative Evangelicalism* (New York: Oxford University Press, 2008), 10–11. This description builds on Bivins's previous work on Christian antiliberalism. See Jason C. Bivins, *The Fracture of Good Order: Christian Antiliberalism and*

the Challenge to American Politics (Chapel Hill: University of North Carolina Press, 2003). For Bivins, mainline to liberal Protestant organizations such as Sojourners "present their activism as a politics beyond politics; their concerns are frequently neither legislative nor programmatic but exemplary of what they call the 'prophetic' nature of Christian activism, which the rigidity of political logic cannot capture" (14).

18. For more, see Norman Lear, "Liberty and its Responsibilities," in *Broadcast Journalism 1979–1981; The Eighth Alfred I. Dupont Columbia University Survey*, ed. Marvin Barrett (New York: Everest, 1982), 236.

19. Leigh Schmidt, *Restless Souls: The Making of American Spirituality* (New York: HarperOne, 2006), 19.

20. Burnidge, "Protestant Liberalism."

21. Most, *Theatrical Liberalism*, 10.

22. This typology can also be found in Most.

23. For more, see Charles S. Liebman, "Toward a Theory of Jewish Liberalism," in *The Religious Situation 1969*, ed. Donald R. Cutler (Boston: Beacon, 1969), 1034. Additionally, see Michael Parenti, "Political Values and Religious Cultures: Jews, Catholics, and Protestants," *Journal for the Scientific Study of Religion* 6, no. (Autumn 1967): 259–69.

24. Matthew Hedstrom, *The Rise of Liberal Religion: Book Culture and American Spirituality in the Twentieth Century* (New York: Oxford University Press, 2013), 9.

25. Most, *Theatrical Liberalism*, 67.

26. Most, 11.

27. The comments concerning Jewish prayers were uttered by then Southern Baptist Convention president Bailey Smith during the Religious Roundtable's National Affairs Briefing in Dallas on August 22, 1980. Smith's words are an example of a particular event or television program that helped catalyze Lear's transition from television producer and writer to nonprofit activist. Another similar incident took place during a Jimmy Swaggart program in which he asked his viewership to pray for the removal of a Supreme Court justice. To Lear, this was a fundamental violation of the civic rules that govern such utterances in public and a violation of the separation of church and state in light of various churches' tax-exempt status.

28. For more, see Jon A. Shields, "Framing the Christian Right: How Progressives and Post-war Liberals Constructed the Religious Right," *Journal of Church and State* 53, no. 4 (Autumn 2011): 635–55.

29. In an interview for the documentary *America in Primetime*, actor Rob Reiner estimated that close to one-quarter of the country had seen an episode of *All in the Family*.

30. For more on Lear's televisual impact, see Martin Kasindorf, "Archie and Maude and Fred and Norman and Alan," *New York Times Magazine*, June 24, 1973; Horace Newcomb, "The Television Artistry of Norman Lear," *Prospects: An American Studies Annual* (1975): 109–25; Horace Newcomb and Paul M. Hirsch, "Television as a Cultural Forum," in *Interpreting Television*, ed. W. D. Rowland and B. Watkins (Beverly Hills, CA: Sage, 1985), 68–73; Newcomb and Alley, *The Producer's Medium*.

31. "King Lear," *Time*, April 5, 1976, 80.

32. The term in quotes reflects Lear's usage as well as that of various journalists who made the similar observation.

33. Norman Lear and Barbara Cady, "Playboy Interview: Norman Lear," *Playboy*, March 1976.

34. Lear's emphasis on academic and religious freedom of speech were foundational emphases of both Protestant liberalism and theatrical liberalism.

35. Newcomb and Alley, *The Producer's Medium*, 14.

36. Newcomb and Alley, 42.

37. For Newcomb and Alley, "He asked the viewer to debate the issues, confront the problems, disagree. . . . In making television comedy a forum for the exploration of ideas about the social order, Lear has placed on the public agenda attitudes about some very serious questions" (178–79).

38. Norman Lear, "Interview with Norman Lear," in Newcomb and Alley, *The Producer's Medium*, 185.

39. Lear's understanding, application, and usage of "civil religion" as a category and tool of civic main-tenance became clearer over the course of the 1970s as he began developing the idea for his non-profit organization People for the American Way. I would argue, however, that whenever Lear argued for greater civility in public life (a call made by numerous concerned members of the mid-dling mainline), he was deploying a nascent form of Robert Bellah's notion of "civil religion" as a uniquely (religious) liberal conception of American public life. For an example, see chapter 1 of Jim Castelli, *A Plea for Common Sense: Resolving the Clash Between Religion and Politics* (New York: Harper and Row, 1988). For Castelli (*A Plea for Common Sense* was a PFAW-published text), "Many of those on the Religious Right today use the language of religion to attack the most fundamental beliefs of the American civil religion" (19).

40. In this usage, "spiritual formation" describes the process through which a medium (television in this case) facilitated the formation of a particular type of citizen (a civil, privately religious one) based on the philosophy or value system of theatrical and religious liberalism. This argument is the spiritual equivalent of the one made by sociologist N. Jay Demerath III in "Cultural Victory and Organizational Defeat in the Paradoxical Decline of Liberal Protestantism," *Journal of the Sci-entific Study of Religion* 34, no. 4 (December 1995): 458–69.

41. For one of the earlier studies of this phenomenon, see Daniel Yankelovich, *The New Morality: A Profile of American Youth in the '70s* (New York: McGraw-Hill, 1974).

42. Two much-viewed media sources, the *Los Angeles Times* and *TV Guide*, hosted extended discus-sions of this shift in moral sensibility during the early 1970s and how it was shaping the interests and purchasing decisions of the nation's youth.

43. Max Gunther, "TV and the New Morality," *TV Guide*, October 14, 1972.

44. Both organizations utilized writing campaigns both to get the word out about their respective orga-nizations and to challenge the networks to broadcast more wholesome programming. Much of this organizational energy can be understood as a nascent form of what would become the Chris-tian Right through the formation of the electronic church and the election of Ronald Reagan as president.

45. Gunther, "TV and the New Morality," 12.

46. This "New Morality" was understood at the time as expressing values antithetical to "traditional values."

47. There will be more on this in the following chapter, "Norman Lear Goes Prime Time."

48. "New Morality on TV Debated," *Los Angeles Times*, March 25, 1976.

49. For more, see Robert Sklar, *Prime-Time America: Life on and Behind the Television Screen* (New York: Oxford University Press, 1982).

50. Robert Sklar, "Electronic Americana," *American Film* 2, no. 5 (March 1977): 61.

51. For American studies scholar Lawrence E. Mintz, characterization within a sitcom tells us a great deal about the social values and beliefs of the writer or production team. This is especially the case when characters and character types take on additional cultural weight due to their popularity across time and space. The "wise fool" or "negative fool" tradition helped audiences understand and comprehend Archie Bunker and his behavior in prime time by reminding the audience on an ideological level that "the wise fool represents the democratic credo that the common man has an innate wisdom superior to the 'book learning' of the upper classes and intellectuals." See Law-rence E. Mintz, "Ideology in the Television Situation Comedy," *Studies in Popular Culture* 8, no. 2 (1985): 46.

52. Sklar, "Electronic Americana," 62.

53. David Marc, "TV Auteurism," *American Film* 7, no. 2 (November 1, 1981): 52. Marc also contends that the most effective way to identify television authorship is to focus on "thematic continuity" across a group of shows.

54. Marc, 54. For a largely conservative and working-class reading of *All in the Family*, see Mike LaVelle, "Biases of All in the Family," *Chicago Tribune*, January 2, 1973. LaVelle's reading of Lear's sitcom is both unrelenting and ruthless. For Lavelle, Lear's comedy is simply a product of money and New Class power, "It seems that we in America have fostered a new class whose members have, like those in Communist countries, taken power to their breasts and their banks and heaped scorn on those below them" (18).

55. Mintz, "Ideology in the Television Situation Comedy," 48.

56. Clarence Petersen, "Scope: Bigoted, Dumb, Clumsy, TV's Archie Bunker," *Chicago Tribune*, April 16, 1972.

57. *All in the Family* was not an immediate success, either critically or popularly, based on reviews and the Nielsen ratings. It also took some time for it to be recognized for what it was—hard-hitting social commentary in the form of a prime-time network sitcom.

58. Numerous articles and studies were written and conducted during the early 1970s out of an effort to discover whether the show ultimately reinforced or challenged bigotry on both societal and individual levels. For one example, see Lear's response in Norman Lear, "Laughing While We Face Our Prejudices,'" *New York Times*, April 11, 1971.

59. Kay Gardella, "Carroll O'Connor: A Tight-Lipped Type of Liberal," *Chicago Tribune*, August 26, 1974. Lear goes so far as to quote a favorable review from an African American source to counteract criticism of his writing style. There is perhaps no better example of liberal patronizing then Lear's method of argumentative defense—cite a favorable minority response in order to defend one's racial innocence while demonstrating one's tolerance of such difference.

60. For more on this school of thought and its history, see Hartman, *A War for the Soul of America*. For a condensed version, see Andrew Hartman, "The Neoconservative Counterrevolution," *Jacobin*, April 23, 2015, accessed April 30, 2015, https://www.jacobinmag.com/2015/04/neoconservatives -kristol-podhoretz-hartman-culture-war/.

61. Gardella's mentioning of "exchange of free ideas" could have been better phrased as "free exchange of ideas" to reflect the criticisms of conservative televangelists such as Jerry Falwell and Pat Robertson, who also attacked Lear and his defense of the fairness doctrine as smoke screens for his own aspirations and those of the federal government and the FCC. There is, in fact, a great deal of resentment in Gardella's writing directed toward liberals, even on talk shows, who cut conservative dialogue off from the get-go. This article is a fantastic snapshot of a developing conservative ressentiment in response to the liberal vision that put a bigoted working-class man on television in order to "throw a humorous light on our frailties" at his own (and others') expense.

62. Gardella, "Carroll O'Connor," B9.

63. For more, see Stephen Schryer, *Fantasies of the New Class: Ideologies of Professionalism in Post– World War II American Fiction* (New York: Columbia University Press, 2006).

64. "The Team Behind Archie Bunker and Co.," *Time*, September 25, 1972.

65. "The Team Behind Archie Bunker and Co.," 9.

66. Horace Newcomb, "The Television Artistry of Norman Lear," *Prospects: An Annual of American Cultural Studies* 2 (October 1977): 109–25.

67. Gerry Nadel, "All in His Family," *New Times*, July 8, 1977.

68. Horace Newcomb, ed. *Television: The Critical View* (New York: Oxford University Press, 1976). The first edition of *Television: The Critical View*, the earliest collection of academic television criticism, featured *All in the Family*, *Maude*, *Sanford and Son*, and *The Jeffersons* in a majority of its chapters.

69. James W. Chesebro and Caroline D. Hamsher, "Communication, Values, and Popular Television Series," in Newcomb, *Television*, 12. For more, see Michael Suman, ed. *Religion and Prime Time Television* (New York: Praeger, 1997). This text features a number of chapters written by scholars of American religion.

70.   Michael Arlen, "The Media Dramas of Norman Lear," in Newcomb, *Television*, 33. This chapter was first published on May 10, 1975, as an essay in the *New Yorker*.

71.   Philip Wander, "Counters in the Social Drama: Some Notes on *All in the Family*," in Newcomb, *Television*, 35.

72.   Wander, 37.

73.   Wander, 38.

74.   Wander, 40.

75.   Carol Taylor Williams, "It's Not So Much 'You've Come a Long Way, Baby'—as 'You're Gonna Make It After All,'" in Newcomb, *Television*, 43–53.

76.   Susan Harding, "Representing Fundamentalism: The Problem of the Repugnant Cultural Other," *Social Research* 58, no. 2 (Summer 1991): 374.

77.   This is to say two things. First, Lear and others in the middling or chattering mainline identified their religious liberalism within the same tradition of progressive Christianity and Judaism that was on the ground marching with King and others. And second, I am also suggesting that Lear's spiritual politics shared a common concern for remaining socially relevant *as* a spiritual value with his fellow supporters in the interfaith and ecumenical communities. See Kathryn Lofton, "Commonly Modern: Rethinking the Modernist-Fundamentalist Controversies," *Church History* 83, no. 1 (March 2014): 137–44.

78.   Neal Koch, "Why Mel Brooks and Bill Moyers Will Always Idolize Norman Lear," HuffPost, November 11, 2014, accessed January 20, 2016, https://www.huffpost.com/entry/norman-lear-pen -award_b_6130620.

79.   Stephen Kercher, *Revel with a Cause: Liberal Satire in Postwar America* (Chicago: University of Chicago Press, 2006), 1.

80.   Carroll O'Connor, "Foreword," in *God, Man, and Archie Bunker*, by Spencer Marsh (New York: Harper and Row, 1975), xii.

81.   The volume of the show's dialogue struck many commentators at the time as strange and out of place. Writers and creators such as Norman Lear, and Jackie Gleason before him, made it a point to model their sets and locations after their own childhood homes in either New York City or New Haven, Connecticut.

82.   The chair from *All in the Family* currently resides in the Smithsonian. Such diatribes and turns of phrase included "meathead," "dingbat," "laziest white boy," "stifle," and countless others. For Lear personally, Archie's chair meant everything to him because it was this chair, the chair of his father, that was first taken when Lear found out that he would be moving out of New Haven because his father had been arrested for selling fake bonds.

83.   Lear's strategy for breaking the show to the American people was to "drench" both the network and the audiences with as much characteristically controversial material as possible. From that point on, audiences would be more inclined to commit their time to watching the show on a week-to-week basis.

84.   Lear later named a People for the American Way primer *Liberty and Justice for Some*, suggesting that certain constituencies within the United States were abusing their First Amendment right to free speech by being religiously intolerant.

85.   While writing *All in the Family*, Lear actually received a Humanitarian Award from the NCCJ in 1976 for his television programming and its promotion of tolerance and religious diversity. Lear's religious sensibilities also reflected those of the NCCJ in its initial formation in the 1930s. As historian Wendy Wall has argued, the NCCJ was responsible for a number of "Tolerance Trios" and promotional campaigns on behalf of religious toleration as part of "the American Way," a phrase that Wall traces back to this very interfaith, interwar moment a quarter of the way into America's twentieth century. Lear would later adopt this phrase as the organizing motif for his nonprofit organization People for the American Way, formed in 1981. The history of this nonprofit is intimately

tied to Wall's narrative of liberal religion and commercial advertisers coming together to defend religions of democracy, consensus ideals, and unity out of diversity. For more, see Wendy Wall, *Inventing the American Way: The Politics of Consensus from the New Deal to the Civil Rights Movement* (New York: Oxford University Press, 2007).

86. For a similarly themed examination of prime-time television, see George Lipsitz, *Time Passages: Collective Memory and American Popular Culture* (Minneapolis: University of Minnesota Press, 1990). In particular, his chapter titled "The Meaning of Memory: Family, Class and Ethnicity in Early Network Television" is an underutilized source in the critical study of television and popular culture.

87. For more, see Jefferson R. Cowie, *Stayin' Alive: The 1970s and the Last Days of the Working Class* (New York: New, 2012).

88. For more, see Koch, "Why Mel Brooks and Bill Moyers Will Always Idolize Norman Lear."

89. Robert A. Schneider, "Church Federation in the Twentieth Century," in *Between the Times: The Travail of the Protestant Establishment in America, 1900–1960*, ed. William R. Hutchison (New York: Cambridge University Press, 1989), 110. For historian Gary Scott Smith, "To the extent that Roosevelt embraced a theological perspective, he largely affirmed the tenets of early twentieth-century liberal Christianity. He most highly valued the Bible's ethical teachings and stressed God's goodness and love, the Ten Commandments, and Christ's Sermon on the Mount. Like other theological liberals, he rejected the doctrine of human depravity and asserted, instead, that people were essentially good." For more, see Gastón Espinosa, ed., *Religion and the American Presidency: George Washington to George W. Bush with Commentary and Primary Sources* (New York: Columbia University Press, 2009), 185–210.

90. Felcher only appeared in one episode of *All in the Family* and, as such, was not a recurring character.

91. For more on this development as understood from the period, see Harold E. Quincy, *The Prophetic Clergy: Social Activism Among Protestant Ministers* (New York: Wiley, 1974).

92. For a concise introduction to the politics of the "New Breed" clergy and how it reflected the religious restructuring outlined by Hadden, Wuthnow, and others, see Harvey Cox, "The 'New Breed' in American Churches: Sources of Social Activism in American Religion," *Daedalus* 96, no. 1 (Winter 1967): 135–50.

93. Jeffrey K. Hadden, "Clergy Involvement in Civil Rights," *Annals of the American Academy of Political and Social Science* 387 (January 1970): 118–27. Various works by sociologists Robert Wuthnow and James Davison Hunter support Hadden's early conclusions in the language of "restructuring."

94. Here, I argue that Lear's organizing shared similar concerns and methods with the civil rights movement, but I would also argue that Lear and his supporters *imagined* themselves into such a tradition both in print and in publicly spoken word.

95. For more, see David Hollinger, "The Realist-Pacifist Summit Meeting of March 1942 and the Political Reorientation of Ecumenical Protestantism in the United States," *Church History* 79, no. 3 (September 2010): 654–77.

96. For more on this transition, see Robert O. Self, *All in the Family: The Realignment of American Democracy Since the 1960s* (New York: Hill and Wang, 2012). For Self, two forms of the breadwinner competed for social acceptance during this period—one liberal and the other conservative. Each possessed its own value system and understanding of the role of the federal government relative to the family that each system lionized.

97. Kathryn C. Montgomery, *Target Prime Time: Advocacy Groups and the Struggle Over Entertainment Television* (New York: Oxford University Press, 1989).

98. Lear, "Liberty and its Responsibilities."

99. Unpublished interview between Lear and director John Rich, "Television : Its Culture, Its Impact, Its Ethics, Its Future," Norman Lear Seminars at the Museum of Broadcasting The Mark

Goodson Seminar Series (June 1986), http://www.normanlear.com/backstory/interviews/tele
vision-its-culture-its-impact-its-ethics-its-future/. For Lear and his writers, Edith's character
exuded the idealized characteristics of the figure of Jesus Christ as teacher rather than source of
salvation. This representation of Jesus was also heavily inflected with a religious liberal emphasis
on Jesus as mediator, moderator, and medium of global communication.

100.   Marsh, *God, Man, and Archie Bunker*, 10–11.

101.   For Lear, to be "born again" was to realize the threat that the Christian Right posed to individuals the country over (to Lear and his supporters) and to act on that realization. In this case, Lear
decided to leave television proper in order to enter into American politics in a more official capacity through the formation of his nonprofit organization People for the American Way. For more,
see Norman Lear, "Why I Am a Born Again American," (speech, Take Back America Conference,
Washington, DC, March 19, 2008), accessed February 12, 2016, http://www.normanlear.com/life
-spirit/why-i-am-a-born-again-american/.

102.   Charles L. Sanders, "Is Archie Bunker the Real White America? Nation's New Hero Is a Beer-
Bellied Bigot with 60 Million Fans," *Ebony*, June 1971.

103.   Sanders, 192.

104.   Sanders, 192.

105.   For a study that examines progressive evangelical organizing that possessed a similar set of political concerns during this period, see Brantley Gassaway, *Progressive Evangelicals and the Pursuit of
Social Justice* (Chapel Hill: University of North Carolina Press, 2014).

106.   Richard Adler, ed., *All in the Family: A Critical Appraisal* (New York: Praeger, 1979), xxxix.

107.   The activist, or "New Breed," preachers of the 1960s and Lear's middling mainline of the 1970s
shared a common cause and method: to act as cultural and spiritual custodians to the nation
through the use of the latest intellectual, scientific, and social developments. The use of media in
this project is ambivalent at best, since many within these communities valued community over
what they deem televisual spectacle as witnessed in the electronic church.

108.   Margaret O'Brien-Steinfels and Peter Steinfels, "The New Awakening: Getting Religion in the
Video Age," *Channels of Communication* 5, no. 2 (January/February 1983): 27.

109.   For earlier examples of liberal programming in the 1960s, see Mike O'Connor, "Liberals in Space:
The 1960s Politics of *Star Trek*," *The Sixties: A Journal of History, Politics, and Culture* 5, no. 2
(December 2012): 185–203.

3. NORMAN LEAR, THE FCC, AND THE HOLY WAR OVER AMERICAN TELEVISION

1.   Numerous commentators at the time commented on how prime-time content post-Lear began to
shift toward edgier, less "family-safe" material. The most common way of identifying this shift was
to name and sometimes list the subject matter of various television programs; such subjects now
include racism, feminism, domestic violence, and nuclear destruction.

2.   For more on how this impacted the political history of this decade, see Robert Self, *All in the Family: The Realignment of American Democracy Since the 1960s* (New York: Hill and Wang, 2013).

3.   There is little governmental or academic consensus on what exactly "the public interest" is and what
it means to act on behalf of it. In 1924, President Herbert Hoover argued that radio itself "is not
to be considered for private gain. . . . It is a public concern impressed with the public trust and is to
be considered primarily from the standpoint of public interest." In 1929, the *Great Lakes Broadcasting* decision defined "public interest" as requiring radio stations to present "all sides of important public questions fairly, objectively, and without bias." A decade later, the FCC argued that

"radio can serve as an instrument of democracy only when devoted to the communication of information and exchange of ideas fairly and objectively presented." In 1946, the FCC's "Public Service Responsibility of Broadcast Licensees" report named fourteen components of the public interest, including educational programs, public affairs programs, news programs, and religious programs. In 1949, the FCC introduced the fairness doctrine, which was intimately connected to "the public interest" because such interest "requires ample play for the free and fair competition of opposing views, and the commission believes that the principle applies to all discussion of importance to the public." This doctrine was interpreted as the primary component of "the public interest." Behavior falling outside of these parameters, including defamation, racial or religious intolerance, and obscenity, did not serve the public interest. Throughout the 1970s, Lear and other religious liberals were not shy in using these federal stipulations to keep some voices off the airwaves and others on in the name of "fairness." The fuzziness surrounding the notion of "the public interest" demands further investigation, especially since much of its content seems to be ideally suited for Lear and his People for the American Way. For more on this history, see Heather Hendershot, "God's Angriest Man: Carl McIntire, Cold War Fundamentalism, and Right-Wing Broadcasting," *American Quarterly* 59, no. 2 (June 2007): 373–96. For more on the public interest, see the FCC's own "Policy and Regulatory Landscape," Federal Communications Commission, https://transition.fcc.gov/osp/inc-report/INoC-26-Broadcast.pdf.

4. My usage of "middling" is shorthand for "chattering," as in the "chattering classes," those who occupied influential positions within US society (in entertainment, universities, or the federal government) that depended on the skillful use of media to achieve much of their political aspirations in a liberal key. For neoconservative writers, this group of individuals was best known as the "knowledge class" or "New Class."

5. Dorothy Stone, "Maude's Abortion Evokes Protests," *Los Angeles Times*, November 29, 1972.

6. The subject of taste is unavoidable in the study of the culture wars. For more, see "Taste" in Raymond Williams, *Keywords: A Vocabulary of Culture and Society* (New York: Oxford University Press, 1983), 313–15.

7. For theorist Raymond Williams, "taste" can be understood as being equivalent to "discrimination": "the word Taste . . . means that quick discerning faculty or power of the mind by which we accurately distinguish the good, bad, or indifferent." I argue that the category of taste assists the study of the religion and politics during the 1970s and 1980s because of the nature of the conflict that unfolded across the decades, which in this case was mostly cultural in terminology. Much of the language of this conflict was also dependent on rhetorical (and ontological) binaries such as good/bad, civil/uncivil, rural/urban, educated/uneducated, and religious/secular. Those in the knowledge industry—the socioeconomic strata that Lear and others in the media occupied—possessed a particular investment in the idea of being the "mainline" or "mainstream," which implied discriminating faculties and learned relationships with similarly accomplished individuals. For more, see Williams, 313.

8. See Paul Cowan, *Tribes of America: Journalistic Discoveries of Our People and Their Cultures* (1971; New York: New, 2004).

9. For more, see Seth Dowland, *Family Values and the Rise of the Christian Right* (Philadelphia: University of Pennsylvania Press, 2015).

10. Whitney Strub, *Perversion for Profit: The Politics of Pornography and the Rise of the New Right* (New York: Columbia University Press, 2011), 118. For Strub, "One of the New Right's major innovations, then, was the conservative cooptation of morality in politics, equating liberalism with libertinism at every available opportunity."

11. Kathryn C. Montgomery, *Target Primetime: Advocacy Groups and the Struggle Over Entertainment Television* (New York: Oxford University Press, 1989), 5.

12. For more, see Norman Lear, *Even This I Get to Experience* (New York: Penguin, 2015).

13.   For more on this understudied topic, see Frederick W. Ford, "The Meaning of the 'Public Interest,' Convenience or Necessity,'" *Journal of Broadcasting* 5, no. 3 (1961): 205–18; Lee Loevinger, "Broadcasting and Religious Liberty," *Journal of Broadcasting* 9, no. 1 (1964): 3–23; Robert R. Smith, "Broadcasting and Religious Freedom," *Journal of Broadcasting* 13, no. 1 (1968): 1–12; Ellen August, "Writers Guild v. FCC: Duty of the Networks to Resist Governmental Regulation," *Syracuse Law Review* 28, no. 2 (1977): 583–607; Charles L. Firestein, "*Red Lion* and the Fairness Doctrine: Regulation of Broadcasting 'in the Public Interest,'" *Arizona Law Review* 11, no. 807 (1969): 807–21; Andrea J. Grefe, "The Family Viewing Hour: An Assault on the First Amendment?," *Hastings Constitutional Law Quarterly* (Fall 1977): 935–89.

14.   While the relationship between Martin Marty and Norman Lear was important for the formation of People for the American Way, another significant partnership was between Lear and journalist Bill Moyers. In fact, at Marty's retirement ceremony, Moyers served as the emcee while Lear spoke as a special guest of Marty's. Lear remarks in his autobiography that Southern Baptists like Moyers influenced how he thought about religion, politics, and censorship in America.

15.   For an example of how global events influenced largely liberal descriptions of conservative religion, see the first lines of Peter Berger, "The Class Struggle in American Religion," *Christian Century*, February 25, 1981, 194–99. For the latest and most original history of this phenomenon, see David Watt, *Antifundamentalism in Modern America* (Ithaca, NY: Cornell University Press, 2017).

16.   Berger, 194.

17.   This monitoring tactic found its culminating application when Lear and others founded People for the American Way.

18.   The history of "the public interest" deserves its own treatment beyond this one. In fact, I would argue that this formulation was as inclusive as it was exclusive in that Lear could wield said "public interest" against those who did not seem to contribute to it (e.g., the televangelists of the late 1970s) while benefiting simultaneously from the protections of the federal government.

19.   Fore is a very important figure during this tumultuous period of federal regulation of the airwaves. He wrote a number of texts and articles on religion and popular culture including a short piece titled "A Short History of Religious Broadcasting." Later in the decade, Fore was intimately involved in the initial meetings that led to the formation of People for the American Way, another indication of how Lear's religious liberalism found support from mainline Protestant church organizations such as the NCC and arguably the FCC itself during the 1970s, which had privileged mainline preachers and speakers on television over their more conservative counterparts dating back to the 1930s.

20.   William Fore, "Religion on the Airwaves: In the Public Interest?" *Christian Century*, September 17, 1975, 782–83, my emphasis.

21.   For more on the FCC and religion, see Marcus Cohen, "Religion and the FCC," *The Reporter*, January 14, 1965, 32–34. See also George Gerbner, "Television: The New State Religion?" *Et Cetera: A Review of General Semantics* (June 1977): 145–50.

22.   Hendershot, "God's Angriest Man."

23.   William F. Fore, "A Short History of Religious Broadcasting," unpublished, 1968, author's private collection.

24.   James A. Brown, "Selling Airtime for Controversy: NAB Self-Regulation and Father Coughlin," *Journal of Broadcasting* 24, no. 2 (1980): 199–224.

25.   Ford, "The Meaning of the 'Public Interest,'" 214, my emphasis. The context of this article is arguably as important as its content in narrating a religious history of American broadcasting after World War II. Three years later, FCC commissioner Lee Loevinger published his own analysis of the history of FCC policy regarding religious broadcasting. By this time, a version of the article had already been presented at a conference of religious broadcasters and generated what was described as "wide attention" (Loevinger's previous professional posts included assistant US

attorney general in charge of the Antitrust Division of the Department of Justice). In a footnote, Loevinger draws his readers' attention to a definition of "the public interest" from 1951 authored by then FCC commissioner Wayne Coy. For Coy, the public interest was public precisely *because* of its religious character as understood and defined by the FCC. "The FCC has always held that adequate time for the religious activities of the community is necessary to a well-rounded program service," argued Coy. "And a well-rounded program service is necessary to meet the statutory requirement that licensees serve the public interest. . . . Serving religious needs is part of the general pattern of public service that we expect from all broadcast licensees." This definition was anything but context specific. "I can envision no time in the future when that requirement will be changed." Once this comment is placed alongside the others cited in these notes, one begins to see the outlines of "the public interest" as both definition and category, content and knowledge generator. For more, see Loevinger, "Broadcasting and Religious Liberty."

26. John Modern, *Secularism in Antebellum America* (Chicago: University of Chicago Press, 2011), 7.

27. David Chidester, *Patterns of Power: Religion & Politics in American Culture* (New York: Prentice Hall, 1988), 270, my emphasis. Chidester's theoretical analysis of civil religion as a "pattern of religio-political power" guides much of my own understanding and discussion of civil religion as both descriptor and category.

28. Cara Burnidge, "Protestant Liberalism," in *Encyclopedia of Religion in America*, ed. Charles H. Lippy and Peter W. Williams (Washington, DC: CQ, 2010), 1783–91, http://dx.doi.org/10.4135 /9781608712427.n301. See also Cara Burnidge, "U.S. Foreign Relations and American Religious Liberalism," *Oxford Research Encyclopedia of Religion*, March 2, 2018, http://religion.oxfordre.com /view/10.1093/acrefore/9780199340378.001.0001/acrefore-9780199340378-e-410.

29. R. Smith, "Broadcasting and Religious Freedom."

30. "Norman Lear vs. the Moral Majority," *Columbia Journalism Review* 20, no. 1 (May/June 1981): 77.

31. Lear, *Even This I Get to Experience*, 284.

32. August, "Writers Guild v. FCC," 593.

33. Grefe, "The Family Viewing Hour," 945, my emphasis.

34. Grefe, 985.

35. James W. Lewis, "Mainline Protestants," in Lippy and Williams, *Encyclopedia of Religion in America*, 1310–18, http://dx.doi.org/10.4135/9781608712427.n212.

36. For historian James W. Lewis, mainline social engagement assumed a "mainline Protestant sense of custodial responsibility for society," which resulted in religious liberals and liberals in general feeling "entitled to speak for the common good, even after their dominance of American religious life had passed away." For more, see Lewis.

37. Red Lion Broadcasting Co. v. FCC, 395 US 367, 382 (1969).

38. This particular reference reveals Lear's awareness of conservative mobilization against his programming during the mid-1970s. I would also argue that this reference located the nascent Christian Right in one of its more grassroots manifestations against an explicitly *social* malady of the times— immoral television. In this sense, to track Lear's movements and their countermovements is to narrate a history of two religio-political movements in America's recent past of cultural warfare—American religious liberalism and the Christian Right. What Lear and others did not realize, however, was how closely related in function and desire the largely liberal "violent television" movement was to the mostly conservative "immoral television" movement. This redeployment of a 1960s single-issue campaign strategy by conservative interests mirrored the larger reappropriation that took place during the 1970s of largely liberal organizing techniques of the movement against poverty and racial injustice by conservative activists and organizers in the name of a silent but moral majority. For more on how the FCC handled "moral" programming, see "Morality and the Broadcast Media: A Constitutional Analysis of FCC Regulatory Standards," *Harvard Law Review* 84, no. 3 (January 1971): 664–99.

39. Norman Lear and Barbara Cady, "Playboy Interview: Norman Lear," *Playboy*, March 1976, 53–71, my emphasis.

40. For more, see Berger, "The Class Struggle in American Religion," 197. Lear's activism fit Berger's description perfectly: "Just as the business class sincerely believed that what is good for business is good for America, the new class believes that its own interests are identical with the 'public interest.'" In addition, Berger's identification of the religious interests of the New Class was equally precise: "One of the easiest empirical procedures to determine very quickly what the agenda of the new class is at any given moment is to look up the latest pronouncements of the National Council of Churches, and to a somewhat lesser extent, of the denominational organizations of mainline Protestantism" (198).

41. Grefe, "The Family Viewing Hour," 988. One document from the period that captured the spiritual front's (New Class's) political agenda in the 1980s, a faction inclusive both of the Protestant mainline and liberal individuals such as Norman Lear, Martin Marty, and Bill Moyers, is titled "The 'Remaking of America': A Message to the Churches." Published in the pages of *Christianity and Crisis* during the summer of 1981, the document originated as a National Council of Churches–authored statement regarding its "fundamental disagreement" with the policies of the newly elected Reagan administration. The statement's adoption by the NCC marked the first time since its founding that it had made "so broad an evaluation of a new Administration's policies." For more, see "The 'Remaking of America': A Message to the Churches," *Christianity and Crisis*, July 20, 1981, 207–10; Edward M. Kennedy, "Tolerance and Truth in America," *Historical Magazine of the Protestant Episcopal Church* 53, no. 1 (March 1984): 7–12.

42. Lear and Cady, "Playboy Interview," 54, emphasis in original.

43. Joan K. Hoyt, "Maude's Abortion Evokes Protests," *Los Angeles Times*, November 29, 1972.

44. Cecil Smith, "Maude's Abortion Evokes Protests," *Los Angeles Times*, November 29, 1972.

45. Aljean Harmetz, "Maude Didn't Leave 'em All Laughing," *New York Times*, December 10, 1972.

46. Material for these episodes found a suitable expressive venue in a contest conducted at the time by the Population Institute, a largely liberal organization that was involved in many of the early attempts to get politics into entertainment programming on behalf of liberal causes.

47. Harmetz, "Maude Didn't Leave 'em All Laughing," D4.

48. Historian Andrew Hartman has described this period as one defined by "epistemologies of liberation." I would add Lear's programming to this list of cultural productions that found their coherence through subversion of hierarchy and social status. For more, see Andrew Hartman, *A War for the Soul of America: A History of the Culture Wars* (Chicago: University of Chicago Press, 2015).

49. Lear, *Even This I Get to Experience*, 265.

50. Lear, 265.

51. Harmetz, "Maude Didn't Leave 'em All Laughing," D3.

52. The Population Institute originated in 1969 and sought to educate the public with information about the perils of an unchecked population. One historian argues that two individuals within this organization, Methodist ministers David Poindexter and Rodney Shaw, came up with the idea of integrating Population Institute material into prime-time television. "The plan to use entertainment television for such educational purposes . . . seemed to be the ideal vehicle for public education." For more, see Montgomery, *Target Primetime*, 30.

53. Montgomery, 33. Montgomery's work is the most extensive on the subject of Lear, *Maude*, and its less than hospitable reception when it comes to both secondary and primary literature. As such, I will reference the work consistently in this section of the chapter.

54. Montgomery, 29.

55. Montgomery, 28.

56. Montgomery, 35.

57.   We will hear more about this tactic later, since it was one of the most effective means Lear had of policing and monitoring televangelist broadcasts in the name of "the public interest."

58.   Montgomery, *Target Primetime*, 36.

59.   Montgomery, 37.

60.   Helen Kruger, "Shame on Maude," *Village Voice*, May 23, 1974. The article concludes by noting that the Shield of Shame hangs in a place of honor in Lear's office. It also notes that the statistics used to demonstrate the national disdain for *All in the Family* also showed that 36 percent of the respondents watched the show regularly, something that Lear mentions consistently when discussing the reception of his programming despite the public opposition to it.

61.   Dan Lewis, "VA Group Says 'Stop Immorality on TV,'" *Lakeland Ledger*, August 12, 1973.

62.   Lewis, 2.

63.   Montgomery, *Target Primetime*, 41.

64.   Montgomery, 44.

65.   Berger, "The Class Struggle in American Religion," 194–99.

66.   Montgomery, *Target Primetime*, 47.

67.   Montgomery, 48.

68.   Lee Margulies, ed., "Proliferation of Pressure Groups in Primetime Symposium, 1981," *Emmy Magazine*, Summer 1981, A1–A32. Despite Lear's advisory role, the symposium was neither in reference to nor did it make references about People for the American Way and its nonprofit work. It was convened by the Academy of Television Arts and Science and the Caucus for Producers, Writers, and Directors. Lear was part of the academy's first hall-of-fame class, and he himself had founded the caucus in the interests of creative and expressive freedom under the First Amendment in the mid-1970s.

69.   David L. Wolper in Margulies, A2.

70.   William Rusher in Margulies, A4.

71.   My understanding of "the Christian Right" emphasizes both the concrete instances of conservative institution building throughout the Bible Belt and Sunbelt following World War II, as well as the term's descriptive character as a discursive catchall for conservatism in the 1970s and 1980s. More often than not, it was individuals like Lear who composed the most influential pieces of film and text that informed fellow political liberals and mainline Protestants from within the knowledge industry about conservative religiosity during the culture wars. In fact, I would argue that "the Christian Right" was a politically expedient interpretive fiction constructed by Lear and others within the bicoastal media who reported on "the electronic church" and its rise to power. The grossly overexaggerated numbers corresponding to the church's viewership regarding its programming also contributed to the formation of the Christian Right as both a concrete entity and a discursive agent.

    While there are countless contemporary texts that examine the Christian Right admirably, much of my own categorical and descriptive analysis finds its grounding in texts produced during the rise of the conservative movement itself. The following is a selection of these sources, ones that have been largely overlooked in the literature and methods of studying the Christian Right: Michael Lienesch, "Right-Wing Religion: Christian Conservatism as a Political Movement," *Political Science Quarterly* 97, no. 3 (Autumn 1982): 403–25; James E. Wood Jr., "Editorial: Religious Fundamentalism and the New Right," *Journal of Church and State* 23 (1981): 409–21; Leo P. Ribuffo, "Liberals and That Old-Time Religion," *The Nation*, November 29, 1980, 570–73; James M. Wall, "The New Right Comes of Age," *Christian Century*, October 22, 1980, 995–96; Tina Rosenberg, "How the Media Made the Moral Majority," *Washington Monthly*, May 1982, 26–34; William Martin, "The Birth of a Media Myth," *The Atlantic*, June 1981, 7–16. Many, if not all, of these sources function as both primary and secondary sources, offering both insight into the Right and evidence for interpretive arguments.

72.   Rusher in Margulies, "Proliferation of Pressure Groups," A4. As political scientist Jean-Francois
      Drolet observes, neoconservatives supported public demonstrations of religion because they made
      up for a morally enervated society. For neoconservative William Bennett, "'Since nothing else has
      been found to substitute for it,' a return to religion in public discourse is necessary to counter the
      'new nihilism' and tame the 'basest appetites, passions, and impulses' of the citizenry." In other
      words, recognizing and supporting the role of "religion" for neoconservatives was a very pragmatic
      and ultimately successful decision politically. For more, see Jean-Francois Drolet, *American Neo-
      conservatism: The Politics and Culture of a Reactionary Idealism* (New York: Columbia University
      Press, 2013), 101.

73.   Rusher in Margulies, "Proliferation of Pressure Groups," A4.

74.   Jerry Falwell, "Let's Be Fair About Fairness," *Journal of Broadcasting* 28, no. 3 (Summer 1984):
      273–74.

75.   Rusher in Margulies, "Proliferation of Pressure Groups," A5.

76.   For symposium attendee Alan Dershowitz, the question of the 1980s read as follows: "Is it possible
      to articulate general rules—rules of civility, rules of morality, rules of law, rules of constitutionality—
      that do not depend on whose ax is being ground or which group is being insulated?" Margulies,
      A14, my emphasis.

77.   Rusher in Margulies, A5.

78.   Richard Levinson in Margulies, A10. Individuals like Levinson and Lear came to a new realiza-
      tion about their programming and its collective significance during these years due to the pressure
      from various advocacy groups both left and right.

79.   Tyrone Brown in Margulies, A7.

80.   For more on how "the market" has ascended in the United States since the 1970s as a form of discur-
      sive contagion, see Daniel Rodgers, *Age of Fracture* (Cambridge, MA: Harvard University Press,
      2011).

81.   Al Schneider in Margulies, "Proliferation of Pressure Groups," A16.

82.   Schneider in Margulies, "A16.

83.   Grant Tinker in Margulies, A22.

84.   Schneider in Margulies, A16.

85.   Harriet Pilpel in Margulies, A31.

86.   Ben Stein, "Norman Lear vs. the Moral Majority: The War to Clean Up TV," *Saturday Review*,
      February 1981.

87.   Maureen Orth, "Religion on TV: Norman Lear Tackles the New Hot Issue," *Vogue*,
      February 1982.

88.   "TV's Latest Listing: Archie vs. Jerry," *Newsweek*, October 18, 1982.

89.   In 1981, Wildmon was the target of a particularly sardonic editorial in the *Los Angeles Times*. Dated
      July 26, the article by Marcia Jacobs suggested a "New Right Moral-Off? Sort of like a bake-off,
      but with questions," as an approved television program based on Wildmon's own standards. The
      questions read as follows: "Who reads the Bible fastest? Who has the longest list of sponsor boy-
      cotts? Who has the biggest flag on July 4th? Who visits the most graves on Memorial Day? Who
      is the Prince of Conservatives?" In addition, as compared to a figure like Falwell, she wrote, "At
      least Norman Lear never asked his audiences to send in money." For more, see Marcia Jacobs, "Open
      Letter to the Rev. Wildmon," *Los Angeles Times*, July 26, 1981.

90.   Robert R. Mendenhall, "Responses to Television from the New Christian Right: The Donald Wild-
      mon Organization's Fight Against Sexual Content," in *Sex, Religion, and Media*, ed. Dane S.
      Claussen (Lanham, MD: Rowman and Littlefield, 2002), 102.

91.   Silverman in Cynthia Cooper, "NBC and the Moral Majority: A Holy War over Violence and Tele-
      vision," in *Violence on Television: Congressional Inquiry, Public Criticism, and Industry Response*
      (Lanham, MD: University Press of America, 1996), 100.

92. The two most notable examples are sociologists James Davison Hunter and Robert Wuthnow.

93. For more, see "The New Right's TV Hit List," *Newsweek*, June 15, 1981; "P&G's Move in a 'Holy War,'" *Newsweek*, June 29, 1981.

94. For sociologist Todd Gitlin, many networks' heads thought their rhetorical victories over Wildmon "succeed in warding off a threat to free expression as serious as book burning." For more, see Todd Gitlin, "The New Crusades: How Fundamentalists Tied Up the Networks," *American Film* (October 1981): 60.

95. Rosenberg, "How the Media Made the Moral Majority," 34. For a more explicit example, former NBC chairman Thomas Wyman called the Moral Majority, "a constitutionally immoral minority." For more, see Gitlin, 60.

96. Carrie Rickey, "Why They Fight: Subjects' Rights and the First Amendment," *American Film* (October 1981): 57.

97. For more on this history, see Kevin Kruse and Julian Zelizer, *Fault Lines: A History of the United States Since 1974* (New York: W. W. Norton, 2019).

98. Quoted in Gitlin, "The New Crusades," 61.

99. Leslie Ward, "Rallying Round the Flag: Norman Lear and the American Way," *American Film* (October 1981): 63. Ward's first observation upon entering Lear's office for the interview was a piece of canvas with the word "TRUTH" painted on it with bright oranges and yellows. I was lucky enough to see this painting in Lear's apartment in New York City during a second interview session. Ward's question remains unanswered, "But is TRUTH dawning or setting?"

100. Ward, 63.

101. For more, see Bethany Moreton, *To Serve God and Walmart: The Making of Christian Free Enterprise* (Cambridge, MA: Harvard University Press, 2009); Axel R. Schäfer, *Piety and Public Funding: Evangelicals and the State in Modern America* (Philadelphia: University of Pennsylvania Press, 2012); Sarah Hammond, "'God Is My Partner': An Evangelical Business Man Confronts Depression and War," *Church History* 80, no. 3 (2011): 498–519; Darren E. Grem, "The Marketplace Missions of S. Truett Cathy and Chick-fil-A," in *Sunbelt Rising: The Politics of Space, Place, and Region*, ed. Michelle Nickerson and Darren Dochuk (Philadelphia: University of Pennsylvania Press, 2011), 293–315. For a more general example of a top-down approach in the study of American religion that cares very little for questions of reception and improvisation, see Kathryn Lofton, *Oprah: Gospel of an Icon* (Berkeley: University of California Press, 2011).

102. Darren Dochuk, *From Bible Belt to Sunbelt: Plain-Folk Religion, Grassroots Politics, and the Rise of Evangelical Conservatism* (New York: W. W. Norton, 2010).

103. Lear in Ward, "Rally Round the Flag," 64.

104. Ward, 81.

105. Johnson in Ward, 81.

106. Rosenberg, "How the Media Made the Moral Majority," 34.

4. PEOPLE FOR THE AMERICAN WAY AND SPIRITUAL POLITICS IN LATE TWENTIETH-CENTURY AMERICA

1. Norman Lear, *Even This I Get to Experience* (New York: Penguin, 2015), 332. By June 1981, the *New York Times* reported that Lear planned to send his public service announcements to "every commercial television station."

2. For more, see Seymour Martin Lipset, ed., *The Third Century: America as a Post-Industrial Society* (Palo Alto, CA: Hoover, 1979); James Davison Hunter, "The New Class and the Young

Evangelicals," *Review of Religious Research* 22, no. 2 (December 1980): 155–69. Lipset's usage of "Post-Industrial" and Hunter's usage of "New Class," respectively, point to another level of analysis that I will deploy in future work on this time period. These terms arguably possess a particular analytical traction in explaining the origins of not only the Christian Right and People for the American Way but also the culture wars themselves. Sociologist Peter Berger has also argued that the New Class emerged with religiously and politically left-leaning tendencies as the culture's most influential manipulators of public symbols. Hunter explores these ideas more succinctly in both the article cited above and in his classic sociological text *The Culture Wars: The Struggle to Define America* (New York: Basic, 1992). For more on the New Class as a product of neoconservative thought, see Jean-Francois Drolet, *American Neoconservatism: The Politics and Culture of a Reactionary Idealism* (New York: Oxford University Press, 2013). For more on 1970s workers' politics, see Jefferson R. Cowie, *Stayin' Alive: The 1970s and the Last Days of the Working Class* (New York: New, 2013). For Berger, see Robert S. Michaelsen and Wade Clark Roof, eds., *Liberal Protestantism: Realities and Possibilities* (New York: Pilgrim, 1986), 19–36.

3. This "about something" points to Lear's desire to educate while entertaining his audiences by exposing them to controversial subjects and news stories of the time. Unlike many of his conservative detractors, Lear avoided taking an explicit stand on any particular social topic, preferring instead to influence and introduce complexity into singular perspectives. His approach reflected what historian Kathryn Montgomery has identified as the social group understanding of how television should operate in American society—namely as "an electronic classroom." For more, see Kathryn C. Montgomery, *Target Primetime: Advocacy Groups and the Struggle Over Entertainment Television* (New York: Oxford University Press, 1989).

4. Wuthnow's term will be explored later in this chapter. For more, see Robert Wuthnow, *The Restructuring of American Religion: Society and Faith Since World War II* (Princeton, NJ: Princeton University Press, 1988).

    The secondary literature on People for the American Way is quite underdeveloped. One of the earlier treatments of PFAW's politics was James Davison Hunter's chapter titled "The Liberal Reaction" in the edited collection *The New Christian Right: Mobilization and Legitimation*. A similarly timed monograph entitled *Prime Time Preachers* by sociologist Jeffrey K. Hadden also explored PFAW and its reactionary politics of civility in light of the rise of televangelism. One of the more compelling analyses produced thus far of PFAW is historian Steven Miller's *Age of Evangelicalism*. His history of evangelicalism as an age versus a subculture includes a colorful cast of characters who were not exclusively evangelical themselves but were nonetheless shaped by the age's collective concerns about the state of religion in American public life and the born-again experience. The most recent study to include PFAW as data is *Righteous Rhetoric: Sex, Speech, and the Politics of Concerned Women for America* by scholar of religion Leslie Dorrough Smith. For more, see James Davison Hunter, "The Liberal Reaction," in *The New Christian Right: Mobilization and Legitimation*, ed. Robert C. Liebman and Robert Wuthnow (New York: Aldine, 1983), 150–61; Jeffrey K. Hadden and Charles E. Swan, eds., *Prime Time Preachers: The Rising Power of Televangelism* (Reading, MA: Addison-Wesley, 1981; Steven P. Miller, *Age of Evangelicalism: America's Born-Again Years* (New York: Oxford University Press, 2014); Leslie Dorrough Smith, *Righteous Rhetoric: Sex, Speech, and the Politics of Concerned Women for America* (New York: Oxford University Press, 2014).

5. There is no question that Lear's mobilizing efforts also had to confront a form of anti-Semitic stereotype concerning rich Jewish Hollywood writers and producers who "ran Hollywood."

6. For more, see Wuthnow, *The Restructuring of American Religion*, 3–13.

7. For more on this tradition, see Wendy Wall, *Inventing the American Way: The Politics of Consensus from the New Deal to the Civil Rights Movement* (New York: Oxford University Press, 2008).

8. As a descriptive and categorical reminder, the term "electronic church" refers to the activities of largely conservative Protestant ministers who began organizing ministries based on the resources

of the airwaves in general and television in particular. Words such as "televangelism" and "televangelist" are closely related to the electronic church and its emergence in American public life in the late 1970s. Typically deployed by centrist to left-leaning political liberals, the term is also suggestively adjudicative in that those churches that were "electronic" were not the same as, and perhaps deficient relative to, physical Protestant churches and the ministries that took place within as products of community.

9.   My association of mainline Protestantism with broadly liberal politics coincides nicely with what historian William Hutchinson argues in his edited collection, *Between the Times*. Despite the fact that associating liberal politics with mainline interests of the early twentieth century is problematic at best, by the late 1970s such shorthand was largely accurate, "but the habit of designating the Protestant mainline churches simply as 'liberal,' which is at least understandable if one has in mind the alignments of the 1970s and 1980s, is problematic for earlier periods" (13). The travails that Hutchinson spoke of for the Protestant mainline were arguably not as disastrous as once thought in an age of disestablishment. In fact, I would argue that mainline interests and power remained rather solidified in the broader American culture through the midcentury up to the early 1980s with the arrival of the Christian Right. In this sense, mainline interests morphed into institutions and communities beyond the confines of the institutional Protestant church to include members of the goodwill movement in the interwar period and individuals such as Norman Lear in the 1970s. In other words, interfaith activism assumed much of the mainline's energy for mobilizing its interests in public in increasingly *secular* spaces. For more on this ecumenical period, see David Hollinger, *After Cloven Tongues of Fire: Protestant Liberalism in Modern American History* (Princeton, NJ: Princeton University Press, 2013). Also see William Hutchinson, *Between the Times: The Travail of the Protestant Establishment in America, 1900–1960* (New York: Cambridge University Press, 1989).

10.   Neil J. Young, *We Gather Together: The Religious Right and the Problem of Interfaith Politics* (New York: Oxford University Press, 2015).

11.   The most disturbing instance of such remarks during this period took place during the National Affairs Briefing held in Dallas in the early 1980s. Although this event is typically remembered for the words of then candidate Ronald Reagan as he endorsed his fellow conservatives' concerns about the country's future, the words of Dr. Bailey Smith resonated strongest with individuals like Lear and Rabbi Marc Tanenbaum, who would go on to serve on PFAW's advisory board. Smith, then president of the Southern Baptist Convention, observed that "God Almighty does not hear the prayer of a Jew." Smith's words were recorded by a member of Tanenbaum's organization at the time on behalf of the American Jewish Committee. Taking a page out of PFAW's awareness-raising handbook, Smith's words were then sent directly to Jewish leaders the week of the briefing. Smith's full quotation reads as such: "It is interesting, at great political rallies, how you have a Protestant to pray, a Catholic to pray, and then you have a Jew to pray. With all due respect to those dear people, my friends, God Almighty does not hear the prayer of a Jew." This formulation was not only anti-Semitic, it also attacked directly the logic of PFAW and Lear's religious liberalism as extensions of the classic sociological categorization of "Protestant-Catholic-Jew" as a viable religio-political platform for nonprofits like Lear's. For more, see "Baptist Leader Claims God 'Does Not Hear the Prayer of a Jew,'" *Jewish Telegraphic Agency*, September 19, 1980, accessed May 10, 2014, http://www .jta.org/1980/09/19/archive/baptist-leader-claims-god-does-not-hear-the-prayer-of-a-jew.

12.   I have examined "culture wars" in a substantive manner in another venue, namely L. Benjamin Rolsky, "Confessions of a Hollywood Liberal: American Sitcoms and the Culture Wars, from Norman Lear to 'Parks and Recreation,'" Marginalia, March 31, 2015, http://marginalia.lareviewofbooks .org/confessions-of-a-hollywood-liberal-american-sitcoms-and-the-culture-wars-from-norman -lear-to-parks-and-recreation-by-l-benjamin-rolsky/.

     In short, I understand Lear and his actions with PFAW as participating in what would eventually become America's culture wars. My contribution is to locate and explicate the liberal interests and activism within these very public contests over various facets of American culture and politics.

13. For more on this transition since America's midcentury, see Daniel Rodgers, *Age of Fracture* (Cambridge, MA: Harvard University Press, 2011); Robert O. Self, *All in the Family: The Realignment of American Democracy Since the 1960s* (New York: Hill and Wang, 2012).

14. For the latest on the "Judeo-Christian" tradition as a subject of academic inquiry, see K. Healan Gaston, "Interpreting Judeo-Christianity in America," *Relegere: Studies in Religion and Reception* 2, no. 2 (2012): 291–304; J. Terry Todd, "The Temple of Religion and the Politics of Religious Pluralism," in *After Pluralism: Reimagining Religious Engagement*, ed. Courtney Bender and Pamela Klassen (New York: Columbia University Press, 2010), 201–24. For more on the goodwill movement, see historian Benny Kraut's chapter in Hutchinson, *Between the Times*, 193–230. For more on Tri-Faith formations, see Kevin Schultz, *Tri-Faith America: How Catholics and Jews Held Postwar America to Its Protestant Promise* (New York: Oxford University Press, 2011). In fact, Lear relied on the popular interwar phrase "Brotherhood of Man" to make an argument about respect and understanding in a moment of vehement political disagreements in his television special *I Love Liberty*, which first aired in 1981. The special was designed by Lear, church historian Martin Marty, and countless others to reclaim what had been appropriated and (to PFAW) exploited by the Christian Right—namely patriotism and moral discourse. The event drew very heavily on Hollywood for much of its appeal, featuring Mary Tyler Moore, Martin Sheen, Christopher Reeve, Walter Matthau, and the Muppets. It utilized the variety show format to defend tolerance and civility in the face of the Right's divisive politics.

15. For more on the relationship between World War II and American Jews, see Deborah Moore, *How World War II Changed a Generation* (Cambridge, MA: Harvard University Press, 2004).

16. Wall, *Inventing the American Way*, 10.

17. For cultural theorist Raymond Williams, this underside of diversity can be understood as the negative sense of consensus itself. For Williams, consensus politics "was intended to describe deliberate evasion of basic conflicts of principle, but also a process in which certain issues were effectively excluded from political argument . . . because there was no room for issues not already [considered] important." For more, see Raymond Williams, *Keywords: A Vocabulary of Culture and Society* (New York: Oxford University Press, 1983), 76–78.

18. Wall, *Inventing the American Way*, 84.

19. Lear's midcentury predecessor was a Hollywood studio president by the name of Barney Balaban. Both men worked with the National Council of Christians and Jews, both were involved in the entertainment industry, and both were of Jewish descent. In addition, both men purchased original copies of America's founding documents (the Bill of Rights and the Declaration of Independence, respectively) in times of national identity formation: the Cold War and post-9/11 America. Balaban even contributed some of his own collection of Americana to the Freedom Train, which ran in the 1940s in order to remind Americans of their own sacred, national history. For more, see Wall, *Inventing the American Way*, 203, 282.

20. For more on interfaith activism, see Katherine E. Knutson, *Interfaith Advocacy: The Role of Religious Coalitions in the Political Process* (New York: Routledge, 2013).

21. The emphasis that Lear and his mainline Protestant supporters placed on the absolutism of the Christian Right was a product of their collective reaction to an antithetical politics that did not require (or even desire) an exchange of ideas or a deliberative encounter with its opposition. Regardless of whether such claims were actually absolutist and thus beyond time and space, Lear and others interpreted televangelists' claims as such and mobilized a significant counteroffensive based on their perception of the Christian Right as exclusionary. A helpful corrective to the scholar adapting such an analysis as her own can be found in scholar of religion Leslie Dorrough Smith's monograph *Righteous Rhetoric: Sex, Speech, and the Politics of Concerned Women for America*. As Smith

points out, absolutist claims such as those made by Concerned Women for America or, arguably, PFAW might rely on an exclusionary politics, yet they also functioned as rhetorical strategy for mobilizing their various constituencies by convincing them of such an agenda's efficacy based largely on its flexibility rather than a rigid consistency. Smith's methodological contribution will be engaged later in this chapter.

22. This observation can be found in an unpublished interview Lear gave as part of a seminar titled "Television: Its Culture, Its Impact, Its Ethics, Its Future." It was copyrighted by the Museum of Broadcasting in 1987.

23. For more on Willard and Mull, see Gary Deeb, "Mull and Willard to Take a Swipe at a Racket via Lear 'Religion' Film," *Chicago Tribune*, March 22, 1979.

24. In Lear's words, the two friends had day jobs as cops. "As clergymen they held Sunday services in their garages or playrooms, which, for tax purposes, they wrote off as sanctuaries. Their family vacations were claimed as religious retreats. All in all, church-related tax write-offs could allow them four thousand dollars more a year in take-home pay, a considerable sum given the salary of the average cop." Lear brought in comedians Richard Pryor and Robin Williams to assist with the story. For more, see Lear, *Even This I Get to Experience*.

25. This story is quite different from the other religion-oriented films that came out in the early 1980s, but they were all united in their effort to lampoon the Christian Right by ridiculing televangelists. Other films that took a similarly critical edge to current events were *Pray TV* and *In God We Tru$t*.

26. In Lear's own words from his speech commemorating the thirtieth anniversary of People for the American Way, "I paid to run it on a local TV station in DC and it caused so much talk that all three networks—there were only three at the time—ran it on their seven o'clock news and, like an act of spontaneous combustion—People for the American Way was born." As Lear remarks in his autobiography, "All of that [staffing PFAW] became easier after we ran the PSA on a local DC station. The national press covered the ad, the nightly news shows played it in its entirety, and I was invited to be interviewed by Tom Brokaw, then on the *Today* show" (333).

27. "I realized that I had lousy credentials for taking on fundamentalist religious figures," Lear admitted in an interview. "I'm Jewish and I'm a product of Hollywood and I'm not going to get a lot of attention that way. I knew I needed the help of mainline church leaders so I went to South Bend, because I had a nice acquaintance with Father Hesburgh at Notre Dame." For more, see Lear, "Television: Its Culture, Its Impact, Its Ethics, Its Future."

28. Lear's memories of his encounter with Hesburgh can be found in Lear, "Television: Its Culture, Its Impact, Its Ethics, Its Future," in the question-and-answer section. This transcript, along with many others referenced in the project, can be found on Norman Lear's website under the heading "Life in the Spirit."

29. For more, see Peggy Shriver, *The Bible Vote: Religion and the New Right* (New York: Pilgrim, 1981).

30. Lear, "Television: Its Culture, Its Impact, Its Ethics, Its Future."

31. Bruce Buursma, "Group Fights 'Voice of Fanaticism,'" *Chicago Tribune*, March 10, 1981.

32. Lear, *Even This I Get to Experience*, 332.

33. Lear, 332. Before moving forward with his nonprofit organizing, Lear consulted another group of influential religious liberals including Rev. George Regas and Rabbi Leonard Beerman, cofounders of Interfaith Communities United for Justice and Peace.

34. Lear, 333.

35. For more on the Hollywood tradition of activism, see Steven J. Ross, *Hollywood Left and Right: How Movie Stars Shaped American Politics* (New York: Oxford University Press, 2011). Countless newspaper articles from the period document the gradual organizing that took place among Hollywood's liberal elite in opposition to a variety of Reagan-led operations including US actions in Central America.

36. Joining such groups in solidarity were fifteen of the largest mainline denominations in the country by way of a cosigned statement titled "Christian Theological Observations on the Religious Right Movement." An excerpt from this statement reads as follows: "There is no place in a Christian manner of political life for arrogance, manipulation, subterfuge, or holding others in contempt.... There is no justification in a pluralistic and democratic society for demands for conformity along religious or ideological lines." For more, see Hadden and Swann, *Prime Time Preachers*, 146–47.

37. For more, see Tina Rosenberg, "How the Media Made the Moral Majority," *Washington Monthly*, May 1982, 26–34; original citation found in Miller, *Age of Evangelicalism*.

38. Lear, *Even This I Get to Experience*, 333.

39. This dynamic speaks to those who argue that the culture wars were and are primarily a product of intellectual, cultural, and political elites.

40. "Smiting the Mighty Right: PAW vs. Political Preachers," *Time*, November 3, 1980.

41. "Smiting the Mighty Right," 103, my emphasis.

42. Stein's comments on Lear and TV do not end here. For more, see Ben Stein, *The View from Sunset Boulevard: America as Brought to You by the People Who Make Television* (New York: Basic, 1979).

43. For another similarly titled article, see "TV's Latest Listing: Archie vs. Jerry," *Newsweek*, October 18, 1982.

44. While various newspapers and journals were publishing articles on the Lear/Falwell story, they were also giving print space to broader and arguably more threatening subject matter including the subject of "born-again" politics itself and its potential in the United States to shift the country to the right. The Lear/Falwell article and this latter type of article should be read as having an intimately connected relationship, with the same cast of characters oftentimes populating the different articles despite their slightly unique narrative concerns. For an example, see Allan J. Mayer, John J. Lindsay, and Howard Fineman, "A Tide of Born-Again Politics," *Newsweek*, September 15, 1980.

45. Maureen Orth, "Religion on TV: Norman Lear Tackles the New Hot Issue," *Vogue*, February 1982.

46. For more similarly titled articles, see Peter W. Kaplan, "Lear vs. Falwell in Morality Armageddon," *Chicago Tribune*, October 1, 1981; John J. Goodman, "Campaign Opens Against Religious New Right," *Los Angeles Times*, October 22, 1980; Keith Love, "Lear Tackles Moral Majority: Producer, Religious Leaders Form Group to Spur Diversity," *Los Angeles Times*, December 13, 1981; Phil Kerby, "Falwell and Lear: Maybe They're Not So Far Apart," *Los Angeles Times*, October 30, 1981; Howard Rosenberg, "Evangelists, Networks: Holy War on Airwaves," *Los Angeles Times*, January 25, 1982; "Lear Assails Religious New Right as a Threat to Spirit of Liberty," *New York Times*, March 27, 1981; Helen Parmley, "Falwell Chides Lear," *Dallas Morning News*, October 23, 1980; Tom Shales, "Norman Lear Takes Aim at Majority," *Wilmington Morning Star*, March 9, 1981; Kenneth R. Clark, "Norman Lear, Clergy Team to Fight Morality Politics," *Pittsburgh Press*, October 25, 1980. For examples of broader articles that address the very same tensions within US society, see Ernest Holsendolph, "Religious Broadcasts Bring Rising Revenues and Create Rivalries," *New York Times*, December 2, 1979; Dudley Clendinen, "Christian New Right's Rush to Power: Test of Strength Lies Ahead," *New York Times*, August 18, 1980.

47. "Mainline Church Leaders Hit for 'Obscene' Political Behavior," *Christianity Today*, April 23, 1982, 42–44.

48. Neuhaus was a well-known Lutheran minister before becoming a Catholic priest.

49. "Mainline Church Leaders Hit for 'Obscene' Political Behavior."

50. Love, "Lear Tackles Moral Majority."

51. The fairness doctrine stated that those who maintained broadcast licenses were obligated to give airtime to issues of public importance (often couched in the terms of the "public interest") while

presenting such discussion in a manner that was balanced or equitable (often referred to as "equal time"). While equal time was not a requirement of this policy, the holders were obliged to present contrasting views of the same issue.

52. Clark, "Norman Lear, Clergy Team to Fight Morality Politics," C5. A number of articles relied on images and tropes from the Middle East in general and the Iranian Revolution in 1979 in particular in order to make sense of the electronic church and its preachers such as Jerry Falwell. More often than not, the author leaned to the middle or to the political left. In these instances, the electronic church as a descriptive category takes on an oppressive tone since most of its purveyors are described by the same author as "media manipulators." For another example of this type of analysis from a significant academic voice then and now, see Peter Berger, "The Class Struggle in American Religion," *Christian Century*, February 25, 1981, 194–99. I will return to this particular article for a more in-depth treatment in a future book project in order to make a broader, sociologically informed argument about the underlying societal tension that undergirded the development of the culture wars along lines of class or, more specifically, along the lines of the New Class and its religious and political predilections.

53. Because the archives at People for the American Way's headquarters in Washington, DC, were being relocated to the Library of Congress during the writing of this monograph, references to primary source material from the organization itself often come from secondhand accounts in newspaper articles and chapters from edited scholarly work on the Christian Right.

54. Jim Castelli, "People for the American Way Aim for Political Participation," *The Dispatch*, February 25, 1981, 17.

55. Becky Theim, "Lear Pushing American Way," *The Bulletin*, October 17, 1982, C3.

56. For more, see "People For's Founding Mission Statement," People for the American Way, accessed March 5, 2015, http://www.pfaw.org/about-us/founding-mission.

57. For more, see Leslie Durrough Smith, *Chaos Rhetoric: Sex, Speech, and the Politics of Concerned Women for America* (New York: Oxford University Press, 2014). For Smith, chaos rhetoric "is a type of speech used by a group to naturalize its own political agendas. It persuades by using fear, threat, and anxiety imagery to generate social sympathy for a position that aligns with the group's own political platforms, which the group offers as the resolution to the very threat it rhetorically created." Four characteristics of chaos rhetoric as demonstrated by Smith are "oversimplification, defensive focus, issue deflection, and urgency." Drawing on the work of theorist Julia Kristeva, Smith argues that chaos rhetoric often responds most effectively to what it does not quite understand. In this sense, that which PFAW did not understand, namely Falwell and others in the electronic church, "disturbed the overarching order that the group [PFAW] presupposes, thus threatening to undo the epistemological basis on which rests the culture's defining power structures."

58. The notion of civility and PFAW will be addressed later in this chapter. In short, a number of concerned members of the Protestant mainline couched their criticisms of the Christian Right in terms of civility/uncivil behavior in public. Most often their calls for greater understanding required either a more respectful atmosphere (as argued by Williams) or a more civil one, which relied most heavily on sociologist Robert Bellah's popular formulation, "civil religion." The adjective "civil" implied both a religious politics that was equally accessible to all who would question it *and* a normative description of how one properly conducted oneself in public that did not depend on parochial reasons for a particular political claim.

59. For more, see "People For's Founding Mission Statement."

60. For more, see "People For's Founding Mission Statement." For scholar of religion Jason Bivins, this claim is evidence of a Christian antiliberal characteristic of politics, namely "political illegibility." As Bivins argues, this term "is suggestive of the ways in which the specificity and robustness of religious beliefs (particularly Christian antiliberal concerns about political order) cannot be 'read' or

understood using the political logic of 'left' and 'right' or perhaps by any political ideology" (10). For more, see Jason Bivins, *The Fracture of Good Order: Christian Antiliberalism and the Challenge to American Politics* (Chapel Hill: University of North Carolina Press, 2003).

61. Evidence can be found online as part of the virtual page for PFAW's archives at the Bancroft Library at the University of California at Berkeley; the finding aid can be found through the Online Archive of California, accessed April 12, 2014, http://www.oac.cdlib.org/findaid/ark:/13030/hb596nb6hz/.

     Additionally, as part of the Center for Right Wing Studies at Berkeley, a number of PFAW primary sources have been made available, including the transcripts of many programs that were recorded by PFAW employees, individually authored notes, and fact sheets on the most troubling issues of the time designed for distribution. A sample of such issues includes censorship, school prayer, creationism, secular humanism, and sex education. These fact sheets typically include a number of newspaper articles addressing the issue in real time along with an introductory note by PFAW meant to give the receiving party the appropriate context for understanding the controversy surrounding the topic in question.

62. For more, see "People For's Founding Mission Statement."

63. For more on this debate, see Norman Lear and Ronald Reagan, "A Debate on Religious Freedom," *Harper's*, October 1984, 15–20.

64. Jim Castelli, *A Plea for Common Sense: Resolving the Clash Between Religion and Politics* (New York: Harper and Row, 1988). Castelli's plea, captured seamlessly by the title, is one thoroughly suffused with aspirations of reestablishing political consensus through calls for a return to common sense. This call is not unlike those made on the Christian and political right for a return to simpler times regarding gender, sexuality, and race.

65. For an analysis of the recent history of civil religion, see Raymond Haberski Jr., *God and War: American Civil Religion Since 1945* (New Brunswick, NJ: Rutgers University Press, 2012).

66. Norman Lear, "Foreword," in Castelli, *A Plea for Common Sense*, x–xi.

67. Despite PFAW's insistence on the distinction between proper and improper usages of religion in public, a distinction mobilized primarily as a defensive measure against the influx of televangelists and conservative strategists into American public life in the late 1970s, each notion remained indebted to a particularly Protestant understanding of civic space. As scholar of religion Chad Seales argues, "In the United States, a public form of liberal Protestantism underwrote the terms of the removal and reentry of religion as a universal category from civil society, dictating the social politics and political workings of secularism." Seales defines secularism in a manner conducive to many of the arguments made in this book, namely "as an epistemological conception of difference and its relationship to American pluralism and diversity." For more, see Chad Seales, *The Secular Spectacle: Performing Religion in a Southern Town* (New York: Oxford University Press, 2014). Seales's insight builds on those of fellow scholar of religion Tracy Fessenden, who argues that Protestantism's expansion within the United States depended on its secularization within the broader culture. For more, see Tracy Fessenden, *Culture and Redemption: Religion, the Secular, and American Literature* (Princeton, NJ: Princeton University Press, 2008).

68. Lear, "Foreword," in Castelli, *A Plea for Common Sense*, x–xi. Lear not only objected to the manner in which the Christian Right conducted itself politically, he also disagreed vehemently with the Right's politics themselves. "When they tell us that putting prayer back in the public schools will solve the problems of teenage suicide and drug use, they are misleading millions of us, blurring our vision of the real problems and causing great damage" (xi). This distinction between method and content challenges Lear's own telling of the story, which usually does not venture beyond firm disagreements with the *manner* and *methods* of conservative religious actors in politics.

69. Castelli, *A Plea for Common Sense*, 19.

70. Castelli, 20–22. For those familiar with the study of liberal democracy, this notion of publicly accessible reasoning is a product of "public reason," a notion developed by philosopher John Rawls.

Based on the work of philosopher of religion Richard Amesbury, both Lear and Rawls can be understood as participating in the same *liberal imaginary* despite their apparent differences. For more, see Richard Amesbury, "Rethinking 'Religion and Politics': Reflections on the Reception and Import of Talal Asad's *Genealogies of Religion,*" *Bulletin for the Study of Religion* 43, no. 1 (February 2014): 2–7.

71. John Rawls, "The Idea of Public Reason Revisited," *University of Chicago Law Review* 64, no. 3 (Summer 1997): 766–67.

72. Drawing on the collective work of Joan Chittister and Martin Marty, Jim Castelli argued that two worldviews tended to dominate the political scene when it came to religious activism and which social and cultural challenges received the most attention. This claim emerged from within the same religio-political moment as Robert Wuthnow's arguments for "two civil religions" and James Davison Hunter's contention that the United States was in a culture war. For Chittister, each side possessed its own agenda for confronting the country's ills, economic or otherwise: "Conservative activists 'are against abortion, sex education in the public schools, the teaching of evolution, the Equal Rights Amendment, and nuclear disarmament' while liberal activists 'were involved in housing, healthcare, human rights programs, education for social change, economic redevelopment, and the peace movement'" (26). Chittister's words suggest that in the wake of the social movements for human rights in the 1960s, conservatives and liberals staked out their respective territories when it came to the defining issues of the last half century. In addition, her words also add credibility to the claim that the New Class did indeed possess a political and religious orientation toward the mainline and its interfaith sensibilities. In short, Chittister and others writing in the 1980s pointed to a fundamental restructuring of American politics along clearly differentiated lines within American society that cut less across denominational divisions and more within denominations themselves. It is in this sense that we can begin speaking of a "new denominationalism" and "new ecumenism" of the recent American religious past.

    Another example of the differences between religious liberals and conservatives during this period reads as such: "Liberals abhor the smugness, the self-righteousness, the absolute certainty, the judgmentalism, the lovelessness of a narrow, dogmatic faith. Conservatives scorn the fuzziness, the marshmallow convictions, the inclusiveness that makes membership meaningless—the 'anything goes' attitude that views even Scripture as relative. Both often caricature the worst in one another and fail to perceive the best." This quotation came from an NCC official quoted in Robert Wuthnow, *The Struggle for America's Soul: Evangelicals, Liberals, and Secularism* (Grand Rapids, MI: Eerdmans, 1989), 22–23. Another way to identify the significance of Norman Lear and PFAW in American religious history is to locate references to him and his work in various works of academic scholarship. Not only did Martin Marty dedicate one of his many texts to Lear and his cause, Wuthnow himself also relied on Lear for the opening of his prologue in *The Struggle for America's Soul*. In particular, Wuthnow opens with an anecdote about a video that was shown in a class on the Christian Right that took place at Princeton in the late 1980s. The video played a number of disturbing images and sound bites by those whom the narrator identified as extremist and dangerous. The video in question was produced and overseen by Lear on behalf of People for the American Way and was narrated by none other than actor Burt Lancaster. The title, "Life and Liberty for All Who Believe," reflected PFAW's literature and activism in defense of American civil liberties. In addition, it also reflected PFAW's tendency to present the conservative and Christian Right in hyperbolic terms that were designed to rally support rather than facilitate understanding despite PFAW's educational aspirations.

73. Castelli, *Plea for Common Sense*, 193.

74. For scholar of religion Chad Seales, civility can be understood as "personal habits of democratic citizenship widely promoted throughout the nation, principally as 'civics' by liberal Protestants in voluntary organizations, such as the YMCA, and by Roman Catholics in their own ecclesiastical

and educational institutions. . . . In the South, white Protestants used it to maintain public control of black bodies." For the purposes of this book, Lear and PFAW relied on the very same discursive powers of civility out of an attempt to define proper and improper usages of religion in public life. For more, see Seales, *The Secular Spectacle.*

75. The title of this text possessed a history of its own. One of the television pilots that Lear wrote for ABC was titled *Justice for All.* This pilot, in its third iteration, went on to become what most know today as *All in the Family* for CBS. Although the titles are not exactly the same, this connection is but one of many between the television work Lear did in the 1970s and his nonprofit organizing in the early 1980s. For more, see David Bollier, *Liberty and Justice for Some: Defending a Free Society from the Radical Right's Holy War on Democracy* (New York: Frederick Ungar, 1982).

76. Both works are particularly important for this study because they identify the most influential religious and social developments that have shaped political activism and mobilization since the 1960s.

77. For more on this transition, see Bivins, *The Fracture of Good Order*; Whitney Strub, *Perversion for Profit: The Politics of Pornography and the Rise of the New Right* (New York: Columbia University Press, 2013).

78. Seth Dowland, *Family Values and the Rise of the Religious Right* (Philadelphia: University of Pennsylvania Press, 2015).

79. The importance of this event in the history of the Christian Right cannot be overstated. Although some argue that abortion itself was the galvanizing issue for the Right and its various political causes, alternative readings of the period suggest that government intervention, either in this case or in the case concerning nonprofit status and the practice of racial discrimination at Bob Jones University, was the primary antagonistic force. More subtle interpretations foreground selective appropriation instead of strict rejection, or "backlash," by the Christian Right of countercultural currents in American society during the 1960s and 1970s. For more on this literature, see the various works of Axel R. Schäfer including *Countercultural Conservatives: American Evangelicalism from the Postwar Revival to the New Christian Right* (Madison: University of Wisconsin Press, 2013); Schäfer, ed., *American Evangelicals and the 1960s* (Madison: University of Wisconsin Press, 2013). For more on the Christian Right, gender, and conservative female leadership, see Emily Johnson, *This Is Our Message: Women's Leadership in the New Christian Right* (New York: Oxford University Press, 2019).

80. For more on the creation of publics, see Michael Warner, "Publics and Counterpublics," *Public Culture* 14, no. 1 (Winter 2002): 49–90. For Warner, a public is "the social space created by the reflexive circulation of discourse" addressed to both personal and impersonal audiences as a form of poetic world making. Additionally, "Writing to a public helps to make a world, insofar as the object of address is brought into being partly by postulating and characterizing it." In this sense, Lear and PFAW assisted in bolstering two separate but interrelated publics—one that corresponded to the Christian Right and the other representing the interests of religious liberals in the early 1980s. Publics fulfill specific needs as well, namely "to concretize the world in which discourse circulates, to offer its members direct and active membership through language, to place strangers on a shared footing." And lastly, publics do not come and go without leaving a mark: "The projection of a public is a new, creative, and distinctively modern mode of power." In order to manifest as a public, discourses or performances "must characterize the world in which it attempts to circulate, projecting for that world a concrete and livable shape, and attempting to realize that world through address."

81. Wuthnow's work is required reading not only for this period in recent US history but also on the emergence of the "third sector" in American politics, which refers to the spaces between individuals and the federal government where politics themselves happen on a national scale. Generally speaking, national organizations and nonprofits typically reside in this space, including the NCC

and PFAW. As scholar of religion Jason Bivins argues, "It is in the political spaces that belong neither to the 'private sphere' nor to the state that Christian antiliberals have attempted to reinvigorate the political process itself, in the struggle for identity through organizing publics, coalescing political identities, and moral suasion" (*The Fracture of Good Order*, 172). For Bivins, most of the verbal protest authored by the Christian Right against the state, not to mention the evangelical Left as evidenced by figures such as Jim Wallis, can be understood as antiliberal speech in the public square.

82.   Wuthnow, *The Struggle for America's Soul*, 10–11.

83.   Drawing on the work of philosopher Jürgen Habermas, Wuthnow argues that the public sphere "is diverse, divided into various subspheres or groupings constituted by interests and expertise.... Above all, it is oriented toward open discussion of basic societal goals" (12). Lear and Falwell not only took part in contributing to such a public, they also engaged its rules and guidelines by either following or rejecting them. Lear tended to defend the basic principles of the public sphere by insisting that there was a proper way to mix religion and politics. Falwell tended to reject these claims since they often resulted in excluding his claims from the wider national discussion of what type of nation would emerge from one of the more contentious decades in recent American political history. "Indeed, the two [liberals and conservatives] often gave lip service to the higher principles held by the other," Wuthnow argues, "but expressed disagreement over the tactics being used" (34). In other words, it wasn't that Falwell's politics were faulty to Lear and PFAW but rather that the means by which he enacted them were an affront to the rules of public deliberation themselves.

84.   Wuthnow, 41.

85.   Wuthnow, 52.

86.   For scholars of religion Courtney Bender and Pamela Klassen, pluralism can be understood as "casting prescriptive norms of identity and engagement, creating new possibilities and curtailing others." In addition, it defines "religion" as that which "is shared between diverse groups, whether as articulated in the language of harmonious interfaith coalitions or in the terminology of secular detractors." Lastly, as deployed by PFAW, notions of pluralism allow organizations to "powerfully articulate the very terms on which religious actors, interests, and understandings are recognized as such." For more, see Bender and Klassen, *After Pluralism*, 1–30.

87.   For sociologist James Davison Hunter, the claims of PFAW can be understood as part of "the liberal reaction" during this period. The authors of such reactions could be found in organizations such as the ACLU, NOW, and the NCC. There are four themes that characterize this reaction according to Hunter: values/ideals, methods, negativism, and substance. Based on these four traits alone, we are able to locate PFAW's accusations concerning the Christian Right's intolerance and antidemocratic tendencies. For more, see James Davison Hunter, "The Liberal Reaction," in Liebman and Wuthnow, *The New Christian Right*, 150–161.

88.   Miller, *Age of Evangelicalism*, 75–76.

89.   By "global" I mean liberals' awareness of the Iranian Revolution of 1979 and its subsequent deployment by Norman Lear, Peter Berger, and others in their attempts to understand conservative Protestantism by way of its fundamentalist, Pentecostal, and evangelical representatives in the American public.

90.   Wuthnow, *The Struggle for America's Soul*, 58.

91.   This is one of many arguments put forth by Wuthnow in *The Restructuring of American Religion*. For Wuthnow, "Special interest groups have arisen for the express purpose of combating, restraining, or promising certain types of government action" (114). This quote not only illuminates America's recent political history, it also shifts analytic emphasis for scholars of religion and historians of American religion by querying the role of the liberal state in cultivating and/or suppressing religious life and practices within the United States instead of beginning with America's religious multiplicity and its subsequent improvisational splendor. For more on the role of the state in

American history, see Gary Gerstle, *Liberty and Coercion: The Paradox of American Government from the Founding to the Present* (Princeton, NJ: Princeton University Press, 2015).

92. For more, see Smith, *Chaos Rhetoric*.

93. For more on this debate, see Lear and Reagan, "A Debate on Religious Freedom," 15–20.

94. Wuthnow, *The Restructuring of American Religion*, 201.

95. Hunter, "The Liberal Reaction," in Liebman and Wuthnow, *The New Christian Right*, 156.

96. Hunter, "The Liberal Reaction," 162.

97. One such call could be found in the pages of *Christianity and Crisis*. Authored in March 1979 by former senator Thomas J. McIntyre, an article titled "Resisting the New Right: The Politics of Civility" attempted to explain why divisive politics were so "dangerously successful" to "liberals and moderates" and why they must not respond to the New Right in kind. "The truth," McIntyre wrote, "is that both sets of absolutes are worthy of respect, and that neither *absolutely* precludes the other." Senator McIntyre's quote comes from a selection of his larger book titled *The Fear Brokers*, published by Pilgrim Press. He was particularly qualified to speak on these issues because he was one of many senators who was unseated during this period by the little-understood Christian Right and its grassroots politics. For more, see Thomas J. McIntyre, "Resisting the New Right: The Politics of Civility," *Christianity and Crisis*, March 5, 1979, 43–48.

98. Among the many characteristics of the Christian Right that offended Lear and PFAW, the certainty of the Bible Scorecard was arguably at the top of the list. Not only did this type of print media evaluate the quality of one's Christianity based on voting records, it also established *the* Christian vote on a particular issue or set of issues regardless of the diversity of opinion. The conversation that in theory was supposed to follow a political claim made in public was unable to get off the ground because the form of the scorecard itself undermined any chance of a dialogue between differing opinions. In short, the scorecard violated many of PFAW's guidelines for properly mixing religion and politics by shutting down conversation in addition to identifying political opinions with the certainty of God.

99. For the definitive work on this topic, see Shultz, *Tri-Faith America*.

100. My tracking of pluralist projects over the course of the twentieth century does not mean to imply that one simply replaced the other. In fact, one could argue that Lear's reliance on the American Way took advantage of the interwar formulation, more so than the Tri-Faith formation, since his frame of biographical reference was the 1930s. He was also known to work with the National Council of Christians and Jews and even received an award from them during the 1970s.

101. Texts that defined the 1980s in such mental terms are as follows: Jerry Falwell, *Listen America!* (New York: Bantam, 1981); Tim LaHaye, *The Battle for the Mind* (Old Tappan, NJ: Fleming H. Revell, 1980); Francis Schaeffer, *The Christian Manifesto* (Wheaton, IL: Crossway, 1981). This emphasis on the mind and ideas was echoed by conservative strategists as well during the early 1980s. "It's a war of ideas," argued Paul Weyrich. "It may not be with rockets and missiles, but it is a war nevertheless. It's a war of ideology, it's a war of ideas, and it is a war about our way of life. And it has to be fought with the same intensity, I think, and dedication as you would fight a shooting war." Think tanks echoed this call to engage one's opponents upon the battlefield of the mind. In 1986, the vice president of the Heritage Foundation described his role as such: "We are the intellectual shock troops of the conservative revolution." For more, see Rodgers, *Age of Fracture*, 1–14.

102. For sociologist James Davison Hunter, civil society in the US context depended on two overriding presuppositions: that there was a proper place *for* religion and that behavior in public would be tolerant of others' rights and freedoms. As Hunter puts it, "In spite of any ideological diversity and any attendant hostilities, the civil society remains intact as long as all parties agree to abide by the procedural norms of tolerance of opposing views, respect for civil liberties, and nonviolent, legally proscribed political action and dissent." For more, see James Davison Hunter, *Evangelicalism: The Coming Generation* (Chicago: University of Chicago Press, 1987), 150.

103. For more, see Susan Harding, "Representing Fundamentalism: The Problem of the Repugnant Cultural Other," *Social Research* 58, no. 2 (Summer 1991): 373–93.

104. Put in a slightly different way, such curtailment functioned as part of the "restraining techniques of public consensus" (Seales, *The Secular Spectacle*, 19).

105. Donald Heinz, "The Struggle to Define America," in Liebman and Wuthnow, *The New Christian Right*, 146–48.

106. For commentary on this topic by scholar of religion Robert Orsi, see his presentation on Walter Capps at UCSB: University of California Television, "Walter Capps: Religious Studies and International Politics," video, YouTube, September 25, 2008, accessed December 15, 2015, https://www .youtube.com/watch?v=y6zuPa7qA9w.

107. Hunter, *Evangelicalism*, 151.

108. Hunter, 152. For anthropologist Susan Harding, "The religious right broke a web of mostly informal restrictions on religious speech in the public arena, in some ways lowered the 'wall of separation' between church and state, and broke the spell of America as a strictly 'secular nation.'" For more, see Susan Harding, "Religious Right," in *Encyclopedia of Religion in America*, ed. Charles Lippy and Peter Williams (New York: Sage, 2010), 1867–80.

109. Seales, *The Secular Spectacle*, 10.

110. Seales, 86.

111. For historian Steven Miller, the "evangelical age" defined the actions of both the Christian Right and those beyond its boundaries who sought their own usages for born-again faith in American politics. In this sense, evangelicals are only one of many protagonists in religious histories of America's recent past. Evangelicalism "was pervasive enough that no one expression of evangelicalism could lay sole claim to it, and it involved more than just avowed born-again Christians." For more, see Miller, *Age of Evangelicalism*, 1–8.

5. LIBERALISM AS VARIETY SHOW

1. Norman Lear, *Even This I Get to Experience* (New York: Penguin, 2017), 334.

2. Lear, 334.

3. Lear, 335.

4. Susan Friend Harding, *The Book of Jerry Falwell: Fundamentalist Language and Politics* (Princeton, NJ: Princeton University Press, 2000).

5. David Watt, *Antifundamentalism in Modern America* (Ithaca, NY: Cornell University Press, 2017). By "ritual" I mean to describe the process by which particular behaviors, self-conceptions, and stereotypes usually understood as "political" come to be naturalized for a given community of citizens.

6. Andrea Most, *Theatrical Liberalism: Jews and Popular Entertainment in America* (New York: New York University Press, 2013).

7. Arlie Russell Hochschild, *Strangers in Their Own Land: Anger and Mourning on the American Right* (New York: New, 2016).

8. Daniel Rodgers, "The Traditions of Liberalism," in *Questions of Tradition*, ed. Mark Phillips and Gordon J. Schochet (Toronto: University of Toronto Press, 2004), 204.

9. Daniel Rodgers, *Age of Fracture* (Cambridge, MA: Harvard University Press, 2011).

10. For more on this largely conservative tradition, see Kevin Kruse, *One Nation Under God: How Corporate America Invented Christian America* (New York: Basic, 2015).

11. J. Brooks Flippen, *Jimmy Carter, the Politics of Family, and the Rise of the Religious Right* (Athens: University of Georgia Press, 2011), 81. For a more detailed description of one such rally, see David Snowball, *Continuity and Change in the Rhetoric of the Moral Majority* (New York: Praeger, 1991).

12.   While numerous studies have been conducted on Falwell, political conservatism, and "the rise of the Christian Right," few if any have effectively or successfully explained how and why Falwell began his career in the public square rejecting the social applicability of the biblical text but then proceeded to defend such applications once organizations like the Christian Voice and the Moral Majority emerged in the 1970s—with his explicit involvement in the latter being essential to its formation. The subsequent manuscript to this one, tentatively titled *Inventing the Christian Right*, will explore these questions more thoroughly by putting forth the following thesis: Falwell and others emerged when they did (or were interpellated as such) because they were subject to a reinvented notion of political engagement designed specifically for and on behalf of conservative causes and actors. In this sense, the "rise of the Christian Right" can and should be understood less as an unprecedented moment in the recent US past and more as a calculated project carried out by a cadre of conservative operatives and strategists as part of a rebranded GOP along the pragmatic, ideologically driven lines of those known as "the New Right." For the latest on Falwell and his sociopolitical impact, see Matthew Avery Sutton, ed., *Jerry Falwell and the Rise of the Religious Right: A Brief History with Documents* (New York: Bedford/St. Martin's, 2012). For a broader sociological study of the same time period and material, see Robert Wuthnow, *Vocabularies of Public Life* (New York: Routledge, 2002). For much of the conceptual architecture for this argument, see Susan Harding and Charles Bright, eds., *Statemaking and Social Movements: Essays in History and Theory* (Ann Arbor: University of Michigan Press, 1984); Stuart Hall, *The Hard Road to Renewal: Thatcherism and the Crisis of the Left* (New York: Verso, 1988).

13.   Jerry Falwell and Elmer Towns, *Church Aflame* (Nashville, TN: Impact, 1971).

14.   Jerry Falwell, *Listen, America!* (New York: Bantam, 1980).

15.   Jeffrey K. Hadden, "Soul-Saving via Video," *Christian Century*, May 28, 1980.

16.   "I Love America Rally Held," *Sarasota Herald-Tribune*, March 4, 1980.

17.   Snowball, *Continuity and Change*, 64–65.

18.   Snowball, 65.

19.   Daniel Bell, *The Radical Right: The New American Right* (New York: Criterion, 1955).

20.   Michael Warner, "Publics and Counterpublics (Abridged)," *Quarterly Journal of Speech* 88, no. 4 (November 2002): 413.

21.   In fact, many credit Falwell's rallies for generating the initial mailing lists and networks of communication that Paul Weyrich, Richard Viguerie, and others used to solidify their control of the GOP in the name of the New Right. For an example, see Frank J. Smith, ed., *Religion and Politics in America: An Encyclopedia of Church and State in American Life* (Santa Barbara, CA: ABC-CLIO, 2016), 295.

22.   Snowball, *Continuity and Change*, 66.

23.   Harding, *The Book of Jerry Falwell*, 10.

24.   For the paradigmatic example in this regard, see Sarah Hammond and Darren Dochuk, eds., *God's Businessmen: Entrepreneurial Evangelicals in Depression and War* (Chicago: University of Chicago Press, 2017).

25.   The 1960s axiom "the personal is the political" added another layer of complexity to this bifurcation onto an already complicated topic of public protest and resistance to white supremacy.

26.   Susan Harding, "A We Like Any Other," Hot Spots, *Cultural Anthropology*, January 18, 2017, https://culanth.org/fieldsights/a-we-like-any-other.

27.   Harding, *The Book of Jerry Falwell*, 12. It was only a matter of time before these channels of God found common cause with similarly thinking conservative strategists, political consultants, and business executives. As a result, Harding's articulation becomes that much more significant when attempting to explain "the rise of the Christian Right" as less a *demographic* reality and more a *discursive* one. As such, "the Christian Right" can be understood less as a description of empirical reality and more the product of a professionally run PR campaign with tactics adapted from the

fields of marketing, advertising, and broadcasting. More important, "the Christian Right" can be understood to have been generated by the single most important electoral development in the last half century of American political history: direct mail. While Harding's work on this subject continues to be underutilized in the study of American conservatism, it remains partially incomplete when attempting to narrate the New Right and the electoral successes of Ronald Reagan. Harding aptly describes the composition of "born-again Christianity" as "more of a mixture than a compound," yet to effectively explain "the rise of a Christian Right" as a "public relations stunt," one has to more thoroughly address the means and aspirations of those composing such cultural productions in the first place—the PR experts themselves.

28. Harding, *The Book of Jerry Falwell*, 62.

29. In this particular encounter between Lear and Falwell, Lear must be understood as defending what Harding describes as modern America's "regime of public religiosity," which could be felt across various levels of socioeconomic strata (21). While seemingly all-pervasive at times as a form of "national common sense," Harding also acknowledges its fragility as a product of thorough contestation in the public arena. As such, this chapter extends Harding's analytical agenda by arguing that *I Love Liberty* was this particular regime's public persona as only Lear could produce it for his prime-time viewership.

30. Tom Shales, "Miss Liberty's Left Hand," *Washington Post*, March 20, 1982.

31. Shales.

32. Richard Zoglin, "Is This Entertainment Special Promoting a Special Interest?" *New York Times*, March 21, 1982.

33. In many ways, this is exactly what happened during the latter part of the twentieth century. Conservative actors in the public square successfully appropriated and deployed the techniques of single-issue advocacy that were initially used on behalf of marginalized communities for "social issue" electoral purposes.

34. John J. O'Connor, "TV Weekend: Lear's 'I Love Liberty' Leads Specials," *New York Times*, March 19, 1982.

35. Arthur Unger, "Norman Lear's 'I Love Liberty': Patriotism and Family Fun," *Christian Science Monitor*, March 19, 1982.

36. Shales, "Miss Liberty's Left Hand." Lear was more than happy to lend his public support to author Gore Vidal for a US Senate seat from California. Lear thought Vidal would "elevate the rhetoric."

37. Shales, "Miss Liberty's Left Hand."

38. Mark Hemingway, "Liberal King Lear," *National Review*, March 25, 2008.

39. For more on Marty's impact on the study of fundamentalism, see Watt, *Antifundamentalism in Modern America*.

40. Martin Marty, "I Love Liberty," *Christian Century*, March 17, 1982, 294.

41. Marty, 294–96, my emphasis. Those events or causes that qualified as a "great religious issue," in addition to the manner in which such an identification took place, are arguably the central narrative catalyst of any story about the recent religious past in the United States since the 1960s. It was in this period, specifically between the mid-1960s and mid-1970s, when religious or spiritual fronts began to form in opposition to their political antitheses in the public square. Marty's selection of education and the Panama Canal as great religious issues was an indication of the restructuring American religious landscape largely in opposition to a determined grassroots mobilization campaign that foregrounded explicitly social and cultural issues as the most significant indicators of America's spiritual vitality and efficacy. In short, Marty's selection said as much about largely liberal, mainline American Protestantism as it did about the broader currents of American religion.

42. Marty, 295. Despite the fact that Marty was working with Lear and PFAW on behalf of *I Love Liberty*, he seemed to enjoy himself most when he was spending time with Senator Goldwater.

"Taking refuge in the familiar," Marty admitted. "I must confess to having had the best time with Senator Barry Goldwater, who was having a good time with his part in *I Love Liberty*" (295).

43.   Marty, 295. Sociologist Nancy Ammerman would more than like identify Marty, Lear, and other mainline supporters as living according to "the golden rule." While Lear is not necessarily Christian, his actions and behavior reflect the concerns of the more "activist wing" of golden-rule Christians, including supporting social justice and working for peace with various nonprofits (PFAW). For more, see her similarly titled chapter in David Hall, ed., *Lived Religion: Toward a History of Practice in America* (Princeton, NJ: Princeton University Press, 1997), 196–216.

44.   Marty, "I Love Liberty," 296.

45.   Charles McCrary and Jeffrey Wheatley, "The Protestant Secular in the Study of American Religion: Reappraisal and Suggestions," *Religion* 47, no. 2 (2017): 256–76.

46.   Most, *Theatrical Liberalism*, 8–9, my emphasis.

47.   Marty, "I Love Liberty," 294. Part of the argument of my next project is that individuals like Marty helped produce the idea of "the Christian Right" from the perspective of the mainline and across the pages of periodicals like the *Christian Century*. The fact that Marty *literally* had to make the New Right a part of his theoretical considerations suggests a great deal about the need for enemies in the liberal imagination in defending the public square. For more on liberal imaginaries, see Richard Amesbury, "Rethinking 'Religion and Politics': Reflections on the Reception and Import of Talal Asad's *Genealogies of Religion*," *Bulletin for the Study of Religion* 43, no. 1 (February 2014): 2–7.

48.   The first four certainly undergirded the variety show's purpose, but more important, they spoke to some of the unacknowledged realities of liberal religious practice and mobilization. Neither single-issue politics nor the "mixing" of religion and politics started off as a conservative invention in the twentieth century. If anything, they were both applied and perfected by religious liberals first as part of "the New Breed" of pastors, priests, and rabbis who took to the streets in the name of social and racial justice.

49.   Leslie Ward, "Rallying Around the Flag: Norman Lear and the American Way," *American Film* (October 1981): 63, 64, 81.

50.   Lear, *Even This I Get to Experience*, 336.

51.   Unger, "Norman Lear's 'I Love Liberty.' " "Parts of this two-hour marathon of American pride, optimism, and goodwill may sound a bit like the dramatic rah-rah radio shows one heard during World War II in order to bring Americans together. As a matter of fact, Norman Corwin, one of the authors of such shows, is credited as consultant."

       We also learn a great deal about the writing of *I Love Liberty* from writer Rita Mae Brown. In her memoir, titled *Rita Will: Memoir of a Literary Rabble-Rouser*, Brown contends that Lear was not the easiest person to work with. "One moment stands out. Norman Lear, king of television at that time, would fire me, then rehire me. He'd heard yes too many times. I said no. Whenever a figure, be it Czar Nicholas II or Norman, becomes muffled in a cocoon of great wealth and obedience, trouble follows." Brown continues, "He fired me. I packed. He called and said, 'Go home this weekend and write a piece with a black, a Jew, a gay person, a woman, a Hispanic. Did I forget anyone?' I did the piece. *Bland* doesn't describe it, but we had to get it through the censors. Norman, bless him, taught me how to combat these guardians of television morality, Broadcast Standards and Practices. Here we were writing a show about the First Amendment, freedom of speech, and we had to pass the censors." For more, see Rita Mae Brown, *Rita Will: Memoir of a Literary Rabble-Rouser* (New York: Bantam, 1997), 366.

52.   Learned Hand, *The Spirit of Liberty: Papers and Addresses* (New York: Vintage, 1959).

53.   In classic Lear style, the end of the song was punctuated by a certain Muppet pig yelling at the top of her lungs, "AND WOMEN!!" in order to remind those at home of the larger reason for their collective presence that evening—racial, gender, and religious representation and protection under

the law as outlined by the American Way. The National Council of Christians and Jews first articulated this type of commitment to such principles in their first mission statement in 1935: "The National Conference exists to promote justice, amity, understanding, and cooperation among Jews, Catholics, and Protestants in the United States, and to analyze, moderate and finally eliminate intergroup prejudices . . . with a view to the establishment of a social order in which the religious ideals of brotherhood and justice shall become the standards of human relationships." For historian Kevin Shultz, the NCCJ sought nothing less than a "new 'social order' centered on brotherhood and justice." The Muppets' concluding song, as authored by Lear and others, was a direct reference back to this interfaith tradition. For more, see Kevin Shultz, *Tri-Faith America: How Catholics and Jews Held Postwar America to its Protestant Promise* (New York: Oxford University Press, 2013), 32.

54. Marty, "I Love Liberty," 295.

55. Tracy Fessenden, *Culture and Redemption: Religion, the Secular, and American Literature* (Princeton, NJ: Princeton University Press, 2007). See also Most, *Theatrical Liberalism*, 67.

56. Jeremy Dauber, *Jewish Comedy: A Serious History* (New York: W. W. Norton, 2017), 94.

57. For more on the eighteenth-century context of American religious liberalism, see Margaret C. Jacob, "Private Beliefs in Public Temples: The New Religiosity of the Eighteenth Century," *Social Research* 59, no. 1 (Spring 1992): 59–84. For Andrea Most, the fourth characteristic of theatrical liberalism as she defines it is "the incontrovertible obligations to the theatrical community" that overrode notions of individual freedom and talk of individual rights. For Most, "there is a palpable tension between a liberal rhetoric of rights and the Judaic rhetoric of obligation." For more, see Most, *Theatrical Liberalism*, 11.

58. For sociologist Arlie Russell Hochschild, the liberal "deep story" is about the public square and its protection. "They are fiercely proud of it," Hochschild says. "Some of them built it, . . . but in the liberal deep story, an alarming event occurs; marauders invade the public square." For more, see Hochschild, *Strangers in Their Own Land*, 235. My reading and analysis of Lear as a contributor to this tradition combines Hochschild's understanding of custodial protection with the explicitly Jewish understanding of obligation (as described by Most) to both the theater and the public square. In this sense, Lear makes a particularly Jewish argument on behalf of religious liberalism based on action and obligation to one's fellow citizen as refracted through the values and epistemics (varied ways of knowing) of liberal democracy.

59. Most, *Theatrical Liberalism*, 9.

60. The sketch's actors included LeVar Burton, Michael Horse, Patty Duke Astin, Desi Arnaz Jr., and Dick Van Patten. Each character articulated a similarly critical observation. For "the angry woman," her plight continued to be the wage gap between men and women. For "the angry Hispanic," too many in his community were working in jobs that were degrading and dehumanizing. Regardless of critique, each character concluded in the same way: "but I love my country."

61. This image of lines can be found in Hochschild, *Strangers in Their Own Land*.

62. "Ask not what your country can do for you," the angry white suggested, "but what you can do for your country. I wish they had heard that one!" This response came after each member of the sketch named a president that spoke to him or her respectively (black/Hispanic/Indian/gay/woman). Some chose Lincoln, others chose Lyndon Johnson, but Patten (the actor) chose Kennedy in order to put the onus on those who were angry to address their own living conditions. Yet again, conservatism is interpreted (by Lear and Marty) as being about personal responsibility and, perhaps most important, accountability, and is thus out of sync within the larger Lear-authored variety show that calls upon America's social institutions to do better when it comes to minority communities. What Lear did not realize was that "the angry white" was just as often a minority as his brown and black brothers and sisters, only a largely hidden one. For more, see Richard Lemon, *The Troubled American* (New York: Simon and Schuster, 1969).

63. One could also argue that the prime-time television show *Parks and Recreation* is guilty of a similar tactic, specifically when it comes to the character Ron Swanson. While he is the source of immense comedic genius in the sitcom, Ron is oftentimes reduced down to either his mustache or his libertarian sensibilities for the sake of a larger joke. Ron certainly counsels Leslie Knope's character in a manner not unlike Lou Grant in *The Mary Tyler Moore Show*, yet, if necessary, Ron-the-character will become the butt of the joke due to his perceived conservatism. The end result is that this dynamic ends up reinforcing the correctness of whatever Leslie says or believes about the role of government (read: *local* government) in American public life.

64. Steven Miller, *The Age of Evangelicalism: America's Born-Again Years* (New York: Oxford University Press, 2014). The earnestness in which the variety show was composed and executed spoke to the somewhat disorganized response marshalled by various liberal actors in America to the presidency of Ronald Reagan and the arrival of the Christian Right.

65. These last two words, "for them," serve as a microcosm for the intellectual shortcomings of liberal religious organizing. The salience may appear to be obvious to those constructing it in the first place (defenders of the public square), but for those on the receiving end (the marauders), it may not be at all. In other words, the inherent salience and applicability of something like "freedom," "religion," or "liberty" in this case could actually be rather arbitrary or detrimental. In this sense, People for the American Way could at times be understood, as Jerry Falwell once put it, as "People for Norman Lear's Way."

66. Shultz, *Tri-Faith America*. As the title indicates, Shultz may intend to argue that such a Tri-Faith articulation helped jettison or challenge the veracity of an overly Protestant notion of a "Christian Nation" in post–World War II America, yet such chronological transitions oftentimes obscure what remains in common between the two, namely a Protestant promise.

67. Jon Shields, "Framing the Christian Right: How Progressives and Post-War Liberals Constructed the Religious Right," *Journal of Church and State* 53, no. 4 (December 2011): 635–55.

68. E. J. Dionne, *Why the Right Went Wrong: Conservatism from Goldwater to the Tea Party and Beyond* (New York: Simon & Schuster, 2016). See also Rick Perlstein, *Before the Storm: Barry Goldwater and the Unmaking of American Consensus* (New York: Nation, 2009).

69. Dionne, 58.

70. Neil Jumonville and Kevin Mattson, eds., *Liberalism for a New Century* (Berkeley: University of California Press, 2007).

71. William A. Rusher, *The Making of the New Majority Party* (Ottawa, IL: Green Hill, 1975). For both Rusher and Dionne, Reagan's electoral successes would not have been possible were it not for Goldwater's failed candidacy for president. "When Goldwater went down to defeat," Rusher explained, "it was inevitable that some conservatives would contemplate the possibility of rebuilding their church on Reagan. By the end of 1965, Reagan had been persuaded to consider running in 1966 for the Governorship of California" (53).

72. Jennifer Burns, "Liberalism and the Conservative Imagination," in Jumonville and Mattson, *Liberalism for a New Century*, 58–74.

73. Jacob, "Private Beliefs in Public Temples," 64.

CONCLUSION

1. Fay Vincent, "Examining the Role of Religion in 'the American Way,'" *Treasure Coast Palm*, October 8, 2015, accessed February 1, 2016, http://www.tcpalm.com/opinion/guest-columns/fay-vincent-examining-the-role-of-religion-in-the-american-way-ep-1309239018-340370181.html.

2. Norman Lear, "Ben Carson and the American Way," Politics, HuffPost, October 21, 2015, accessed February 1, 2016, https://www.huffpost.com/entry/ben-carson-and-the-americ_b_8353156.

3. David Watt, *Antifundamentalism in Modern America* (Ithaca, NY: Cornell University Press, 2017).

4. Peter Coviello, "Plural: Mormon Polygamy and the Biopolitics of Secularism," *History of the Present* 7, no. 2 (Fall 2017): 219–41.

5. Coviello, 238, my emphasis.

6. Robert Self, *All in the Family: The Realignment of American Democracy Since the 1960s* (New York: Hill and Wang, 2013).

7. Jon Shields, "Framing the Christian Right: How Progressives and Postwar Liberals Constructed the Religious Right," *Journal of Church and State* 53, no. 4 (December 2011): 635–55.

8. Darren Dochuk, *From Bible Belt to Sunbelt: Plainfolk Religion, Grassroots Politics, and the Rise of Evangelical Conservatism* (New York: W. W. Norton, 2011).

9. Andrea Most, *Theatrical Liberalism: Jews and Popular Entertainment in America* (New York: New York University Press, 2013).

10. For more on ecumenical Protestantism as "a halfway house," see David Hollinger, *After Cloven Tongues of Fire: Protestant Liberalism in Modern American History* (Princeton, NJ: Princeton University Press, 2013).

11. This argument may not need to be made to those studying the Christian Right, but many still argue that liberal progressive organizing made its own contributions to the unfolding of American secularization over the course of the twentieth century. For an example, see Kevin M. Schultz, *Tri-Faith America: How Catholics and Jews Held Postwar America to Its Protestant Promise* (New York: Oxford University Press, 2011).

12. For a much-needed reconsideration of the notion of charisma, see Vincent Lloyd, *In Defense of Charisma* (New York: Columbia University Press, 2018).

13. Historian of American religion Mark Edwards has called for a similar study, one that would examine the "parallel lives" of seemingly oppositional communities. "I am not entirely convinced yet of the purpose or value of stressing liberal and conservative Protestant commonality. . . . I'm most intrigued by the historiographical possibilities: Might we be able to craft new narratives that place the Protestant left, right, and center in conversation all at the same time? The Culture Warriors will say we can't and we shouldn't. Nuts to them." For more, see Mark Edwards, "The Theft of the (Christian) Century," *Society of US Intellectual History Blog*, March 1, 2013, accessed February 19, 2018, https://s-usih.org/2013/03/the-theft-of-the-christian-century/.

14. John Modern, "My Evangelical Conviction," *Religion* 42, no. 3 (2012): 439–57.

15. Finbarr Curtis, "The Study of American Religions: Critical Reflections on a Specialization," *Religion* 42, no. 3 (2012): 11.

16. Tracy Fessenden, "The Objects of Religious Studies," *Religion* 42, no. 3 (2012): 375.

17. Courtney Bender, "The Power of Pluralist Thinking," in *Politics of Religious Freedom*, ed. Winnifred Sullivan, Elizabeth Shakman Hurd, Saba Mahmood, and Peter G. Danchin (Chicago: University of Chicago Press, 2015), 66–77.

18. Bender, 73.

19. Robert Bellah, "Civil Religion in America," *Daedalus* 96, no. 1 (Winter 1967): 1–21.

20. By the time this monograph is published, some of this material will have been published as part of an Immanent Frame forum at the Social Science Research Council on "The Religious Left" in American public life. The forum is organized around the following online piece: Nadia Marzouki, "Does the United States Need a Religious Left?" Social Science Research Council, January 23, 2019, accessed February 22, 2019, https://tif.ssrc.org/2019/01/23/does-the-united-states-need-a-religious-left/.

21. Michael Rogin, "Politics, Emotion, and the Wallace Vote," *British Journal of Sociology* 20, no. 1 (March 1969): 39.

Bibliography

ARCHIVES, EPHEMERA, AND VIDEO COLLECTIONS

"Life of the Spirit." Personal Collection of Norman Lear. http://www.normanlear.com/life-spirit/.
Paley Center for Media. New York, NY.
"People for the American Way Collection of Conservative Political Ephemera, 1980–2004." University
 of California, Berkeley, Bancroft Library. Berkeley, CA.

PRIMARY SOURCES (SELECTED)

Blumenthal, Sidney. "The Righteous Empire." *New Republic* 191, no. 16 (October 1984): 18.
Bollier, David. *Liberty and Justice for Some: Defending a Free Society from the Radical Right's Holy War on
 Democracy.* New York: Frederick Ungar, 1982.
Brown, Rita Mae. *Rita Will: Memoir of a Literary Rabble-Rouser.* New York: Bantam, 1997.
Buckley, William F. "The Nightmare of Norman Lear." *National Review,* November 27, 1981, 1441–42.
Butts, Freeman R. *Religion, Education, and the First Amendment: The Appeal to History.* Washington, DC:
 People for the American Way, 1986.
Buursma, Bruce. "The National Affairs Briefing: Evangelicals Give Reagan a 'Non-partisan' Stump." *Chris-
 tianity Today,* September 19, 1980.
Castelli, Jim. "People for the American Way Aim for Political Participation." *The Dispatch,* February 25,
 1981, 17.
——. *A Plea for Common Sense: Resolving the Clash Between Religion and Politics.* New York: Harper and
 Row, 1988.
Callahan, Daniel. "The Quest for Social Relevance." *Daedalus* 96, no. 1 (Winter 1967): 151–79.
Clark, Kenneth R. "Norman Lear, Clergy Team to Fight Morality Politics." *Pittsburgh Press,* October 25,
 1980.
Clendinen, Dudley. "Christian New Right's Rush to Power: Test of Strength Lies Ahead." *New York Times,*
 August 18, 1980.
Cohen, Marcus. "Religion and the FCC." *The Reporter,* January 14, 1965, 32–34.

Cox, Harvey. "The 'New Breed' in American Churches: Sources of Social Activism in American Religion," *Daedalus* 96, no. 1 (Winter 1967): 135–50.

Crawford, Alan. "Richard Viguerie's Bid for Power." *The Nation*, January 29, 1977, 104–8.

——. *Thunder on the Right: The 'New Right' and the Politics of Resentment.* New York: Pantheon, 1980.

Cutler, Donald R., ed. *The Religious Situation 1969.* Boston: Beacon, 1969.

Deeb, Gary. "Mull and Willard to Take a Swipe at a Racket via Lear 'Religion' Film." *Chicago Tribune*, March 22, 1979.

Falwell, Jerry. "Let's Be Fair About Fairness." *Journal of Broadcasting* 28, no. 3 (Summer 1984): 273–74.

——. *Listen America!* New York: Bantam, 1981.

Firestein, Charles L. "*Red Lion* and the Fairness Doctrine: Regulation of Broadcasting 'In the Public Interest.'" *Arizona Law Review* 11, no. 807 (1969): 807–21.

Ford, Frederick W. "The Meaning of the 'Public Interest,' Convenience or Necessity.'" *Journal of Broadcasting* 5, no. 3 (1961): 205–18.

Fore, William. "Religion on the Airwaves: In the Public Interest?" *Christian Century*, September 17, 1975, 782–83.

Friedman, Milton. *Capitalism and Freedom.* Chicago: University of Chicago Press, 1982.

Frishman, Bob. *American Families: Responding to the Pro-family Movement.* Washington, DC: People for the American Way, 1984.

Gardella, Kay. "Carroll O'Connor: A Tight-Lipped Type of Liberal." *Chicago Tribune*, August 26, 1974.

Gitlin, Todd. "The New Crusades: How Fundamentalists Tied Up the Networks." *American Film* (October 1981): 52–60.

Goodman, John J. "Campaign Opens Against Religious New Right." *Los Angeles Times*, October 22, 1980.

Grefe, Andrea J. "The Family Viewing Hour: An Assault on the First Amendment?" *Hastings Constitutional Law Quarterly* (Fall 1977): 935–89.

Gunther, Max. "TV and the New Morality." *TV Guide*, October 14, 1972, 8–13.

Hand, Learned. *The Spirit of Liberty: Papers and Addresses.* New York: Vintage, 1959.

Harmetz, Aljean. "Maude Didn't Leave 'em All Laughing." *New York Times*, December 10, 1972.

Holsendolph, Ernest. "Religious Broadcasts Bring Rising Revenues and Create Rivalries." *New York Times*, December 2, 1979.

Hoyt, Joan K. "Maude's Abortion Evokes Protests." *Los Angeles Times*, November 29, 1972.

Hunter, James Davison. "The New Class and the Young Evangelicals." *Review of Religious Research* 22, no. 2 (December 1980): 155–69.

Hutcheson, Richard G. *Mainline Churches and the Evangelicals: A Challenging Crisis?* Atlanta: John Knox, 1981.

Jacobs, Marcia. "Open Letter to the Rev. Wildmon." *Los Angeles Times*, July 26, 1981.

Jorstad, Erling. *The Politics of Doomsday: Fundamentalists of the Far Right.* New York: Abingdon, 1970.

——. *The Politics of Moralism: The New Christian Right in American Life.* Minneapolis: Augsburg, 1981.

Kaplan, Peter W. "Lear vs. Falwell in Morality Armageddon." *Chicago Tribune*, October 1, 1981.

Kasindorf, Martin. "Archie and Maude and Fred and Norman and Alan." *New York Times Magazine*, June 24, 1973, 12–13, 15–19.

Kennedy, Edward M. "Tolerance and Truth in America." *Historical Magazine of the Protestant Episcopal Church* 53, no. 1 (March 1984): 7–12.

Kerby, Phil. "Falwell and Lear: Maybe They're Not So Far Apart." *Los Angeles Times*, October 30, 1981.

"King Lear." *Time*, April 5, 1976, 80.

Kruger, Helen. "Shame on Maude." *Village Voice*, May 23, 1974, 56.

LaHaye, Tim. *The Battle for the Mind.* Old Tappan, NJ: Fleming H. Revell, 1980.

Landy, Thomas M. "What's Missing from This Picture: Norman Lear Explains." *Commonweal* 119, no. 17 (October 1992): 17–20.

LaVelle, Mike. "Biases of All in the Family." *Chicago Tribune*, January 2, 1973.

Lear, Norman. "A Church for People Like Us." HuffPost, May 1, 2010. Accessed November 11, 2015. https://www.huffpost.com/entry/mamaloshen-a-church-for-p_b_480896.

——. "Does TV Have the Courage to Pioneer a New Commercial Ethic?" *Television Quarterly* 21, no. 4 (1985): 7–14.

——. "Education for the Human Spirit." *Virginia Journal of Education* 84 (October 1990): 6–13.

——. "Essay." In *More Reflections on the Meaning of Life*. New York: Life Magazine, 1992.

——. "Foreword." In *Aiming Higher: 25 Stories of How Companies Prosper by Combining Sound Management and Social Vision*, by David Bollier, vii–x, 1–7. New York: Amacom, 1996.

——. "Introduction." In *Being God's Partner: How to Find the Hidden Link Between Spirituality and Your Work*, by Jeffrey K. Salkin, 21–28. New York: Jewish Lights, 1997.

——. "Laughing While We Face Our Prejudices." *New York Times*, April 11, 1971.

——. "Liberty and Its Responsibilities." In *Broadcast Journalism 1979–1981: The Eighth Alfred I. DuPont Columbia University Survey*, ed. Marvin Barrett, 10–15. New York: Everest, 1982.

——. "Nurturing our Spiritual Imagination in an Age of Science and Technology." *Religion and Public Education* 16, no. 3 (Fall 1989): 395–408.

——. "Our Political Leaders Mustn't Be Evangelists." *USA Today*, August 17, 1984.

——. "Rewriting the Bottom Line: Hollywood, Profits, and the Life of the Spirit." *Image* 27 (Summer 2000): 117–23.

——. "The Search for E Pluribus Unum." Speech, National Press Club, Washington, DC, December 9, 1993.

——. "Social Responsibility: A Cure for the Loneliness in our Time." *Harvard Divinity Bulletin* 22, no. 2 (1992): 13–16.

——. "Why I Am a Born Again American." Take Back America Conference, Washington, DC, March 19, 2008.

Lear, Norman, and Barbara Cady. "Playboy Interview: Norman Lear." *Playboy*, March 1976, 53–69.

Lear, Norman, and Ronald Reagan. "A Debate on Religious Freedom." *Harper's*, October 1984, 15–20.

Lemon, Richard. *The Troubled American*. New York: Simon and Schuster, 1969.

Lewis, Dan. "VA Group Says 'Stop Immorality on TV.'" *Lakeland Ledger*, August 12, 1973.

Loevinger, Lee. "Broadcasting and Religious Liberty." *Journal of Broadcasting* 9, no. 1 (1964): 3–23.

Love, Keith. "Lear Tackles Moral Majority: Producer, Religious Leaders Form Group to Spur Diversity." *Los Angeles Times*, December 13, 1981.

"Mainline Church Leaders Hit for 'Obscene' Political Behavior." *Christianity Today*, April 23, 1982: 42–44.

Marc, David. "TV Auteurism." *American Film* 7, no. 2 (November 1, 1981): 52–53.

——. "Understanding Television." *The Atlantic*, August 1984, 35–37.

Margulies, Lee, ed. "Proliferation of Pressure Groups in Primetime Symposium, 1981." *Emmy Magazine*, Summer 1981, A1–A32.

Martin, William. "The Birth of a Media Myth." *The Atlantic*, June 1981, 7–16.

Marty, Martin. *Church-State Separation in America: The Tradition Nobody Knows*. Washington, DC: People for the American Way, 1982.

——. "Fundamentalism as a Social Phenomenon." *Bulletin of the American Academy of Arts and Sciences* 42, no. 2 (November 1988): 15–29.

——. "Fundamentalism Reborn." *Saturday Review*, May 1980, 37–43.

——. "I Love Liberty." *Christian Century*, March 1982, 294–96.

——. "A Profile of Norman Lear: Another Pilgrim's Progress." *Christian Century*, January 21, 1987, 55–58.

——. "Religion in America Since Mid-century." *Daedalus* 111, no. 1 (Winter 1982): 149–63.

Mayer, Allan J., John J. Lindsay, and Howard Fineman. "A Tide of Born-Again Politics." *Newsweek*, September 15, 1980.

McIntyre, Thomas J. "Resisting the New Right: The Politics of Civility." *Christianity and Crisis*, March 5, 1979, 43–48.

"Meanwhile: Norman Lear on Spirituality." *Christianity Today*, April 23, 1982, 42–44.

Mills, C. Wright. *The Power Elite*. New York: Oxford University Press, 1956.

"Morality and the Broadcast Media: A Constitutional Analysis of FCC Regulatory Standards." *Harvard Law Review* 84, no. 3 (January 1971): 664–99.

Nadel, Gerry. "All in His Family." *New Times*, July 9, 1977.

Neuhaus, Richard John. *The Naked Public Square: Religion and Democracy in America*. Grand Rapids, MI: W. B. Eerdmans, 1984.

Newcomb, Horace. "The Television Artistry of Norman Lear." *Prospects: An American Studies Annual* (1975): 109–25.

"New Morality on TV Debated." *Los Angeles Times*, March 25, 1976.

"Norman Lear vs. the Moral Majority." *Columbia Journalism Review* 20, no. 1 (May/June 1981): 77.

Novak, Michael. "Norman Lear's Failed Experiment." *Christian Century*, March 8, 1978, 246–49.

O'Brien-Steinfels, Margaret, and Peter Steinfels. "The New Awakening: Getting Religion in the Video Age." *Channels of Communication* 5, no. 2 (January/February 1983): 24–27, 62.

O'Connor, Carroll. "Foreword." In *God, Man, and Archie Bunker*, by Spencer Marsh, v–xii. New York: Harper and Row, 1975.

O'Connor, John J. "TV Weekend; Lear's 'I Love Liberty' Leads Specials." *New York Times*, March 19, 1982.

Opton, Frank G. *Liberal Religion: Principles and Practices*. New York: Prometheus, 1982.

Orth, Maureen. "Religion on TV: Norman Lear Tackles the New Hot Issue." *Vogue*, February 1982, 177–80.

Parenti, Michael. "Political Values and Religious Cultures: Jews, Catholics, and Protestants." *Journal for the Scientific Study of Religion* 6, no. 2 (Autumn 1967): 259–69.

Petersen, Clarence. "Scope: Bigoted, Dumb, Clumsy, TV's Archie Bunker." *Chicago Tribune*, April 16, 1972.

Phillips, Kevin. *The Emerging Republican Majority*. James Madison Library in American Politics. 1969. Rev. ed. Princeton, NJ: Princeton University Press, 2015.

——. *Mediacracy: American Parties and Politics in the Communications Age*. New York: Doubleday, 1975.

Plowman, Edward E. "Is Morality All Right?" *Christianity Today*, November 2, 1979, 76–85.

"The Remaking of America: A Message to the Churches." *Christianity and Crisis*, July 20, 1981, 207–10.

Ribuffo, Leo P. "Liberals and That Old-Time Religion." *The Nation*, November 29, 1980, 570–73.

Rickey, Carrie. "Why They Fight: Subjects' Rights and the First Amendment." *American Film* (October 1981): 57–60.

Rosenberg, Howard. "Evangelists, Networks: Holy War on Airwaves." *Los Angeles Times*, January 25, 1982.

Rosenberg, Tina. "How the Media Made the Moral Majority." *Washington Monthly*, May 1982, 26–34.

Rusher, William A. *The Making of the New Majority Party*. Ottawa, IL: Green Hill, 1975.

Sanders, Charles L. "Is Archie Bunker the Real White America? Nation's New Hero Is a Beer-Bellied Bigot with 60 Million Fans." *Ebony*, June 1971, 186–92.

Schaeffer, Francis. *The Christian Manifesto*. Wheaton, IL: Crossway, 1981.

Shriver, Peggy. *The Bible Vote: Religion and the New Right*. New York: Pilgrim, 1981.

Smith, Robert R. "Broadcasting and Religious Freedom." *Journal of Broadcasting* 13, no. 1 (1968): 1–12.

"Smiting the Mighty Right." *Time*, November 3, 1980, 103.

Spring, Beth. "Norman Lear's Lobbying Style Troubles Some Supporters." *Christianity Today*, November 12, 1982, 78–81.

Stein, Ben. "Norman Lear vs. the Moral Majority: The War to Clean Up TV." *Saturday Review*, February 1981, 22–27.

——. *The View from Sunset Boulevard: America as Brought to You by the People Who Make Television*. New York: Basic, 1979.

Stone, Dorothy. "Maude's Abortion Evokes Protests." *Los Angeles Times*, November 29, 1972.

"The Team Behind Archie Bunker and Co." *Time*, September 25, 1972, 9.

Theim, Becky. "Lear Pushing American Way." *The Bulletin*, October 17, 1982, C3.

"The Troubled American." *Newsweek*, October 6, 1969, 29–73.

"TV's Latest Listing: Archie vs. Jerry." *Newsweek*, October 18, 1982, 41.

Van Horne, Harriet. "The Moral Majority and Us." *National Academy of Television Arts and Sciences* 18, no. 1 (Spring 1981): 65–66.

Vecsey, George. "Militant Television Preachers Try to Wield Fundamentalist Christian's Political Power." *New York Times*, January 21, 1980.

Viguerie, Richard A. *The Establishment vs. the People: Is a New Populist Revolt on the Way?* Washington, DC: Regnery Gateway, 1984.

——. *The New Right: We're Ready to Lead.* Falls Church, VA: Viguerie, 1981.

Wall, James M. "The New Right Comes of Age." *Christian Century*, October 22, 1980, 995–96.

——. "Norman Lear in His Pulpit: Editorial Correspondence." *Christian Century*, November 12, 1975, 1019–20.

Ward, Leslie. "Rallying Round the Flag: Norman Lear and the American Way." *American Film* (October 1981): 63–66.

Williamson, Rene de Visme. "Conservatism and Liberalism in American Protestantism." *Annals of the American Academy of Political and Social Science* 344 (November 1962): 76–84.

Wood, James E., Jr. "Editorial: Religious Fundamentalism and the New Right." *Journal of Church and State* 23 (1981): 409–21.

Yankelovich, Daniel. *The New Morality: A Profile of American Youth in the '70s.* New York: McGraw-Hill, 1974.

Zoglin, Richard. "Is This Entertainment Special Promoting a Special Interest?" *New York Times*, March 21, 1982.

ARTWORK AND FILM

Feldman, Marty, dir. *In God We Tru$t.* DVD. Universal City, CA: Universal Pictures, 1980.

Friedberg, Rick, dir. *Pray TV.* DVD. Los Angeles, CA: Filmways Pictures, 1980.

Larson, Susan. "Life and Liberty for All Who Believe." Video. YouTube, May 2, 2012. http://www.youtube.com/watch?v=is_fhyhbAa4.

Lear, Norman, dir. *I Love Liberty.* DVD. Los Angeles, CA: ABC, 1982.

PFAWdotorg. Video collection. YouTube. https://www.youtube.com/user/PFAWdotorg/videos?flow=grid&view=0&sort=p.

BOOKS AND ARTICLES

Acham, Christine. *Revolution Televised: Prime Time and the Struggle for Black Power.* Minneapolis: University of Minnesota Press, 2004.

Adler, Richard P. *All in the Family: A Critical Appraisal.* New York: Praeger, 1979.

Adorno, Theodor. *The Culture Industry: Selected Essays on Mass Culture.* New York: Routledge, 1991.

——. *The Psychological Technique of Martin Luther Thomas' Radio Addresses.* Palo Alto, CA: Stanford University Press, 2000.

Allen, Robert C., ed. *Channels of Discourse, Reassembled: Television and Contemporary Criticism.* Chapel Hill: University of North Carolina Press, 1992.

Amesbury, Richard. "Rethinking 'Religion and Politics': Reflections on the Reception and Import of Talal Asad's Genealogies of Religion." *Bulletin for the Study of Religion* 43, no. 1 (February 2014): 2–7.

Anderson, Amanda. "The Liberal Aesthetic." In *Theory After Theory*, ed. Jane Elliott and Derek Attridge, 249–61. New York: Routledge, 2011.

Apostolildis, Paul. *Stations of the Cross: Adorno and Christian Right Radio.* Durham, NC: Duke University Press, 2000.

August, Ellen. "Writers Guild v. FCC: Duty of the Networks to Resist Governmental Regulation." *Syracuse Law Review* 28, no. 2 (1977): 583–607.

Bailey, Beth, and David Farber, eds. *America in the Seventies.* Lawrence: University Press of Kansas, 2004.

Bates, Stephen. *Battleground: One Mother's Crusade, the Religious Right, and the Struggle for Control of our Classrooms.* New York: Poseidon, 1993.

Bell, Daniel, ed. *The Radical Right.* 1955. 3rd ed. New Brunswick, NJ: Transaction, 2002.

Bender, Courtney. *The New Metaphysicals: Spirituality and the American Religious Imagination.* New York: Columbia University Press, 2010.

Bender, Courtney, and Pamela Klassen. *After Pluralism: Reimagining Religious Engagement* New York: Columbia University Press, 2014.

Bercovitch, Sacvan. *The Rites of Assent: Transformations in the Symbolic Construction of America.* New York: Routledge, 1993.

Berger, Peter. "The Class Struggle in American Religion." *Christian Century*, February 25, 1981, 194–99.

Bivins, Jason. *The Fracture of Good Order: Christian Antiliberalism and the Challenge to American Politics.* Chapel Hill: University of North Carolina Press, 2003.

——. *Religion of Fear: The Politics of Horror in Conservative Evangelicalism.* New York: Oxford University Press, 2008.

Blankholm, Joe. "The Political Advantages of a Polysemous Secular." *Journal for the Scientific Study of Religion* 53, no. 4 (December 2014): 775–90.

Borstelmann, Thomas. *The 1970s: A New Global History from Civil Rights to Economic Inequality.* Princeton, NJ: Princeton University Press, 2012.

Briggs-Bruce, B., ed. *The New Class?* New York: McGraw-Hill, 1979.

Brown, James A. "Selling Airtime for Controversy: NAB Self-Regulation and Father Coughlin." *Journal of Broadcasting* 24, no. 2 (1980): 199–224.

Brown, Wendy. *Undoing the Demos: Neoliberalism's Stealth Revolution.* New York: Zone, 2015.

Burnidge, Cara. "Protestant Liberalism." In *Encyclopedia of Religion in America*, ed. Charles H. Lippy and Peter W. Williams, 1783–91. Washington, DC: CQ, 2010. http://dx.doi.org/10.4135/9781608712427.n301.

Butler, Jon. "Jack-in-the-Box Faith: The Religion Problem in Modern American History." *Journal of American History* 90, no. 4 (March 2004): 1357–78.

Capps, Walter. "Contemporary Socio-Political Change and the Work of Religious Studies." *Council on the Study of Religion Bulletin* 12, no. 4 (October 1981): 93–95.

——. *The New Religious Right: Piety, Patriotism, and Politics.* Columbia: University of South Carolina Press, 1990.

Chidester, David. *Authentic Fakes: Religion and American Popular Culture.* Berkeley: University of California Press, 2005.

——. *Patterns of Power: Religion & Politics in American Culture.* New York: Prentice Hall, 1988.

Clecak, Peter. *America's Quest for the Ideal Self: Dissent and Fulfillment in the 60s and 70s.* New York: Oxford University Press, 1995.

Coffman, Elesha. J. *The Christian Century and the Rise of the Protestant Mainline.* New York: Oxford University Press, 2013.

Collins, Robert M. *Transforming America: Politics and Culture During the Reagan Years.* New York: Columbia University Press, 2007.

Connolly, William. "The Evangelical-Capitalist Resonance Machine." *Political Theory* 33, no. 6 (December 2005): 869–86.

Cook, Deborah. *The Culture Industry Revisited: Theodor W. Adorno on Mass Culture*. New York: Rowman and Littlefield, 1996.

Cooper, Cynthia. *Violence on Television: Congressional Inquiry, Public Criticism, and Industry Response*. Lanham, MD: University Press of America, 1996.

Cowan, Paul. *The Tribes of America: Journalistic Discoveries of Our People and Their Cultures*. 1971. New York: New, 2008.

Cowie, Jefferson R. *Stayin' Alive: The 1970s and the Last Days of the Working Class*. New York: New, 2012.

Currid-Halkett, Elizabeth. *The Sum of Small Things: A Theory of the Aspirational Class*. Princeton, NJ: Princeton University Press, 2017.

Curtis, Finbarr. *The Production of Religious Freedom*. New York: New York University Press, 2017.

Curts, Kati. "Temples and Turnpikes in the World of Tomorrow: Religious Assemblage and Automobility at the 1939 New York World's Fair." *Journal of the American Academy of Religion* 83, no. 3 (2015): 722–49.

Dauber, Jeremy. *Jewish Comedy: A Serious History*. New York: W. W. Norton, 2017.

Demerath, N. J., III. "Cultural Victory and Organizational Defeat in the Paradoxical Decline of Liberal Protestantism." *Journal for the Scientific Study of Religion* 34, no. 4 (December 1995): 458–69.

Diamond, Sara. *Spiritual Warfare: The Politics of the Christian Right*. Montreal: Black Rose, 1990.

Dionne, E. J. *Why the Right Went Wrong: From Goldwater to the Tea Party and Beyond*. New York: Simon & Schuster, 2016.

Dochuk, Darren, and Michelle Nickerson, eds. *Sunbelt Rising: The Politics of Space, Place, and Region*. Philadelphia: University of Pennsylvania Press, 2011.

Douglas, Mary. "The Effects of Modernization on Religious Change." *Daedalus* 111, no. 1 (Winter 1982): 1–19.

Douglas, Mary, and Steven M. Tipton, eds. *Religion and America: Spirituality in a Secular Age*. Boston: Beacon, 1982.

Dowland, Seth. *Family Values and the Rise of the Christian Right*. Philadelphia: University of Pennsylvania Press, 2015.

Drolet, Jean-Francois. *American Neoconservatism: The Politics and Culture of a Reactionary Idealism*. New York: Columbia University Press, 2013.

Eaton, Mick. "Television Situation Comedy." *Screen: The Journal of the Society for Education in Film and Television* 19, no. 4 (1978): 61–90.

Edgerton, Gary R. *The Columbia History of American Television*. New York: Columbia University Press, 2007.

Espinosa, Gastón, ed., *Religion and the American Presidency: George Washington to George W. Bush with Commentary and Primary Sources*. New York: Columbia University Press, 2009.

——. *Religion, Race, and the American Presidency*. New York: Rowman and Littlefield, 2010.

Ferre, John P., ed. *Channels of Belief: Religion and American Commercial Television*. Ames: Iowa State University Press, 1990.

Fessenden, Tracy. *Culture and Redemption: Religion, the Secular, and American Literature*. Princeton, NJ: Princeton University Press, 2009.

Fitzgerald, Francis. *The Evangelicals: The Struggle to Shape America*. New York: Simon & Schuster, 2017.

Flippen, J. Brooks. *Jimmy Carter, the Politics of Family, and the Rise of the Religious Right*. Athens: University of Georgia Press, 2011.

Fox, Richard W. "The Culture of Liberal Protestant Progressivism, 1875–1925." *Journal of Interdisciplinary History* 23, no. 3 (Winter, 1993): 639–60.

Frank, Thomas. *The Conquest of Cool: Business Culture, Counterculture, and the Rise of Hip Consumerism*. Chicago: Chicago University Press, 1997.

Frankiel, Sandra S. *California's Spiritual Frontiers: Religious Alternatives in Anglo-Protestantism.* Berkeley: University of California Press, 1988.

Fraser, Steve, and Gary Gerstle. *The Rise and Fall of the New Deal Order, 1930–1980.* Princeton, NJ: Princeton University Press, 1989.

Gasaway, Brantley. *Progressive Evangelicals and the Pursuit of Social Justice.* Chapel Hill: University of North Carolina Press, 2011.

Gaston, Healan K. "Interpreting Judeo-Christianity in America." *Relegere: Studies in Religion and Reception* 2, no. 2 (2012): 291–304.

Geismer, Lily. *Don't Blame Us: Suburban Liberals and the Transformation of the Democratic Party.* Princeton, NJ: Princeton University Press, 2015.

Gerstle, Gary. *Liberty and Coercion: The Paradox of American Government from the Founding to the Present.* Princeton, NJ: Princeton University Press, 2015.

Gitlin, Todd. *Inside Prime Time.* Berkeley: University of California Press, 1994.

——. "Prime Time Ideology: The Hegemonic Process in Television Entertainment." *Social Problems* 26, no. 3 (February 1979): 251–66.

Gloege, Timothy E. W. *Guaranteed Pure: The Moody Bible Institute, Business, and the Making of Modern Evangelicalism.* Chapel Hill: University of North Carolina Press, 2015.

Gorski, Philip. *American Covenant: A History of Civil Religion from the Puritans to the Present.* Princeton, NJ: Princeton University Press, 2017.

Grem, Darren. *The Blessings of Business: How Corporations Shaped Conservative Christianity.* New York: Oxford University Press, 2016.

Grem, Darren, Amanda Porterfield, and John Corrigan, eds. *The Business Turn in American Religious History.* New York: Oxford University Press, 2017.

Griffith, Marie. *Moral Combat: How Sex Divided American Christians and Fractured American Politics.* New York: Basic, 2017.

Haberski, Raymond, Jr. *God and War: American Civil Religion Since 1945.* New Brunswick, NJ: Rutgers University Press, 2012.

Hadden, Jeffrey K. "Clergy Involvement in Civil Rights." *Annals of the American Academy of Political and Social Science* 387 (January 1970): 118–27.

——. "Religious Broadcasting and the Mobilization of the New Christian Right." *Journal for the Scientific Study of Religion* 26, no. 1 (March 1987): 1–24.

——. "The Rise and Fall of American Televangelism." *Annals of the American Academy of Political and Social Sciences* 527 (May 1993): 113–30.

Hadden, Jeffrey, and Charles E. Swan, eds. *Prime Time Preachers: The Rising Power of Televangelism.* Reading, MA: Addison-Wesley, 1981.

Hall, David D. *Lived Religion: Toward a History of Practice in America.* Princeton, NJ: Princeton University Press, 1997.

——, ed. *Worlds of Wonder, Days of Judgment: Popular Religious Belief in Early New England.* New York: Knopf, 1989.

Hall, Stuart. *The Hard Road to Renewal: Thatcherism and the Crisis of the Left.* New York: Verso, 1988.

Halle, David. *America's Working Man: Work, Home, and Politics Among Blue Collar Property-Owners.* Chicago: University of Chicago Press, 1984.

Hamamoto, Darrell Y. *Nervous Laughter: Television Situation Comedy and Liberal Democratic Ideology.* Santa Barbara, CA: Praeger, 1989.

Hammond, Sarah, and Darren Dochuk, eds. *God's Businessmen: Entrepreneurial Evangelicals in Depression and War.* Chicago: University of Chicago Press, 2017.

Hangen, Tona J. *Redeeming the Dial: Radio, Religion, and Popular Culture in America.* Chapel Hill: University of North Carolina Press, 2002.

Harding, Susan. "American Protestant Moralism and the Secular Imagination: From Temperance to the Moral Majority." *Social Research* 76, no. 4 (Winter 2009): 1277–306.

——. *The Book of Jerry Falwell: Fundamentalist Language and Politics*. Princeton, NJ: Princeton University Press, 2001.

——. "Representing Fundamentalism: The Problem of the Repugnant Cultural Other." *Social Research* 58, no. 2 (Summer 1991): 373–93.

——. "A We Like Any Other." Hot Spots, *Cultural Anthropology* website, January 18, 2017. https://culanth.org/fieldsights/1036-a-we-like-any-other.

Hartman, Andrew. *A War for the Soul of America: A History of the Culture Wars*. Chicago: University of Chicago Press, 2015.

Hazard, Sonia. "The Material Turn in the Study of Religion." *Religion and Society: Advances in Research* 4 (2013): 58–78.

Hedstrom, Matthew. *The Rise of Liberal Religion: Book Culture and American Spirituality in the Twentieth Century*. New York: Oxford University Press, 2013.

Hendershot, Heather. "God's Angriest Man: Carl McIntire, Cold War Fundamentalism, and Right-Wing Broadcasting." *American Quarterly* 59, no. 2 (June 2007): 373–96.

——. *Open to Debate: How William F. Buckley Put Liberal America on the Firing Line*. New York: Harper Collins, 2017.

Himmelstein, Hal. *Television Myth and the American Mind*. New York: Praeger, 1994.

Hixon, William B. *Search for the American Right: An Analysis of the Social Science Record, 1955–1987*. Princeton, NJ: Princeton University Press, 1992.

Hochschild, Arlie Russell. *Strangers in Their Own Land: Anger and Mourning on the American Right*. New York: New, 2016.

Hollinger, David. *After Cloven Tongues of Fire: Protestant Liberalism in Modern American History*. Princeton, NJ: Princeton University Press, 2013.

——. "The Realist-Pacifist Summit Meeting of March 1942 and the Political Reorientation of Ecumenical Protestantism in the United States." *Church History* 79, no. 3 (September 2010): 654–77.

——. *Science, Jews, and Secular Culture: Studies in Mid-twentieth Century American Intellectual History*. Princeton, NJ: Princeton University Press, 1996.

Hoover, Stewart. *Mass Media Religion: The Social Sources of the Electronic Church*. New York: Sage, 1988.

Hunter, James Davison. *The Culture Wars: The Struggle to Define America*. New York: Basic, 1991.

——. *Evangelicalism: The Coming Generation*. Chicago: University of Chicago Press, 1987.

——. "The New Class and Young Evangelicals." *Review of Religious Research* 22, no. 2 (December 1980): 155–69.

Hunter, James Davison, and Alan Wolfe. *Is There a Culture War? A Dialogue on Values and American Public Life*. Washington, DC: Brookings Institution, 2006.

Hutchinson, William. *Between the Times: The Travail of the Protestant Establishment in America, 1900–1960*. New York: Cambridge University Press, 1990.

Israel, Jeffrey. *Living with Hate in American Politics and Religion: How Popular Culture Can Defuse Intractable Differences*. New York: Columbia University Press, 2019.

Jacob, Margaret C. "Private Beliefs in Public Temples: The New Religiosity of the Eighteenth Century." *Social Research* 59, no. 1 (Spring 1992): 59–84.

Jhally, Sut. *The Spectacle of Accumulation: Essays in Culture, Media, and Politics*. New York: Peter Lang, 2006.

Johnson, Emily. *This Is Our Message: Women's Leadership in the New Christian Right*. New York: Oxford University Press, 2019.

Jumonville, Neil, and Kevin Mattson, eds. *Liberalism for a New Century*. Berkeley: University of California Press, 2007.

Kaufmann, Karen. "Culture Wars, Secular Realignment, and the Gender Gap in Party Identification." *Political Behavior* 24, no. 3 (September 2002): 283–307.

Kellner, Douglas. "Critical Perspectives on Television from the Frankfurt School to Postmodernism." In *A Companion to Television*, ed. Janet Wasko, 29–50. New York: Wiley-Blackwell, 2009.

Kercher, Stephen. *Revel with a Cause: Liberal Satire in Postwar America*. Chicago: University of Chicago Press, 2006.

Kertzer, David. *Ritual, Politics, and Power*. New Haven, CT: Yale University Press, 1988.

Kintz, Linda, and Julia Lesage, eds. *Media, Culture, and the Religious Right*. Minneapolis: University of Minnesota Press, 1998.

Kittelstrom, Amy. *Religion of Democracy: Seven Liberals and the American Moral Tradition*. New York: Penguin, 2016.

Knutson, Katherine E. *Interfaith Advocacy: The Role of Religious Coalitions in the Political Process*. New York: Routledge, 2013.

Koch, Neal. "Why Mel Brooks and Bill Moyers Will Always Idolize Norman Lear." HuffPost, November 11, 2014. http://www.huffingtonpost.com/neal-koch/norman-lear-pen-award_b_6130620.html.

Kruse, Kevin. *One Nation Under God: How Corporate America Invented Christian America*. New York: Basic, 2015.

Landsberg, Alison. *Engaging the Past: Mass Culture and the Production of Historical Knowledge*. New York: Columbia University Press, 2015.

Lane, Christopher. *Surge of Piety: Norman Vincent Peale and the Remaking of American Religious Life*. New Haven, CT: Yale University Press, 2016.

Lear, Norman. *Even This I Get to Experience*. New York: Penguin, 2015.

Leege, David C., Kenneth Wald, Brian Krueger, and Paul Mueller. *The Politics of Cultural Difference: Social Change and Voter Mobilization Strategies in the Post–New Deal Period*. Princeton, NJ: Princeton University Press, 2002.

Lembo, Ron. *Thinking Through Television*. New York: Cambridge University Press, 2000.

Levitt, Laura. "Judeo-Christian Traditions Reconsidered." Essay 16, Section 3, "World's Religions in America." In *The Cambridge History of Religions in America*, ed. Stephen Stein, 285–307. New York: Cambridge University Press, 2012.

Lewis, James W. "Mainline Protestants." In *Encyclopedia of Religion in America*, ed. Charles H. Lippy and Peter W. Williams, 1310–18. Washington, DC: CQ, 2010. http://dx.doi.org/10.4135/9781608712427.n212.

Lichter, Robert S., and Linda S. Lichter, eds. *Prime Time: How TV Portrays American Culture*. Washington, DC: Regnery, 1994.

Liebman, Robert C., and Robert Wuthnow. *The New Christian Right: Mobilization and Legitimation*. New York: Aldine, 1983.

Lienesch, Michael. "Right-Wing Religion: Christian Conservatism as a Political Movement." *Political Science Quarterly* 97, no. 3 (Autumn 1982): 403–25.

Lipset, Seymour Martin, ed. *The Third Century: America as a Post-industrial Society*. Palo Alto, CA: Hoover, 1979.

Lipsitz, George. *Time Passages: Collective Memory and American Popular Culture*. Minneapolis: University of Minnesota Press, 1990.

Lofton, Kathryn. "Commonly Modern: Rethinking the Modernist-Fundamentalist Controversies." *Church History* 83, no. 1 (March 2014): 137–44.

——. *Consuming Religion*. Chicago: University of Chicago Press, 2017.

——. *Oprah: The Gospel of an Icon*. Berkeley: University of California Press, 2011.

Luhr, Eileen. "Seeker Surfer, Yogi: The Progressive Religious Imagination and the Cultural Politics of Place in Encinitas, California." *American Quarterly* 67, no. 4 (December 2015): 1169–93.

Marc, David. *Comic Visions: Television Comedy and American Culture*. Boston: Blackwell, 1997.

McCrary, Charles, and Jeffrey Wheatley. "The Protestant Secular in the Study of American Religion: Reappraisal and Suggestions." *Religion* 47, no. 2 (2017): 256–76.

Mendenhall, Robert R. "Responses to Television from the New Christian Right: The Donald Wildmon Organization's Fight against Sexual Content." In *Sex, Religion, and Media*, ed. Dane S. Claussen, 101–14. Lanham, MD: Rowman and Littlefield, 2002.

Michaelsen, Robert S., and Wade Clark Roof, eds. *Liberal Protestantism: Realities and Possibilities.* New York: Pilgrim, 1986.

Miller, Steven P. *The Age of Evangelicalism: America's Born-Again Years.* New York: Oxford University Press, 2014.

Mintz, Lawrence E. "Ideology in the Television Situation Comedy." *Studies in Popular Culture* 8, no. 2 (1985): 42–51.

Mislin, David. *Saving Faith: Making Religious Pluralism an American Value at the Dawn of the Secular Age.* Ithaca, NY: Cornell University Press, 2015.

Mitchell, Kerry. "The Politics of Spirituality: Liberalizing the Definition of Religion." In *Secularism and Religion-Making*, ed. Markus Dressler and Arvind Mandair, 125–40. New York: Oxford University Press, 2011.

Modern, John L. "Institutional Dreams." *Church History* 83, no. 4 (December 2014): 988–96.

——. *Secularism in Antebellum America.* Chicago: Chicago University Press, 2011.

Montgomery, Kathryn C. *Target Prime Time: Advocacy Groups and the Struggle Over Entertainment Television.* New York: Oxford University Press, 1989.

Moore, Deborah. *How World War II Changed a Generation.* Cambridge, MA: Harvard University Press, 2004.

Moore, R. Laurence. "Religion, Secularization and the Shaping of the Culture Industry in Antebellum America." *American Quarterly* 41 (1989): 216–42.

——. *Selling God: American Religion in the Marketplace of Culture.* New York: Oxford University Press, 1994.

Moreton, Bethany. *To Serve God and Walmart: The Making of Christian Free Enterprise.* Cambridge, MA: Harvard University Press, 2009.

Morreale, Joanne, ed. *Critiquing the Sitcom: A Reader.* Syracuse, NY: Syracuse University Press, 2003.

Most, Andrea. *Theatrical Liberalism: Jews and Popular Entertainment in America.* New York: New York University Press, 2013.

Newcomb, Horace, ed. *Television: The Critical View.* New York: Oxford University Press, 1976.

Newcomb, Horace, and Robert S. Alley. *The Producer's Medium: Conversations with Creators of American TV.* New York: Oxford University Press, 1983.

Newcomb, Horace, and Paul M. Hirsch. "Television as a Cultural Forum." In *Interpreting Television*, ed. W. D. Rowland and B. Watkins, 68–73. Thousand Oaks, CA: Sage, 1985.

Noll, Mark, ed. *Religion and American Politics: From the Colonial Period to the Present.* New York: Oxford University Press, 2007.

Nussbaum, Emily. "The Great Divide: Norman Lear, Archie Bunker, and the Rise of the Bad Fan." *New Yorker*, April 7, 2014.

O'Connor, Mike. "Liberals in Space: The 1960s Politics of *Star Trek*." *The Sixties: A Journal of History, Politics, and Culture* 5, no. 2 (December 2012): 185–203.

Orsi, Robert. *Between Heaven and Earth: The Religious Worlds People Make and the Scholars Who Study Them.* Princeton, NJ: Princeton University Press, 2006.

——. *History and Presence.* Cambridge, MA: Harvard University Press, 2016.

Ozersky, Josh. *Archie Bunker's America: TV in an Era of Change, 1968–1978.* Carbondale: Southern Illinois University Press, 2003.

Petro, Anthony. *After the Wrath of God: AIDS, Sexuality, and American Religion.* New York: Oxford University Press, 2016.

Phillips-Fein, Kim. *Fear City: New York's Fiscal Crisis and the Rise of Austerity Politics.* New York: Henry Holt, 2017.

Porterfield, Amanda. *The Transformation of American Religion: The Story of a Late Twentieth-Century Awakening.* New York: Oxford University Press, 2001.

Poster, Mark. "Foucault and History." *Social Research* 49, no. 1 (Spring 1982): 116–42.

Preston, Andrew, Bruce Schulman, and Julian Zelizer, eds. *Faithful Republic: Religion and Politics in Modern America.* Philadelphia: University of Pennsylvania Press, 2015.

Prothero, Stephen. *Why Liberals Win the Culture Wars (Even when They Lose Elections): The Battles That Define America from Jefferson's Heresies to Gay Marriage.* New York: Harper Collins, 2016.

Quinley, Harold E. *The Prophetic Clergy: Social Activism Among Protestant Ministers.* New York: John Wiley, 1974.

Rawls, John. "The Idea of Public Reason Revisited." *University of Chicago Law Review* 64, no. 3 (Summer 1997): 766–67.

Rodgers, Daniel. *Age of Fracture.* Cambridge, MA: Harvard University Press, 2012.

Rogin, Michael. *Ronald Reagan the Movie, and Other Episodes in Political Demonology.* Berkeley: University of California Press, 1987.

Rolsky, Louis Benjamin. "Are Comedians the Political Vanguard?" *Christian Century,* July 8, 2015.

——. "Confessions of a Hollywood Liberal: American Sitcoms and the Culture Wars from Norman Lear to Parks and Recreation." Marginalia, March 31, 2015. http://marginalia.lareviewofbooks.org /confessions-of-a-hollywood-liberal-american-sitcoms-and-the-culture-wars-from-norman-lear-to -parks-and-recreation-by-l-benjamin-rolsky/.

——. "The Struggle Is Real, Indeed: American Cultural Warfare and the Recent Religious Past." Martin Marty Center: Religion and Culture Forum, July 25, 2017.

——. "Taking Conservatism Seriously in the Age of #MAGA." Martin Marty Center: Religion and Culture Forum, March 8, 2017.

——. "Wall Street Goes to War: Hardhat Politics and the Culture War of Everything Since the 1960s." Marginalia, February 29, 2016.

Roof, Wade Clark. "America's Voluntary Establishment: Mainline Religion in Transition." *Daedalus* 111, no. 1 (Winter 1982): 165–84.

Rosenthal, Michele. *American Protestants and TV in the 1950s: Responses to a New Medium.* New York: Palgrave MacMillan, 2007.

Ross, Steven J. *Hollywood Left and Right: How Movie Stars Shaped American Politics.* New York: Oxford University Press, 2011.

Schäfer, Axel R., ed. *American Evangelicals and the 1960s.* Madison: University of Wisconsin Press, 2013.

——. *Countercultural Conservatives: American Evangelicalism from the Postwar Revival to the New Christian Right.* Madison: University of Wisconsin Press, 2011.

——. *Piety and Public Funding: Evangelicals and the State in Modern America.* Philadelphia: University of Pennsylvania Press, 2012.

Schmidt, Leigh. *Restless Souls: The Making of American Spirituality.* New York: HarperOne, 2006.

Schmidt, Leigh, and Sally Promey, eds. *American Religious Liberalism.* Bloomington: Indiana University Press, 2012.

Schryer, Stephen. *Fantasies of the New Class: Ideologies of Professionalism in Post–World War II American Fiction.* New York: Columbia University Press, 2006.

Schulman, Bruce J., ed. *Making the American Century: Essays on the Political Culture of Twentieth-Century America.* New York: Oxford University, 2015.

Schulman, Bruce J., and Julian E. Zelizer, eds. *Rightward Bound: Making America Conservative in the 1970s.* Cambridge, MA: Harvard University Press, 2008.

Schultz, Kevin. *Tri-Faith America: How Catholics and Jews Held Postwar America to Its Protestant Promise.* New York: Oxford University Press, 2011.

Seales, Chad. *The Secular Spectacle: Performing Religion in a Southern Town*. New York: Oxford University Press, 2014.

Self, Robert O. *All in the Family: The Realignment of American Democracy Since the 1960s*. New York: Hill and Wang, 2012.

Shields, Jon A. "Framing the Christian Right: How Progressives and Post-war Liberals Constructed the Religious Right." *Journal of Church and State* 53, no. 4 (Autumn 2011): 635–55.

Shields, Jon A., and Joshua M. Dunn, eds. *Passing on the Right: Conservative Professors in the Progressive University*. New York: Oxford University Press, 2016.

Shulman, Bruce. *The Seventies: The Great Shift in American Culture, Society, and Politics*. New York: Da Capo, 2001.

Silk, Mark. *Spiritual Politics: Religion and America Since World War II*. New York: Touchstone, 1989.

Sklar, Robert. *Prime-Time America: Life on and Behind the Television Screen*. New York: Oxford University Press, 1980.

Smith, Christian. *Resisting Reagan: The US Central America Peace Movement*. Chicago: University of Chicago Press, 1996.

Smith, Leslie Dorrough. *Righteous Rhetoric: Sex, Speech, and the Politics of Concerned Women for America*. New York: Oxford University Press, 2014.

Snowball, David. *Continuity and Change in the Rhetoric of the Moral Majority*. New York: Praeger, 1991.

Sorett, Josef. *Spirit in the Dark: A Religious History of Racial Aesthetics*. New York: Oxford University Press, 2017.

Spigel, Lynn, and Michael Curtin, eds. *The Revolution Wasn't Televised: Sixties Television and Social Conflict*. New York: Routledge, 1997.

Stevens, Jason. *God Fearing and Free: A Spiritual History of America's Cold War*. Cambridge, MA: Harvard University Press, 2010.

Stolow, Jeremy. "Religion and/as Media." *Theory, Culture, and Society* 22, no. 4 (2005): 119–45.

Strub, Whitney. *Perversion for Profit: The Politics of Pornography and the Rise of the New Right*. New York: Columbia University Press, 2011.

Sullivan, Winnifred, Elizabeth Shakman Hurd, Saba Mahmood, and Peter G. Danchin, eds. *Politics of Religious Freedom*. Chicago: University of Chicago Press, 2015.

Suman, Michael ed. *Religion and Prime Time Television*. New York: Praeger, 1997.

Sutton, Matthew. *American Apocalypse: A History of Modern Evangelicalism*. Cambridge, MA: Harvard University Press, 2014.

——, ed. *Jerry Falwell and the Rise of the Religious Right: A Brief History with Documents*. New York: Bedford/St. Martin's, 2012.

——. "Was FDR the Antichrist? The Birth of Fundamentalist Antiliberalism in a Global Age." *Journal of American History* 98, no. 4 (2012): 1052–74.

Taylor, Ella. *Prime-Time Families: Television Culture in Postwar America*. Berkeley: University of California Press, 1989.

Thompson, Nato. *Culture as Weapon: The Art of Influence in Everyday Life*. New York: Melville House, 2017.

Thompson, Robert J. *Adventures on Prime Time: The Television Programs of Stephen J. Cannell*. New York: Greenwood, 1990.

Todd, Terry J. "Mainline Protestants and the News Narratives of Declension." In *The Oxford Handbook of Religion and the American New Media*, ed. Diane Winston, 185–98. New York: Oxford University Press, 2012.

Tweed, Thomas. *Retelling U.S. Religious History*. Berkeley: University of California Press, 2007.

Wall, Wendy. *Inventing the "American Way": The Politics of Consensus from the New Deal to the Civil Rights Movement*. New York: Oxford University Press, 2008.

Warner, Michael. "Publics and Counterpublics." *Public Culture* 14, no. 1 (Winter 2002): 49–90.

Watt, David. *Antifundamentalism in Modern America*. Ithaca, NY: Cornell University Press, 2017.

Weiner, Isaac. "Calling Everyone to Pray: Pluralism, Secularism, and the Adhan in Hamtramck, Michigan." *Anthropological Quarterly* 87, no. 4 (Fall 2014): 1049–78.

Weisenfeld, Judith. *Hollywood Be Thy Name: African American Religion in American Film, 1929–1949*. Berkeley: University of California Press, 2007.

White, Heather. *Reforming Sodom: Protestants and the Rise of Gay Rights*. Chapel Hill: University of North Carolina Press, 2015.

Williams, Raymond. *Keywords: A Vocabulary of Culture and Society*. New York: Oxford University Press, 1983.

Williams, Rhys H., ed. *Cultural Wars in American Politics: Critical Reviews of a Popular Myth*. New York: Aldine de Gruyter, 1997.

Winston, Diane, ed. *Small Screen, Big Picture: Television and Lived Religion*. Waco, TX: Baylor University Press, 2009.

Witkin, Robert W. *Adorno on Popular Culture* New York: Routledge, 2002.

Wittebols, James H. *Watching MASH, Watching America: A Social History of the 1972–1983 Television Series*. Jefferson, NC: McFarland, 1998.

Wolfe, Alan. *One Nation, After All: What Americans Really Think About God, Country, Family, Racism, Welfare, Immigration, Homosexuality, Work, the Right, the Left and Each Other*. New York: Penguin, 1999.

Woodword, Kenneth L. *Getting Religion: Faith, Culture, and Politics from the Age of Eisenhower to Era of Obama*. New York: Random House, 2016.

Worthen, Molly. *Apostles of Reason: The Crisis of Authority in American Evangelicalism*. New York: Oxford University, 2015.

——. "Faithless." Review of *The Twilight of the American Enlightenment: The 1950s and the Crisis of Liberal Belief*, by George Marsden. *Democracy: A Journal of Ideas* 32 (Spring 2014): 77–85.

Wuthnow, Robert. *Left Behind: Decline and Rage in Rural America*. Princeton, NJ: Princeton University Press, 2018.

——. *The Restructuring of American Religion: Society and Faith Since World War II*. Princeton, NJ: Princeton University Press, 1988.

——. *The Struggle for America's Soul: Evangelicals, Liberals, and Secularism*. Grand Rapids, MI: Eerdmans, 1989.

Young, Neil J. *We Gather Together: The Religious Right and the Problem of Interfaith Politics*. New York: Oxford University Press, 2015.

Zimmerman, Jonathan. *Whose America? Culture Wars in the Public Schools*. Cambridge, MA: Harvard University Press, 2005.

DISSERTATIONS AND THESES

Andrae, Thomas S. "The End of Innocence: Prime-Time Television and the Politics of the Sixties." PhD diss., University of California, Berkeley, 2002.

Lapook, Corinne Beth. "Norman Lear: His Impact on American Television and Society." Senior Honors Thesis, Brandeis University, 1980.

Index

CPSIA information can be obtained
at www.ICGtesting.com
Printed in the USA
JSHW080940251122
33666JS00002BA/8

9 780231 193634